MS. MARVEL
TIME AND AGAIN

MS. MARVEL #31

writers
G. WILLOW WILSON (PP. 1-5, 11-12, 19-20, 26-30), SALADIN AHMED (PP. 6-10),
RAINBOW ROWELL (PP. 13-18) & HASAN MINHAJ (PP. 21-25)

artists
NICO LEON (PP. 1-5, 11-12, 19-20, 26-30), GUSTAVO DUARTE (PP. 6-10),
BOB QUINN (PP. 13-18) & ELMO BONDOC (PP. 21-25)

color artist
IAN HERRING

cover art
VALERIO SCHITI & RACHELLE ROSENBERG

MS. MARVEL #32-37

writer	artist
G. WILLOW WILSON	NICO LEON
color artist	cover art
IAN HERRING	VALERIO SCHITI & RACHELLE ROSENBERG

MS. MARVEL #38

story
G. WILLOW WILSON

writers
G. WILLOW WILSON (PP. 1-9), DEVIN GRAYSON (PP. 10-12),
EVE L. EWING (PP. 13-15), JIM ZUB (PP. 16-18) & SALADIN AHMED (PP. 19-21)

artists
NICO LEON (PP. 1-9), TAKESHI MIYAZAWA (PP. 10-12),
JOEY VAZQUEZ (PP. 13-15), KEVIN LIBRANDA (PP. 16-18)
AND MINKYU JUNG & JUAN VLASCO (PP. 19-21)

color artist
IAN HERRING

cover art
VALERIO SCHITI & RACHELLE ROSENBERG

letterer
VC's JOE CARAMAGNA

PREVIOUSLY

WHEN A STRANGE TERRIGEN MIST DESCENDED UPON JERSEY CITY, KAMALA KHAN WAS IMBUED WITH POLYMORPH POWERS. USING HER NEW ABILITIES TO FIGHT EVIL AND PROTECT JERSEY CITY, SHE BECAME THE ALL-NEW MS. MARVEL. HER LIFE WAS CHANGED FOREVER...AND SO WERE THE LIVES OF HER FAMILY AND FRIENDS.

AND THINGS CONTINUE TO CHANGE. KAMALA'S BECOME AN AUNTIE. SHE KISSED A BOY. THAT BOY WAS RED DAGGER, A PAKISTANI SUPER HERO WHO WAS OPERATING IN JERSEY CITY FOR A WHILE. HER RELATIONSHIPS WITH HER FRIENDS HAVE BECOME STRAINED AND ALTERED. BUT KAMALA REALIZES IT'S TIME TO REACH OUT TO HER FRIENDS AND SET THINGS RIGHT.

collection editor
JENNIFER GRÜNWALD

assistant editor
CAITLIN O'CONNELL

associate managing editor
KATERI WOODY

editor, special projects
MARK D. BEAZLEY

vp production & special projects
JEFF YOUNGQUIST

svp print, sales & marketing
DAVID GABRIEL

editor in chief
C.B. CEBULSKI

chief creative officer
JOE QUESADA

president
DAN BUCKLEY

executive producer
ALAN FINE

MS. MARVEL VOL. 10: TIME AND AGAIN. Contains material originally published in magazine form as MS. MARVEL #31-38. First printing 2018. ISBN 978-1-302-91269-7. Published by MARVEL WORLDWIDE, INC., a subsidiary of MARVEL ENTERTAINMENT, LLC. OFFICE OF PUBLICATION: 135 West 50th Street, New York, NY 10020. Copyright © 2018 MARVEL No similarity between any of the names, characters, persons, and/or institutions in this magazine with those of any living or dead person or institution is intended, and any such similarity which may exist is purely coincidental. **Printed in the U.S.A.** DAN BUCKLEY, President, Marvel Entertainment; JOHN NEE, Publisher; JOE QUESADA, Chief Creative Officer; TOM BREVOORT, SVP of Publishing; DAVID BOGART, SVP of Business Affairs & Operations, Publishing & Partnership; DAVID GABRIEL, SVP of Sales & Marketing, Publishing; JEFF YOUNGQUIST, VP of Production & Special Projects; DAN CARR, Executive Director of Publishing Technology; ALEX MORALES, Director of Publishing Operations; DAN EDINGTON, Managing Editor; SUSAN CRESPI, Production Manager; STAN LEE, Chairman Emeritus. For information regarding advertising in Marvel Comics or on Marvel.com, please contact Vit DeBellis, Custom Solutions & Integrated Advertising Manager, at vdebellis@marvel.com. For Marvel subscription inquiries, please call 888-511-5480. Manufactured between 2/6/2019 and 3/5/2019 by LSC COMMUNICATIONS INC., KENDALLVILLE, IN, USA.

10 9 8 7 6 5 4 3 2 1

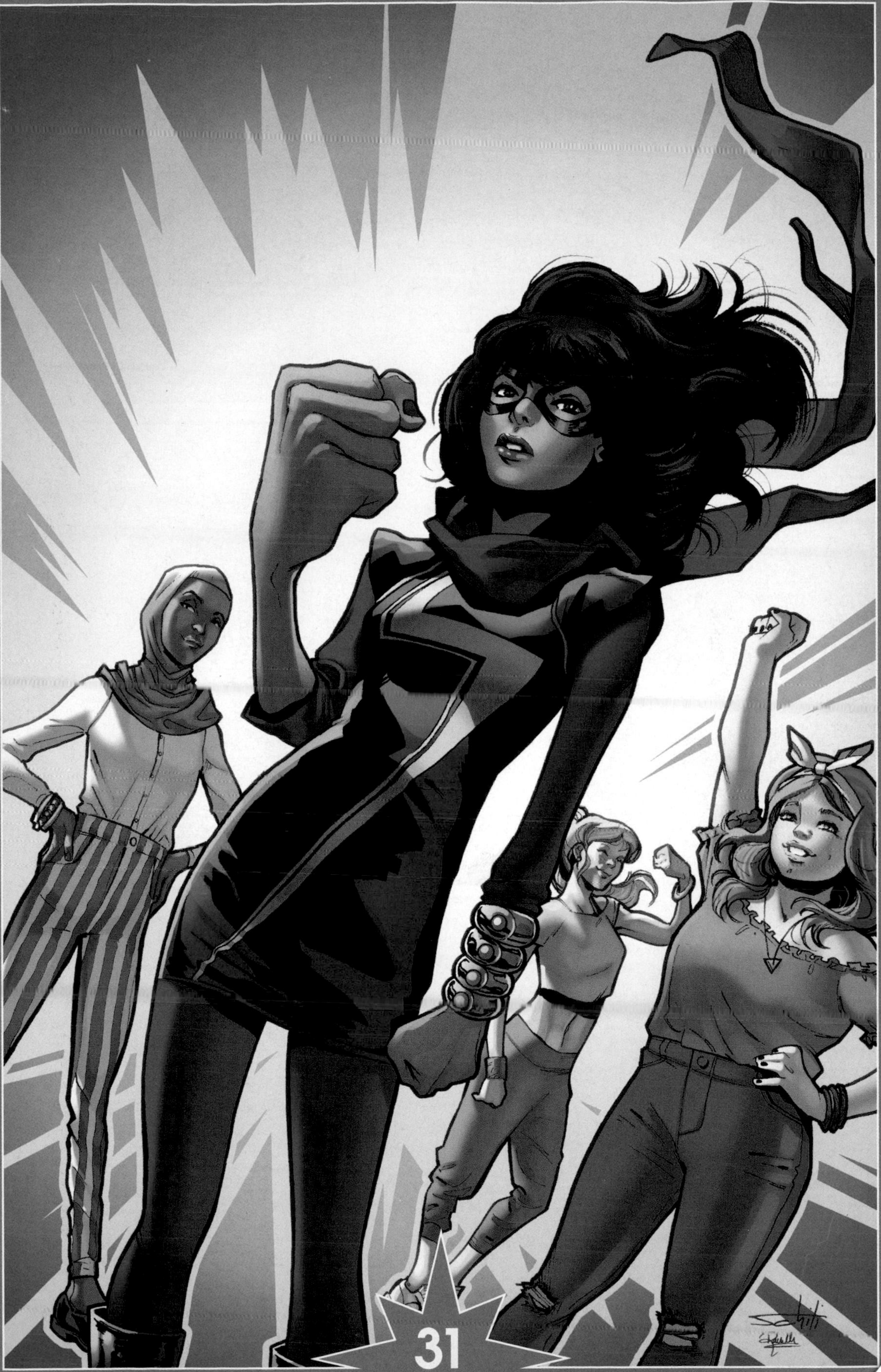
31

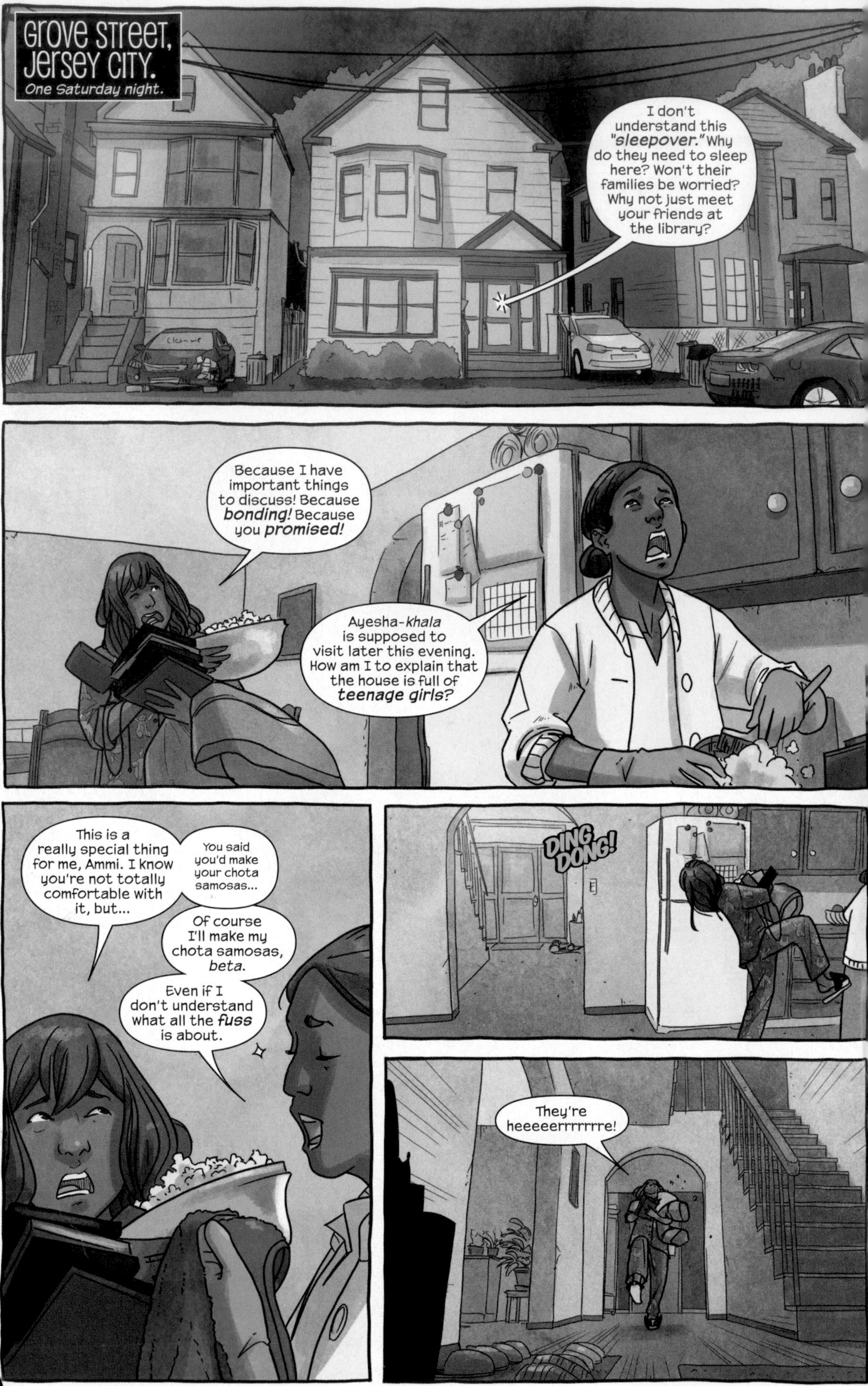

GROVE STREET, JERSEY CITY.
One Saturday night.
I don't understand this "sleepover." Why do they need to sleep here? Won't their families be worried? Why not just meet your friends at the library?
Because I have important things to discuss! Because bonding! Because you promised!
Ayesha-khala is supposed to visit later this evening. How am I to explain that the house is full of teenage girls?
This is a really special thing for me, Ammi. I know you're not totally comfortable with it, but...
You said you'd make your chota samosas...
Of course I'll make my chota samosas, beta.
Even if I don't understand what all the fuss is about.
DING DONG!
They're heeeeerrrrrrre!

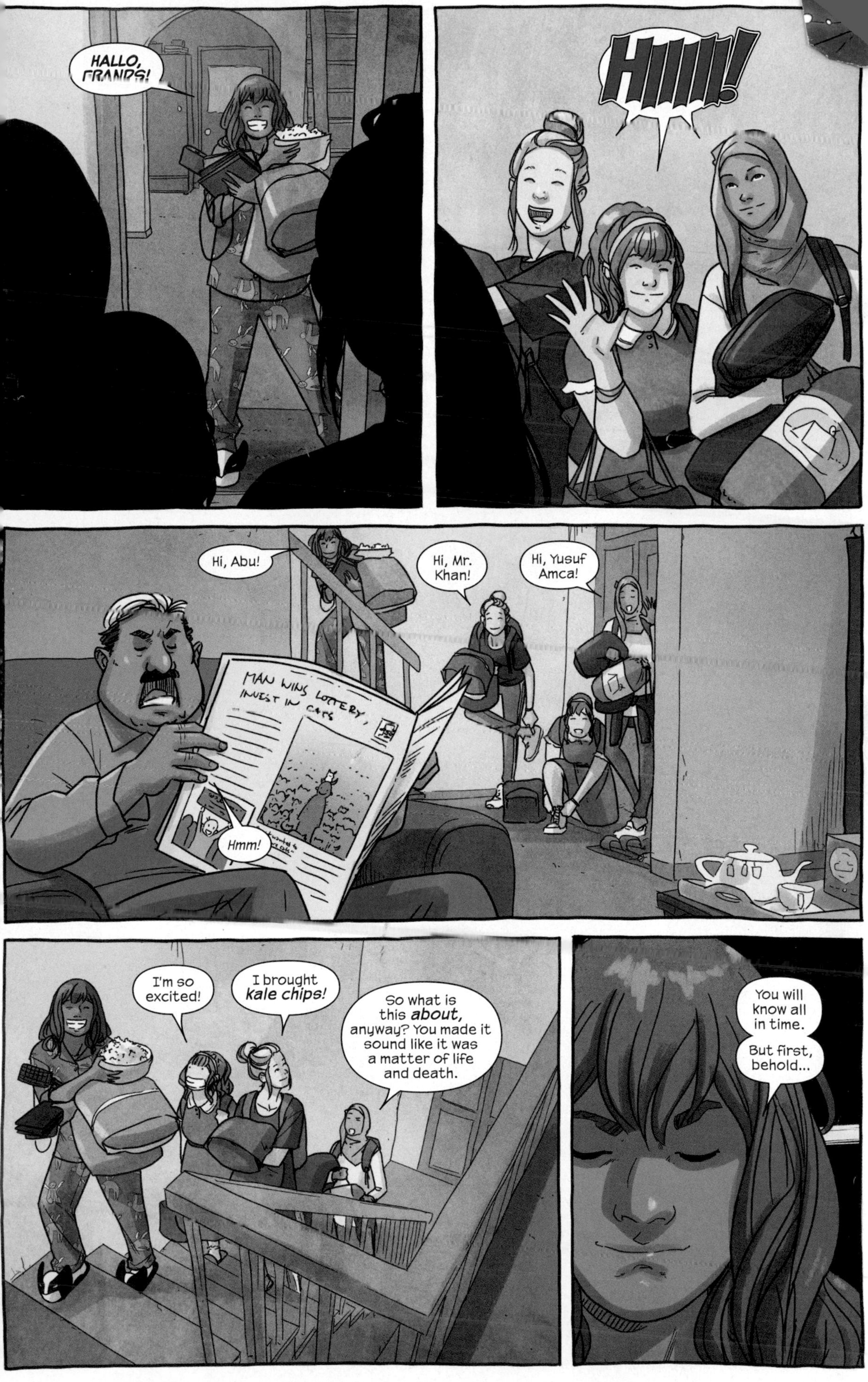
HALLO, FRANDS!
HIIIII!
Hi, Abu!
Hi, Mr. Khan!
Hi, Yusuf Amca!
MAN WINS LOTTERY, INVEST IN CATS
Hmm!
I'm so excited!
I brought kale chips!
So what is this about, anyway? You made it sound like it was a matter of life and death.
You will know all in time.
But first, behold...

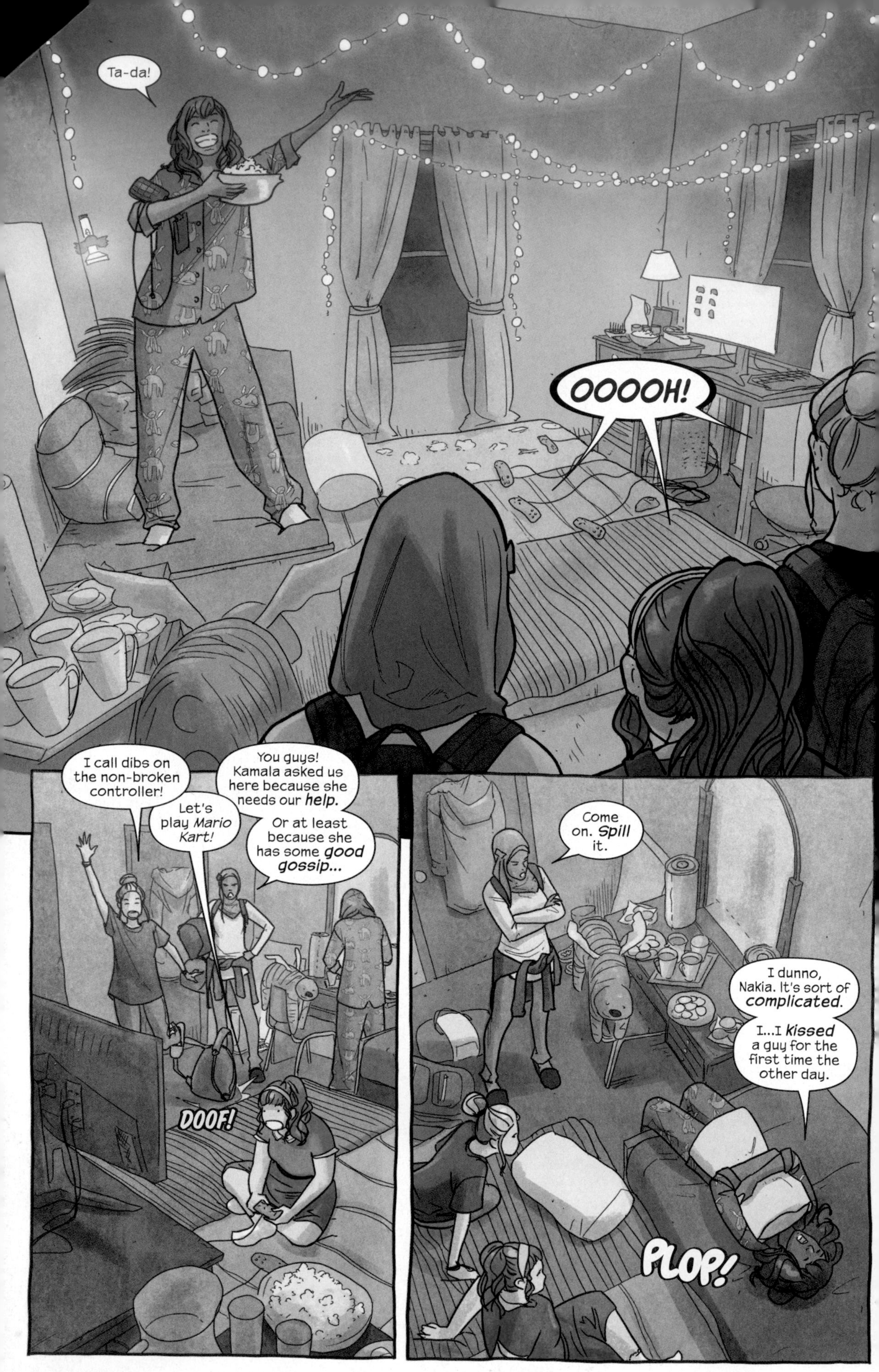
Ta-da!
OOOOH!
I call dibs on the non-broken controller!
Let's play *Mario Kart!*
You guys! Kamala asked us here because she needs our **help.**
Or at least because she has some ***good gossip...***
DOOF!
Come on. ***Spill*** it.
I dunno, Nakia. It's sort of ***complicated.***
I...I ***kissed*** a guy for the first time the other day.
PLOP!

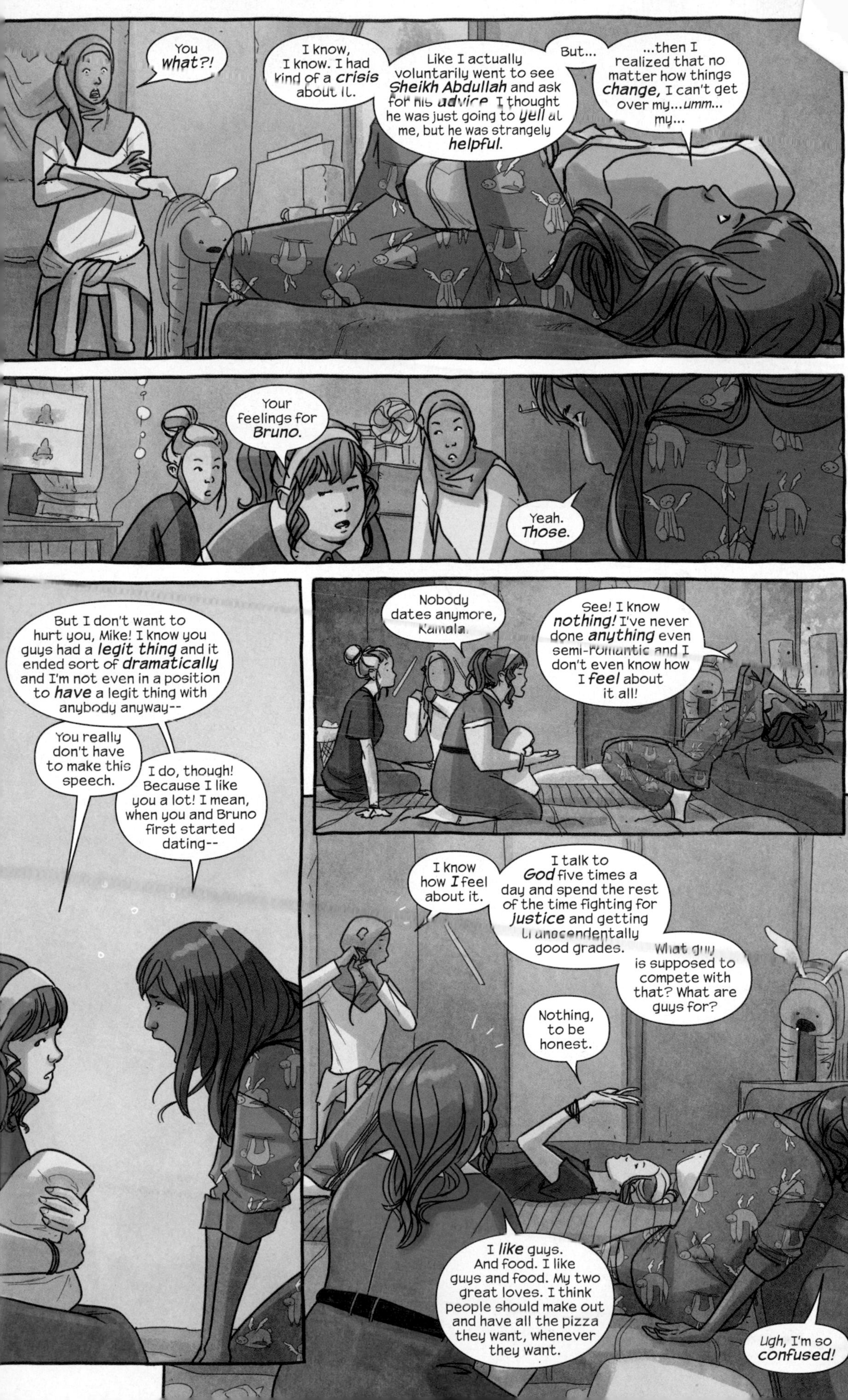
You what?!
I know, I know. I had kind of a crisis about it.
Like I actually voluntarily went to see Sheikh Abdullah and ask for his advice. I thought he was just going to yell at me, but he was strangely helpful.
But...
...then I realized that no matter how things change, I can't get over my...umm... my...
Your feelings for Bruno.
Yeah. Those.
But I don't want to hurt you, Mike! I know you guys had a legit thing and it ended sort of dramatically and I'm not even in a position to have a legit thing with anybody anyway--
You really don't have to make this speech.
I do, though! Because I like you a lot! I mean, when you and Bruno first started dating--
Nobody dates anymore, Kamala.
See! I know nothing! I've never done anything even semi-romantic and I don't even know how I feel about it all!
I know how I feel about it.
I talk to God five times a day and spend the rest of the time fighting for justice and getting transcendentally good grades.
What guy is supposed to compete with that? What are guys for?
Nothing, to be honest.
I like guys. And food. I like guys and food. My two great loves. I think people should make out and have all the pizza they want, whenever they want.
Ugh, I'm so confused!

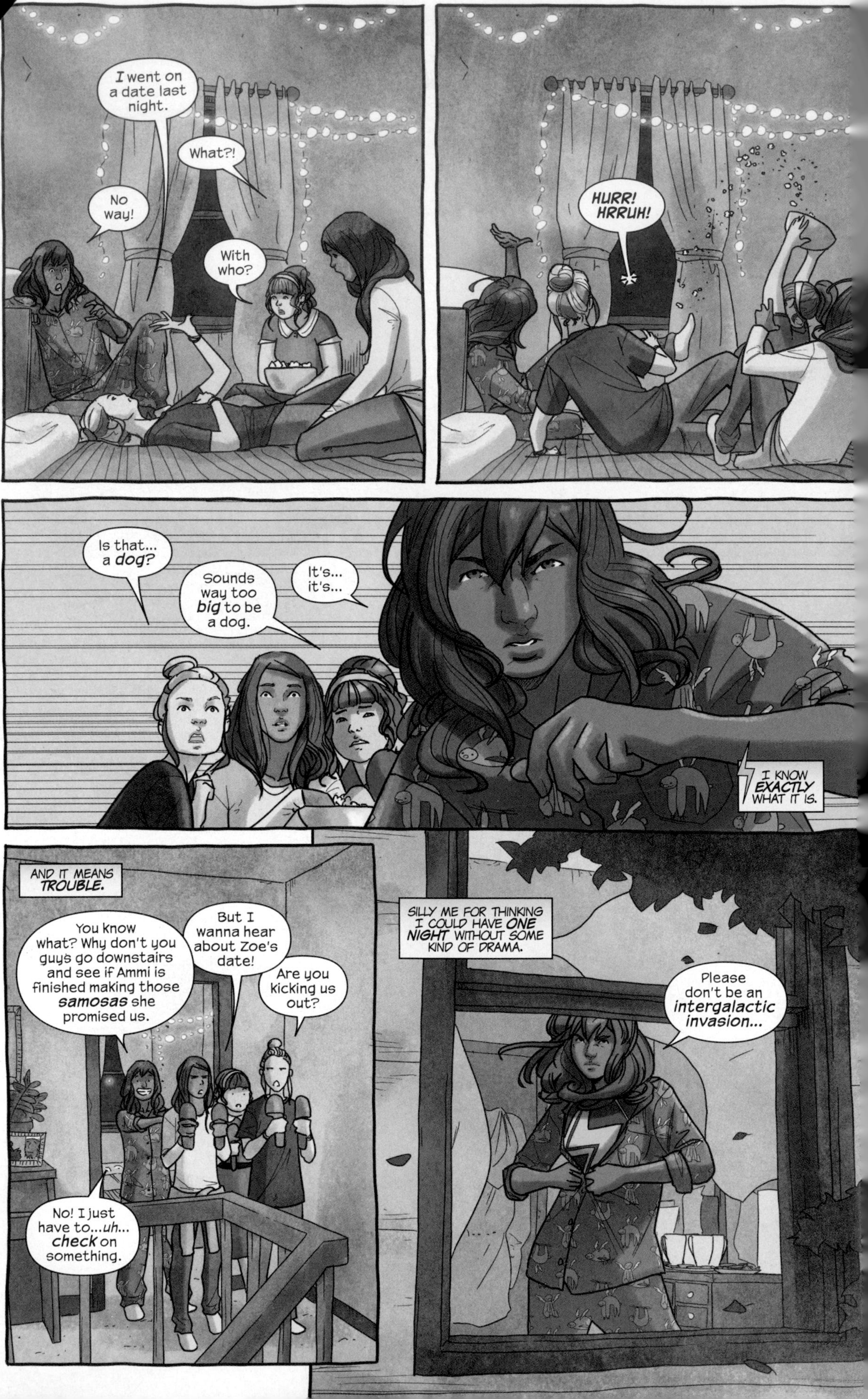
I went on a date last night.
What?!
No way!
With who?
HURR! HRRUH!
Is that... a dog?
Sounds way too big to be a dog.
It's... it's...
I KNOW EXACTLY WHAT IT IS.
AND IT MEANS TROUBLE.
You know what? Why don't you guys go downstairs and see if Ammi is finished making those samosas she promised us.
But I wanna hear about Zoe's date!
Are you kicking us out?
No! I just have to...uh... check on something.
SILLY ME FOR THINKING I COULD HAVE ONE NIGHT WITHOUT SOME KIND OF DRAMA.
Please don't be an intergalactic invasion...

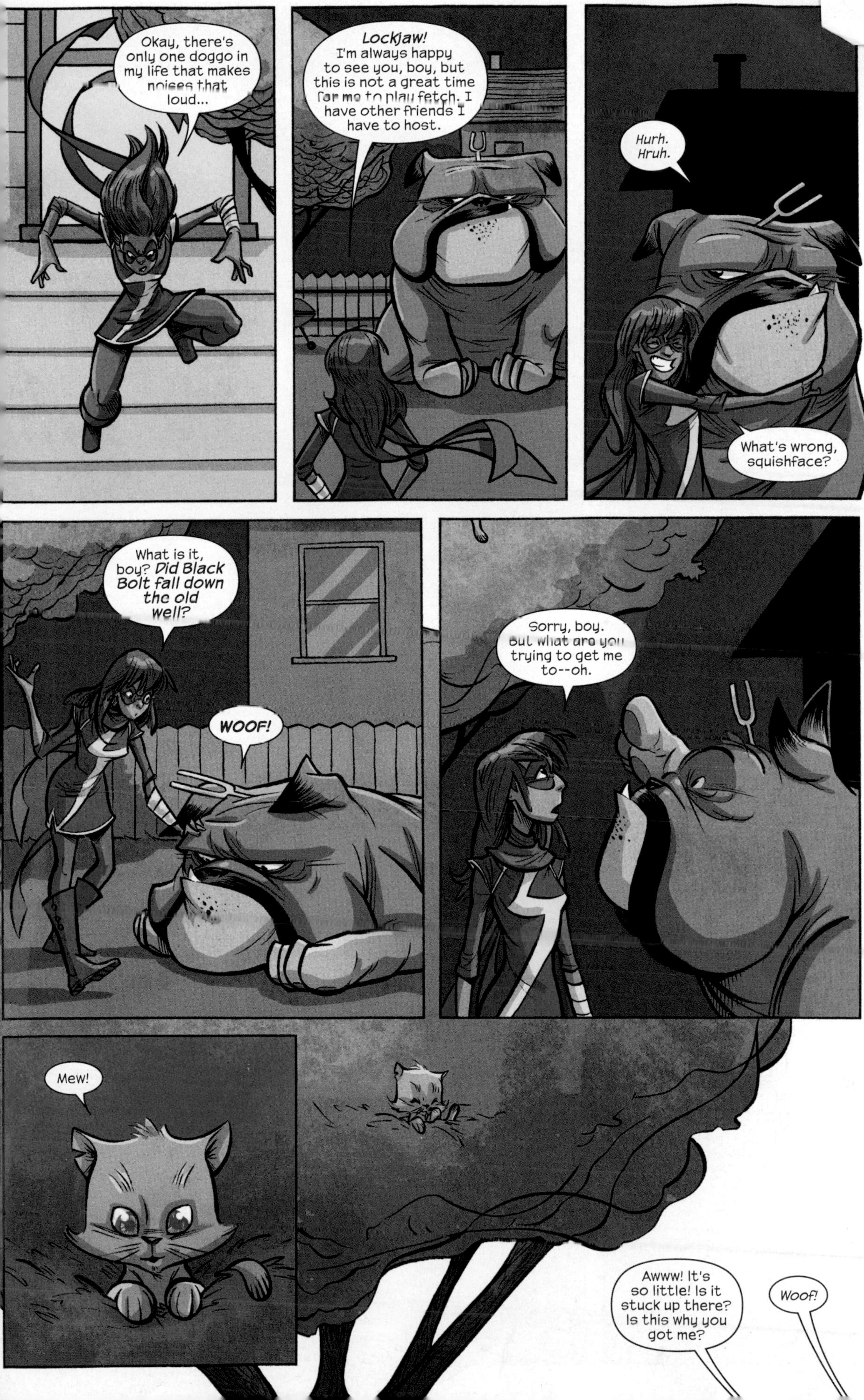

Okay, there's only one doggo in my life that makes noises that loud...
Lockjaw! I'm always happy to see you, boy, but this is not a great time for me to play fetch. I have other friends I have to host.
Hurh. Hruh.
What's wrong, squishface?
What is it, boy? Did Black Bolt fall down the old well?
WOOF!
Sorry, boy. But what are you trying to get me to--oh.
Mew!
Awww! It's so little! Is it stuck up there? Is this why you got me?
Woof!

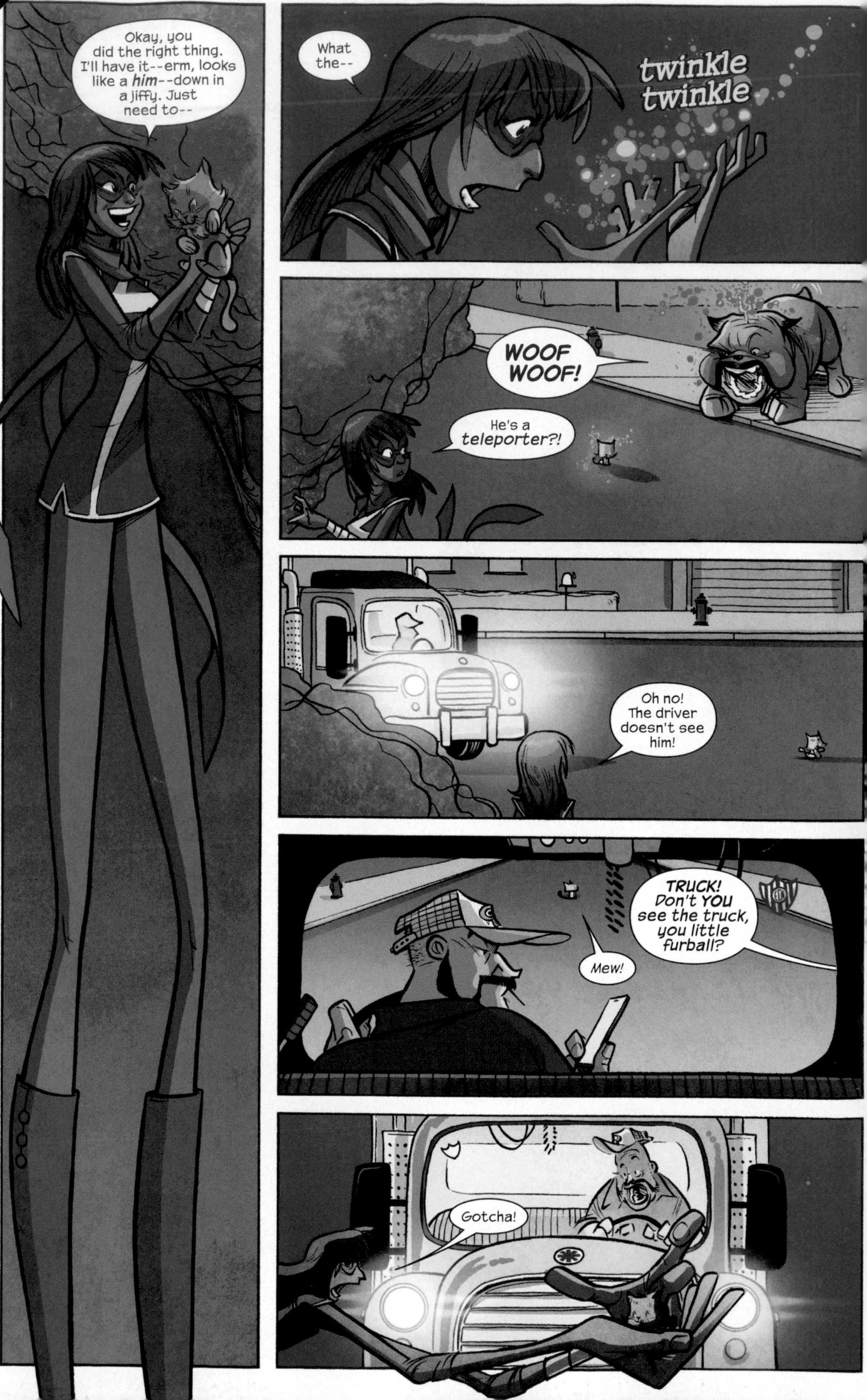
Okay, you did the right thing. I'll have it--erm, looks like a *him*--down in a jiffy. Just need to--
What the--
twinkle twinkle
WOOF WOOF!
He's a *teleporter?!*
Oh no! The driver doesn't see him!
TRUCK! Don't YOU see the truck, you little furball?
Mew!
Gotcha!

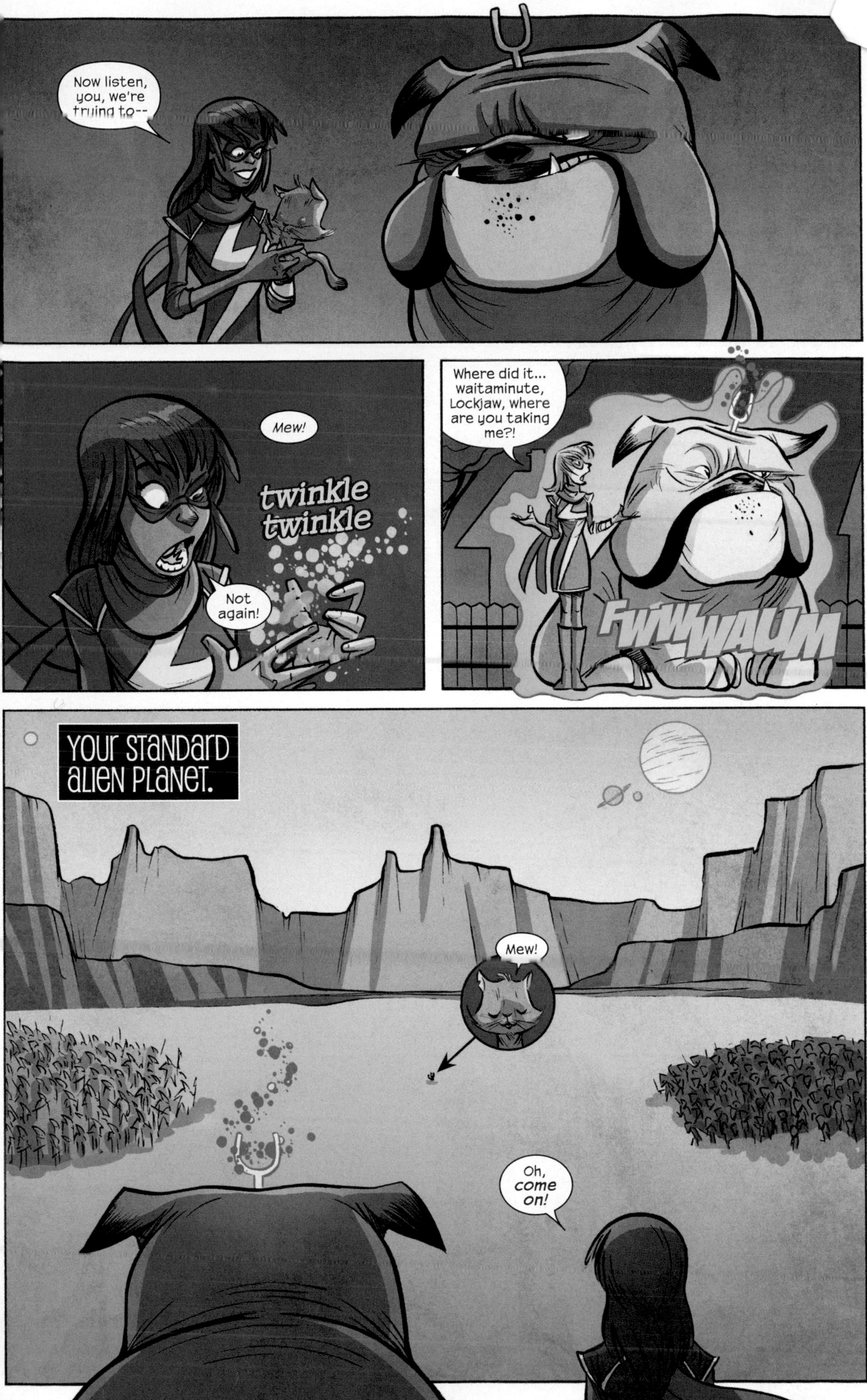

Now listen, you, we're trying to--
Mew!
twinkle twinkle
Not again!
Where did it... waitaminute, Lockjaw, where are you taking me?!
FWWWAUM
YOUR STANDARD ALIEN PLANET.
Mew!
Oh, come on!

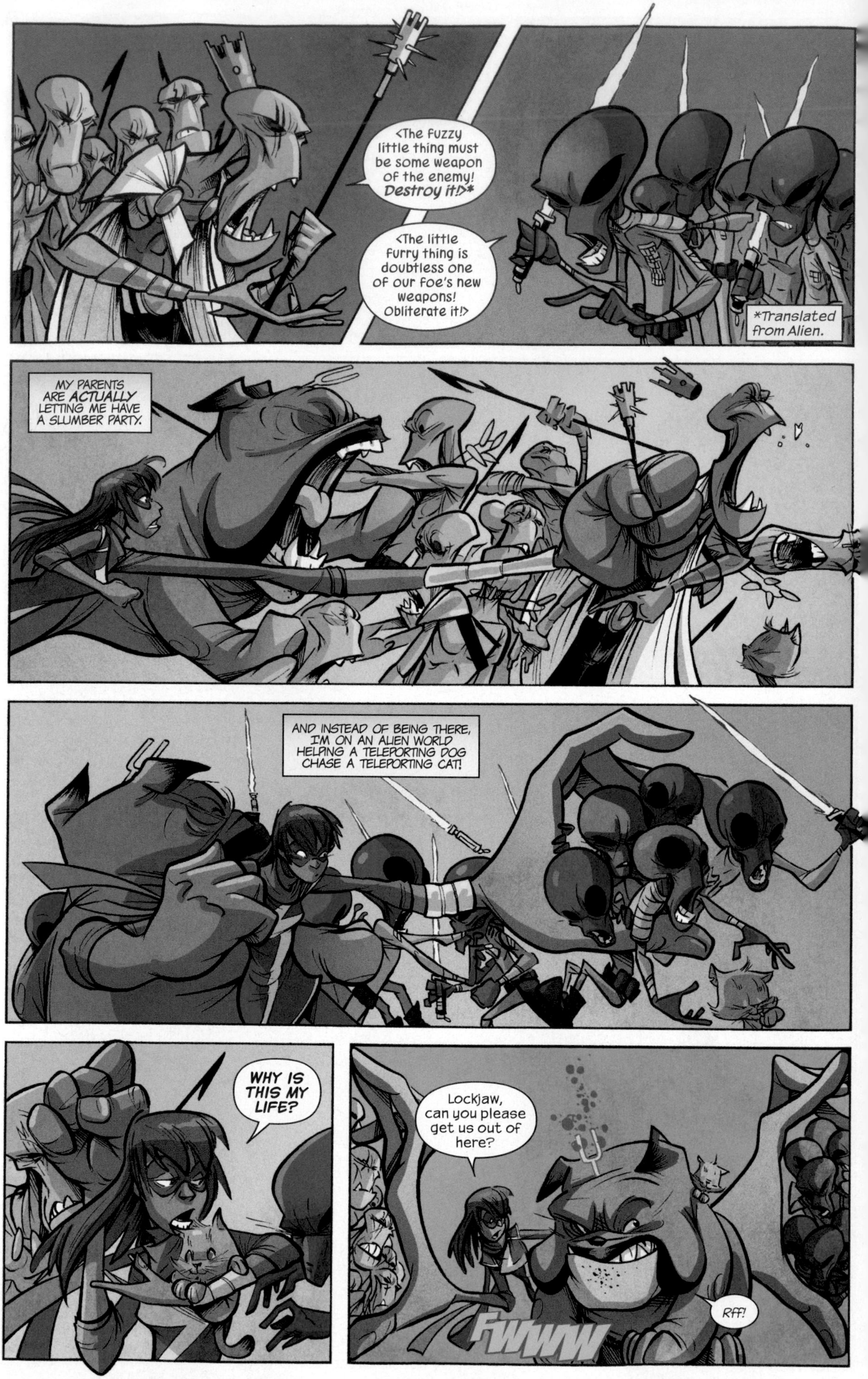
<The fuzzy little thing must be some weapon of the enemy! Destroy it!>*
<The little furry thing is doubtless one of our foe's new weapons! Obliterate it!>
*Translated from Alien.
MY PARENTS ARE ACTUALLY LETTING ME HAVE A SLUMBER PARTY.
AND INSTEAD OF BEING THERE, I'M ON AN ALIEN WORLD HELPING A TELEPORTING DOG CHASE A TELEPORTING CAT!
WHY IS THIS MY LIFE?
Lockjaw, can you please get us out of here?
Rff!
FWWW

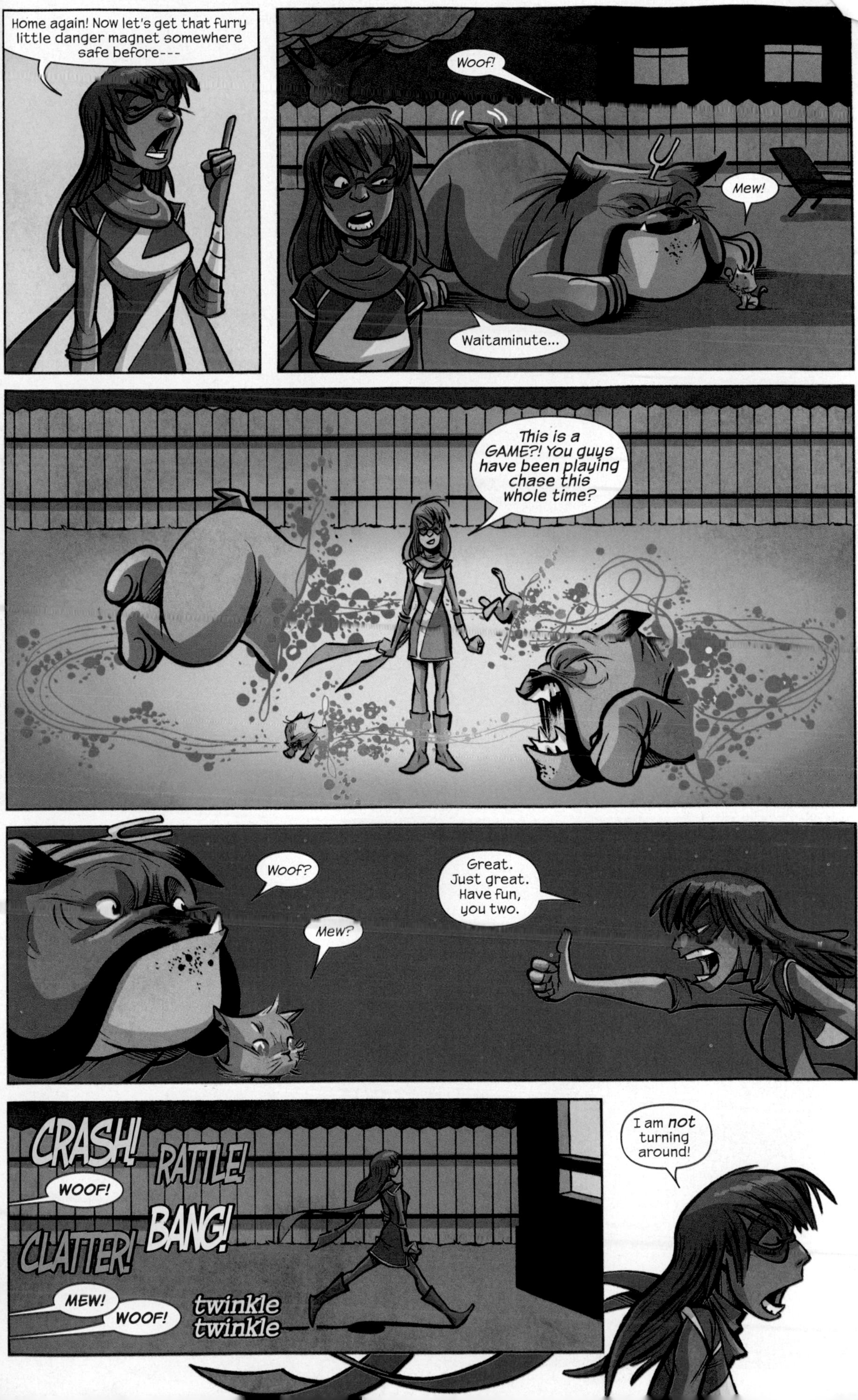
Home again! Now let's get that furry little danger magnet somewhere safe before---
Woof!
Mew!
Waitaminute...
This is a GAME?! You guys have been playing chase this whole time?
Woof?
Mew?
Great. Just great. Have fun, you two.
CRASH!
RATTLE!
WOOF!
BANG!
CLATTER!
MEW!
WOOF!
twinkle twinkle
I am *not* turning around!

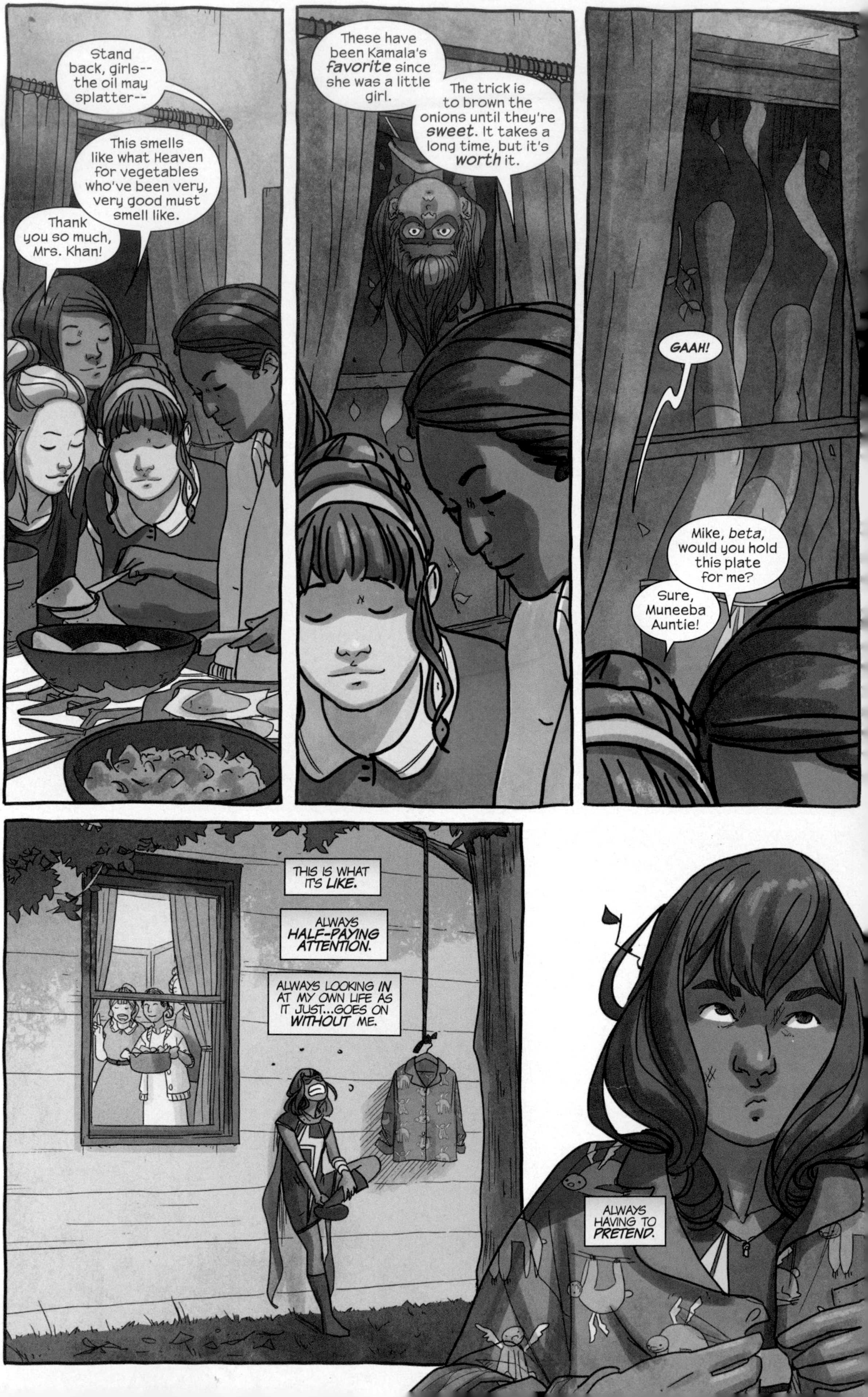
Stand back, girls-- the oil may splatter--
This smells like what Heaven for vegetables who've been very, very good must smell like.
Thank you so much, Mrs. Khan!
These have been Kamala's favorite since she was a little girl.
The trick is to brown the onions until they're sweet. It takes a long time, but it's worth it.
GAAH!
Mike, beta, would you hold this plate for me?
Sure, Muneeba Auntie!
THIS IS WHAT IT'S LIKE.
ALWAYS HALF-PAYING ATTENTION.
ALWAYS LOOKING IN AT MY OWN LIFE AS IT JUST...GOES ON WITHOUT ME.
ALWAYS HAVING TO PRETEND.

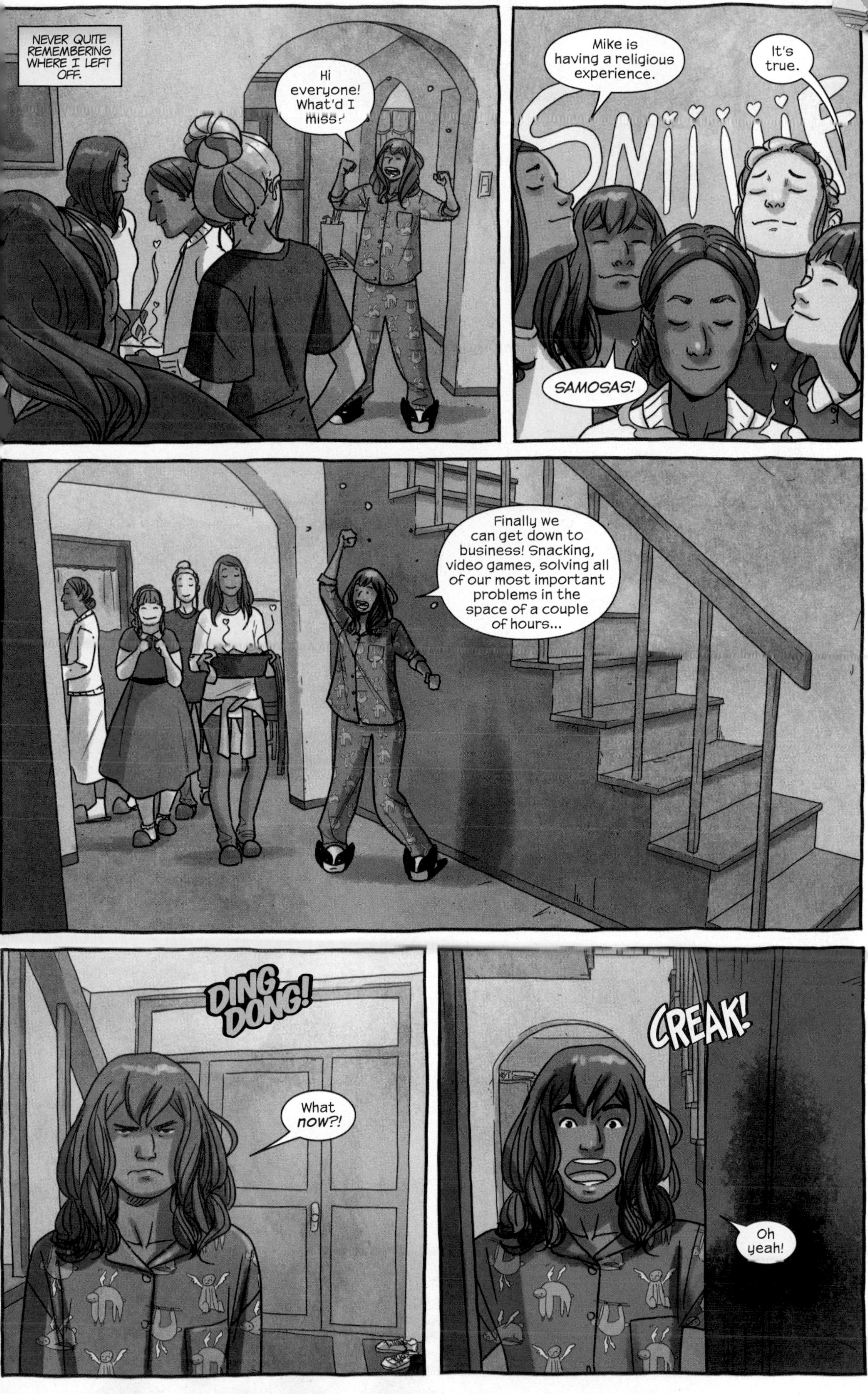
NEVER QUITE REMEMBERING WHERE I LEFT OFF.
Hi everyone! What'd I miss?
Mike is having a religious experience.
It's true.
SNIIIIFF
SAMOSAS!
Finally we can get down to business! Snacking, video games, solving all of our most important problems in the space of a couple of hours...
DING DONG!
What now?!
CREAK!
Oh yeah!

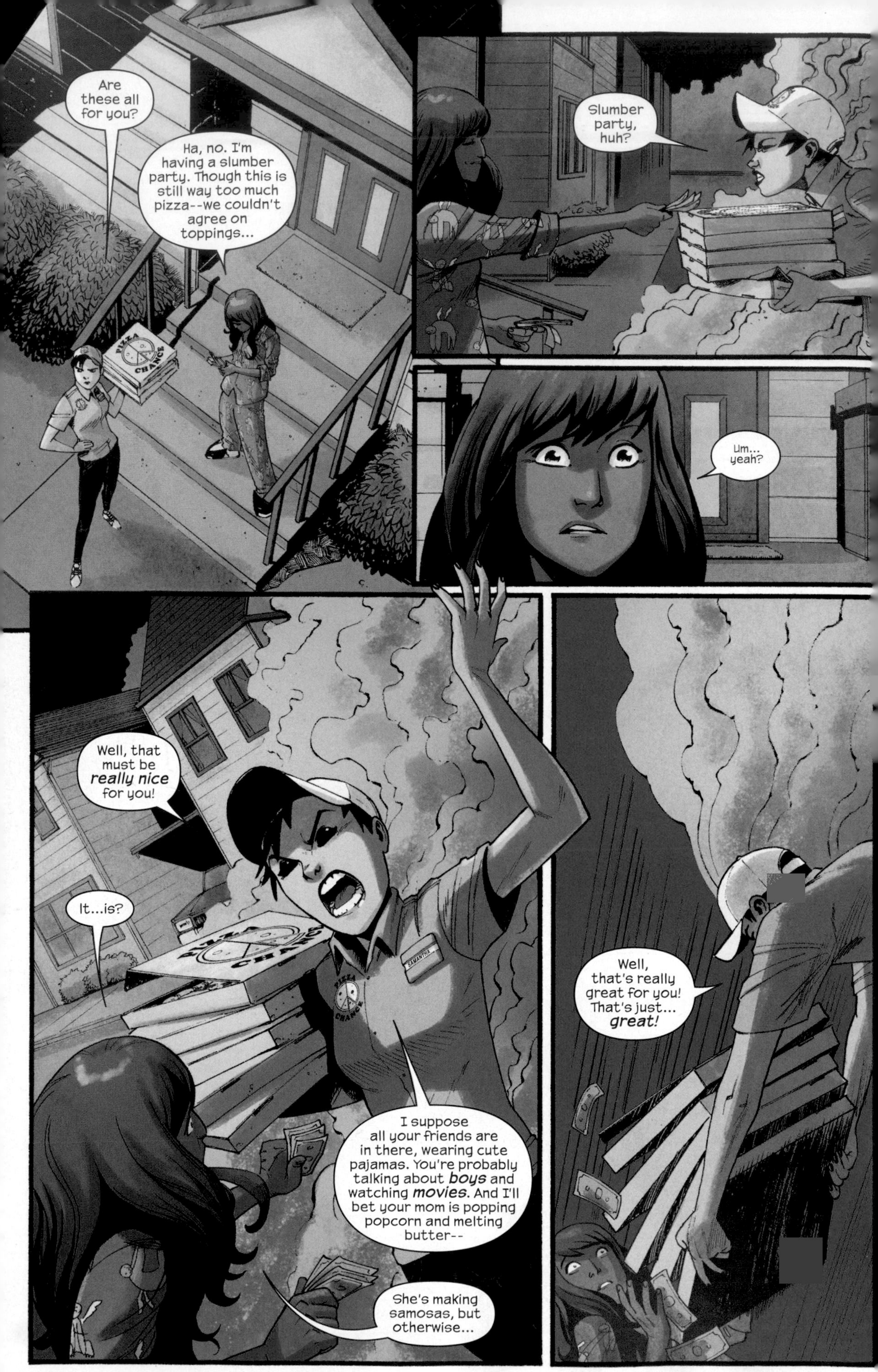

Are these all for you?
Ha, no. I'm having a slumber party. Though this is still way too much pizza--we couldn't agree on toppings...
PIZZA CHANCE
Slumber party, huh?
Um... yeah?
Well, that must be *really nice* for you!
It...is?
SAMANTHA
I suppose all your friends are in there, wearing cute pajamas. You're probably talking about *boys* and watching *movies*. And I'll bet your mom is popping popcorn and melting butter--
She's making samosas, but otherwise...
Well, that's really great for you! That's just... *great!*

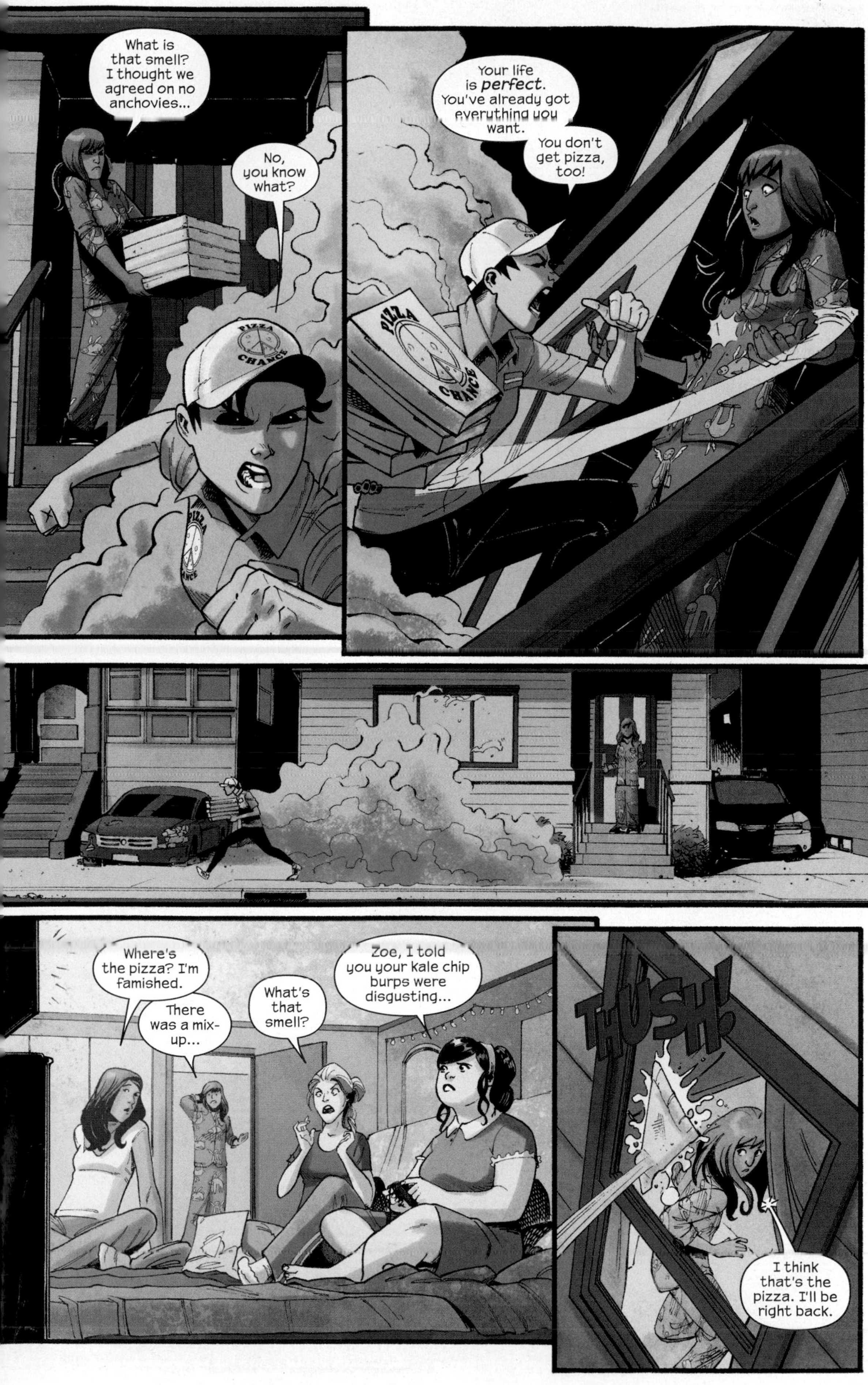

What is that smell? I thought we agreed on no anchovies...
No, you know what?
Your life is *perfect*. You've already got everything you want.
You don't get pizza, too!
PIZZA CHANCE
Where's the pizza? I'm famished.
There was a mix-up...
What's that smell?
Zoe, I told you your kale chip burps were disgusting...
THUSH!
I think that's the pizza. I'll be right back.

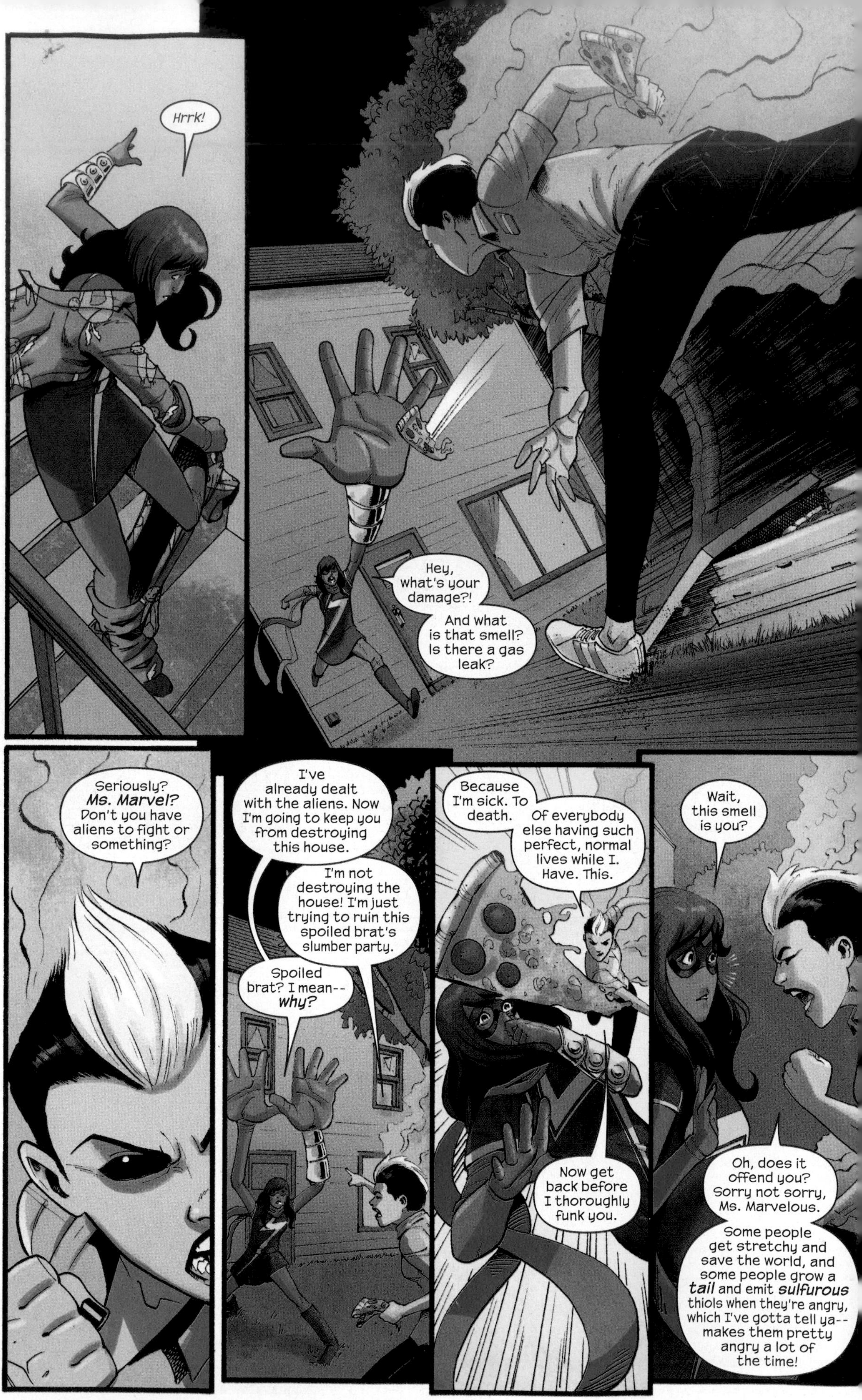
Hrrk!
Hey, what's your damage?!
And what is that smell? Is there a gas leak?
Seriously? Ms. Marvel? Don't you have aliens to fight or something?
I've already dealt with the aliens. Now I'm going to keep you from destroying this house.
I'm not destroying the house! I'm just trying to ruin this spoiled brat's slumber party.
Spoiled brat? I mean-- why?
Because I'm sick. To death.
Of everybody else having such perfect, normal lives while I. Have. This.
Now get back before I thoroughly funk you.
Wait, this smell is you?
Oh, does it offend you? Sorry not sorry, Ms. Marvelous.
Some people get stretchy and save the world, and some people grow a tail and emit sulfurous thiols when they're angry, which I've gotta tell ya-- makes them pretty angry a lot of the time!

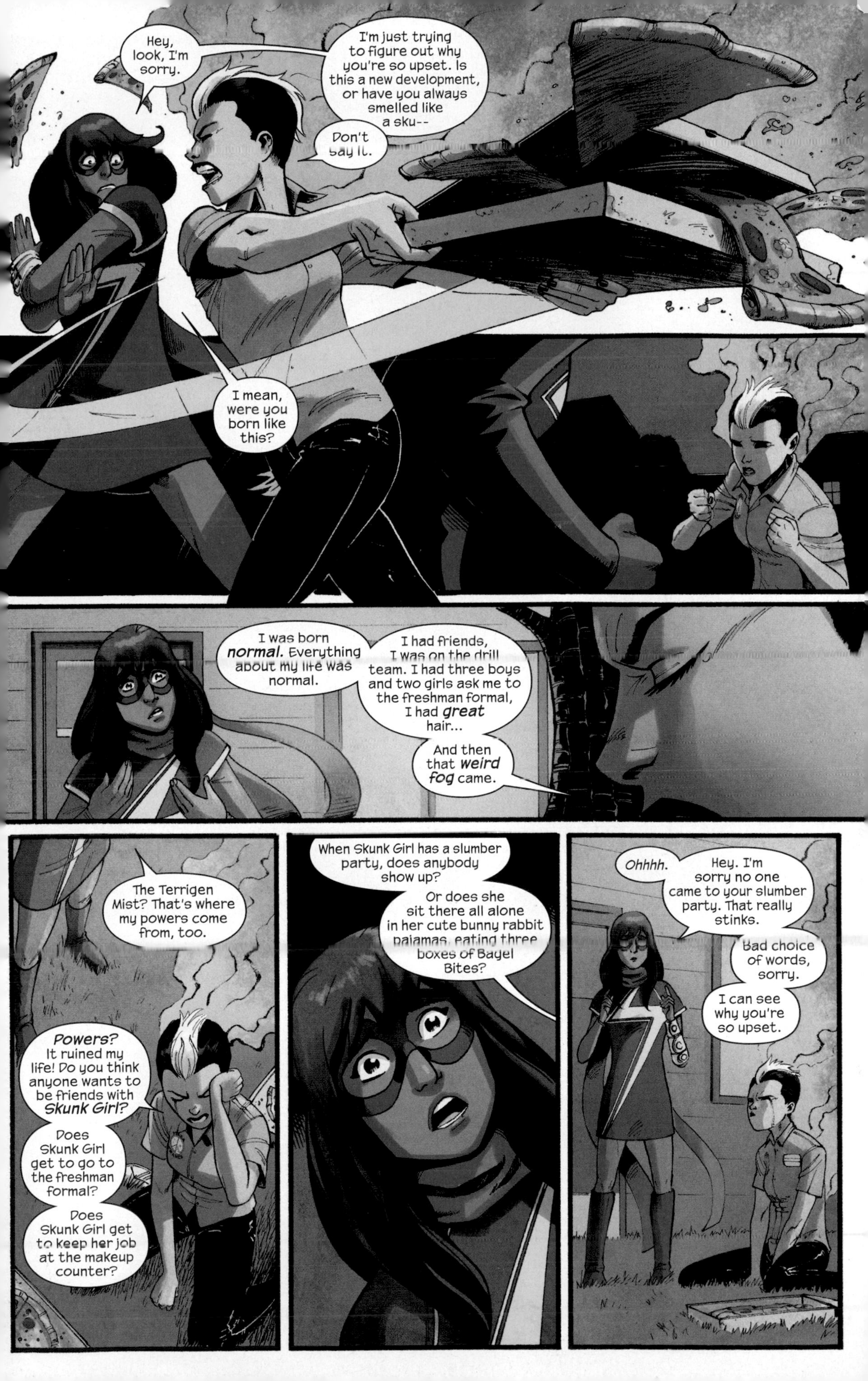
Hey, look, I'm sorry.
I'm just trying to figure out why you're so upset. Is this a new development, or have you always smelled like a sku--
Don't say it.
I mean, were you born like this?
I was born normal. Everything about my life was normal.
I had friends, I was on the drill team. I had three boys and two girls ask me to the freshman formal, I had great hair...
And then that weird fog came.
The Terrigen Mist? That's where my powers come from, too.
Powers? It ruined my life! Do you think anyone wants to be friends with Skunk Girl?
Does Skunk Girl get to go to the freshman formal?
Does Skunk Girl get to keep her job at the makeup counter?
When Skunk Girl has a slumber party, does anybody show up?
Or does she sit there all alone in her cute bunny rabbit pajamas, eating three boxes of Bagel Bites?
Ohhhh.
Hey. I'm sorry no one came to your slumber party. That really stinks.
Bad choice of words, sorry.
I can see why you're so upset.

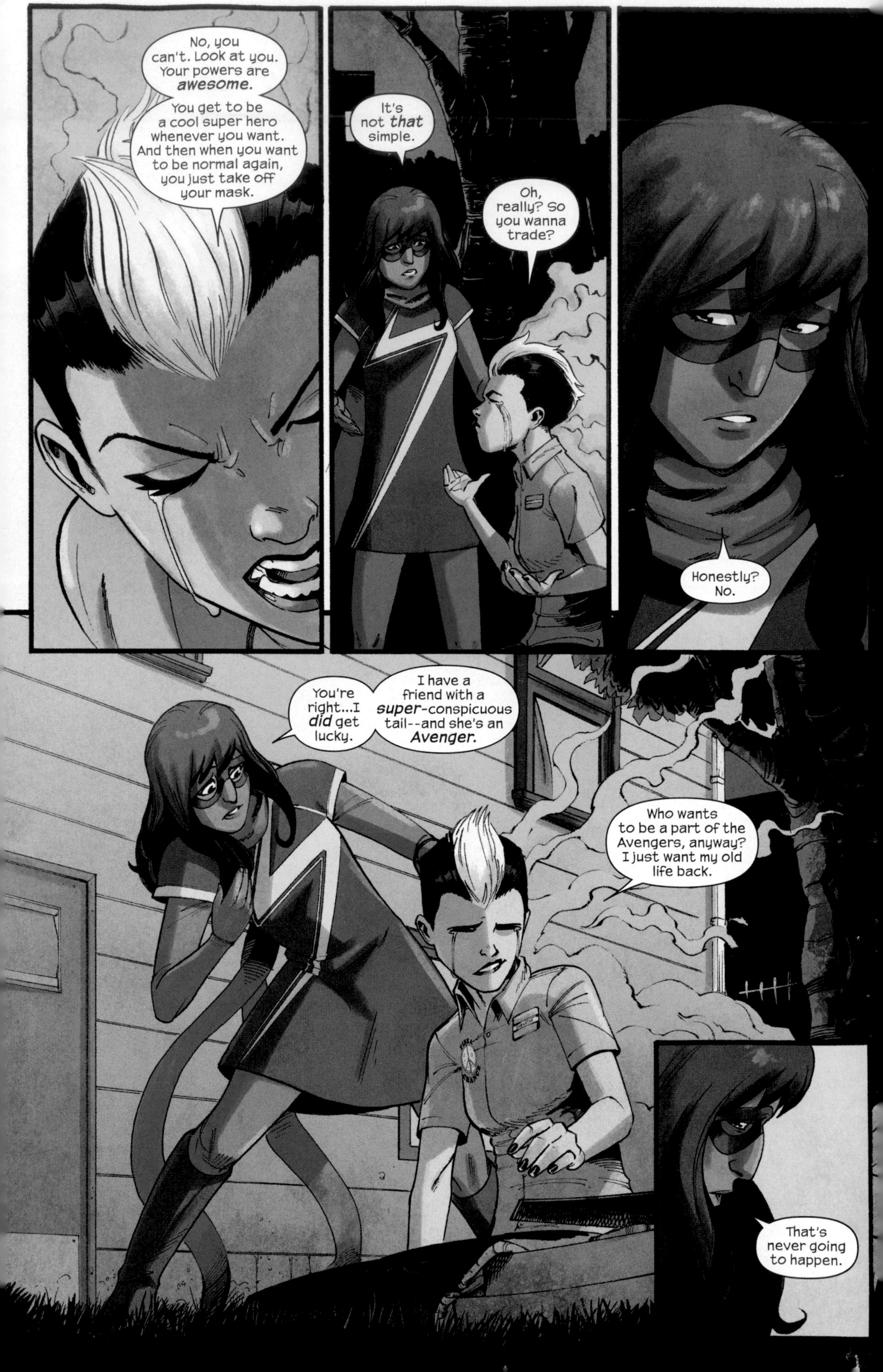
No, you can't. Look at you. Your powers are awesome.
You get to be a cool super hero whenever you want. And then when you want to be normal again, you just take off your mask.
It's not that simple.
Oh, really? So you wanna trade?
Honestly? No.
You're right...I did get lucky.
I have a friend with a super-conspicuous tail--and she's an Avenger.
Who wants to be a part of the Avengers, anyway? I just want my old life back.
That's never going to happen.

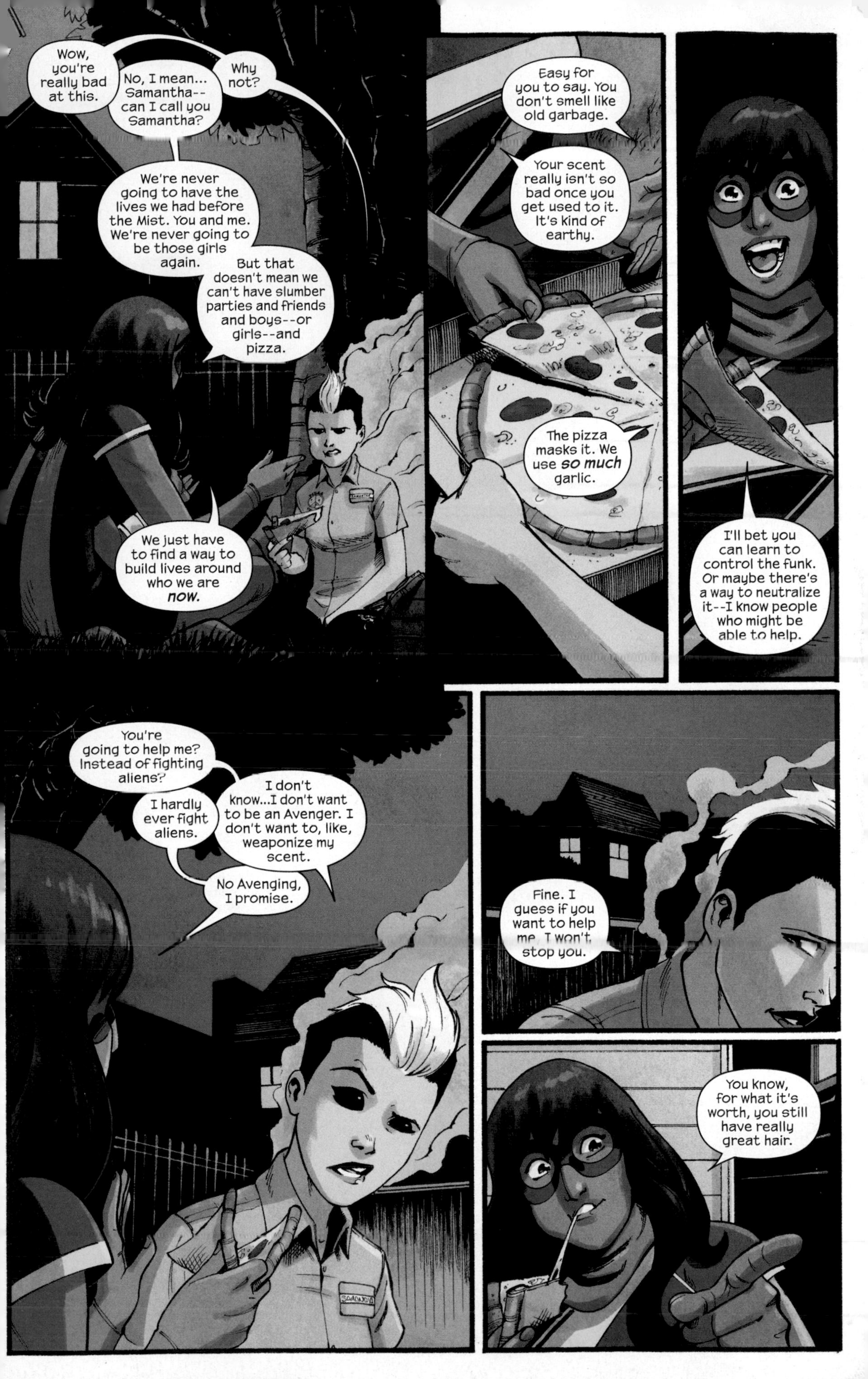

Wow, you're really bad at this.
Why not?
No, I mean... Samantha--can I call you Samantha?
We're never going to have the lives we had before the Mist. You and me. We're never going to be those girls again.
But that doesn't mean we can't have slumber parties and friends and boys--or girls--and pizza.
We just have to find a way to build lives around who we are *now.*
Easy for you to say. You don't smell like old garbage.
Your scent really isn't so bad once you get used to it. It's kind of earthy.
The pizza masks it. We use *so much* garlic.
I'll bet you can learn to control the funk. Or maybe there's a way to neutralize it--I know people who might be able to help.
You're going to help me? Instead of fighting aliens?
I hardly ever fight aliens.
I don't know...I don't want to be an Avenger. I don't want to, like, weaponize my scent.
No Avenging, I promise.
Fine. I guess if you want to help me, I won't stop you.
You know, for what it's worth, you still have really great hair.

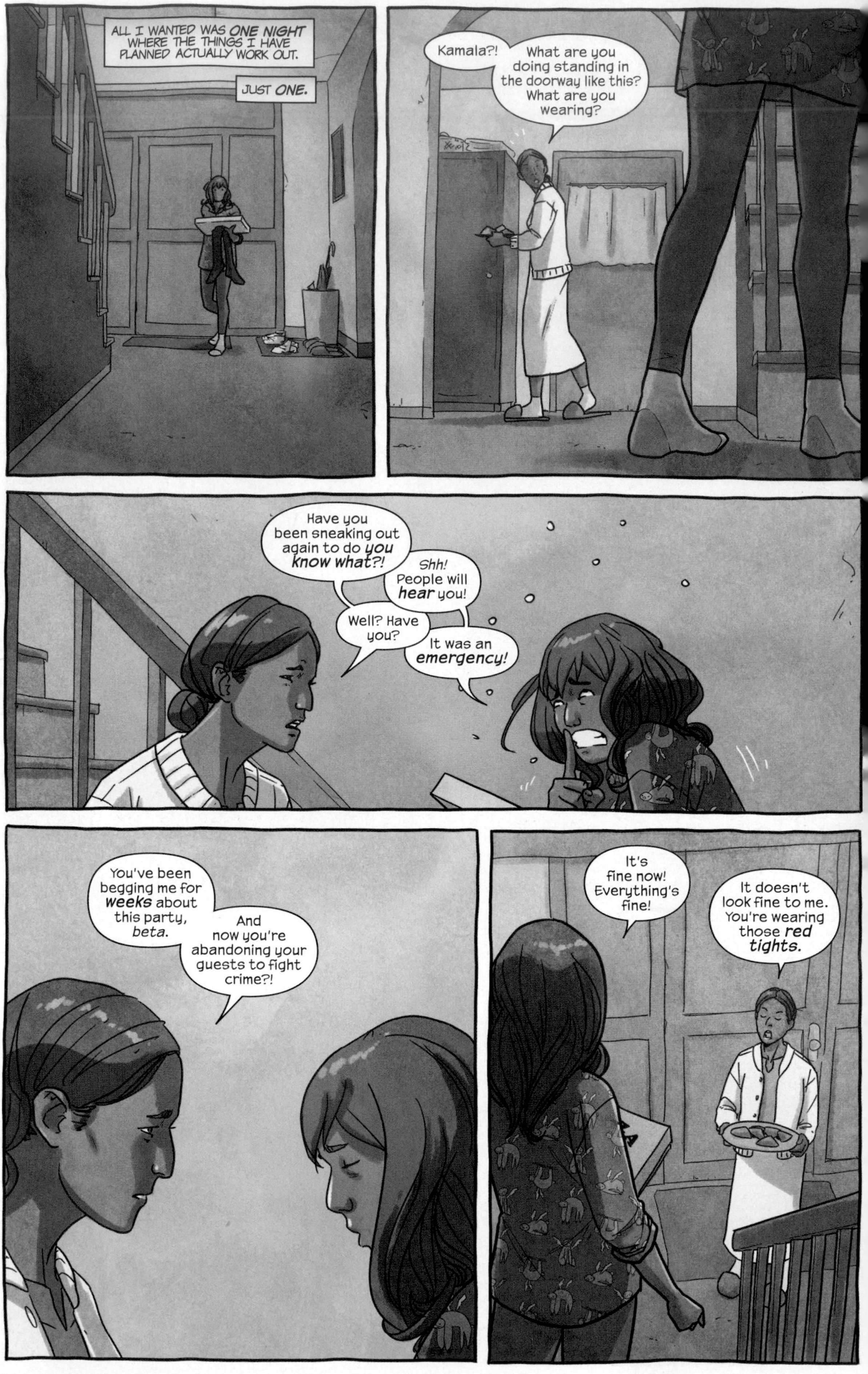

ALL I WANTED WAS ONE NIGHT WHERE THE THINGS I HAVE PLANNED ACTUALLY WORK OUT.
JUST ONE.
Kamala?!
What are you doing standing in the doorway like this? What are you wearing?
Have you been sneaking out again to do you know what?!
Shh! People will hear you!
Well? Have you?
It was an emergency!
You've been begging me for weeks about this party, beta.
And now you're abandoning your guests to fight crime?!
It's fine now! Everything's fine!
It doesn't look fine to me. You're wearing those red tights.

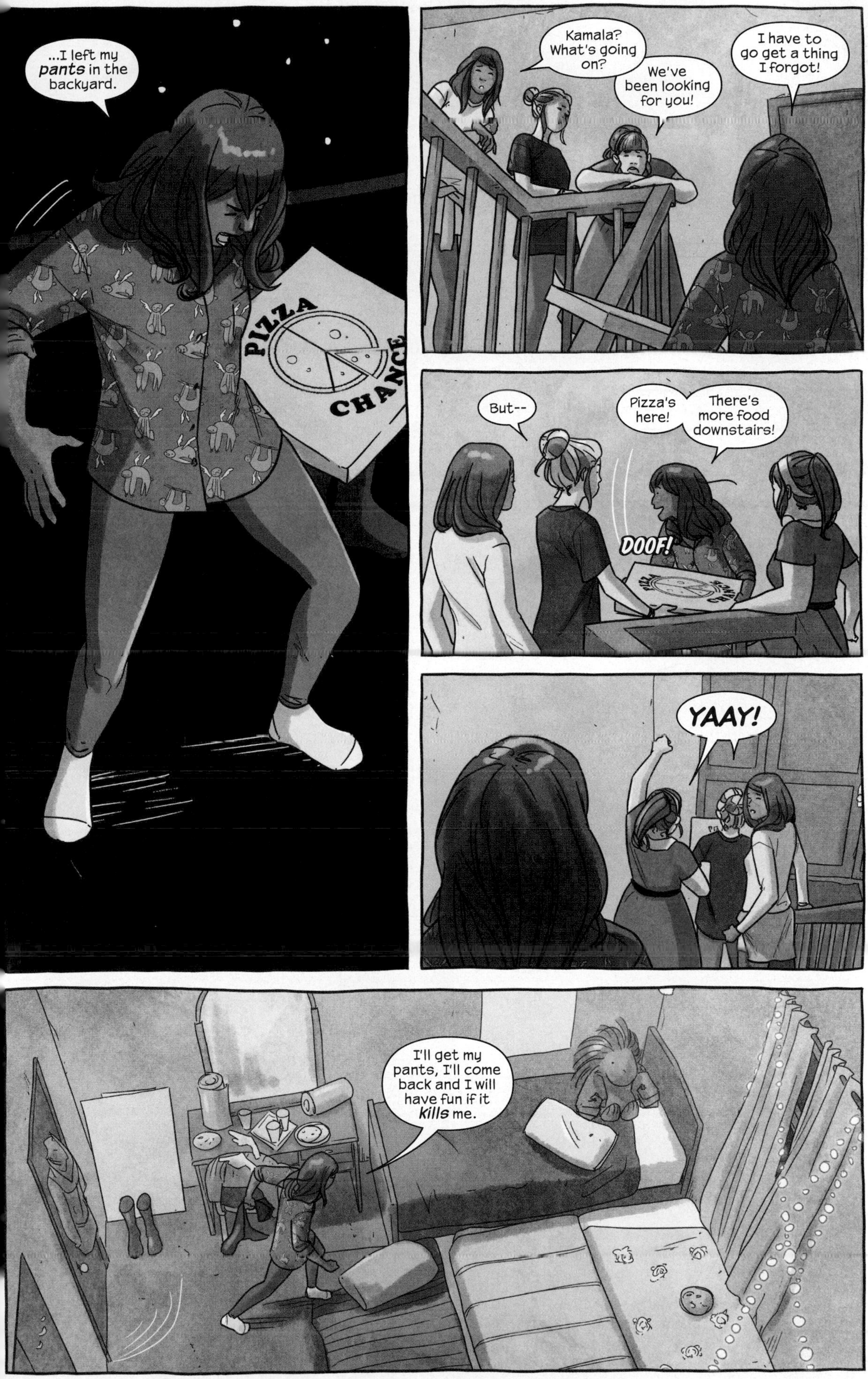

...I left my *pants* in the backyard.
PIZZA CHANCE
Kamala? What's going on?
We've been looking for you!
I have to go get a thing I forgot!
But--
Pizza's here!
There's more food downstairs!
DOOF!
YAAY!
I'll get my pants, I'll come back and I will have fun if it *kills* me.

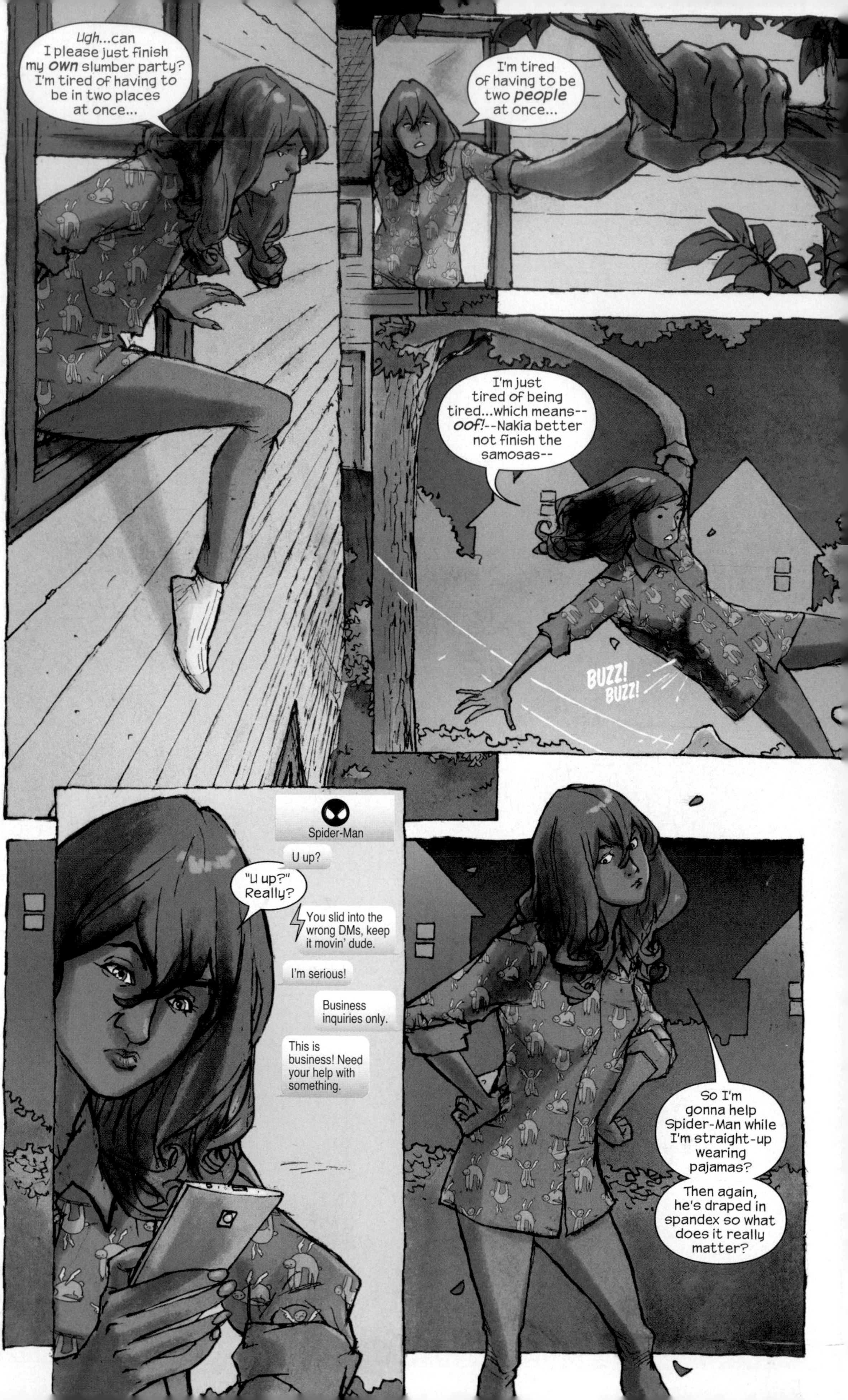

Ugh...can I please just finish my OWN slumber party? I'm tired of having to be in two places at once...
I'm tired of having to be two people at once...
I'm just tired of being tired...which means--oof!--Nakia better not finish the samosas--
BUZZ! BUZZ!
Spider-Man
U up?
"U up?" Really?
You slid into the wrong DMs, keep it movin' dude.
I'm serious!
Business inquiries only.
This is business! Need your help with something.
So I'm gonna help Spider-Man while I'm straight-up wearing pajamas?
Then again, he's draped in spandex so what does it really matter?

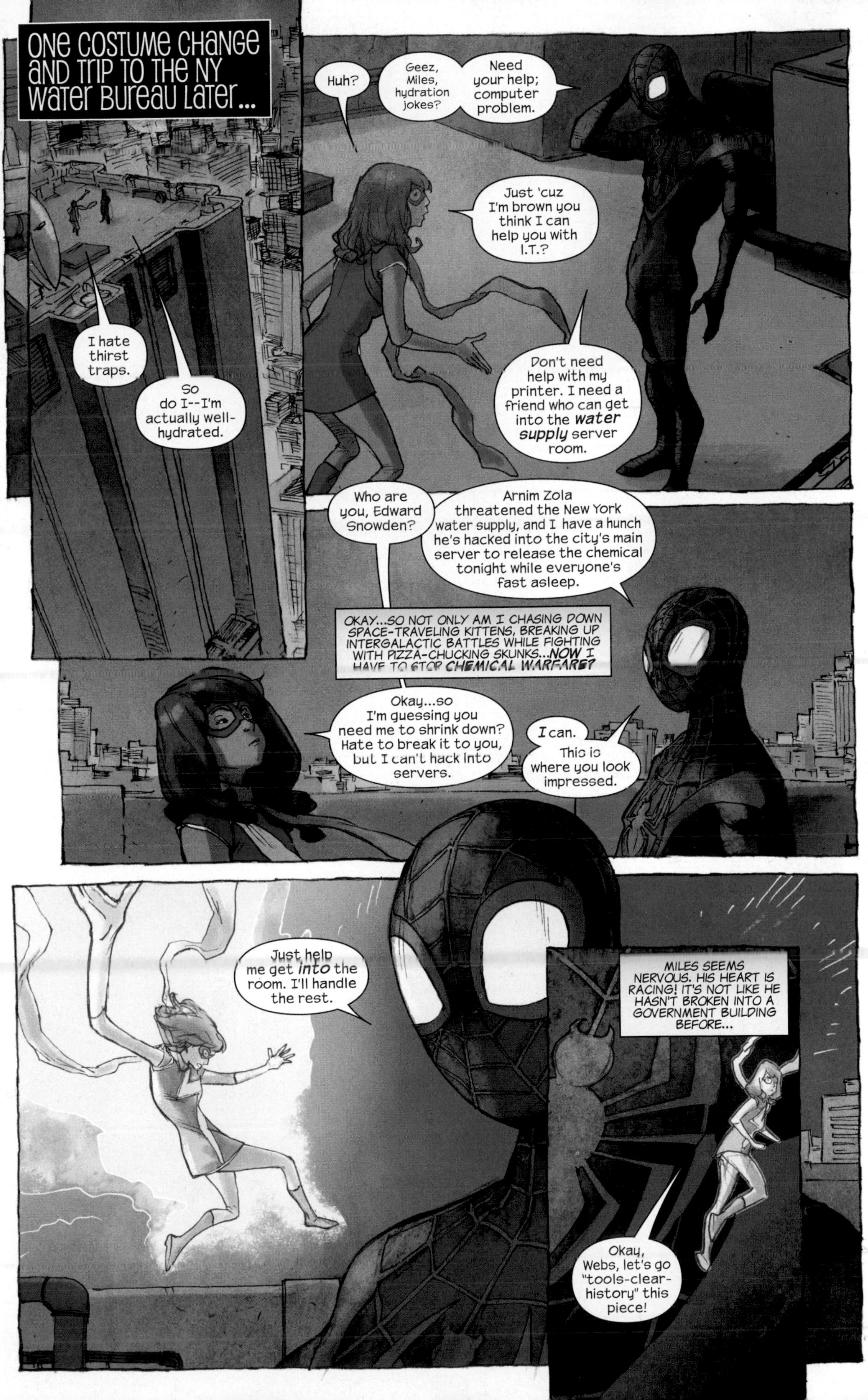
ONE COSTUME CHANGE AND TRIP TO THE NY WATER BUREAU LATER...
Huh?
Geez, Miles, hydration jokes?
Need your help; computer problem.
I hate thirst traps.
So do I--I'm actually well-hydrated.
Just 'cuz I'm brown you think I can help you with I.T.?
Don't need help with my printer. I need a friend who can get into the water supply server room.
Who are you, Edward Snowden?
Arnim Zola threatened the New York water supply, and I have a hunch he's hacked into the city's main server to release the chemical tonight while everyone's fast asleep.
OKAY...SO NOT ONLY AM I CHASING DOWN SPACE-TRAVELING KITTENS, BREAKING UP INTERGALACTIC BATTLES WHILE FIGHTING WITH PIZZA-CHUCKING SKUNKS...NOW I HAVE TO STOP CHEMICAL WARFARE?
Okay...so I'm guessing you need me to shrink down? Hate to break it to you, but I can't hack into servers.
I can.
This is where you look impressed.
Just help me get into the room. I'll handle the rest.
MILES SEEMS NERVOUS. HIS HEART IS RACING! IT'S NOT LIKE HE HASN'T BROKEN INTO A GOVERNMENT BUILDING BEFORE...
Okay, Webs, let's go "tools-clear-history" this piece!

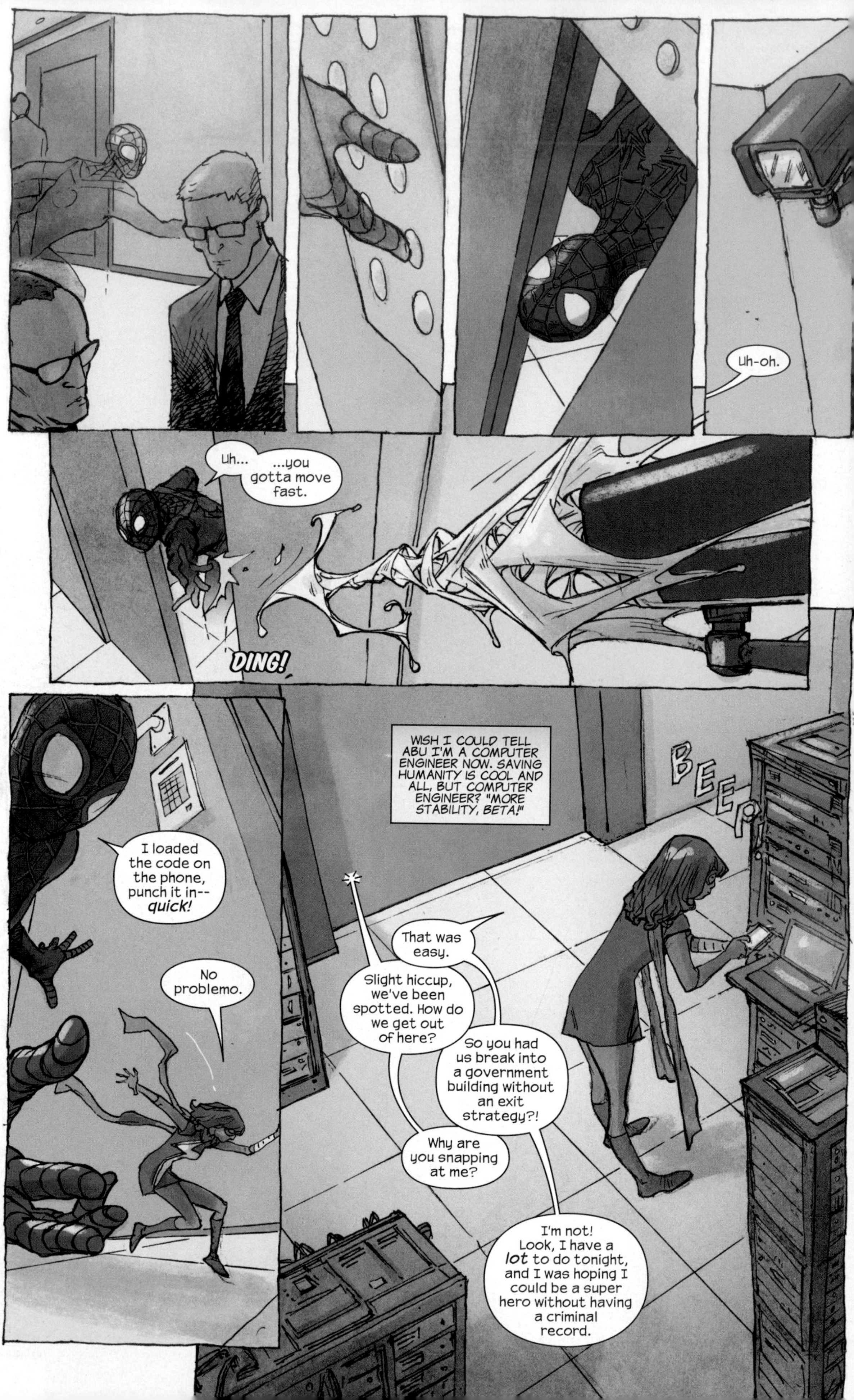
Uh-oh.
Uh...
...you gotta move fast.
DING!
WISH I COULD TELL ABU I'M A COMPUTER ENGINEER NOW. SAVING HUMANITY IS COOL AND ALL, BUT COMPUTER ENGINEER? "MORE STABILITY, BETA!"
BEEP
I loaded the code on the phone, punch it in--*quick!*
No problemo.
That was easy.
Slight hiccup, we've been spotted. How do we get out of here?
So you had us break into a government building without an exit strategy?!
Why are you snapping at me?
I'm not! Look, I have a *lot* to do tonight, and I was hoping I could be a super hero without having a criminal record.

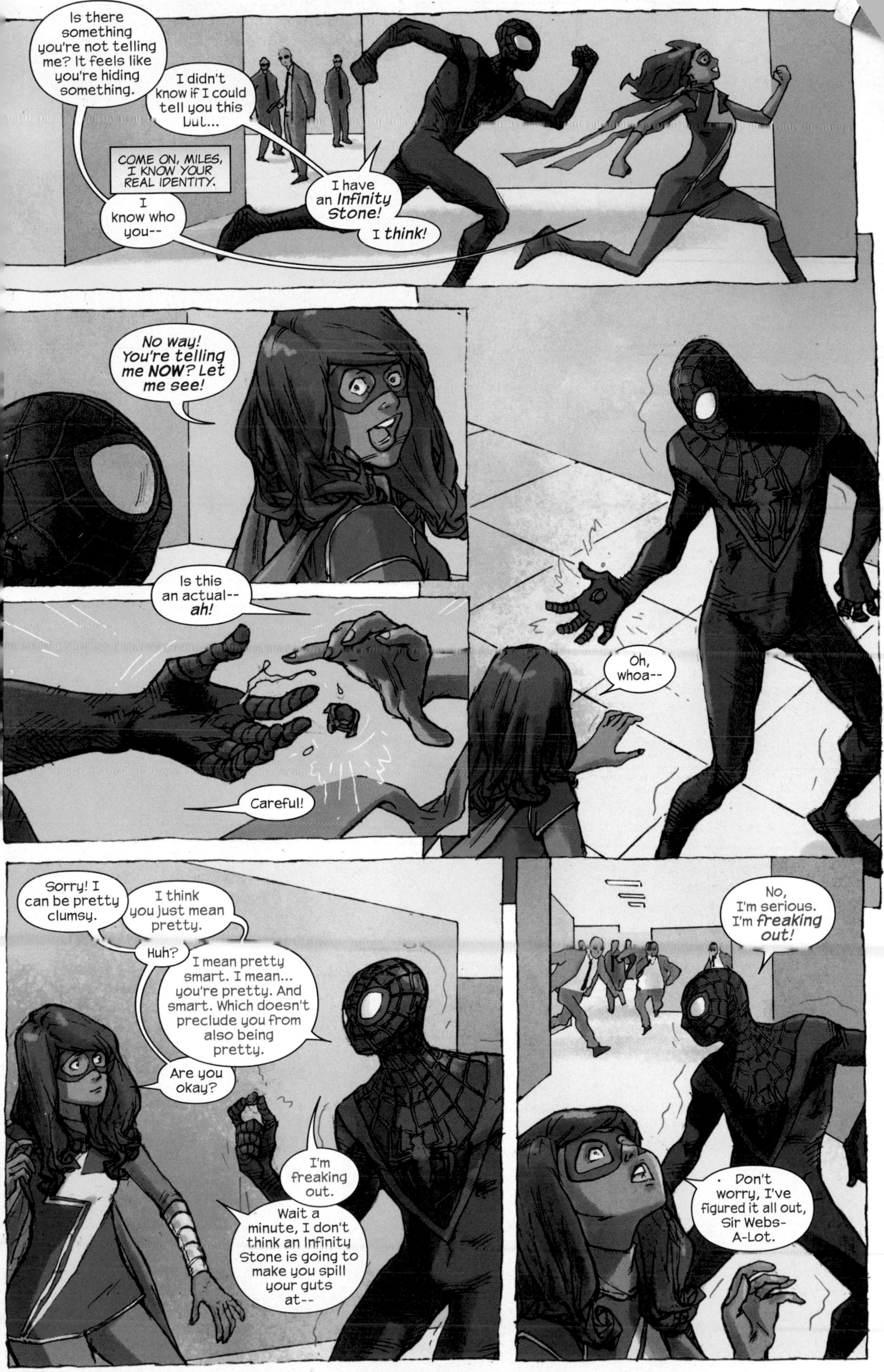

Is there something you're not telling me? It feels like you're hiding something.
I didn't know if I could tell you this but...
COME ON, MILES, I KNOW YOUR REAL IDENTITY.
I know who you--
I have an *Infinity Stone!*
I *think!*
No way! You're telling me NOW? Let me see!
Is this an actual-- *ah!*
Careful!
Oh, whoa--
Sorry! I can be pretty clumsy.
I think you just mean pretty.
Huh?
I mean pretty smart. I mean... you're pretty. And smart. Which doesn't preclude you from also being pretty.
Are you okay?
I'm freaking out.
Wait a minute, I don't think an Infinity Stone is going to make you spill your guts at--
No, I'm serious. I'm *freaking out!*
Don't worry, I've figured it all out, Sir Webs-A-Lot.

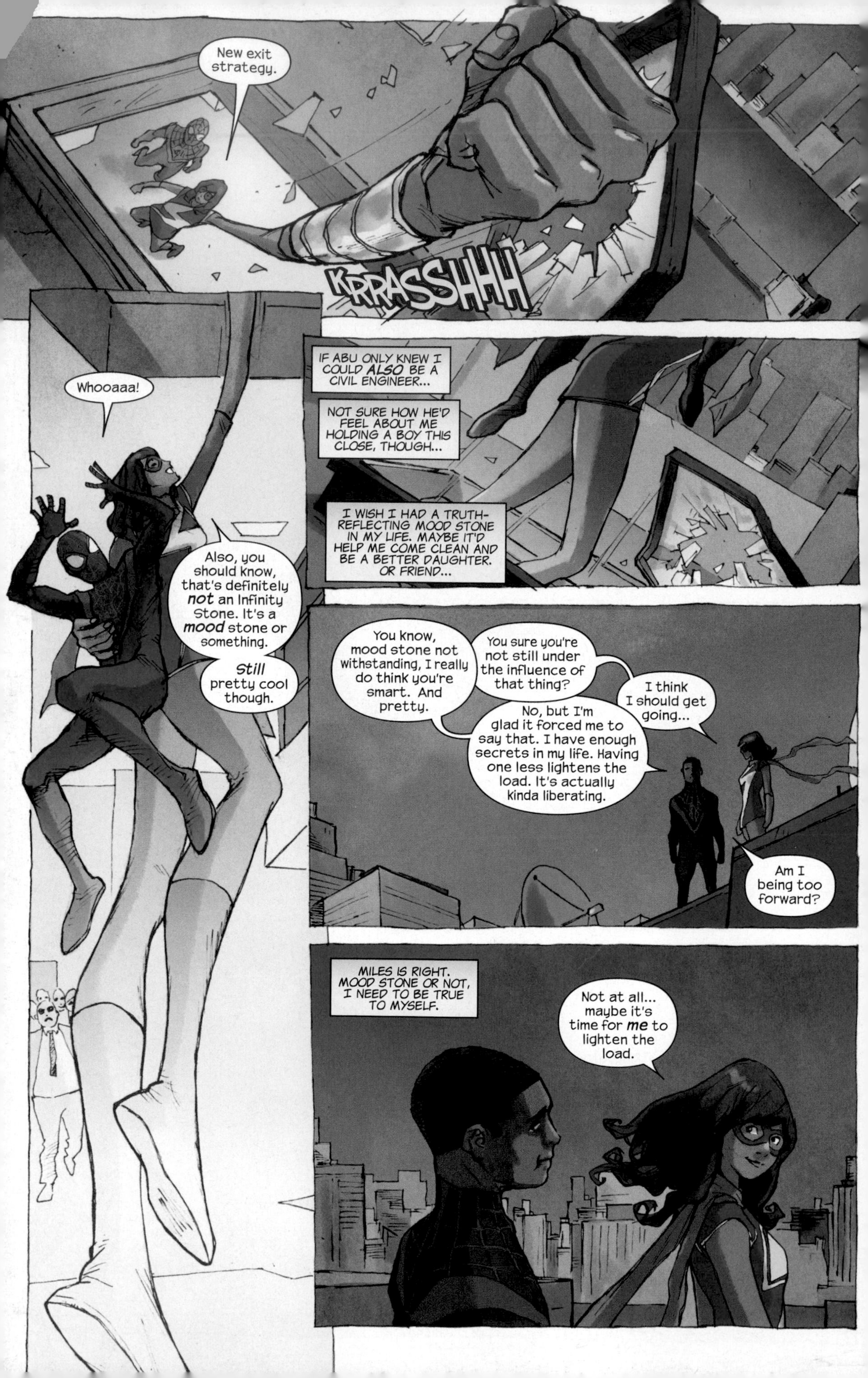
New exit strategy.
KRRASSHHH
Whooaaa!
IF ABU ONLY KNEW I COULD ALSO BE A CIVIL ENGINEER...
NOT SURE HOW HE'D FEEL ABOUT ME HOLDING A BOY THIS CLOSE, THOUGH...
I WISH I HAD A TRUTH-REFLECTING MOOD STONE IN MY LIFE. MAYBE IT'D HELP ME COME CLEAN AND BE A BETTER DAUGHTER. OR FRIEND...
Also, you should know, that's definitely not an Infinity Stone. It's a mood stone or something.
Still pretty cool though.
You know, mood stone not withstanding, I really do think you're smart. And pretty.
You sure you're not still under the influence of that thing?
No, but I'm glad it forced me to say that. I have enough secrets in my life. Having one less lightens the load. It's actually kinda liberating.
I think I should get going...
Am I being too forward?
MILES IS RIGHT. MOOD STONE OR NOT, I NEED TO BE TRUE TO MYSELF.
Not at all... maybe it's time for me to lighten the load.

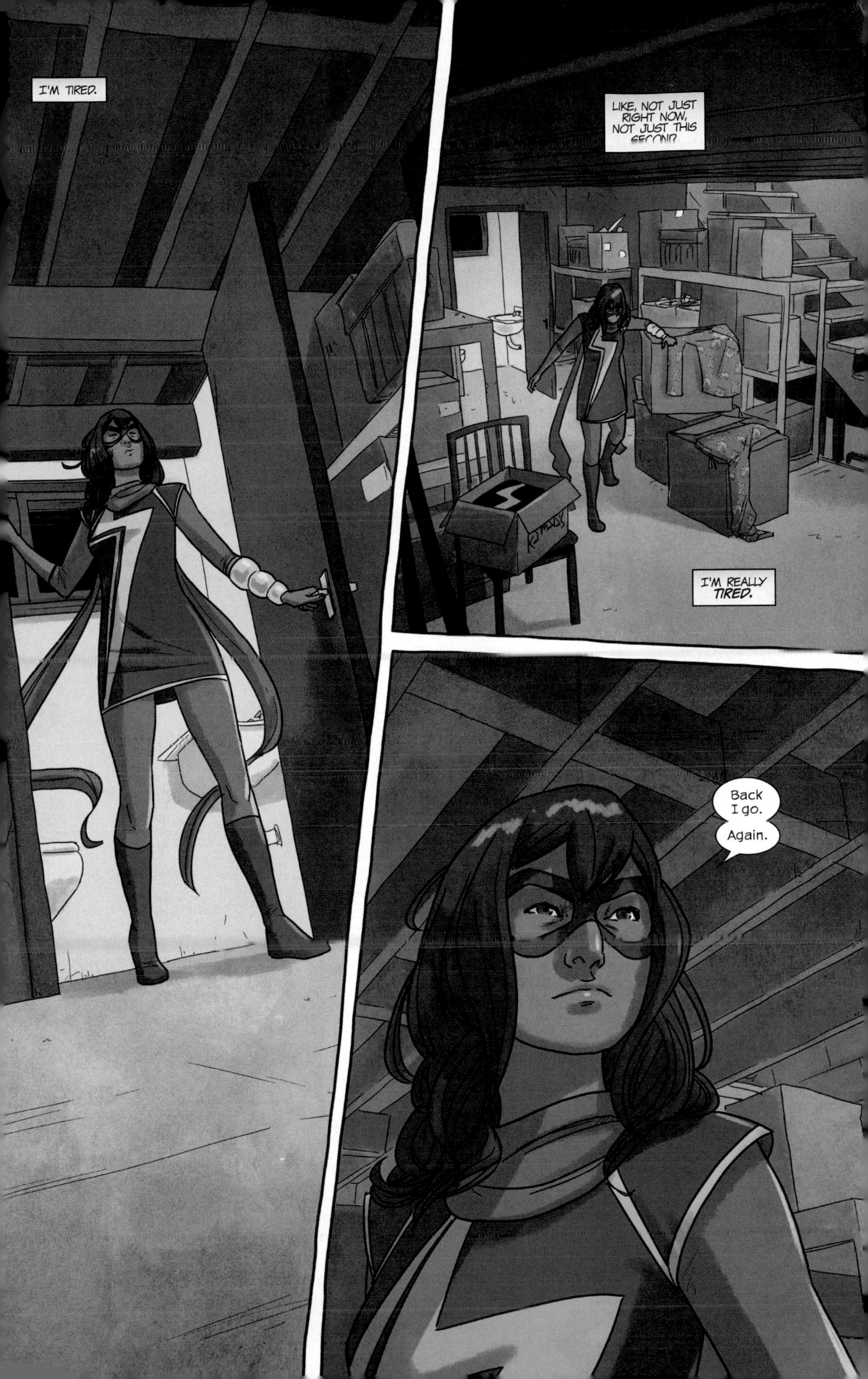
I'M TIRED.
LIKE, NOT JUST RIGHT NOW, NOT JUST THIS SECOND?
I'M REALLY *TIRED.*
Back I go.
Again.

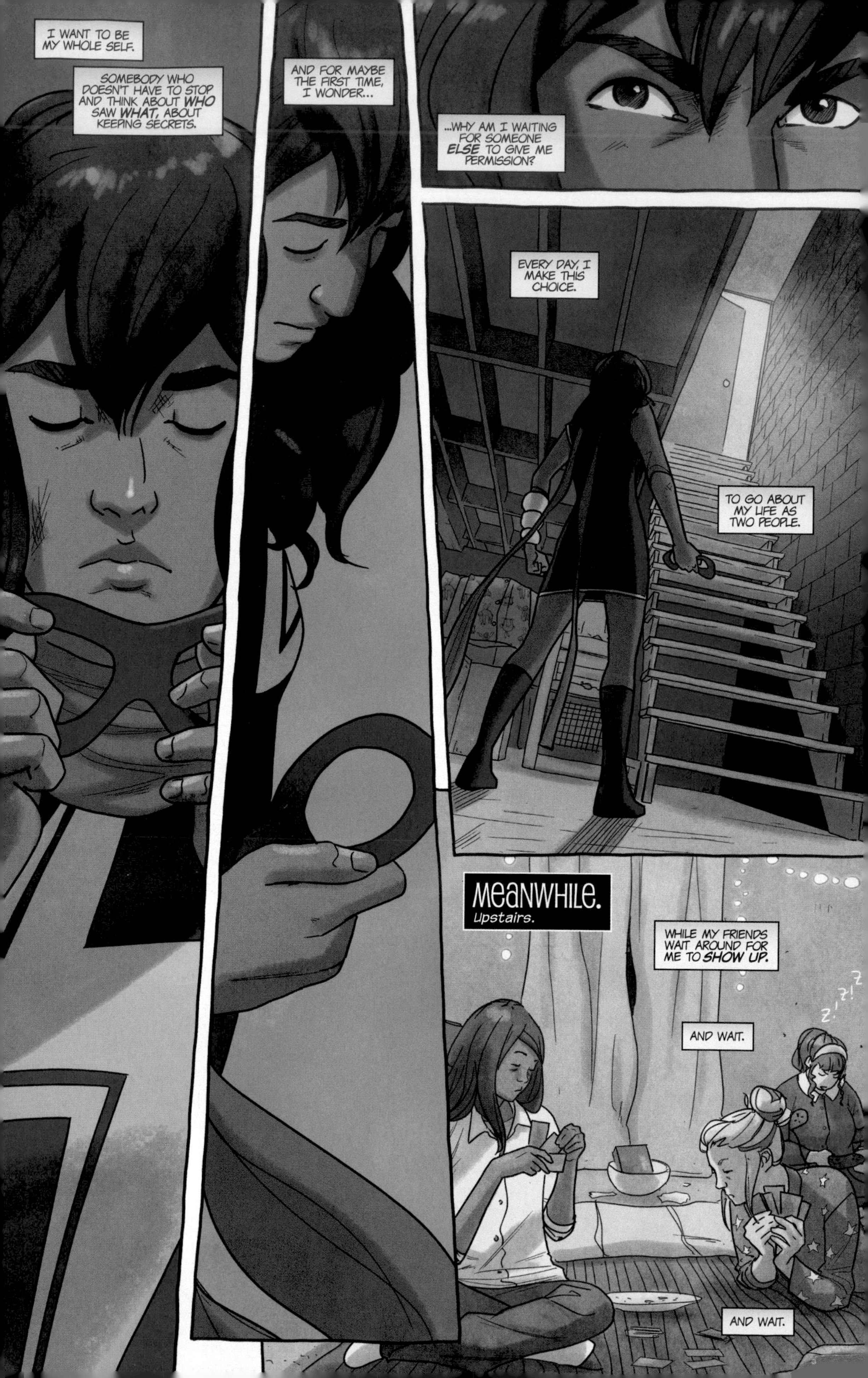
I WANT TO BE MY WHOLE SELF.
SOMEBODY WHO DOESN'T HAVE TO STOP AND THINK ABOUT WHO SAW WHAT, ABOUT KEEPING SECRETS.
AND FOR MAYBE THE FIRST TIME, I WONDER...
...WHY AM I WAITING FOR SOMEONE ELSE TO GIVE ME PERMISSION?
EVERY DAY, I MAKE THIS CHOICE.
TO GO ABOUT MY LIFE AS TWO PEOPLE.
MEANWHILE.
Upstairs.
WHILE MY FRIENDS WAIT AROUND FOR ME TO SHOW UP.
Z! Z! Z
AND WAIT.
AND WAIT.

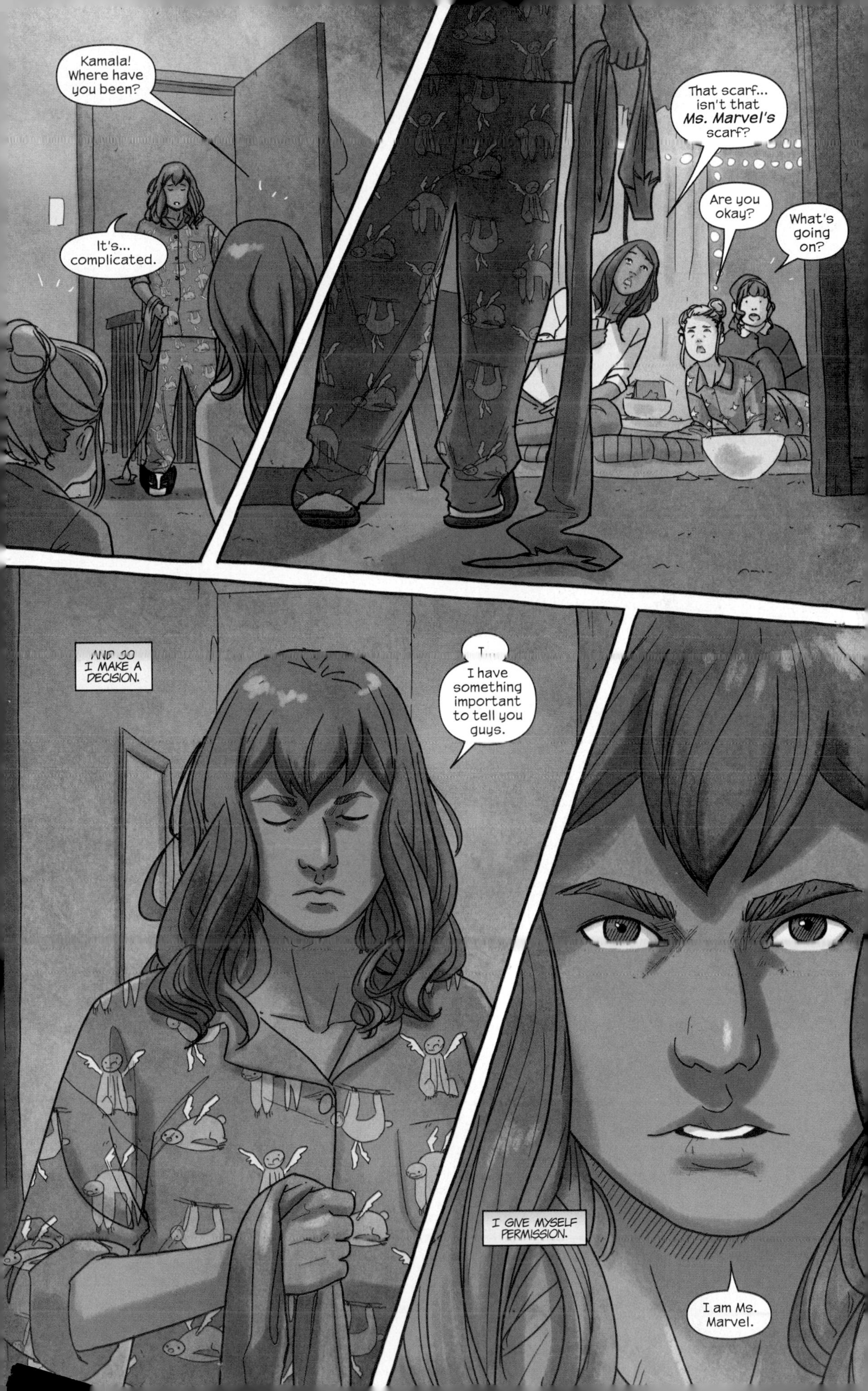
Kamala! Where have you been?
It's... complicated.
That scarf... isn't that *Ms. Marvel's* scarf?
Are you okay?
What's going on?
AND SO I MAKE A DECISION.
I... I have something important to tell you guys.
I GIVE MYSELF PERMISSION.
I am Ms. Marvel.

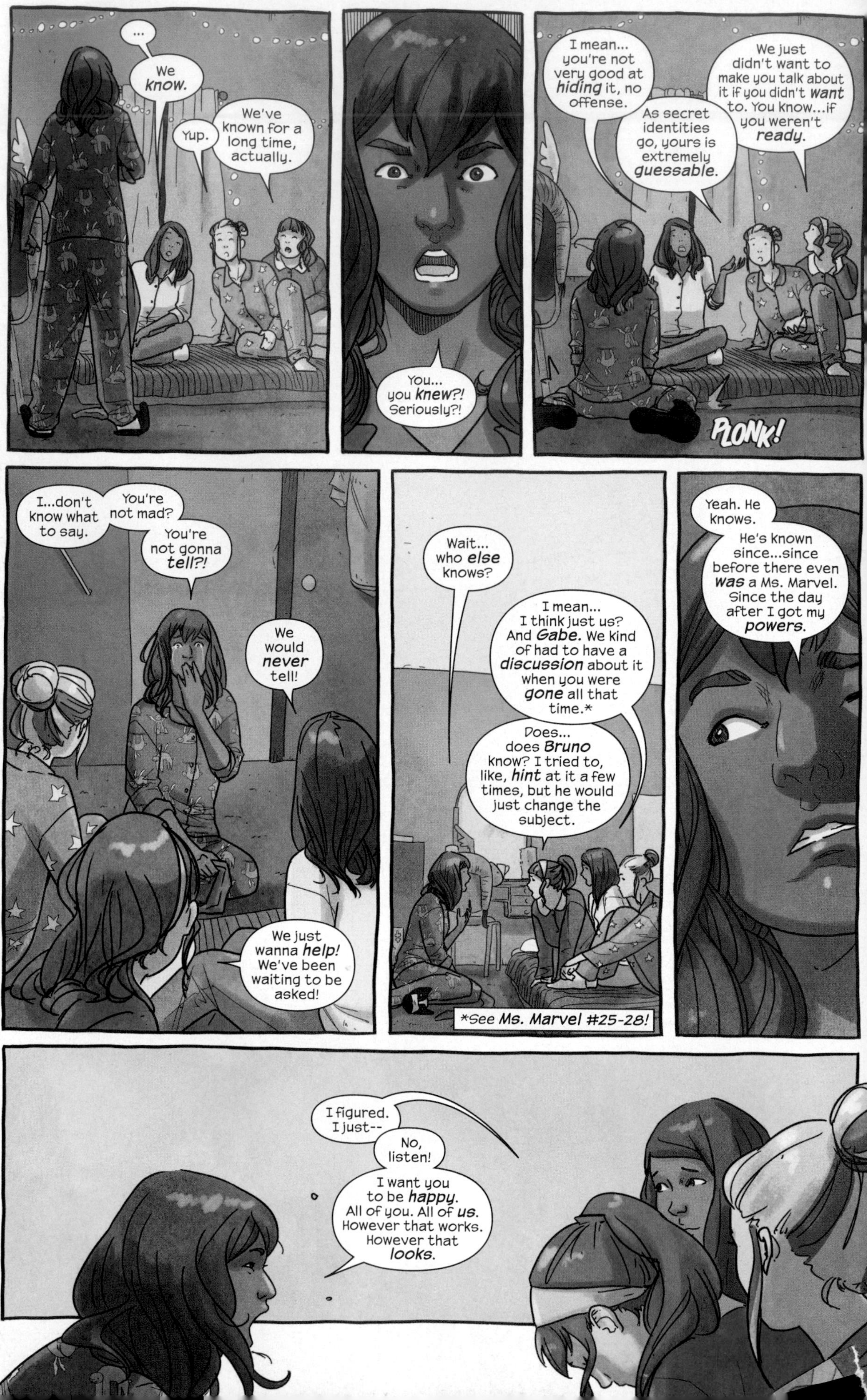
...
We know.
Yup.
We've known for a long time, actually.
You... you knew?! Seriously?!
I mean... you're not very good at hiding it, no offense.
As secret identities go, yours is extremely guessable.
We just didn't want to make you talk about it if you didn't want to. You know...if you weren't ready.
PLONK!
I...don't know what to say.
You're not mad?
You're not gonna tell?!
We would never tell!
We just wanna help! We've been waiting to be asked!
Wait... who else knows?
I mean... I think just us? And Gabe. We kind of had to have a discussion about it when you were gone all that time.*
Does... does Bruno know? I tried to, like, hint at it a few times, but he would just change the subject.
*See Ms. Marvel #25-28!
Yeah. He knows.
He's known since...since before there even was a Ms. Marvel. Since the day after I got my powers.
I figured. I just--
No, listen!
I want you to be happy. All of you. All of us. However that works. However that looks.

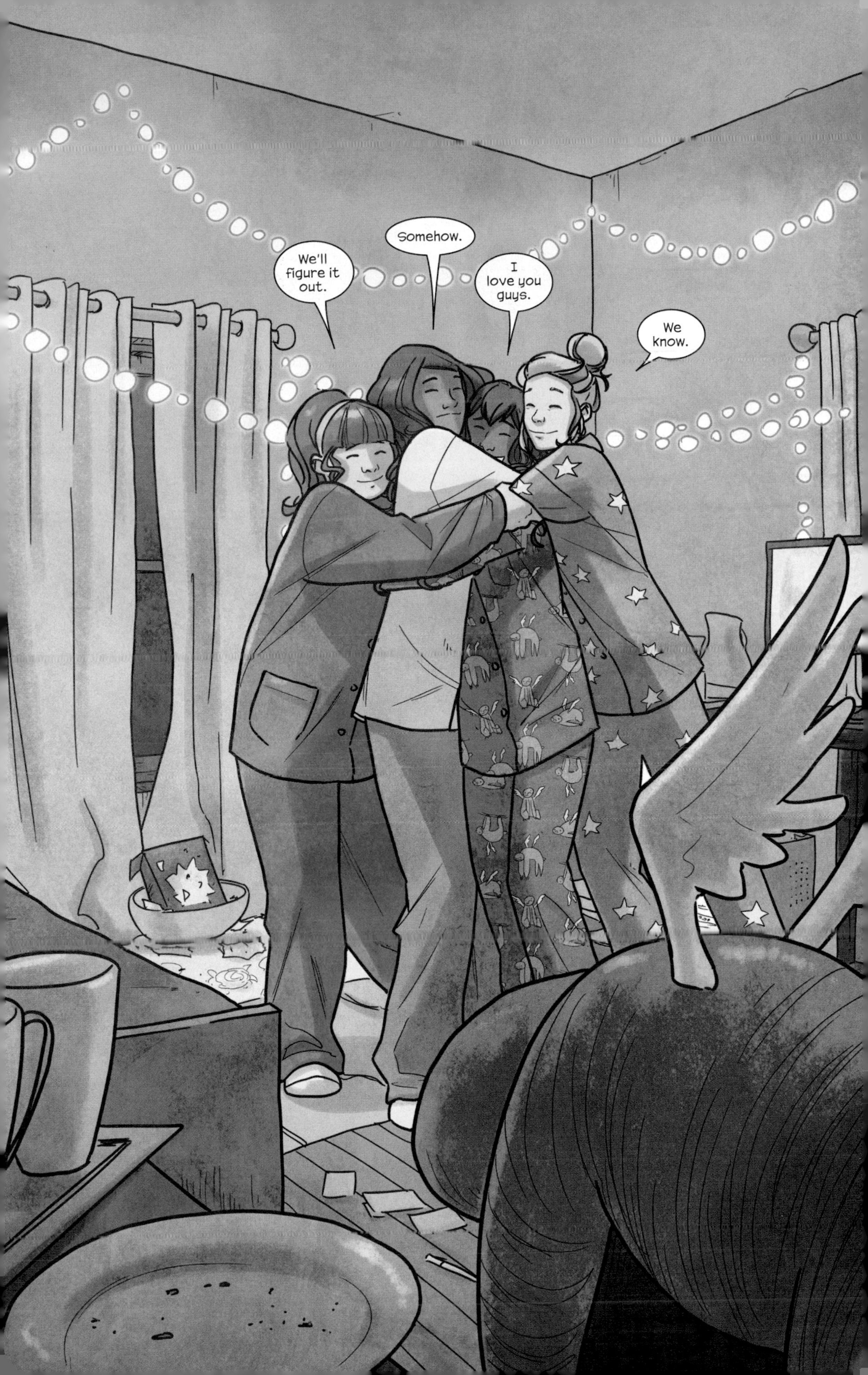
We'll figure it out.
Somehow.
I love you guys.
We know.

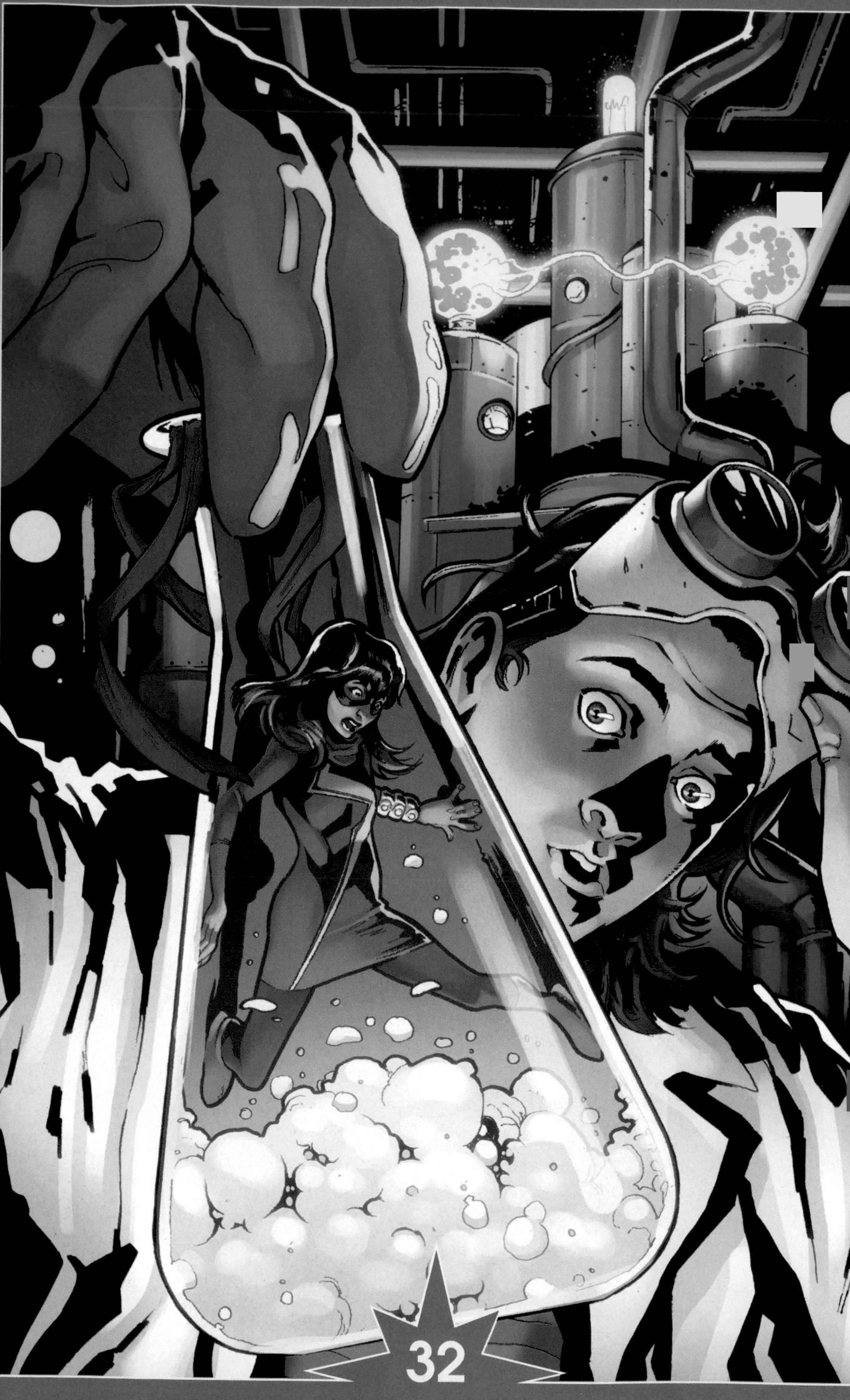
32

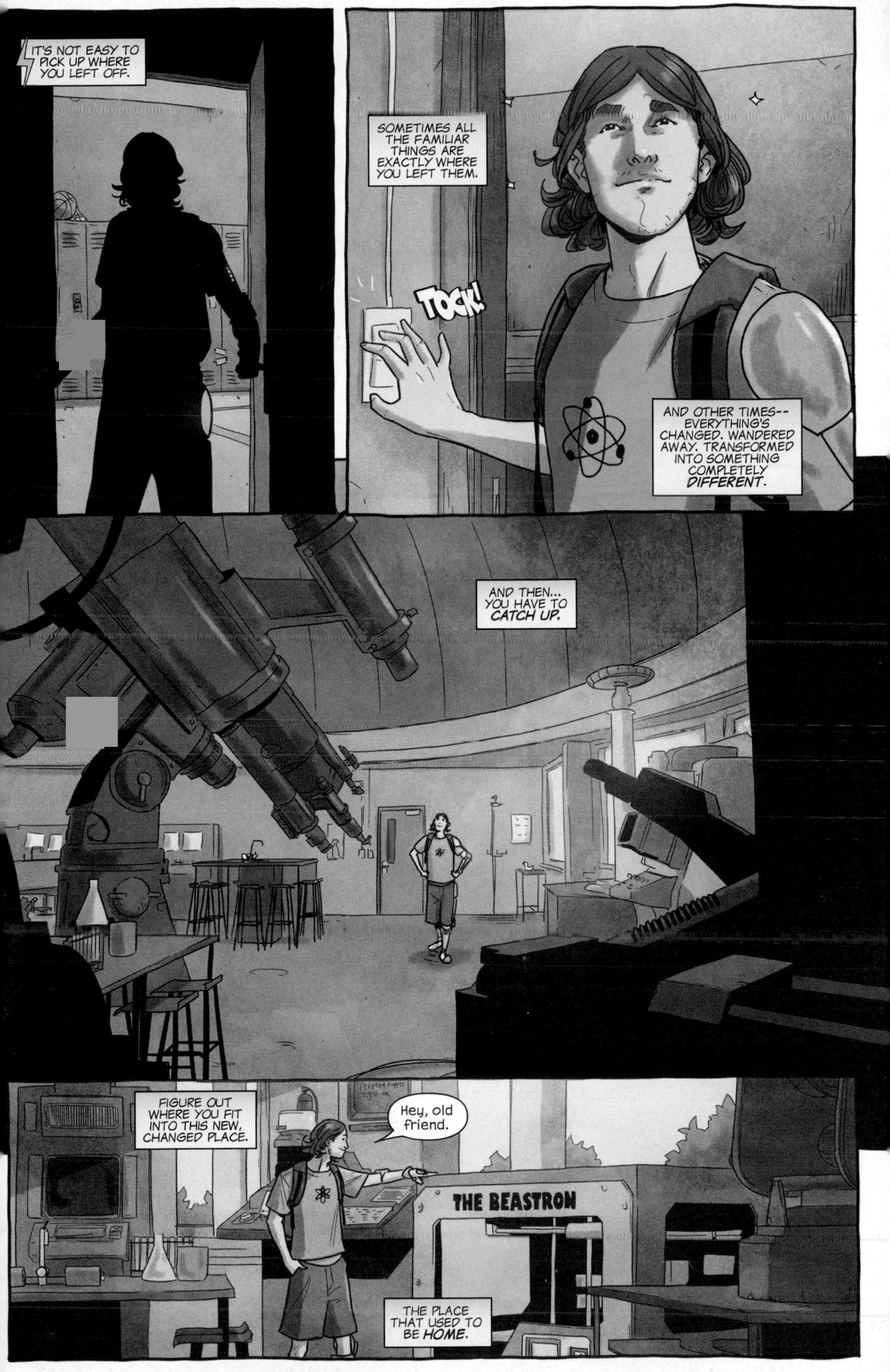
IT'S NOT EASY TO PICK UP WHERE YOU LEFT OFF.
SOMETIMES ALL THE FAMILIAR THINGS ARE EXACTLY WHERE YOU LEFT THEM.
TOCK!
AND OTHER TIMES-- EVERYTHING'S CHANGED. WANDERED AWAY. TRANSFORMED INTO SOMETHING COMPLETELY DIFFERENT.
AND THEN... YOU HAVE TO CATCH UP.
FIGURE OUT WHERE YOU FIT INTO THIS NEW, CHANGED PLACE.
Hey, old friend.
THE BEASTRON
THE PLACE THAT USED TO BE HOME.

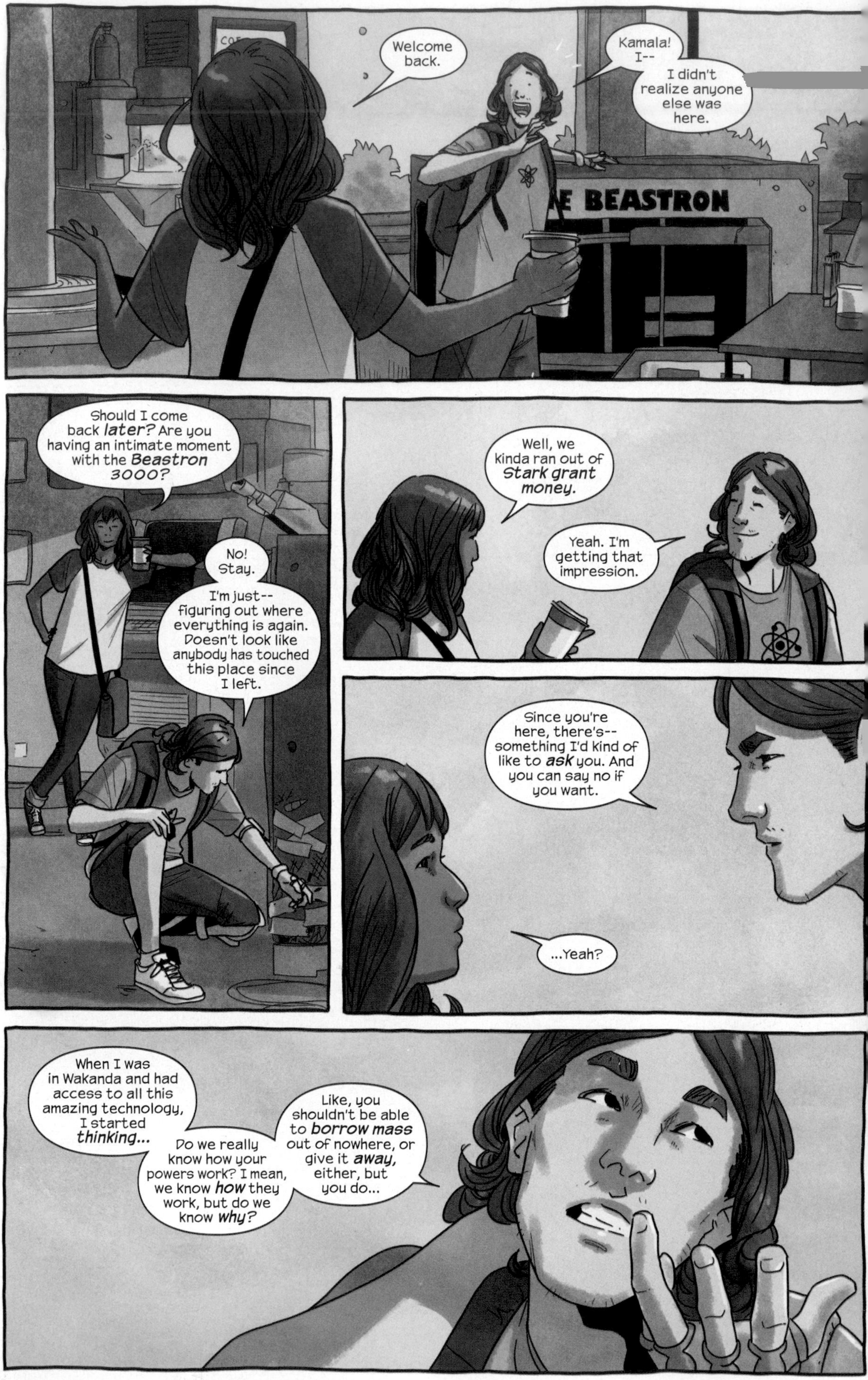

Welcome back.
Kamala! I--
I didn't realize anyone else was here.
BEASTRON
Should I come back later? Are you having an intimate moment with the Beastron 3000?
No! Stay.
I'm just-- figuring out where everything is again. Doesn't look like anybody has touched this place since I left.
Well, we kinda ran out of Stark grant money.
Yeah. I'm getting that impression.
Since you're here, there's-- something I'd kind of like to ask you. And you can say no if you want.
...Yeah?
When I was in Wakanda and had access to all this amazing technology, I started thinking...
Do we really know how your powers work? I mean, we know how they work, but do we know why?
Like, you shouldn't be able to borrow mass out of nowhere, or give it away, either, but you do...

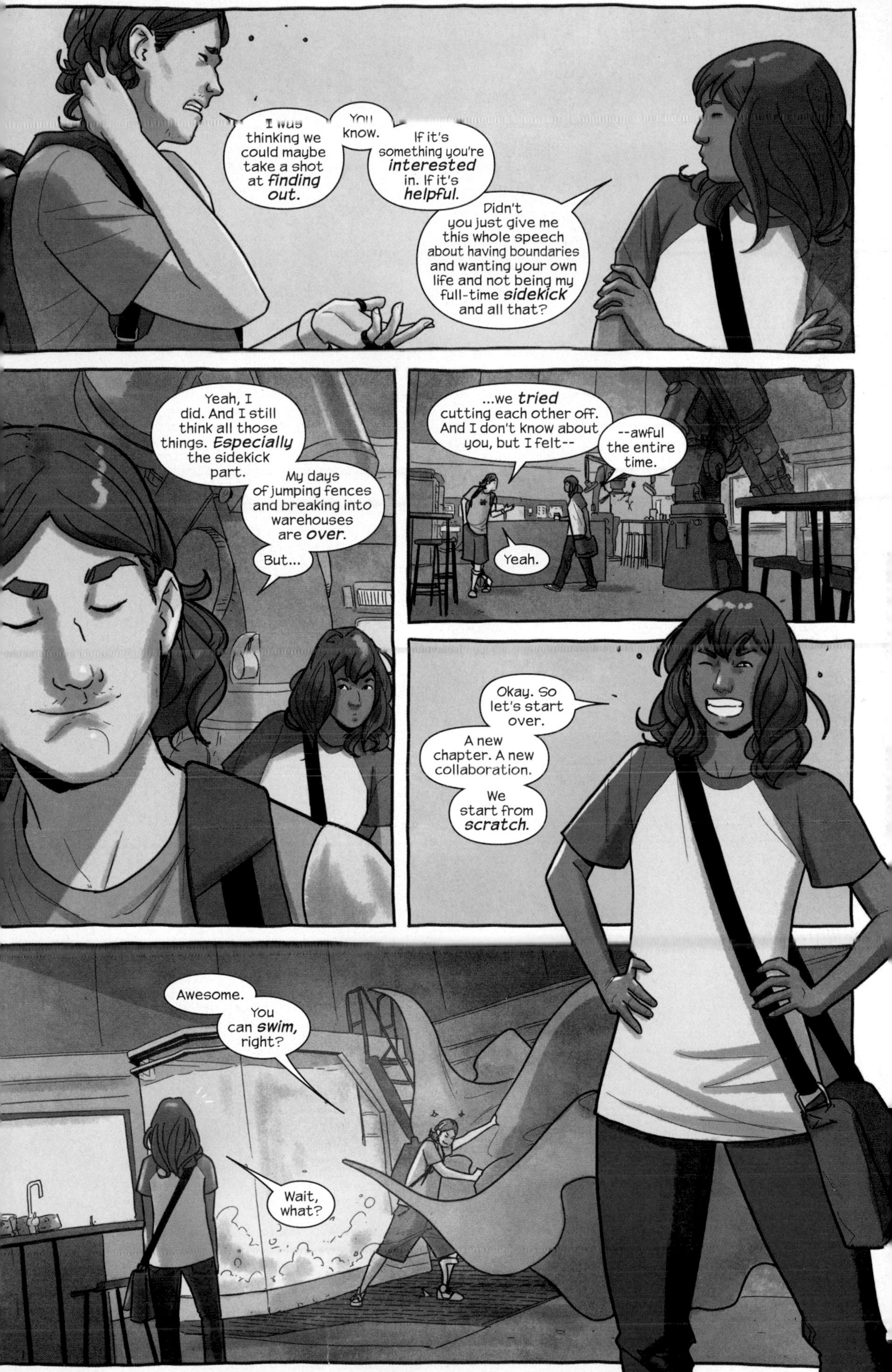

I was thinking we could maybe take a shot at *finding out.*
You know.
If it's something you're *interested* in. If it's *helpful.*
Didn't you just give me this whole speech about having boundaries and wanting your own life and not being my full-time *sidekick* and all that?
Yeah, I did. And I still think all those things. *Especially* the sidekick part.
My days of jumping fences and breaking into warehouses are *over.*
But...
...we *tried* cutting each other off. And I don't know about you, but I felt--
--awful the entire time.
Yeah.
Okay. So let's start over.
A new chapter. A new collaboration.
We start from *scratch.*
Awesome.
You can *swim,* right?
Wait, what?

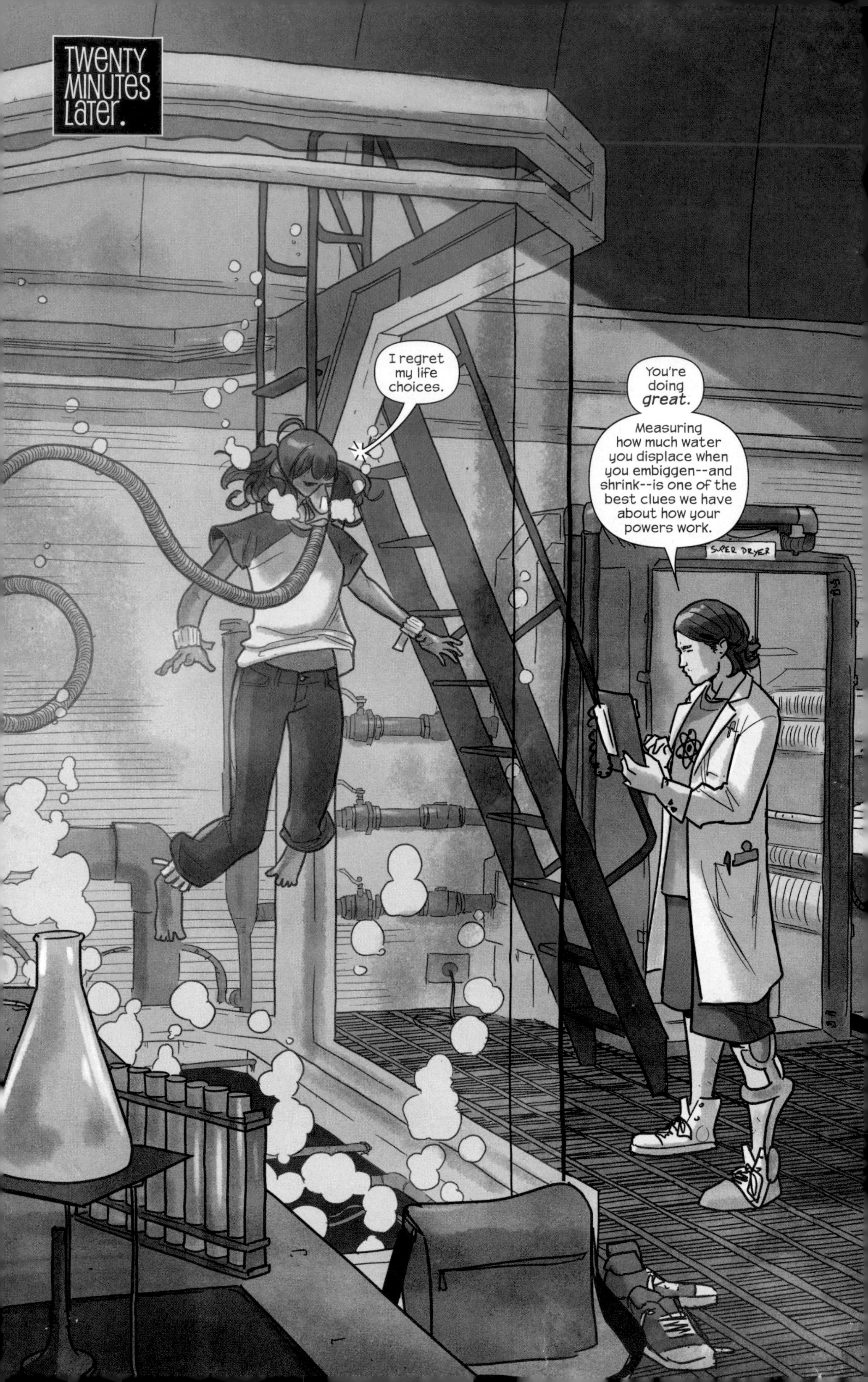
TWENTY MINUTES LATER.
I regret my life choices.
You're doing *great.*
Measuring how much water you displace when you embiggen--and shrink--is one of the best clues we have about how your powers work.
SUPER DRYER

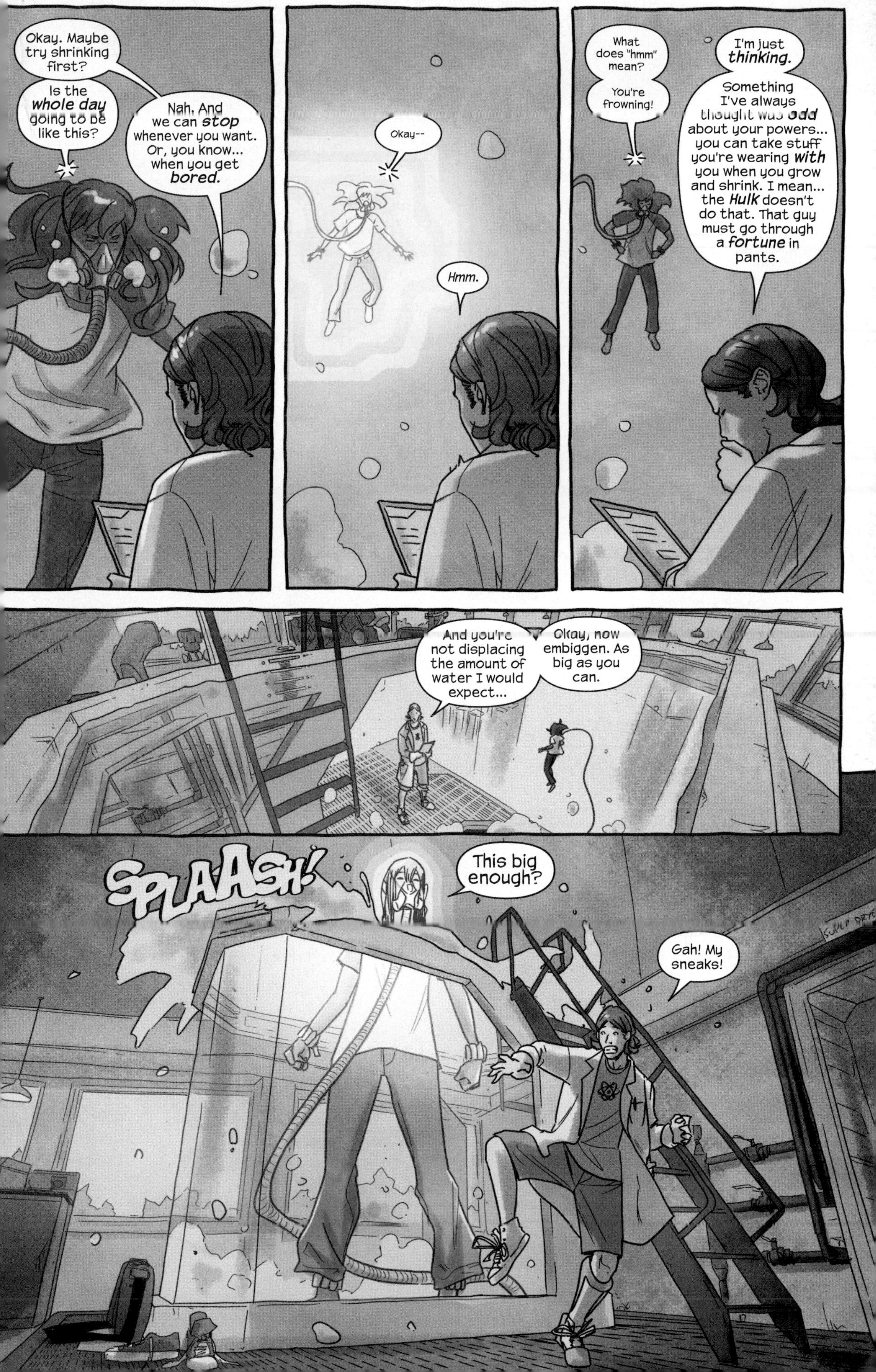
Okay. Maybe try shrinking first?
Is the whole day going to be like this?
Nah. And we can stop whenever you want. Or, you know... when you get bored.
Okay--
Hmm.
What does "hmm" mean?
You're frowning!
I'm just thinking.
Something I've always thought was odd about your powers... you can take stuff you're wearing with you when you grow and shrink. I mean... the Hulk doesn't do that. That guy must go through a fortune in pants.
And you're not displacing the amount of water I would expect...
Okay, now embiggen. As big as you can.
SPLAASH!
This big enough?
Gah! My sneaks!

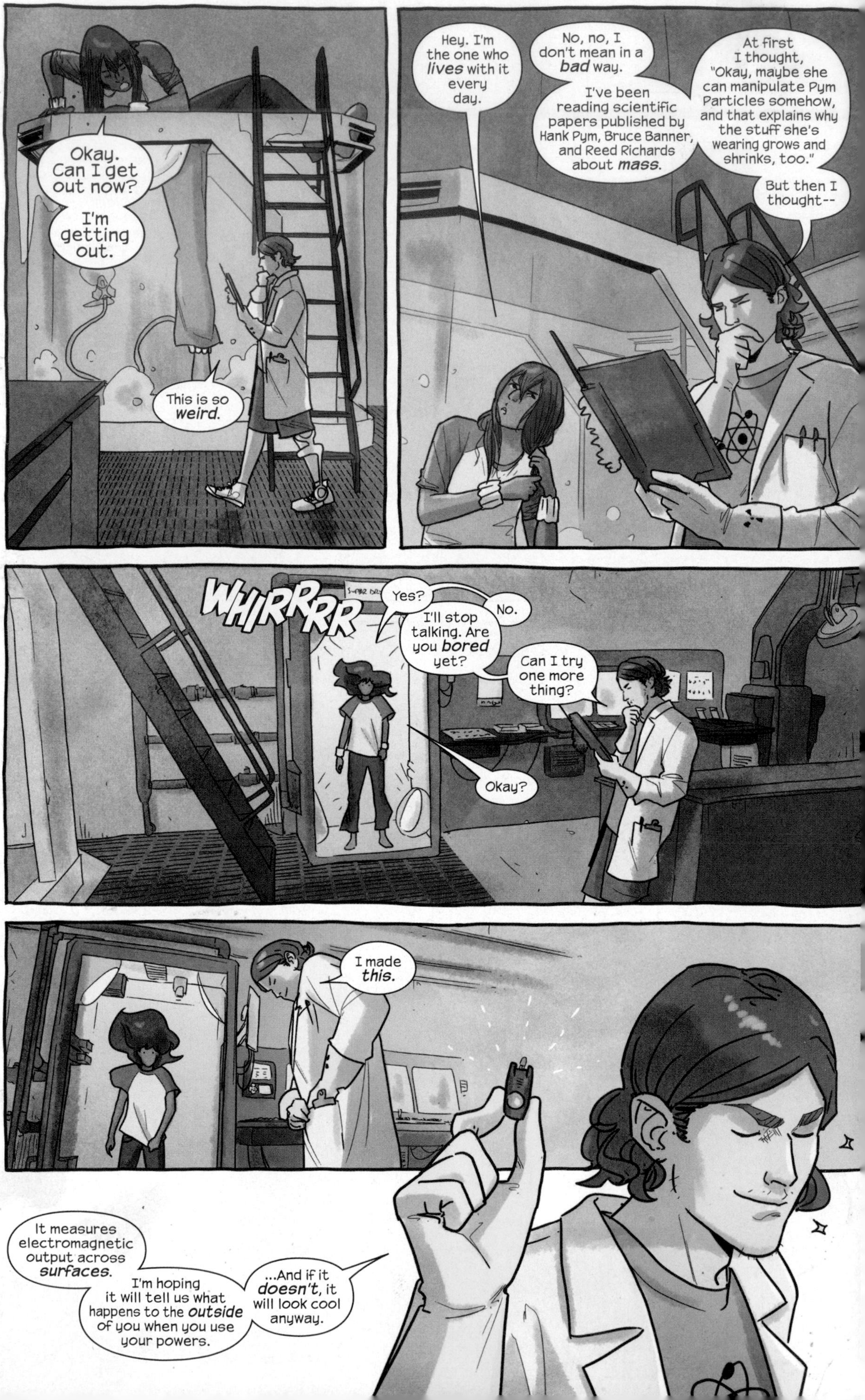
Okay. Can I get out now?
I'm getting out.
This is so weird.
Hey. I'm the one who lives with it every day.
No, no, I don't mean in a bad way.
I've been reading scientific papers published by Hank Pym, Bruce Banner, and Reed Richards about mass.
At first I thought, "Okay, maybe she can manipulate Pym Particles somehow, and that explains why the stuff she's wearing grows and shrinks, too."
But then I thought--
WHIRRRR
Yes?
No.
I'll stop talking. Are you bored yet?
Can I try one more thing?
Okay?
I made this.
It measures electromagnetic output across surfaces.
I'm hoping it will tell us what happens to the outside of you when you use your powers.
...And if it doesn't, it will look cool anyway.

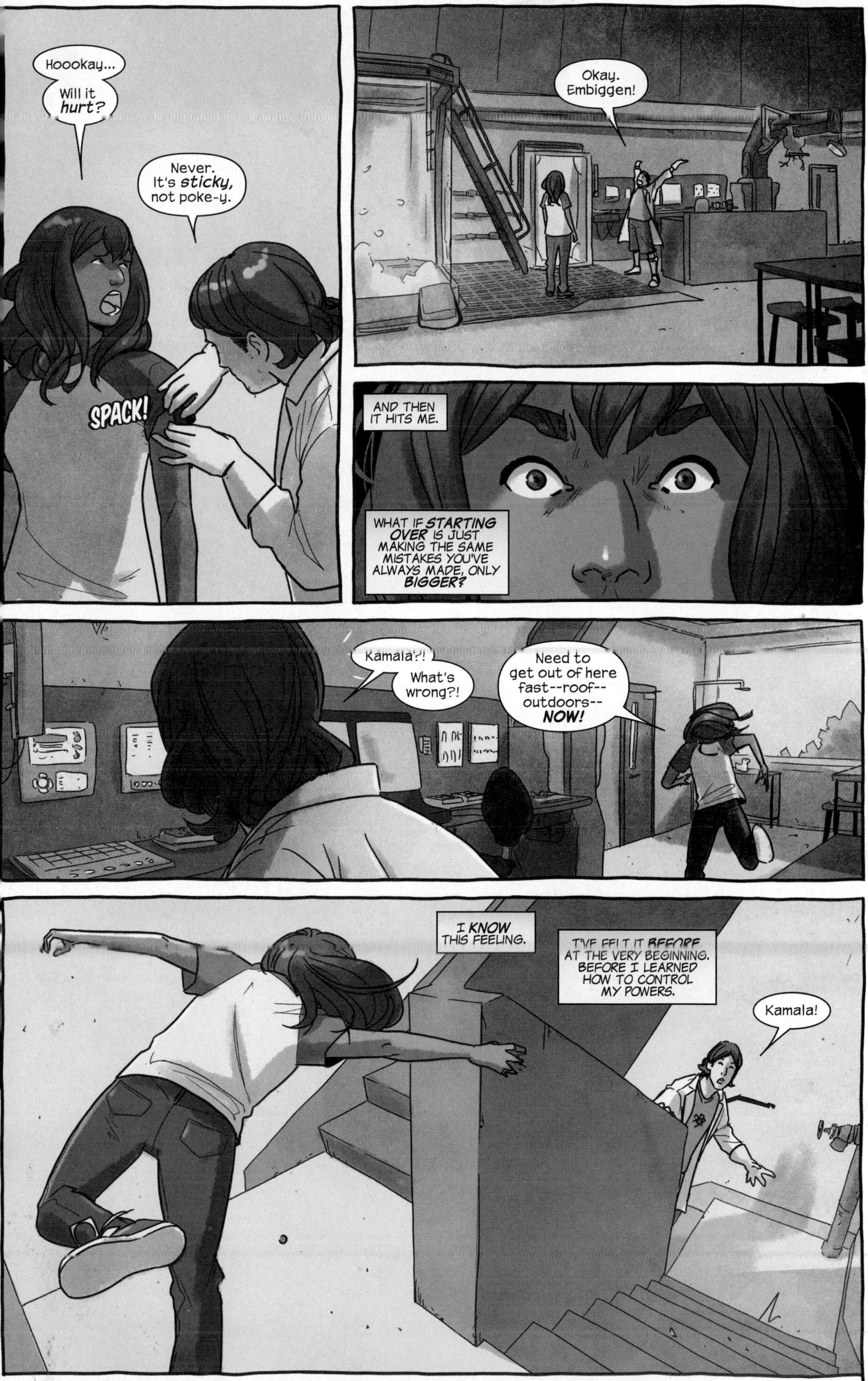

Hooookay...
Will it *hurt?*
Never. It's *sticky,* not poke-y.
SPACK!
Okay. Embiggen!
AND THEN IT HITS ME.
WHAT IF *STARTING OVER* IS JUST MAKING THE SAME MISTAKES YOU'VE ALWAYS MADE, ONLY *BIGGER?*
Kamala?!
What's wrong?!
Need to get out of here fast--roof--outdoors--*NOW!*
I *KNOW* THIS FEELING.
I'VE FELT IT *BEFORE* AT THE VERY BEGINNING. BEFORE I LEARNED HOW TO CONTROL MY POWERS.
Kamala!

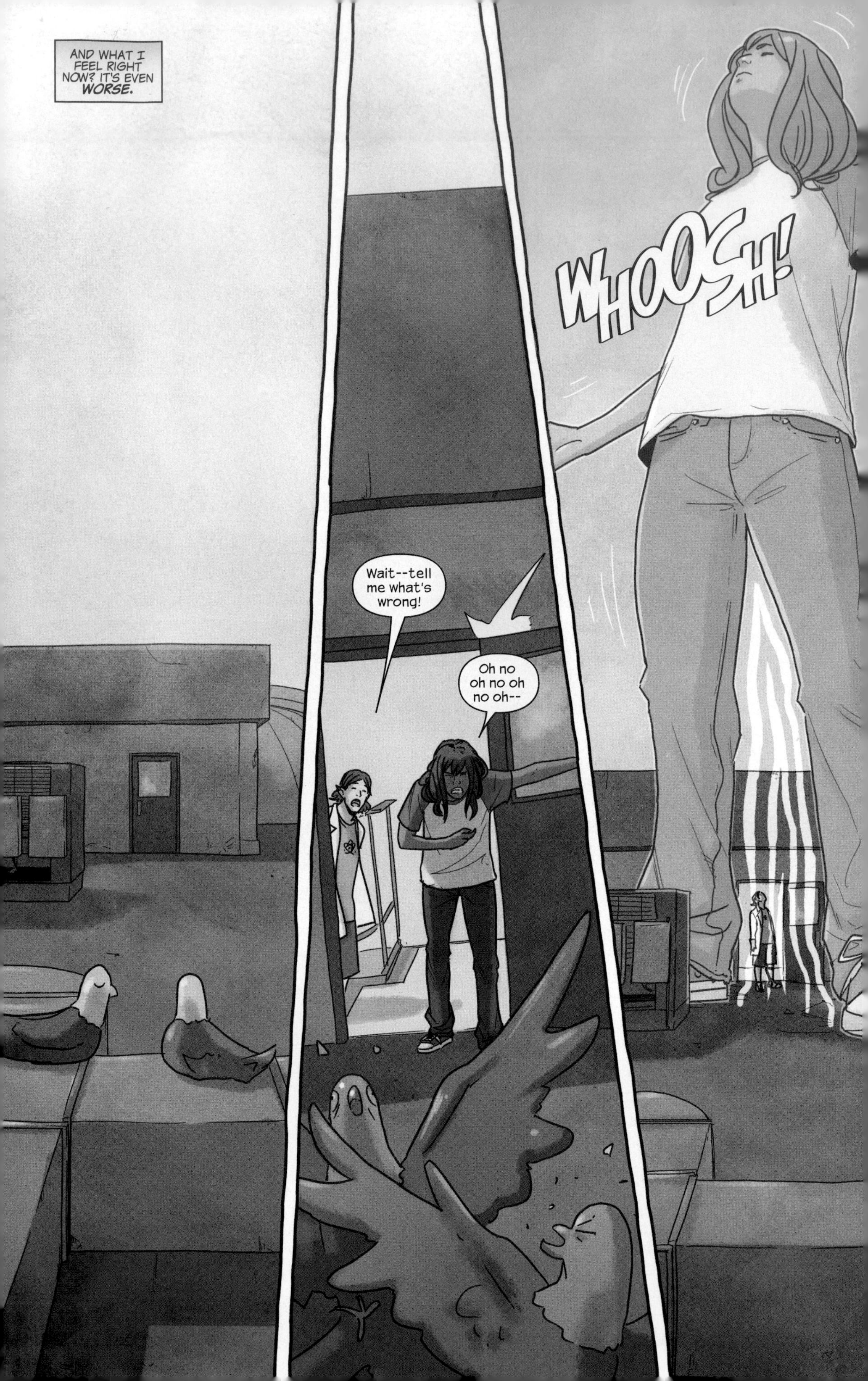
AND WHAT I FEEL RIGHT NOW? IT'S EVEN WORSE.
WHOOSH!
Wait--tell me what's wrong!
Oh no oh no oh no oh--

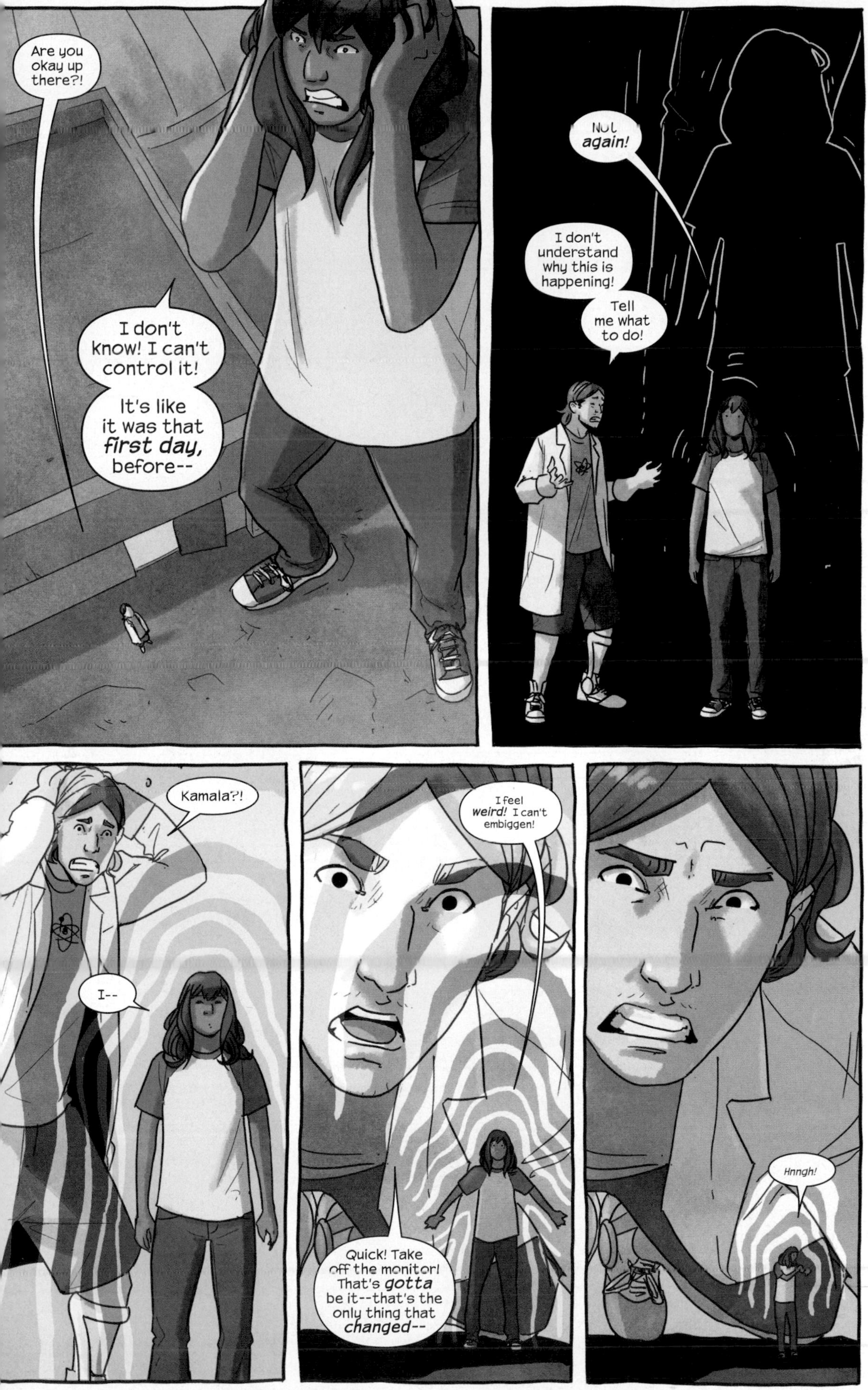

Are you okay up there?!
I don't know! I can't control it!
It's like it was that *first day,* before--
NO! *again!*
I don't understand why this is happening!
Tell me what to do!
Kamala?!
I--
I feel *weird!* I can't embiggen!
Quick! Take off the monitor! That's *gotta* be it--that's the only thing that *changed*--
Hnngh!

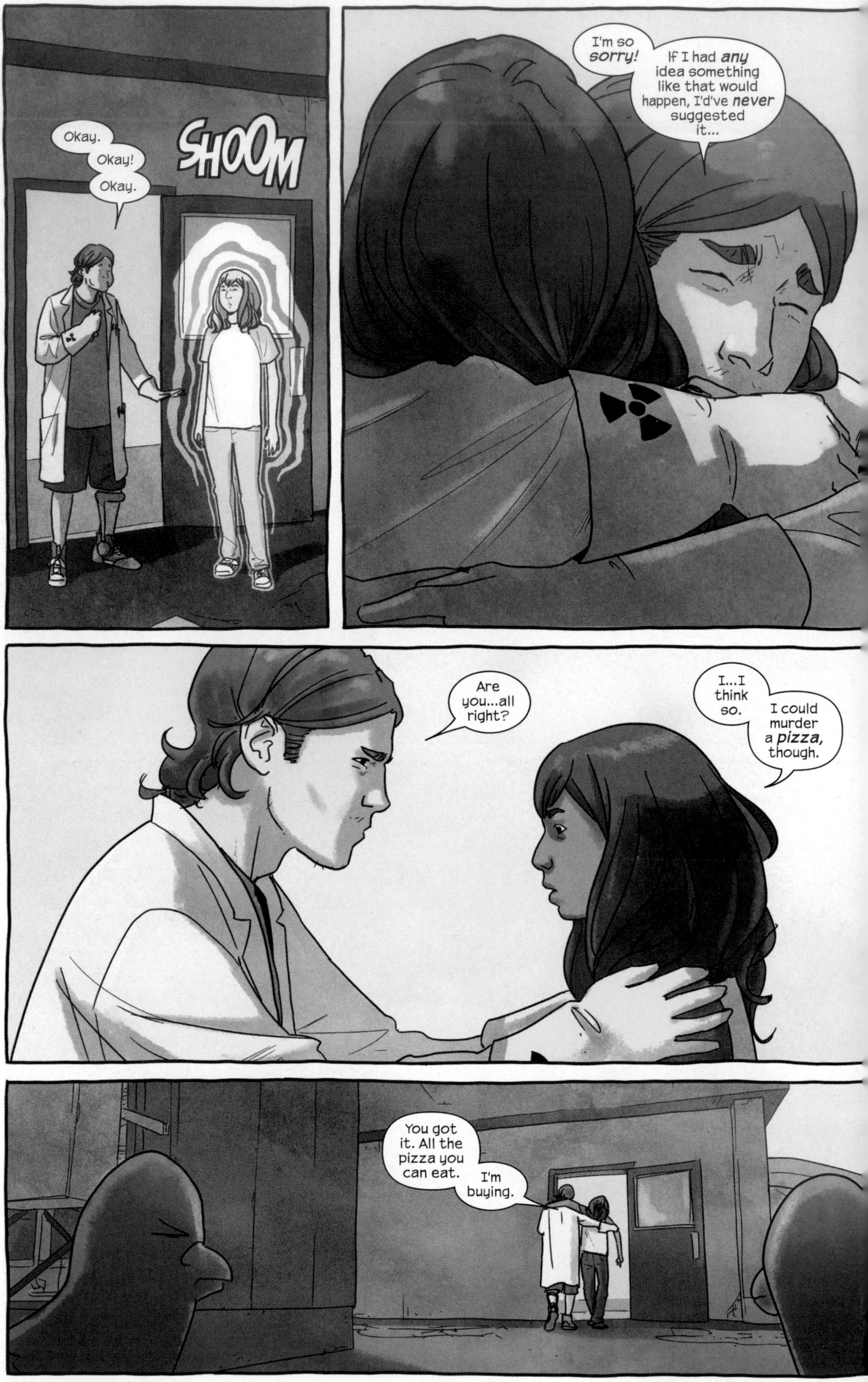
Okay.
Okay!
Okay.
SHOOM
I'm so sorry!
If I had any idea something like that would happen, I'd've never suggested it...
Are you...all right?
I...I think so.
I could murder a pizza, though.
You got it. All the pizza you can eat.
I'm buying.

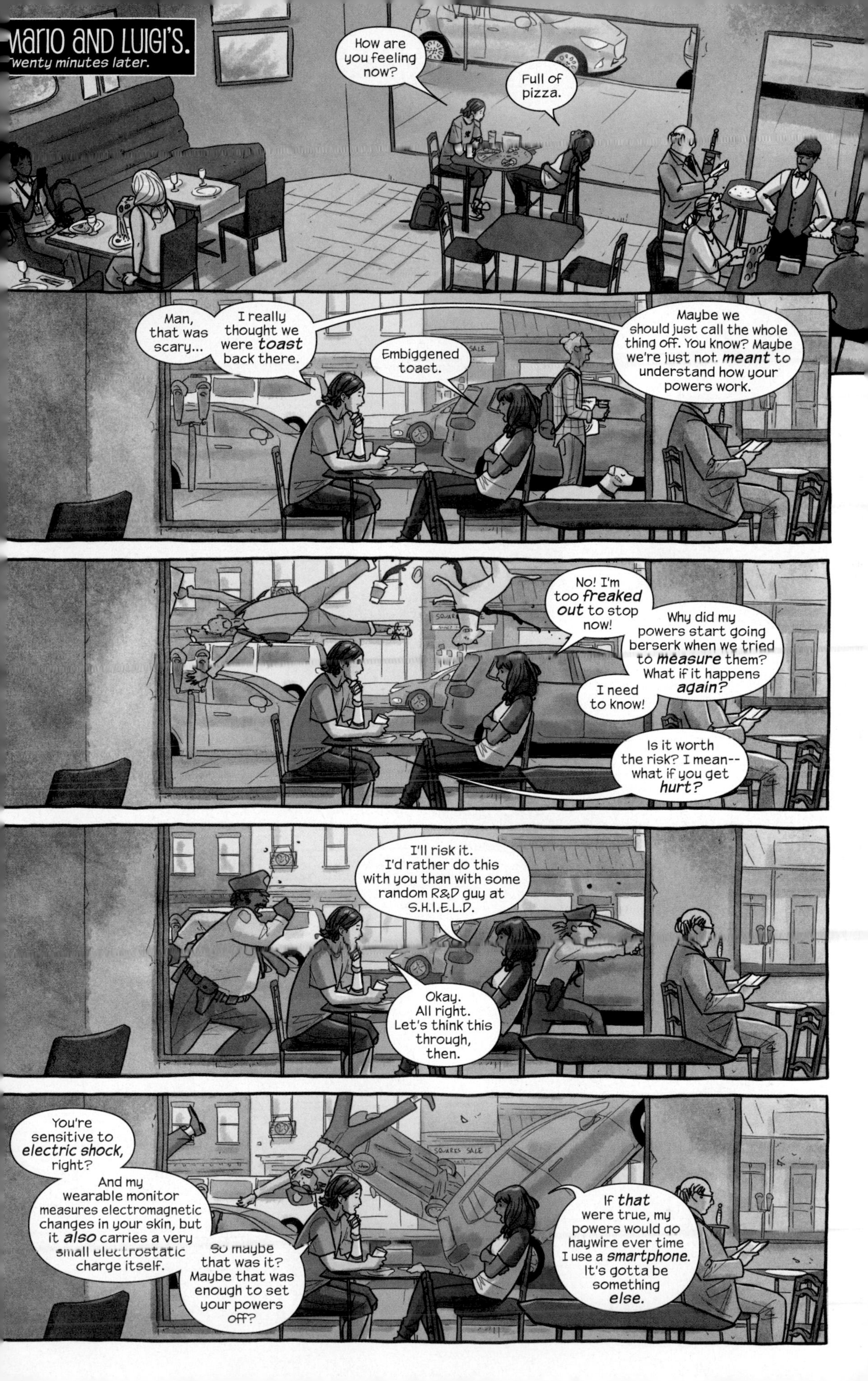
Mario and Luigi's.
Twenty minutes later.
How are you feeling now?
Full of pizza.
Man, that was scary...
I really thought we were toast back there.
Embiggened toast.
Maybe we should just call the whole thing off. You know? Maybe we're just not meant to understand how your powers work.
No! I'm too freaked out to stop now!
Why did my powers start going berserk when we tried to measure them? What if it happens again?
I need to know!
Is it worth the risk? I mean-- what if you get hurt?
I'll risk it. I'd rather do this with you than with some random R&D guy at S.H.I.E.L.D.
Okay. All right. Let's think this through, then.
You're sensitive to electric shock, right?
And my wearable monitor measures electromagnetic changes in your skin, but it also carries a very small electrostatic charge itself.
So maybe that was it? Maybe that was enough to set your powers off?
If that were true, my powers would go haywire ever time I use a smartphone. It's gotta be something else.

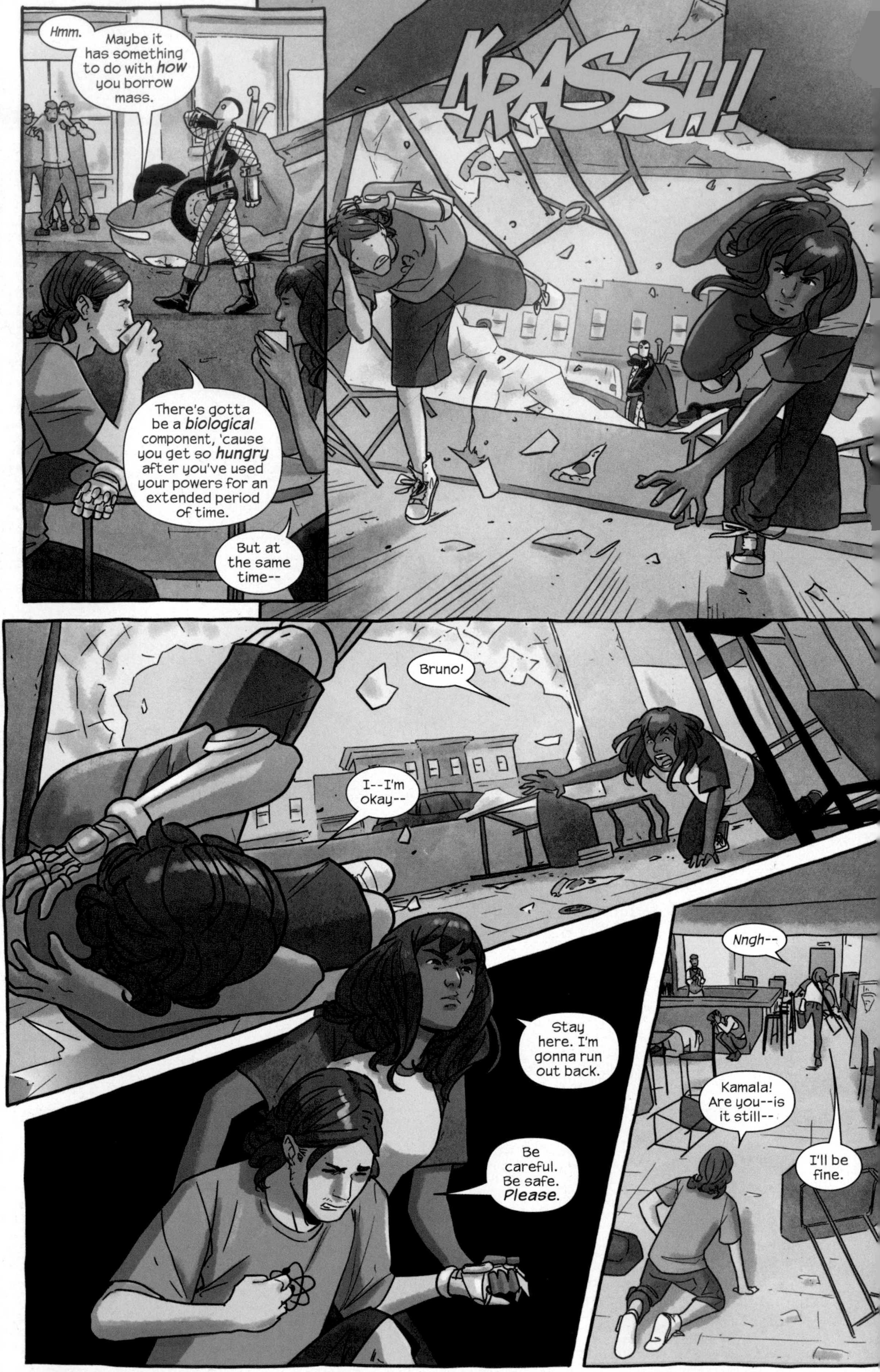

Hmm.
Maybe it has something to do with *how* you borrow mass.
There's gotta be a *biological* component, 'cause you get so *hungry* after you've used your powers for an extended period of time.
But at the same time--
KRASSH!
Bruno!
I--I'm okay--
Stay here. I'm gonna run out back.
Be careful. Be safe. *Please.*
Nngh--
Kamala! Are you--is it still--
I'll be fine.

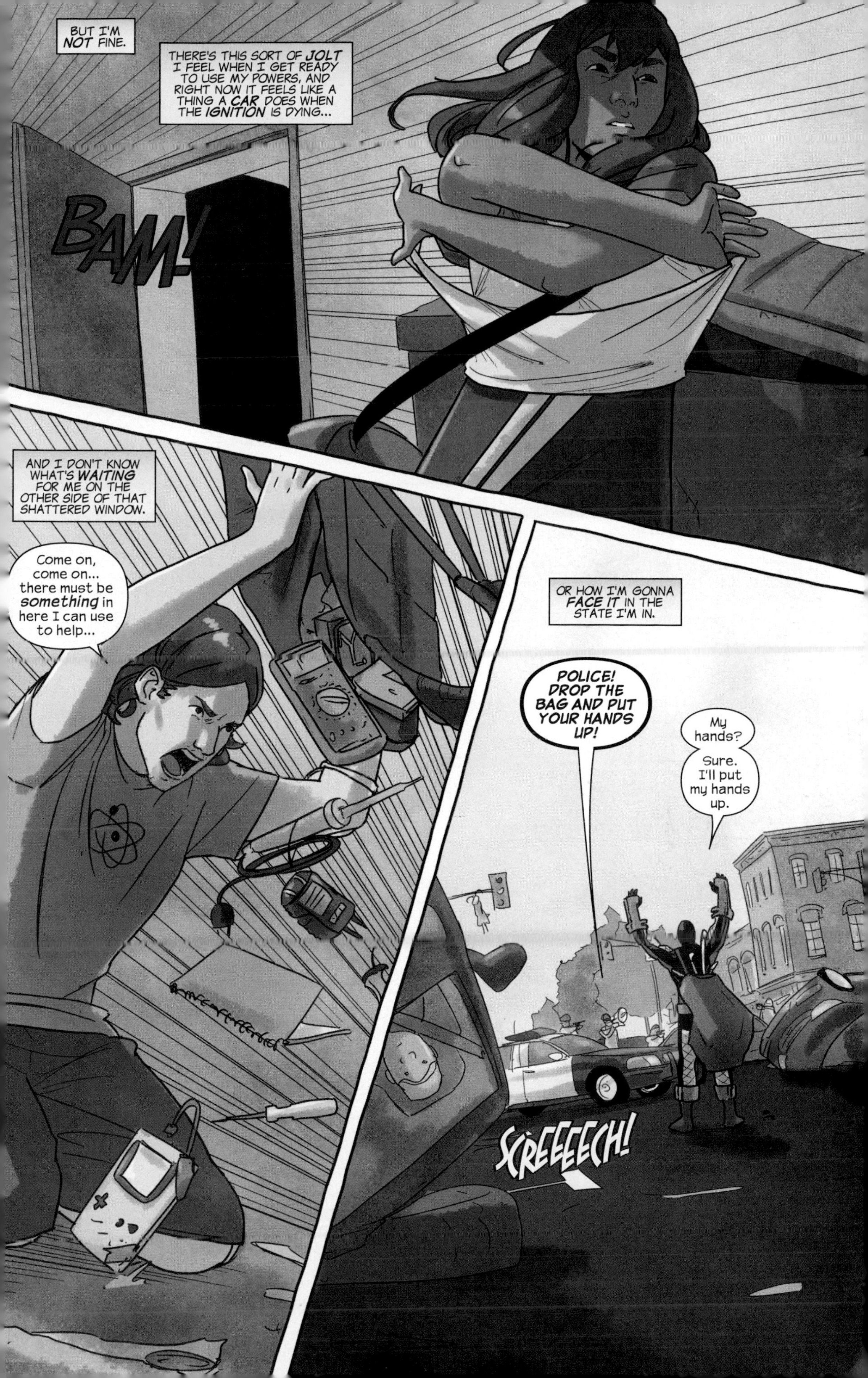
BUT I'M NOT FINE.
THERE'S THIS SORT OF JOLT I FEEL WHEN I GET READY TO USE MY POWERS, AND RIGHT NOW IT FEELS LIKE A THING A CAR DOES WHEN THE IGNITION IS DYING...
BAM!
AND I DON'T KNOW WHAT'S WAITING FOR ME ON THE OTHER SIDE OF THAT SHATTERED WINDOW.
Come on, come on... there must be something in here I can use to help...
OR HOW I'M GONNA FACE IT IN THE STATE I'M IN.
POLICE! DROP THE BAG AND PUT YOUR HANDS UP!
My hands?
Sure. I'll put my hands up.
SCREEEECH!

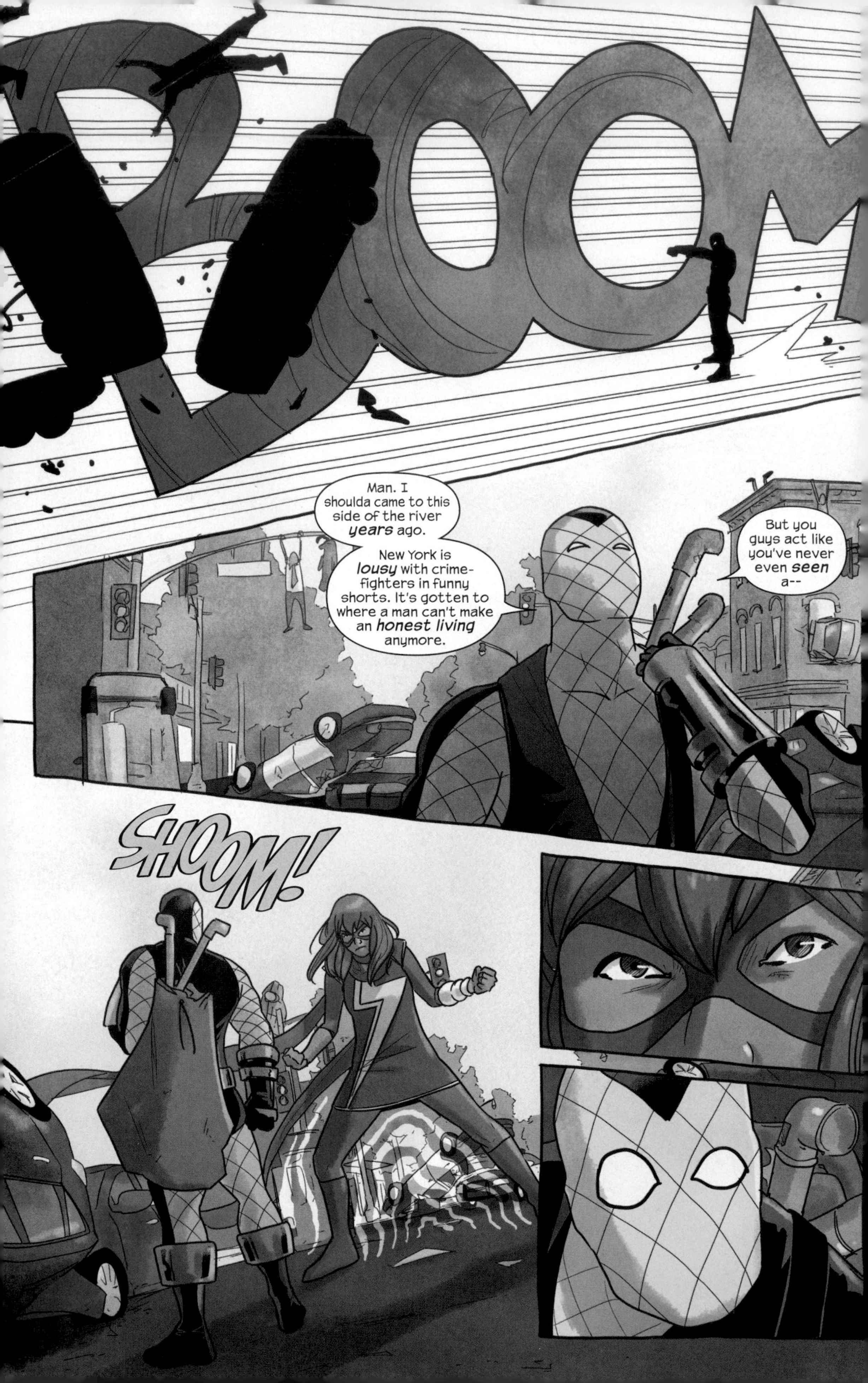

BLOOOM
Man. I shoulda came to this side of the river years ago.
New York is lousy with crime-fighters in funny shorts. It's gotten to where a man can't make an honest living anymore.
But you guys act like you've never even seen a--
SHOOM!

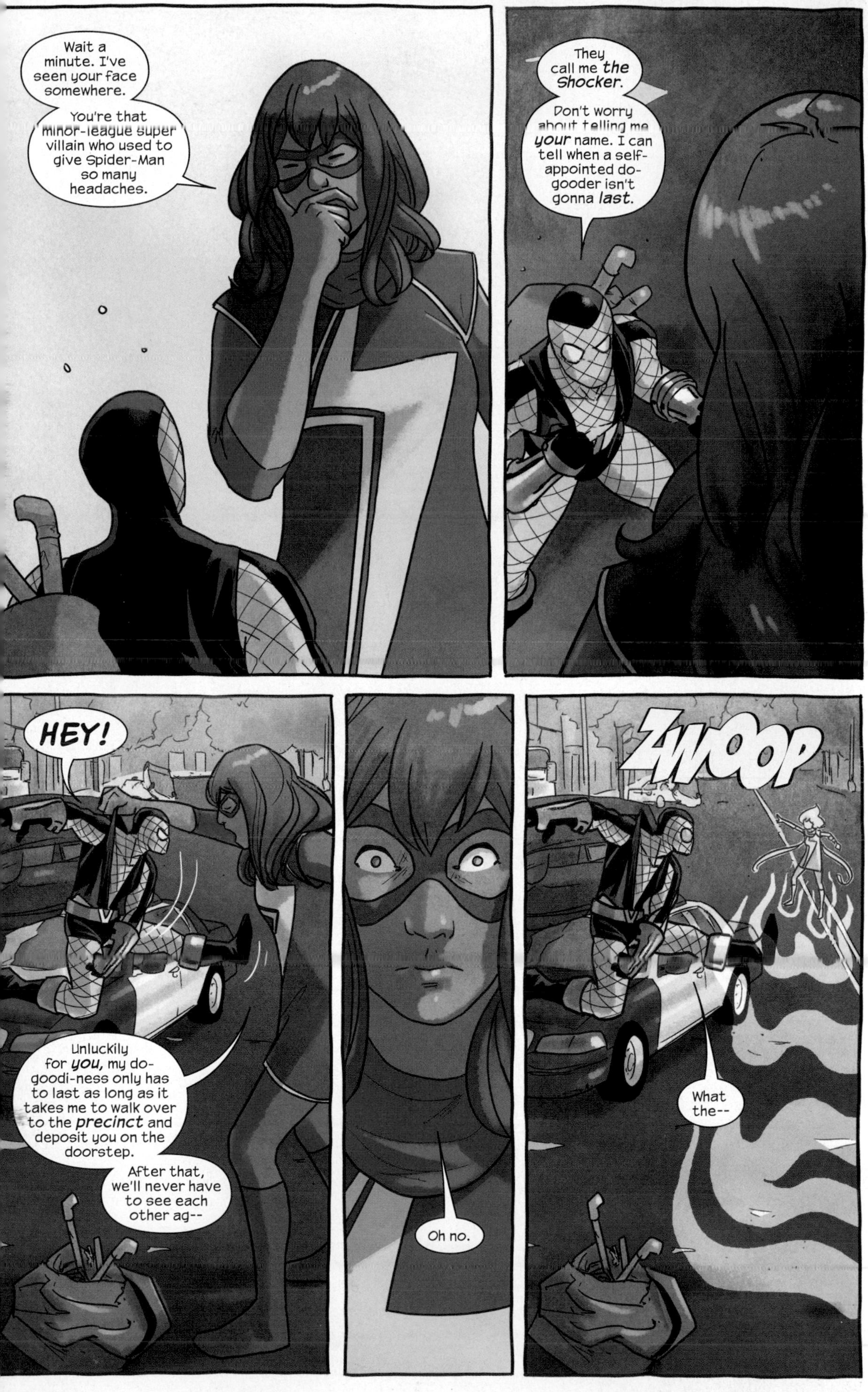
Wait a minute. I've seen your face somewhere.
You're that minor-league super villain who used to give Spider-Man so many headaches.
They call me *the Shocker*.
Don't worry about telling me *your* name. I can tell when a self-appointed do-gooder isn't gonna *last*.
HEY!
Unluckily for *you*, my do-goodi-ness only has to last as long as it takes me to walk over to the *precinct* and deposit you on the doorstep.
After that, we'll never have to see each other ag--
Oh no.
ZWOOP
What the--

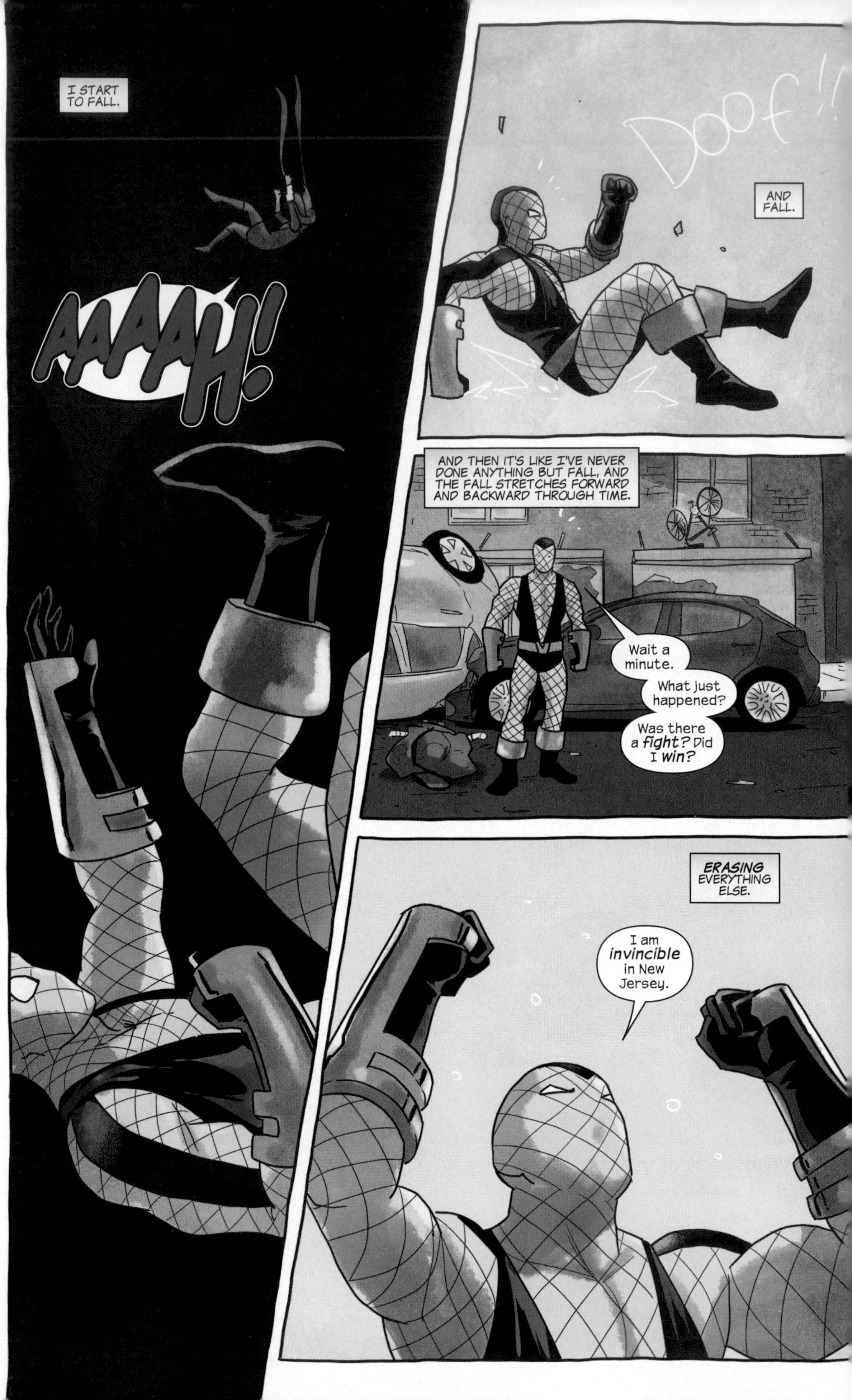
I START TO FALL.
AAAAH!
DOOF!!!
AND FALL.
AND THEN IT'S LIKE I'VE NEVER DONE ANYTHING BUT FALL, AND THE FALL STRETCHES FORWARD AND BACKWARD THROUGH TIME.
Wait a minute.
What just happened?
Was there a fight? Did I win?
ERASING EVERYTHING ELSE.
I am invincible in New Jersey.

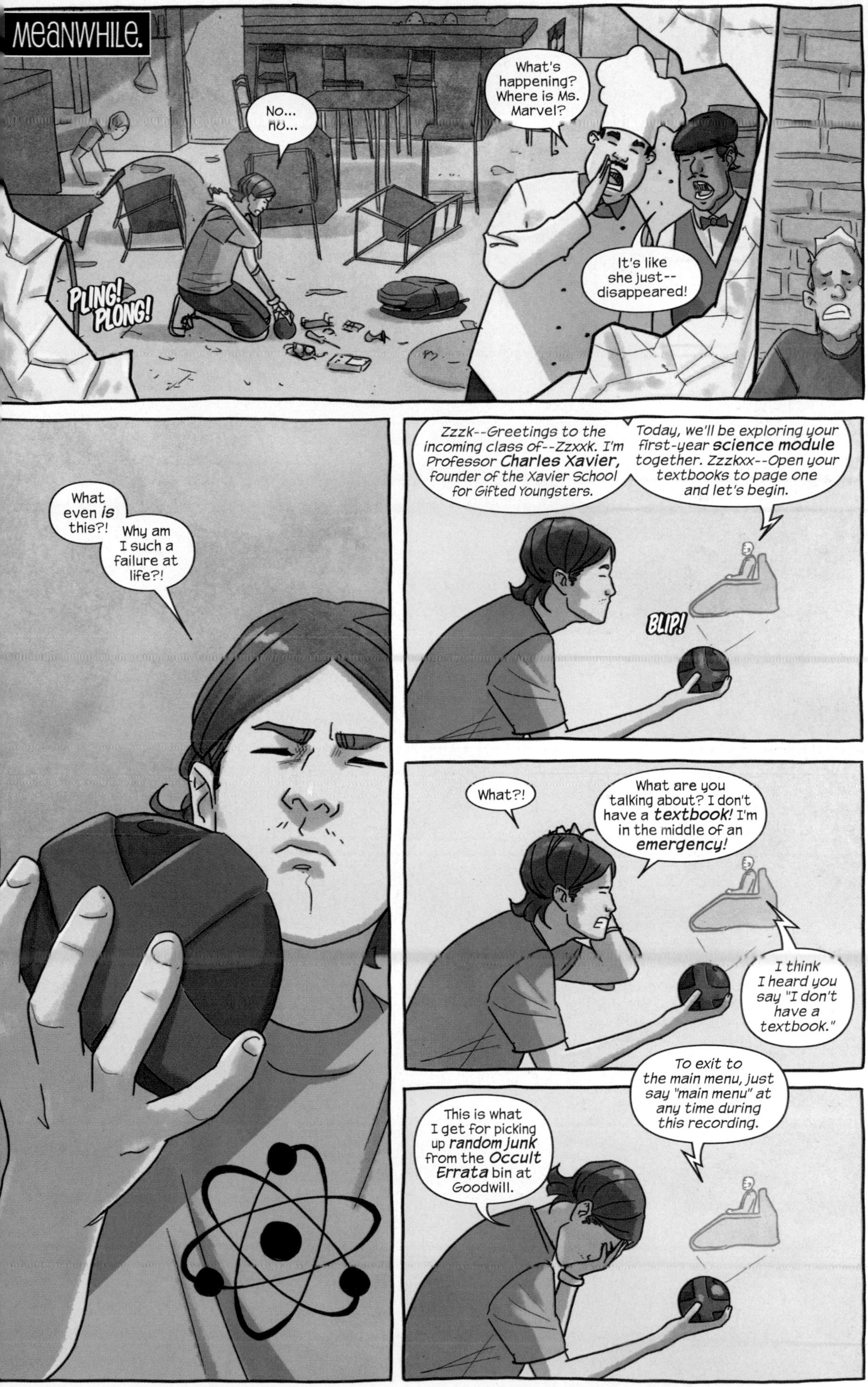
MEANWHILE.
No... no...
What's happening? Where is Ms. Marvel?
It's like she just--disappeared!
PLING! PLONG!
What even is this?!
Why am I such a failure at life?!
Zzzk--Greetings to the incoming class of--Zzxxk. I'm Professor Charles Xavier, founder of the Xavier School for Gifted Youngsters.
Today, we'll be exploring your first-year science module together. Zzzkxx--Open your textbooks to page one and let's begin.
BLIP!
What?!
What are you talking about? I don't have a textbook! I'm in the middle of an emergency!
I think I heard you say "I don't have a textbook."
To exit to the main menu, just say "main menu" at any time during this recording.
This is what I get for picking up random junk from the Occult Errata bin at Goodwill.

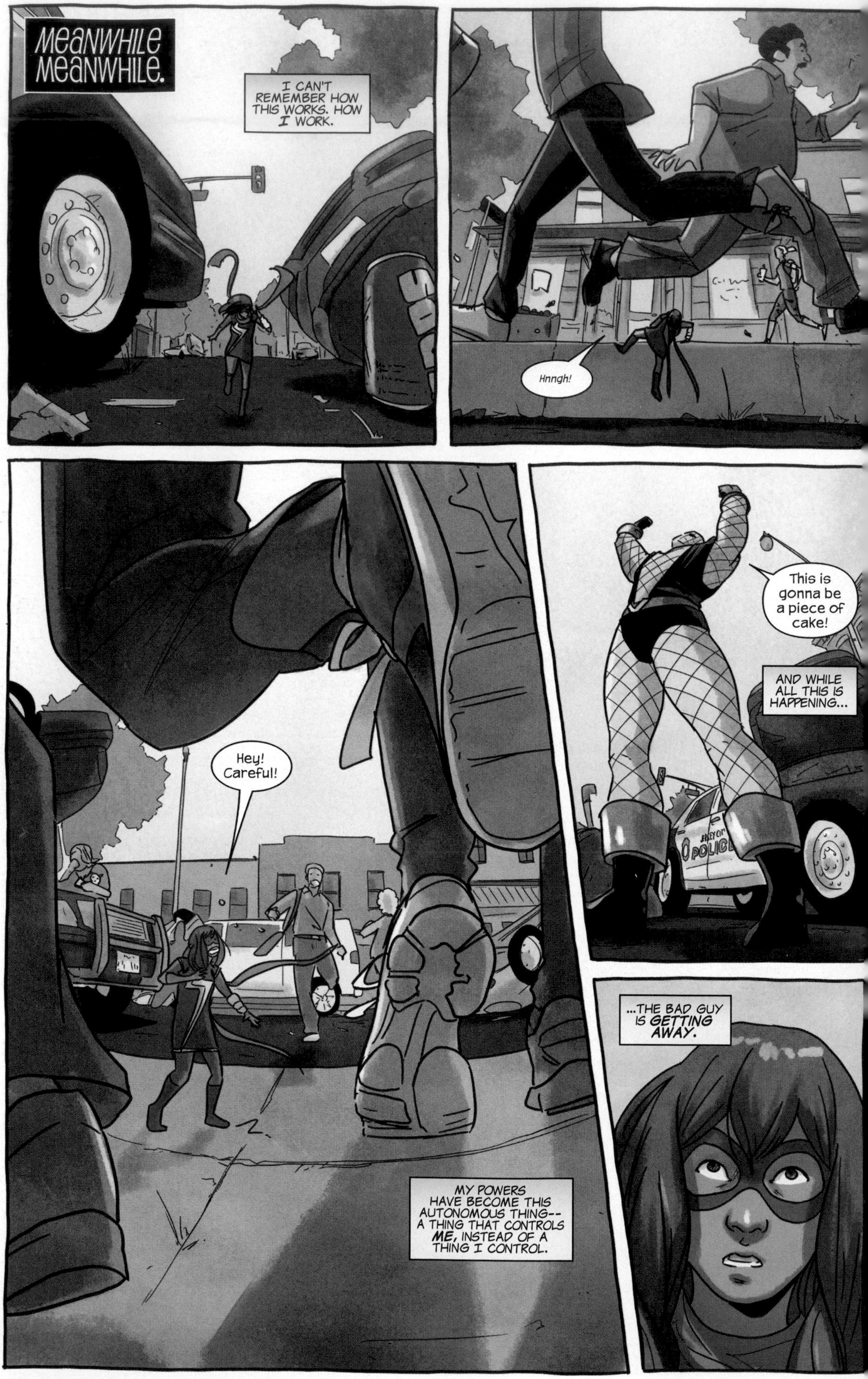
MEANWHILE MEANWHILE.
I CAN'T REMEMBER HOW THIS WORKS. HOW I WORK.
Hnngh!
Hey! Careful!
MY POWERS HAVE BECOME THIS AUTONOMOUS THING-- A THING THAT CONTROLS ME, INSTEAD OF A THING I CONTROL.
This is gonna be a piece of cake!
AND WHILE ALL THIS IS HAPPENING...
...THE BAD GUY IS GETTING AWAY.

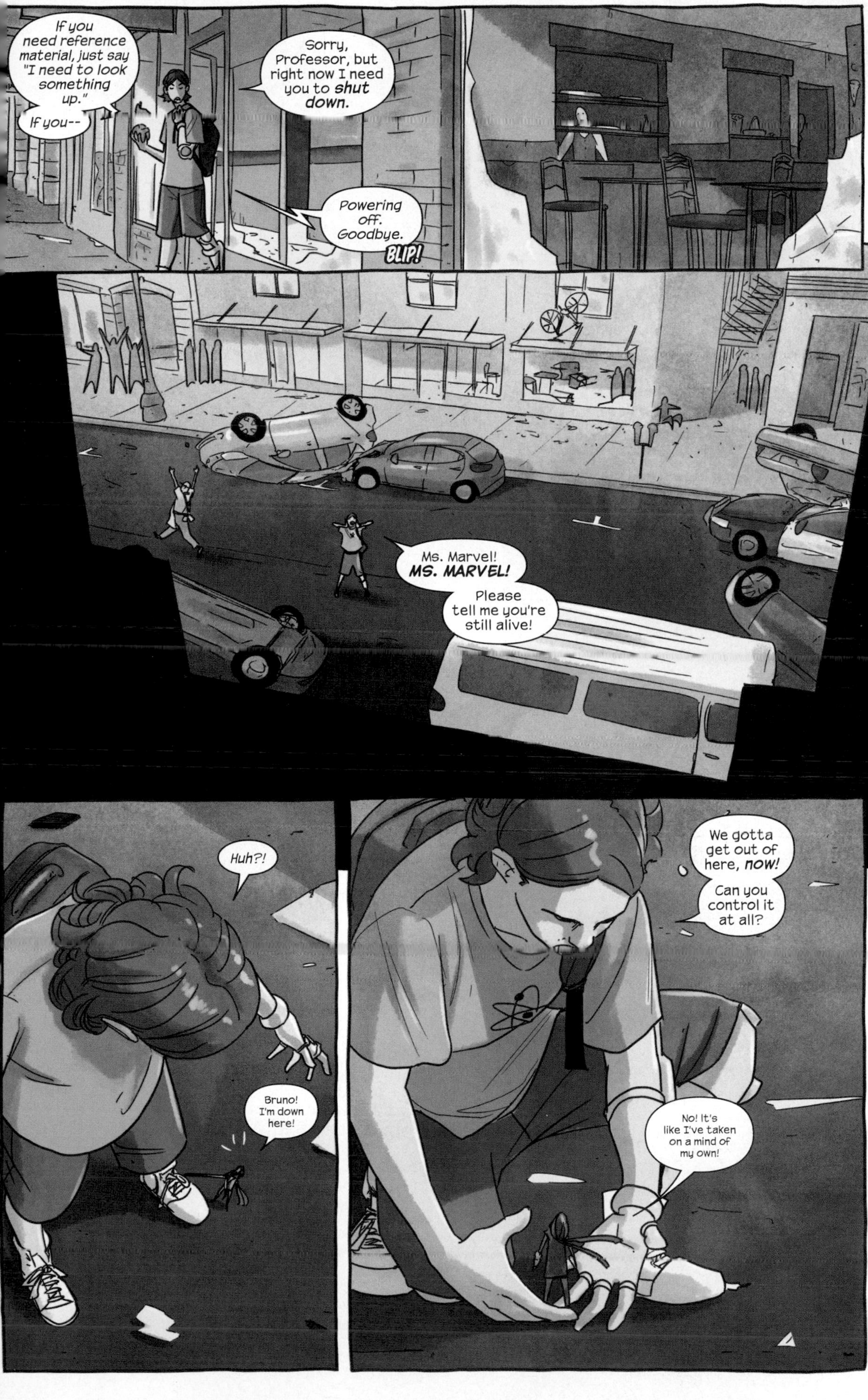

If you need reference material, just say "I need to look something up."
If you--
Sorry, Professor, but right now I need you to shut down.
Powering off. Goodbye.
BLIP!
Ms. Marvel! MS. MARVEL!
Please tell me you're still alive!
Huh?!
Bruno! I'm down here!
We gotta get out of here, NOW!
Can you control it at all?
No! It's like I've taken on a mind of my own!

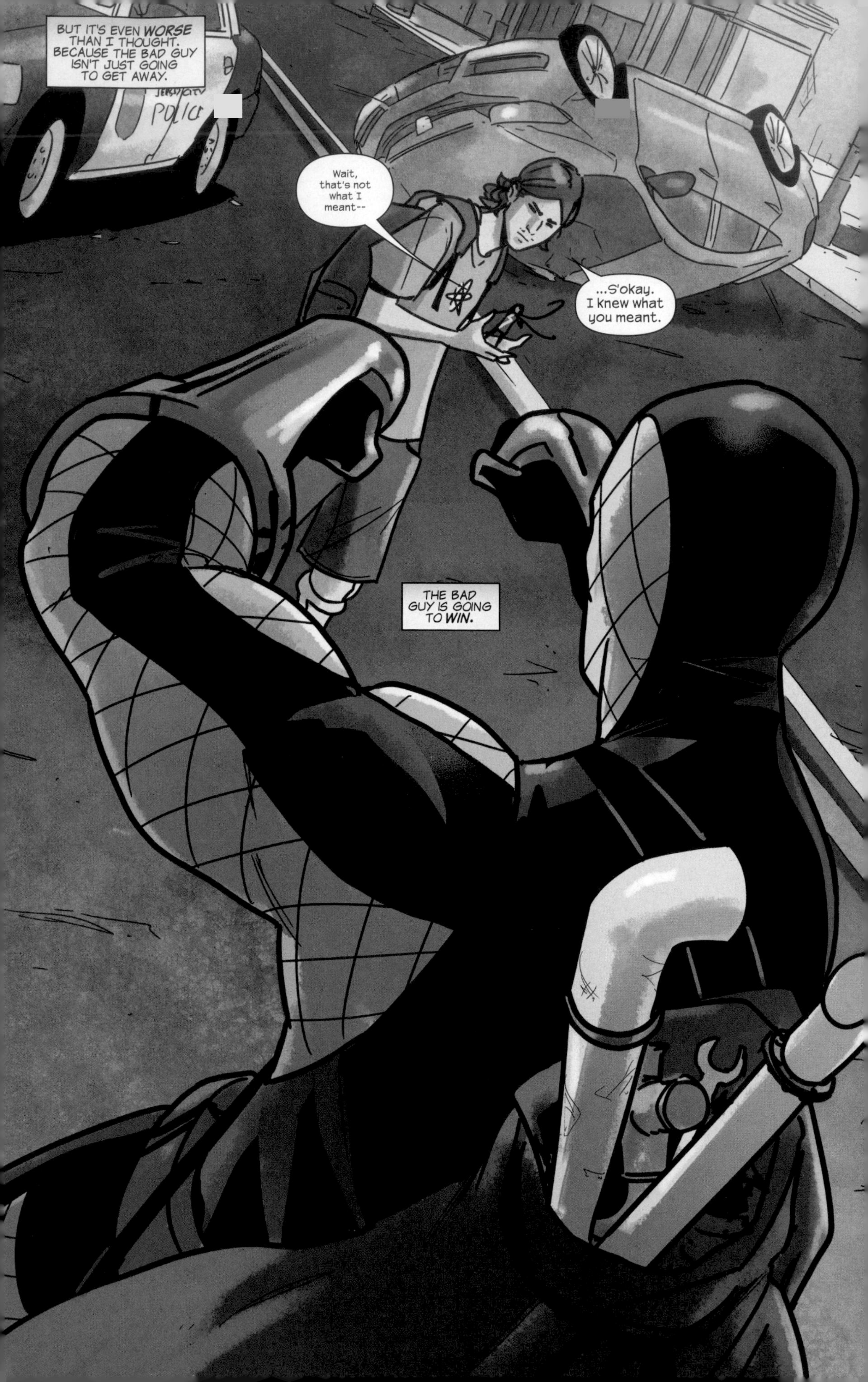
BUT IT'S EVEN WORSE THAN I THOUGHT. BECAUSE THE BAD GUY ISN'T JUST GOING TO GET AWAY.
Wait, that's not what I meant--
...S'okay. I knew what you meant.
THE BAD GUY IS GOING TO WIN.

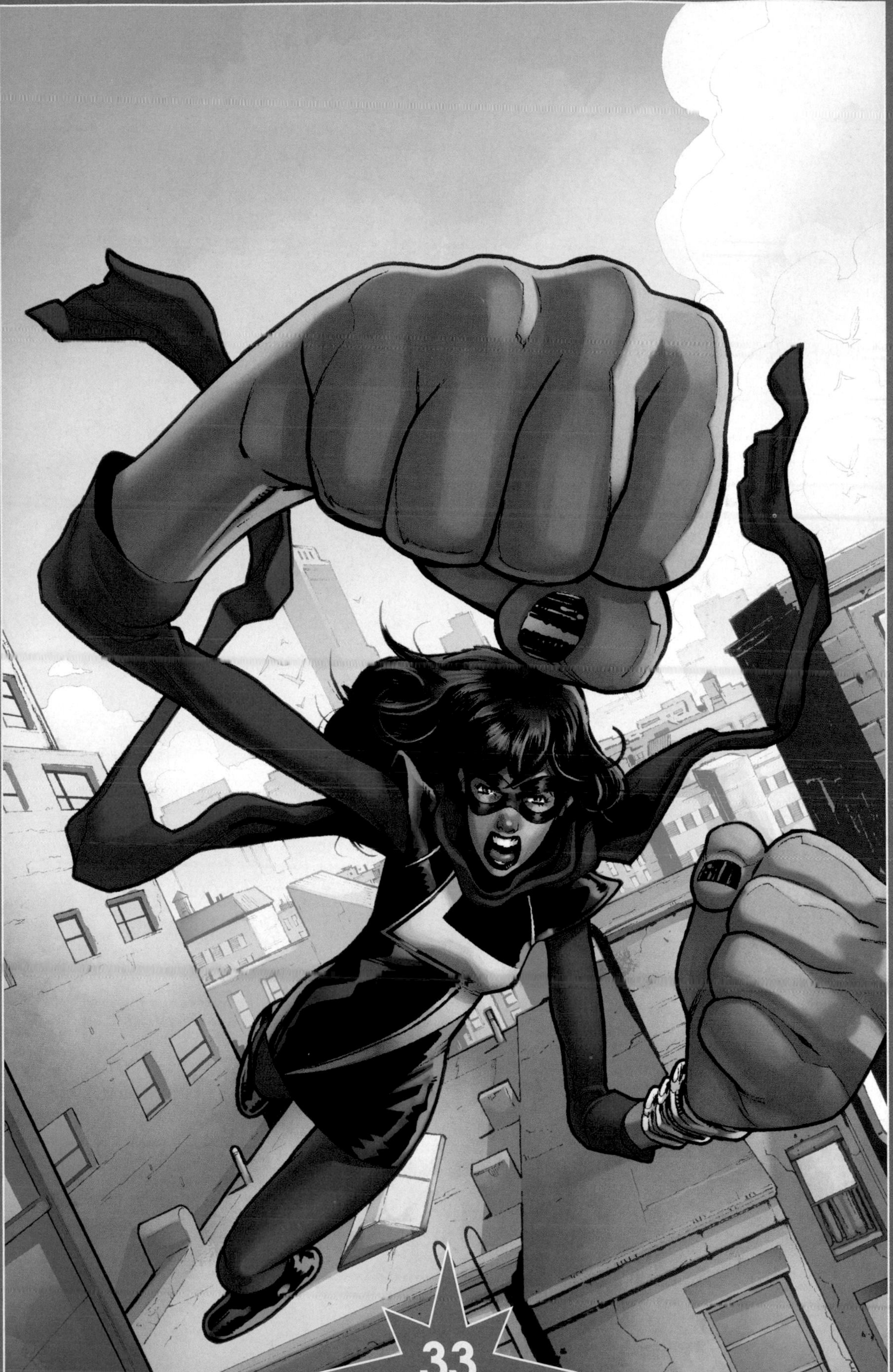
33

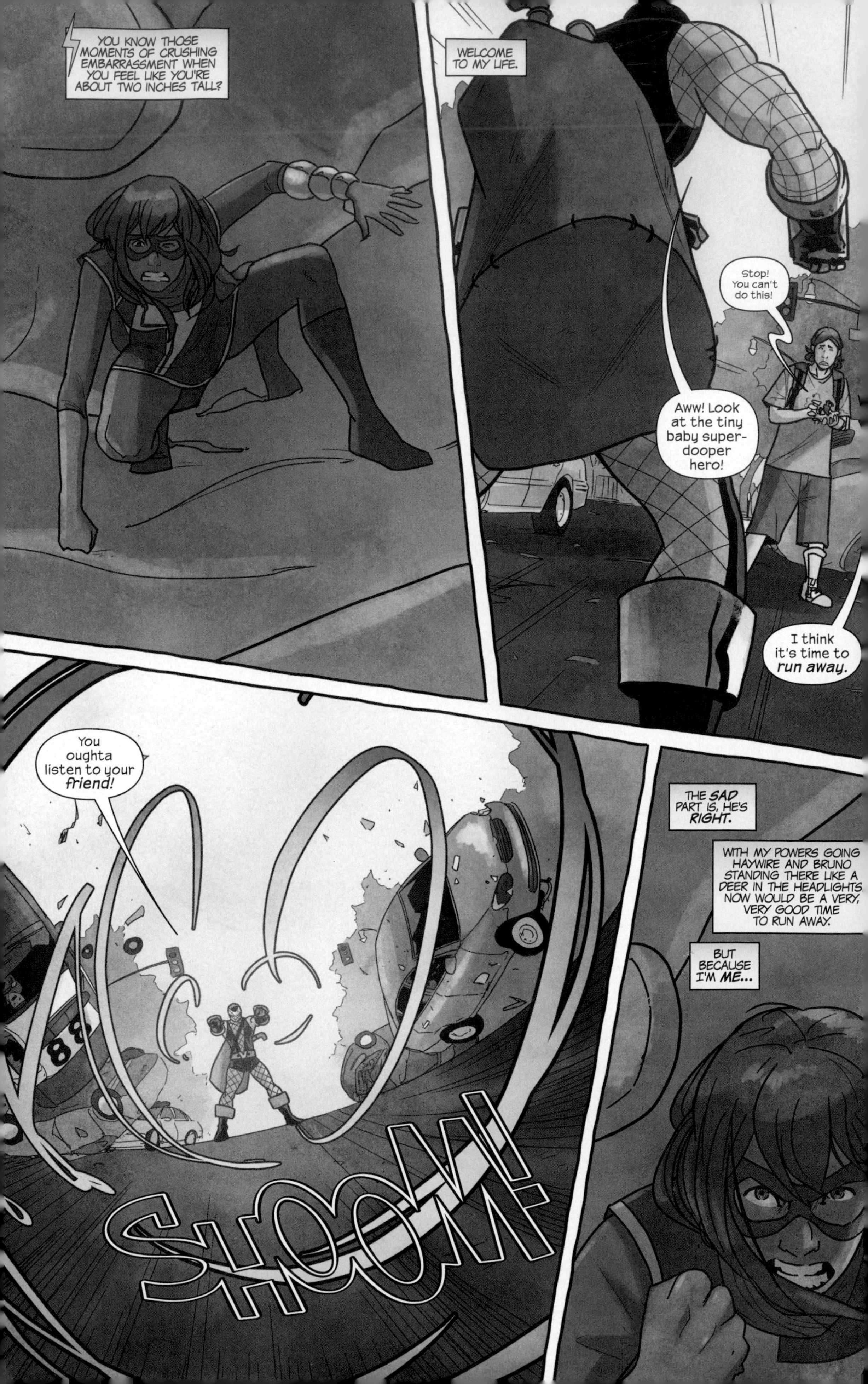
YOU KNOW THOSE MOMENTS OF CRUSHING EMBARRASSMENT WHEN YOU FEEL LIKE YOU'RE ABOUT TWO INCHES TALL?
WELCOME TO MY LIFE.
Stop! You can't do this!
Aww! Look at the tiny baby super-dooper hero!
I think it's time to run away.
You oughta listen to your friend!
SHOOOM!
THE SAD PART IS, HE'S RIGHT.
WITH MY POWERS GOING HAYWIRE AND BRUNO STANDING THERE LIKE A DEER IN THE HEADLIGHTS NOW WOULD BE A VERY, VERY GOOD TIME TO RUN AWAY.
BUT BECAUSE I'M ME...

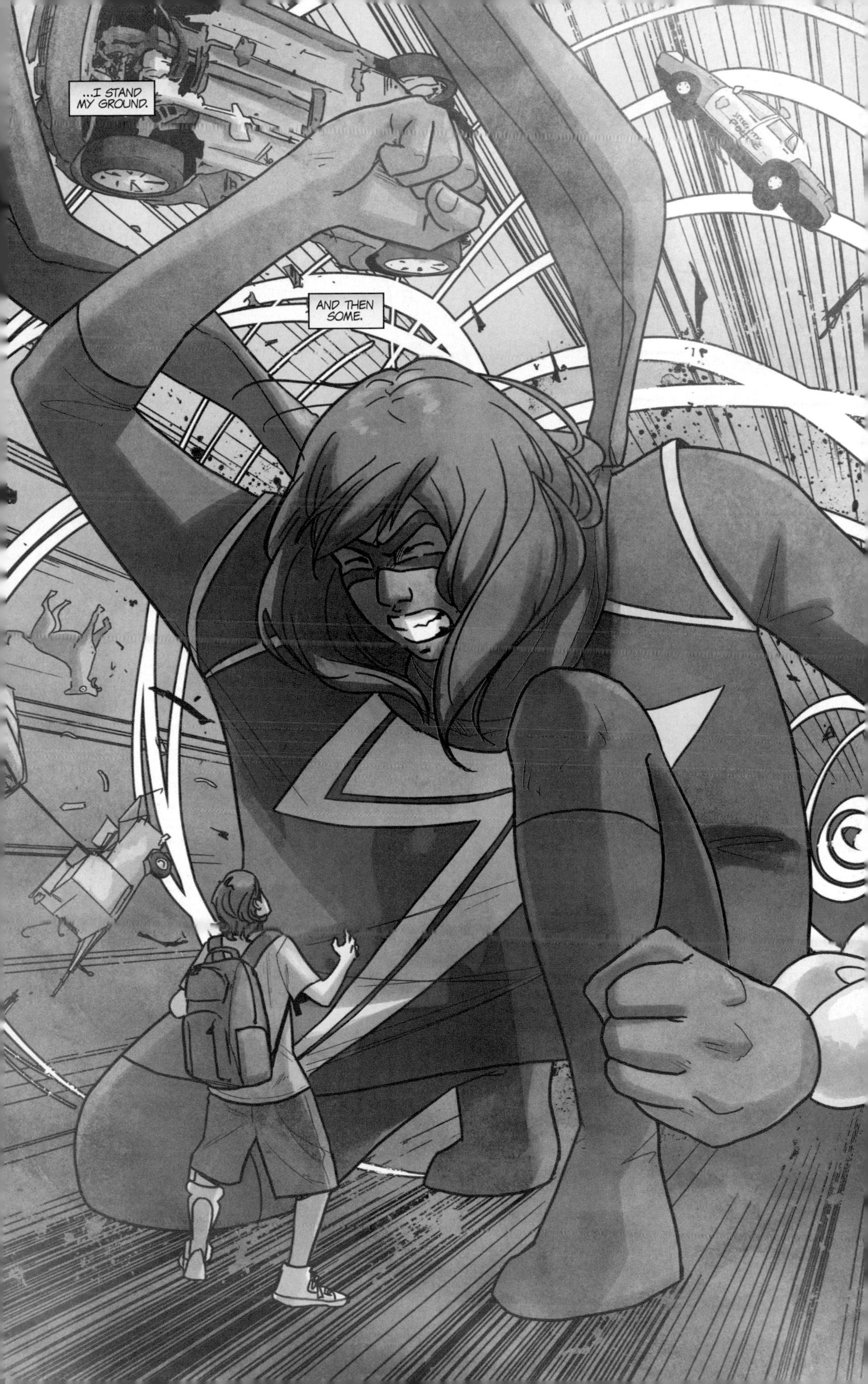

...I STAND MY GROUND.
AND THEN SOME.

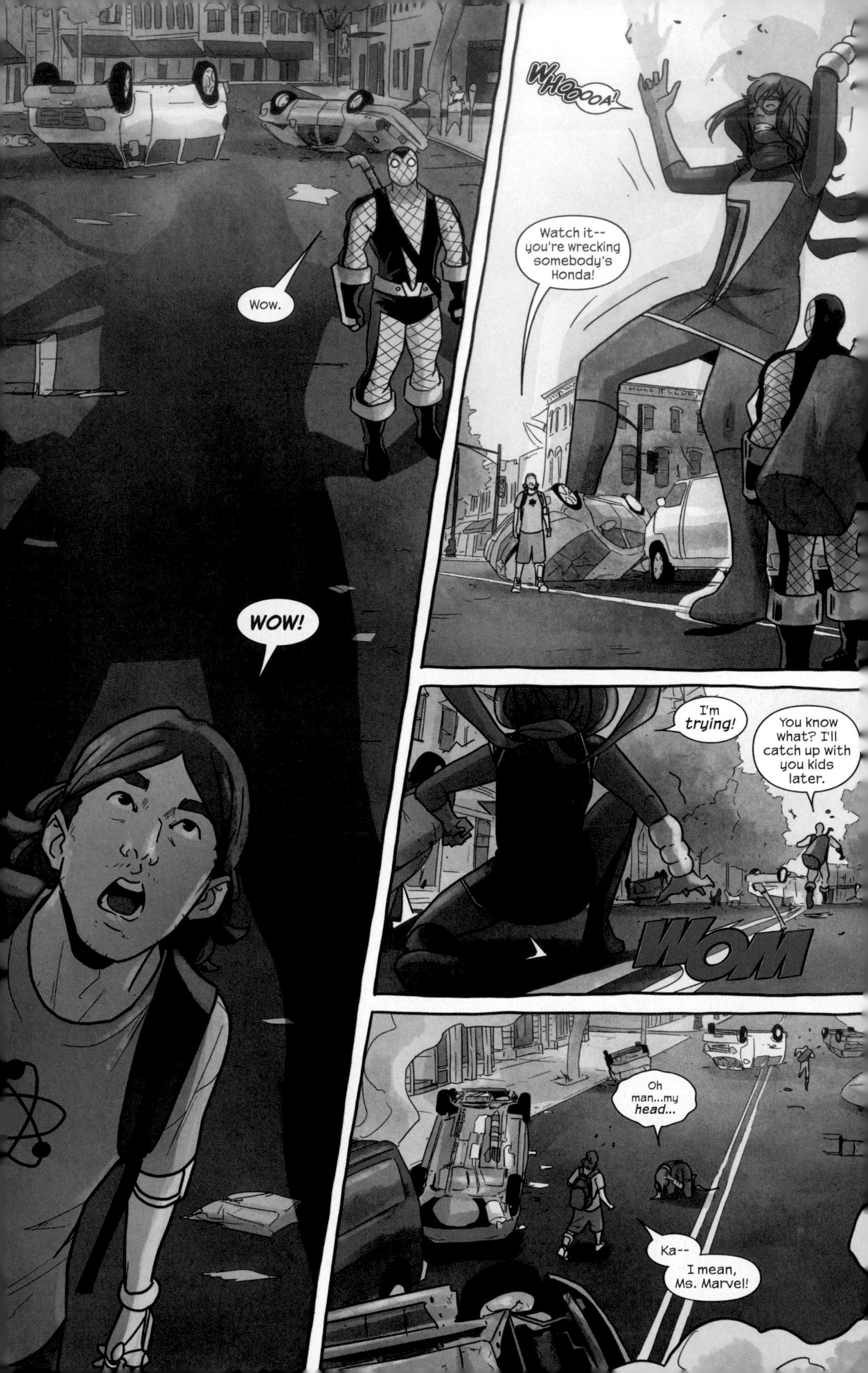
Wow.
WOW!
WHOOOOA!
Watch it--you're wrecking somebody's Honda!
I'm trying!
You know what? I'll catch up with you kids later.
WOM
Oh man...my head...
Ka--
I mean, Ms. Marvel!

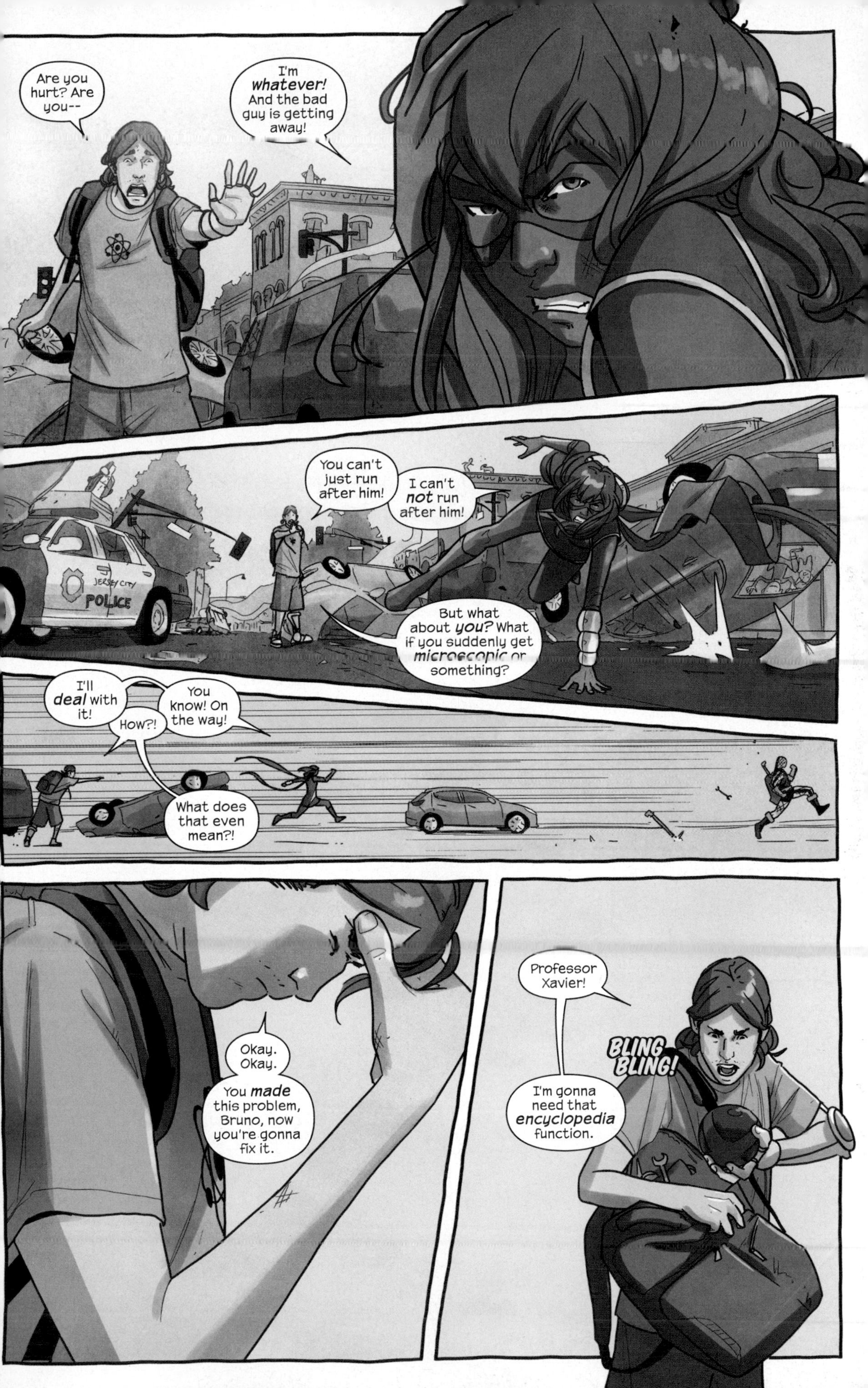
Are you hurt? Are you--
I'm *whatever!* And the bad guy is getting away!
You can't just run after him!
I can't *not* run after him!
But what about *you?* What if you suddenly get *microscopic* or something?
I'll *deal* with it!
You know! On the way!
How?!
What does that even mean?!
Okay. Okay.
You *made* this problem, Bruno, now you're gonna fix it.
Professor Xavier!
BLING BLING!
I'm gonna need that *encyclopedia* function.

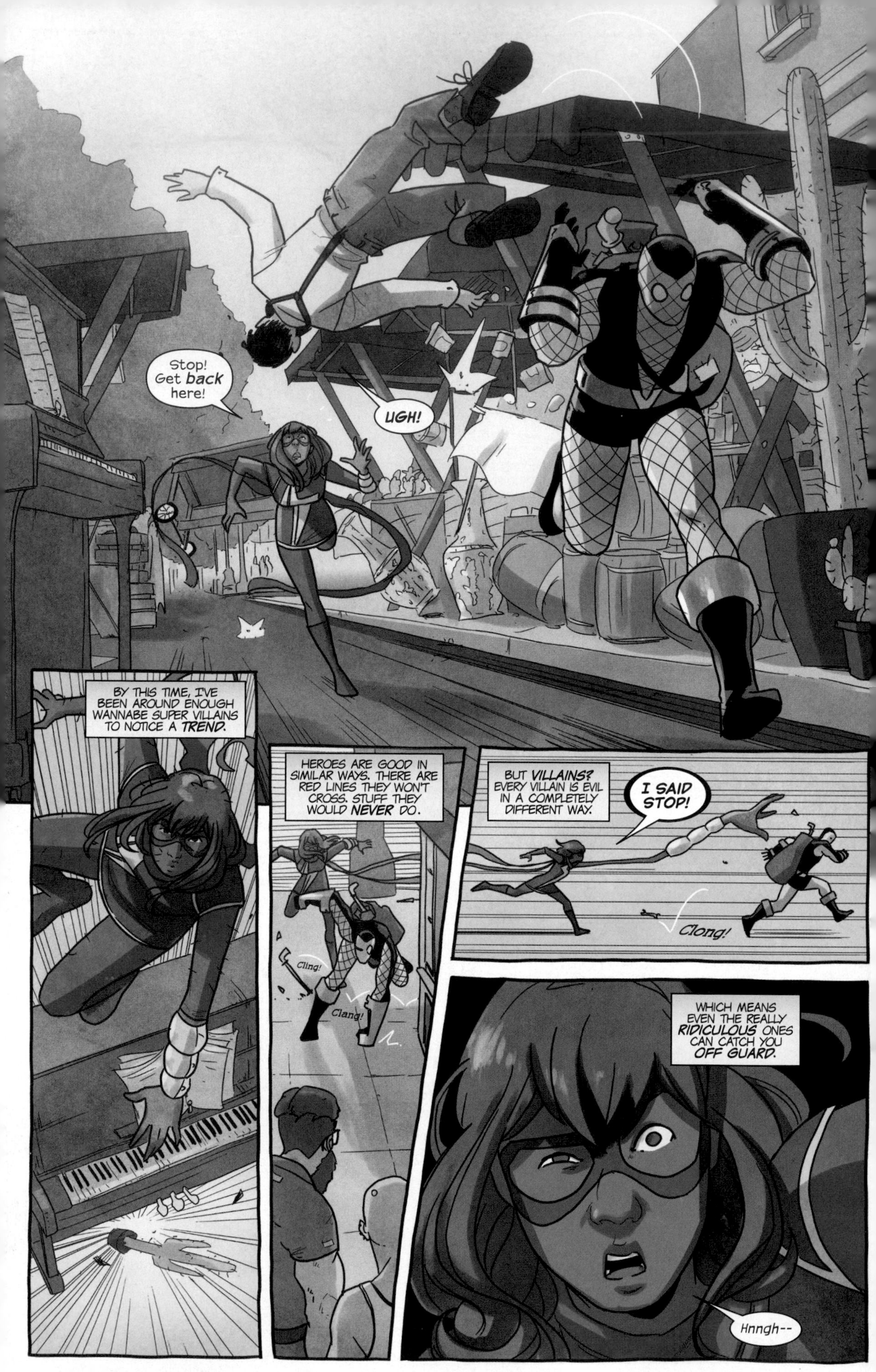
Stop! Get back here!
UGH!
BY THIS TIME, I'VE BEEN AROUND ENOUGH WANNABE SUPER VILLAINS TO NOTICE A TREND.
HEROES ARE GOOD IN SIMILAR WAYS. THERE ARE RED LINES THEY WON'T CROSS. STUFF THEY WOULD NEVER DO.
Cling!
Clang!
BUT VILLAINS? EVERY VILLAIN IS EVIL IN A COMPLETELY DIFFERENT WAY.
I SAID STOP!
Clong!
WHICH MEANS EVEN THE REALLY RIDICULOUS ONES CAN CATCH YOU OFF GUARD.
Hnngh--

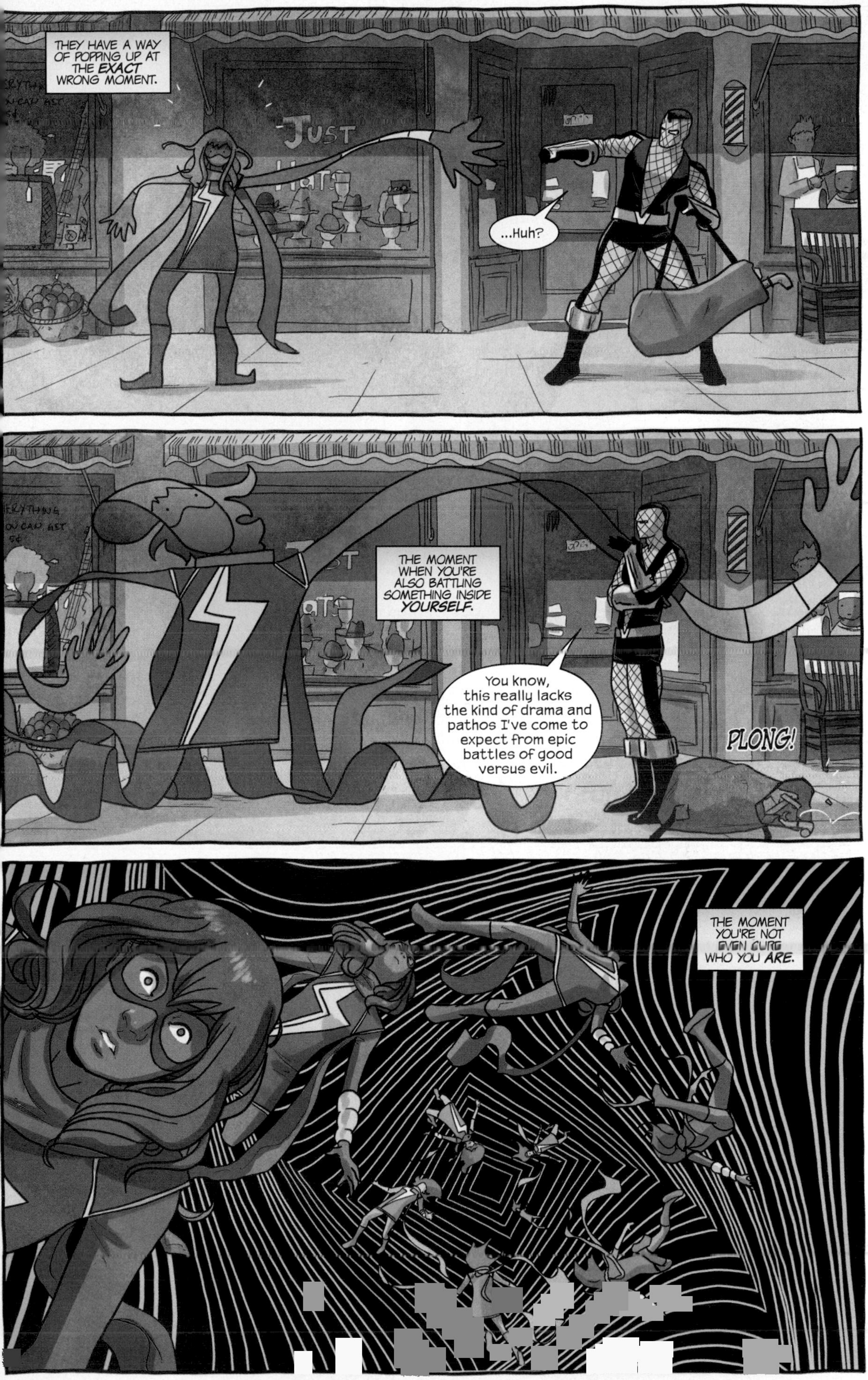
THEY HAVE A WAY OF POPPING UP AT THE EXACT WRONG MOMENT.
...Huh?
THE MOMENT WHEN YOU'RE ALSO BATTLING SOMETHING INSIDE YOURSELF.
You know, this really lacks the kind of drama and pathos I've come to expect from epic battles of good versus evil.
PLONG!
THE MOMENT YOU'RE NOT EVEN SURE WHO YOU ARE.

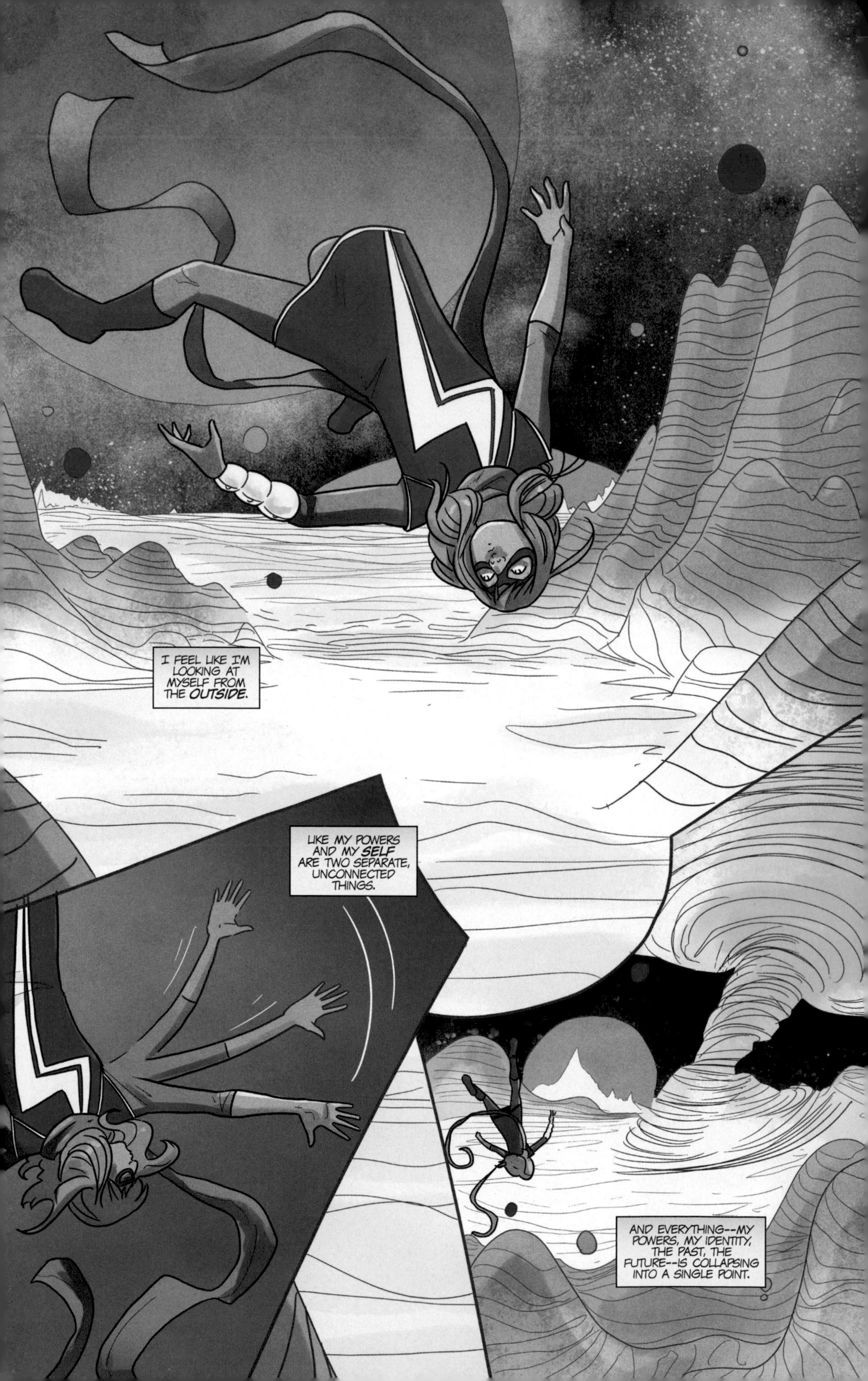
I FEEL LIKE I'M LOOKING AT MYSELF FROM THE OUTSIDE.
LIKE MY POWERS AND MY SELF ARE TWO SEPARATE, UNCONNECTED THINGS.
AND EVERYTHING--MY POWERS, MY IDENTITY, THE PAST, THE FUTURE--IS COLLAPSING INTO A SINGLE POINT.

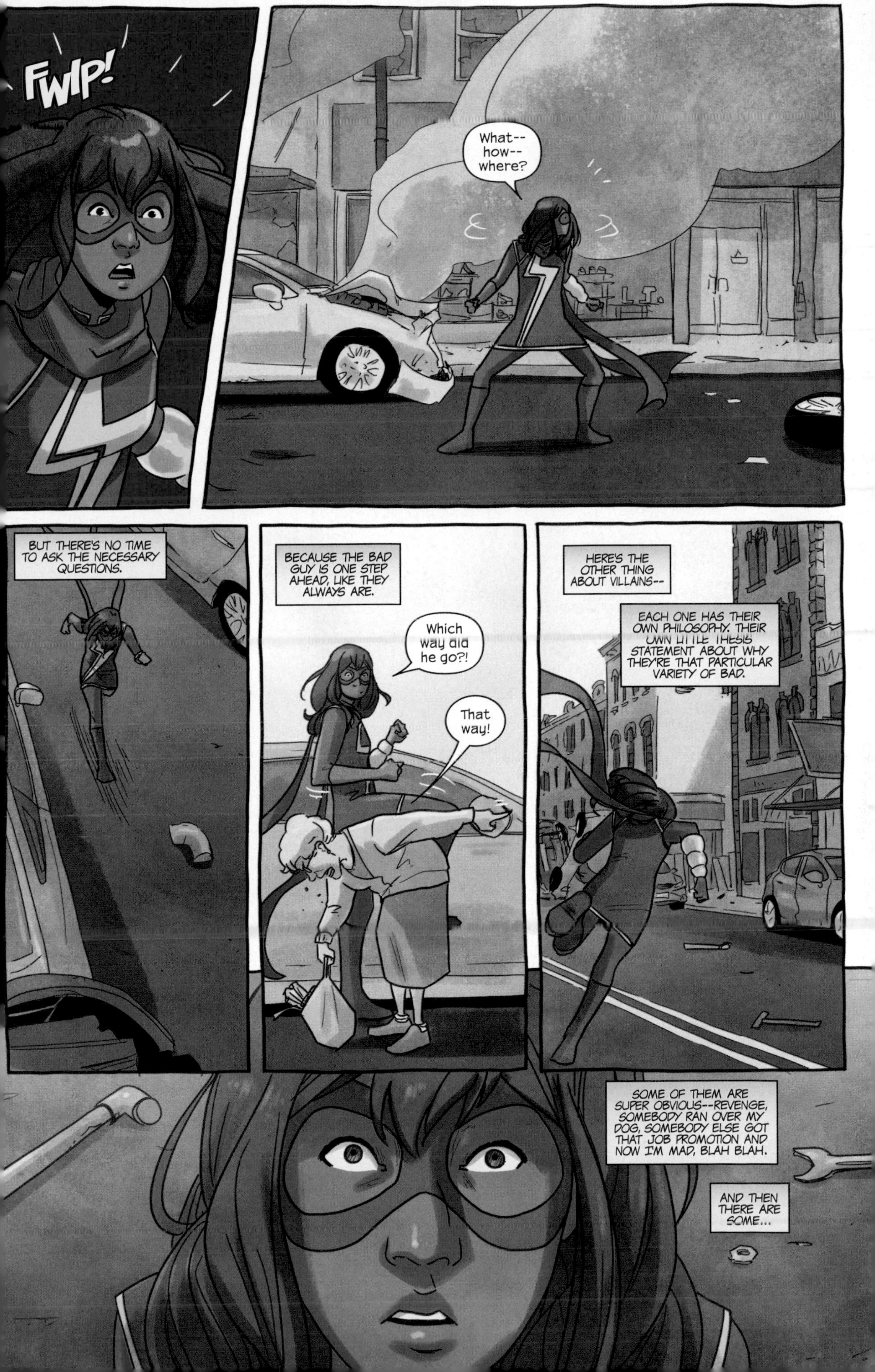
FWIP!
What-- how-- where?
BUT THERE'S NO TIME TO ASK THE NECESSARY QUESTIONS.
BECAUSE THE BAD GUY IS ONE STEP AHEAD, LIKE THEY ALWAYS ARE.
Which way did he go?!
That way!
HERE'S THE OTHER THING ABOUT VILLAINS--
EACH ONE HAS THEIR OWN PHILOSOPHY. THEIR OWN LITTLE THESIS STATEMENT ABOUT WHY THEY'RE THAT PARTICULAR VARIETY OF BAD.
SOME OF THEM ARE SUPER OBVIOUS--REVENGE, SOMEBODY RAN OVER MY DOG, SOMEBODY ELSE GOT THAT JOB PROMOTION AND NOW I'M MAD, BLAH BLAH.
AND THEN THERE ARE SOME...

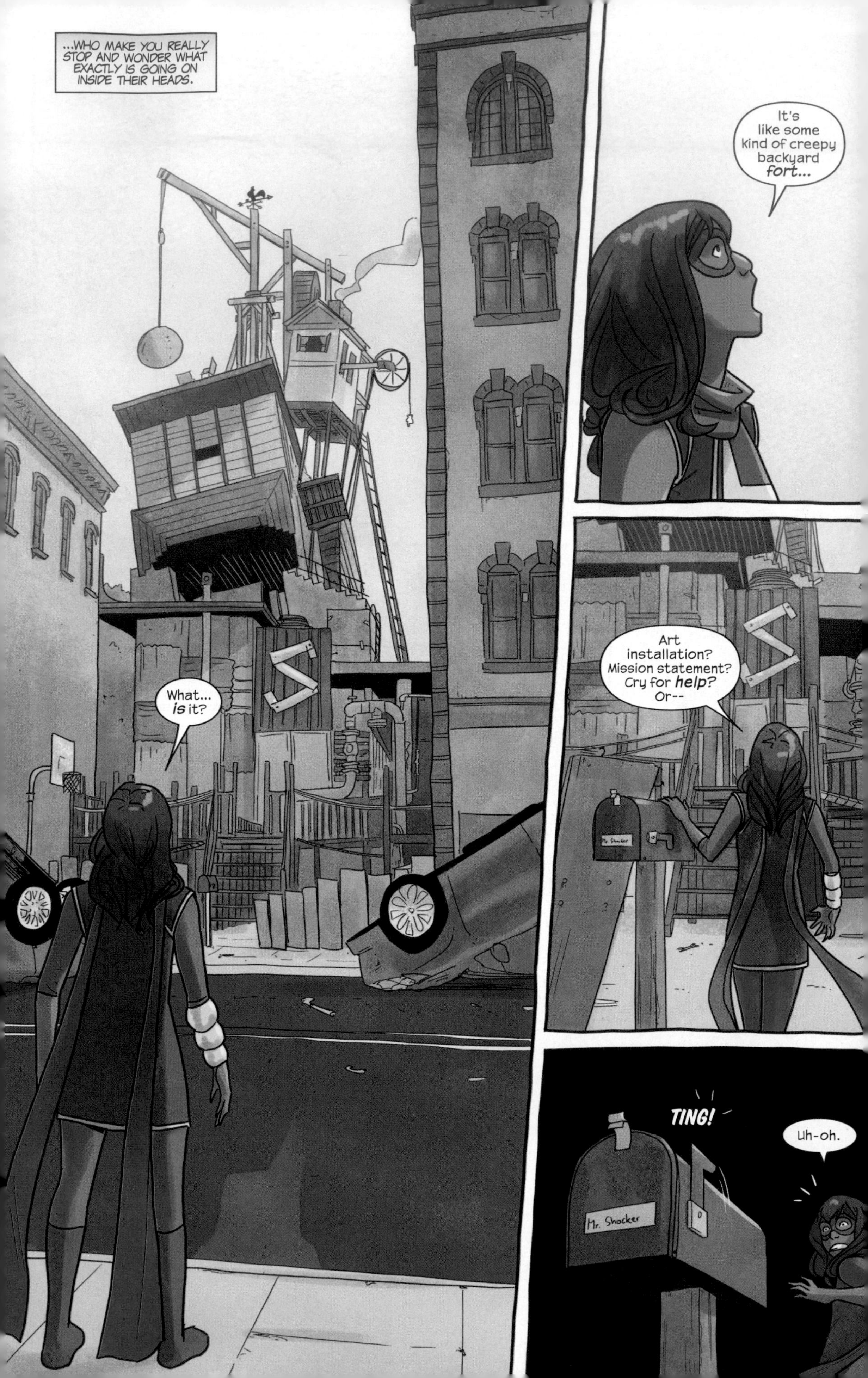
...WHO MAKE YOU REALLY STOP AND WONDER WHAT EXACTLY IS GOING ON INSIDE THEIR HEADS.
What... is it?
It's like some kind of creepy backyard fort...
Art installation? Mission statement? Cry for help? Or--
Mr. Shocker
TING!
Mr. Shocker
Uh-oh.

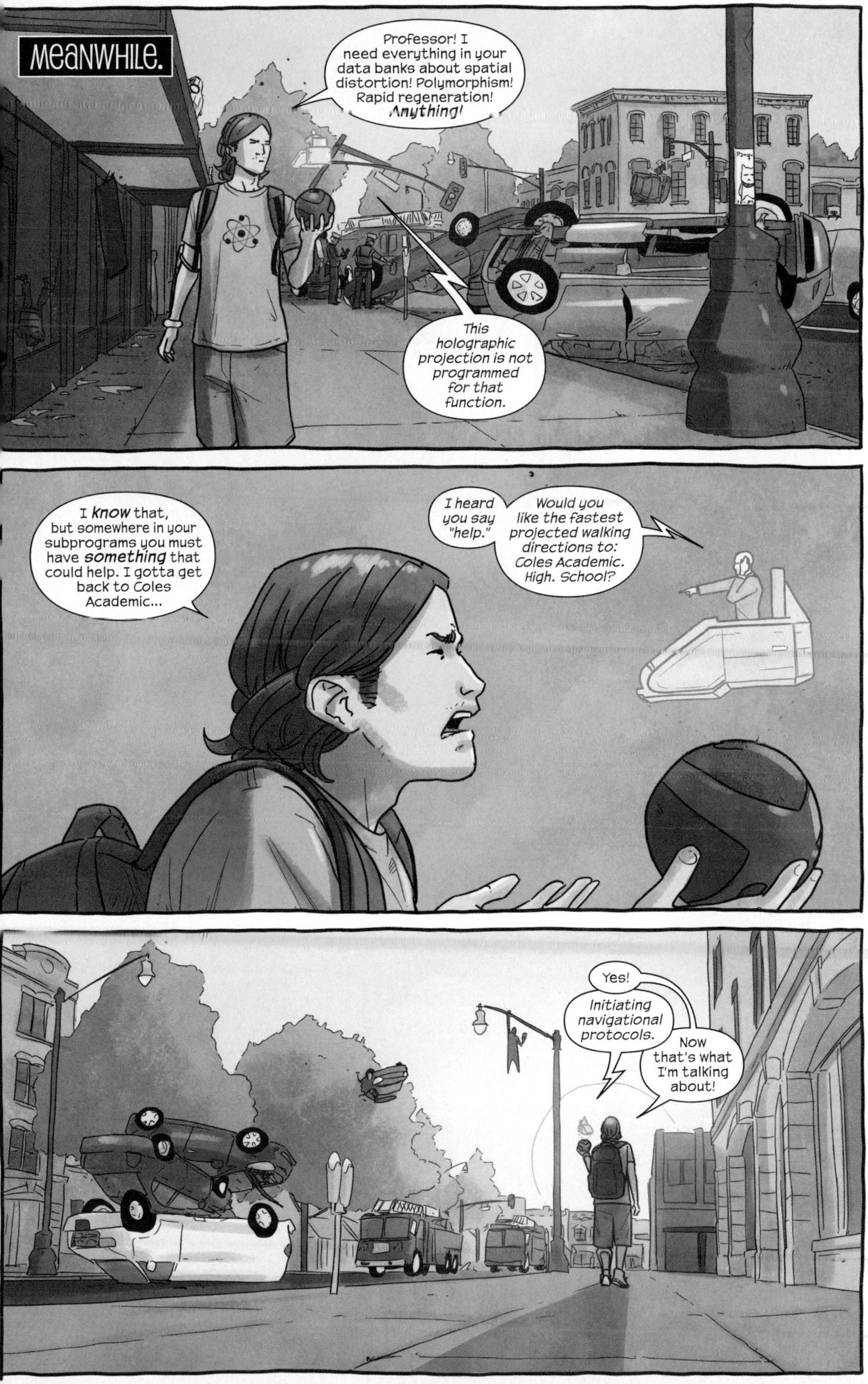
MEANWHILE.
Professor! I need everything in your data banks about spatial distortion! Polymorphism! Rapid regeneration! Anything!
This holographic projection is not programmed for that function.
I know that, but somewhere in your subprograms you must have something that could help. I gotta get back to Coles Academic...
I heard you say "help."
Would you like the fastest projected walking directions to: Coles Academic. High. School?
Yes!
Initiating navigational protocols.
Now that's what I'm talking about!

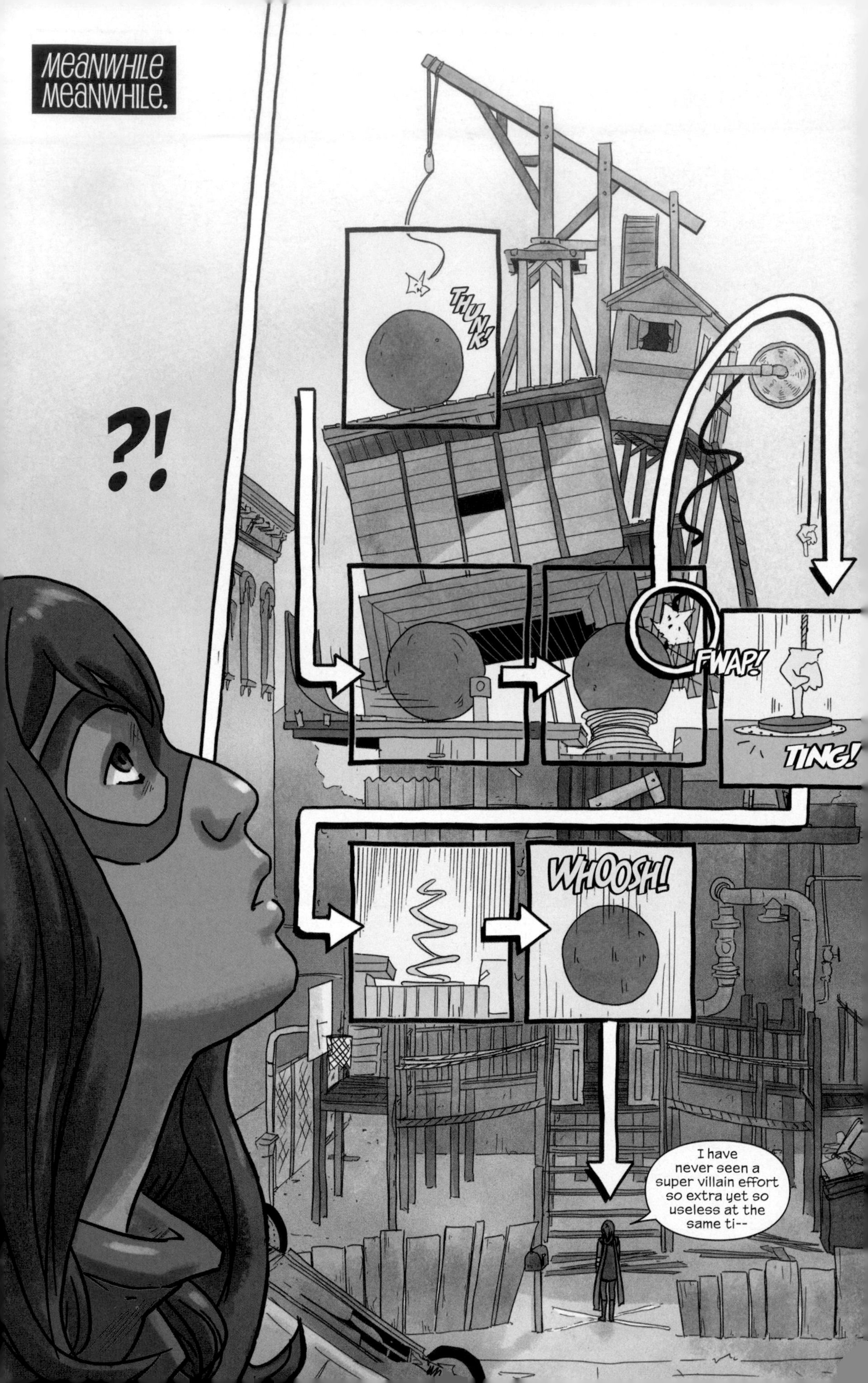
MEANWHILE MEANWHILE.
?!
THUNK!
FWAP!
TING!
WHOOSH!
I have never seen a super villain effort so extra yet so useless at the same ti--

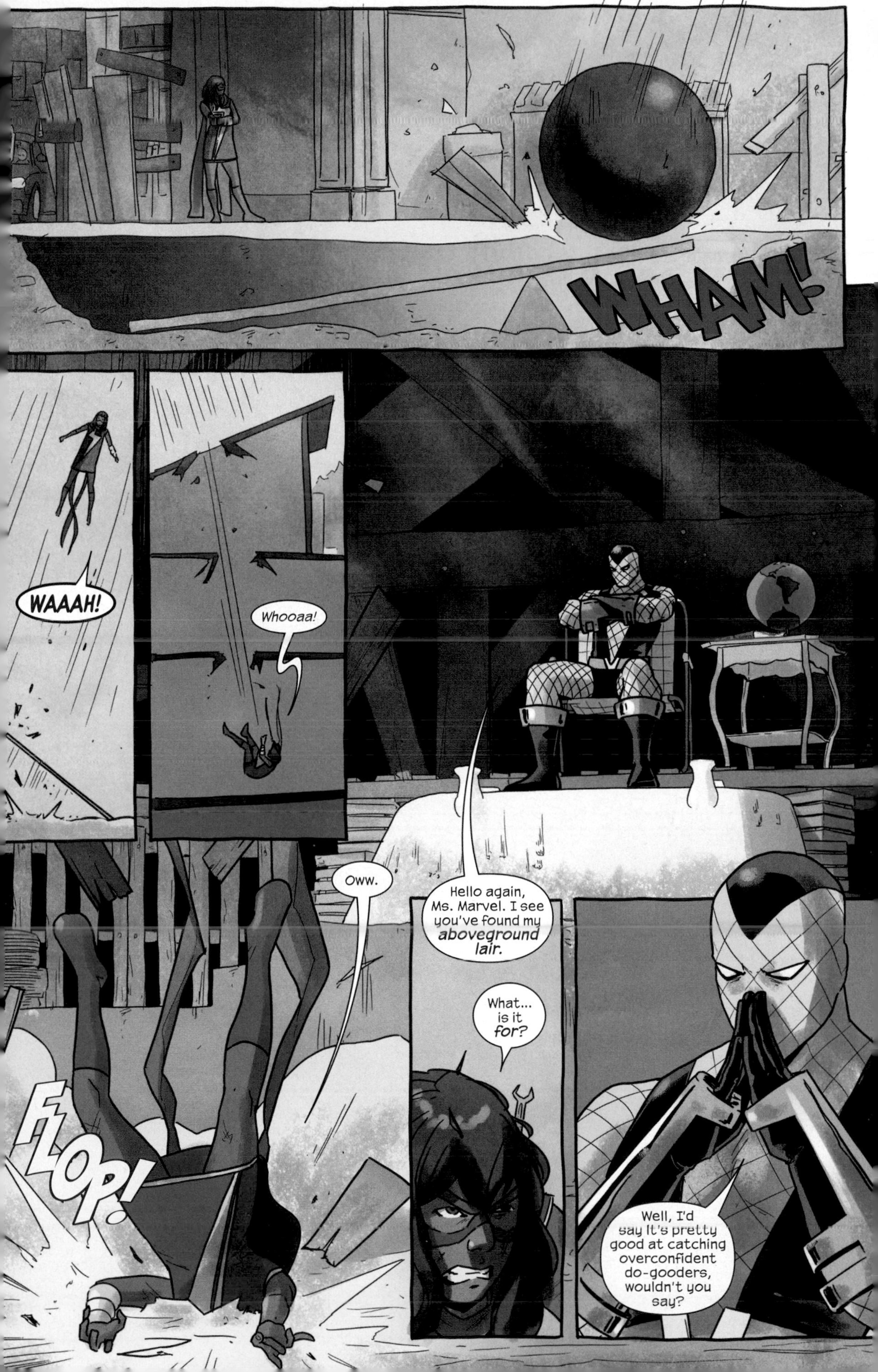
WHAM!
WAAAH!
Whooaa!
Hello again, Ms. Marvel. I see you've found my *aboveground lair.*
Oww.
FLOP!
What... is it *for?*
Well, I'd say it's pretty good at catching overconfident do-gooders, wouldn't you say?

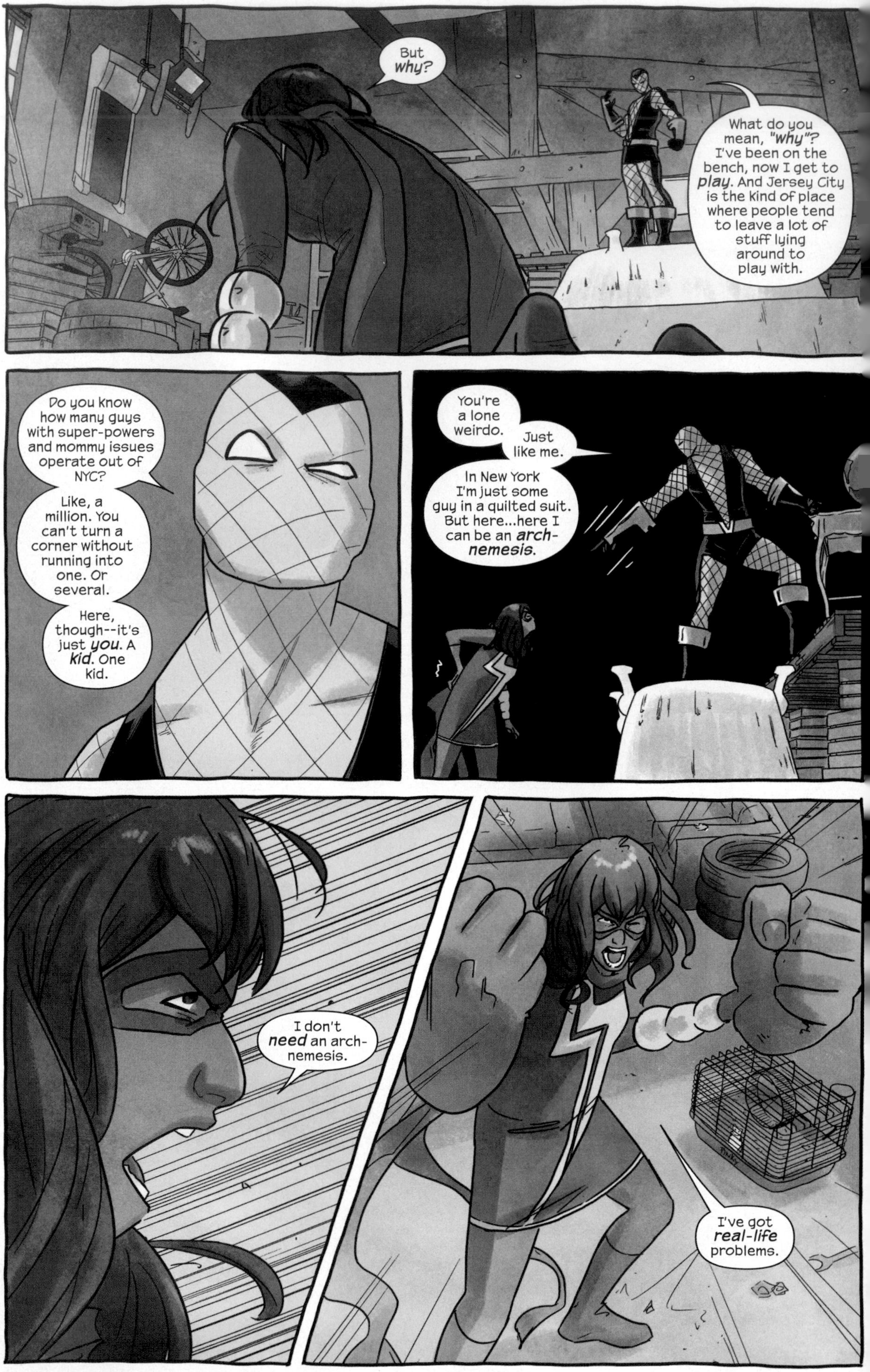
But *why*?
What do you mean, "*why*"? I've been on the bench, now I get to *play*. And Jersey City is the kind of place where people tend to leave a lot of stuff lying around to play with.
Do you know how many guys with super-powers and mommy issues operate out of NYC?
Like, a million. You can't turn a corner without running into one. Or several.
Here, though--it's just *you*. A *kid*. One kid.
You're a lone weirdo.
Just like me.
In New York I'm just some guy in a quilted suit. But here...here I can be an *arch-nemesis*.
I don't *need* an arch-nemesis.
I've got *real-life* problems.

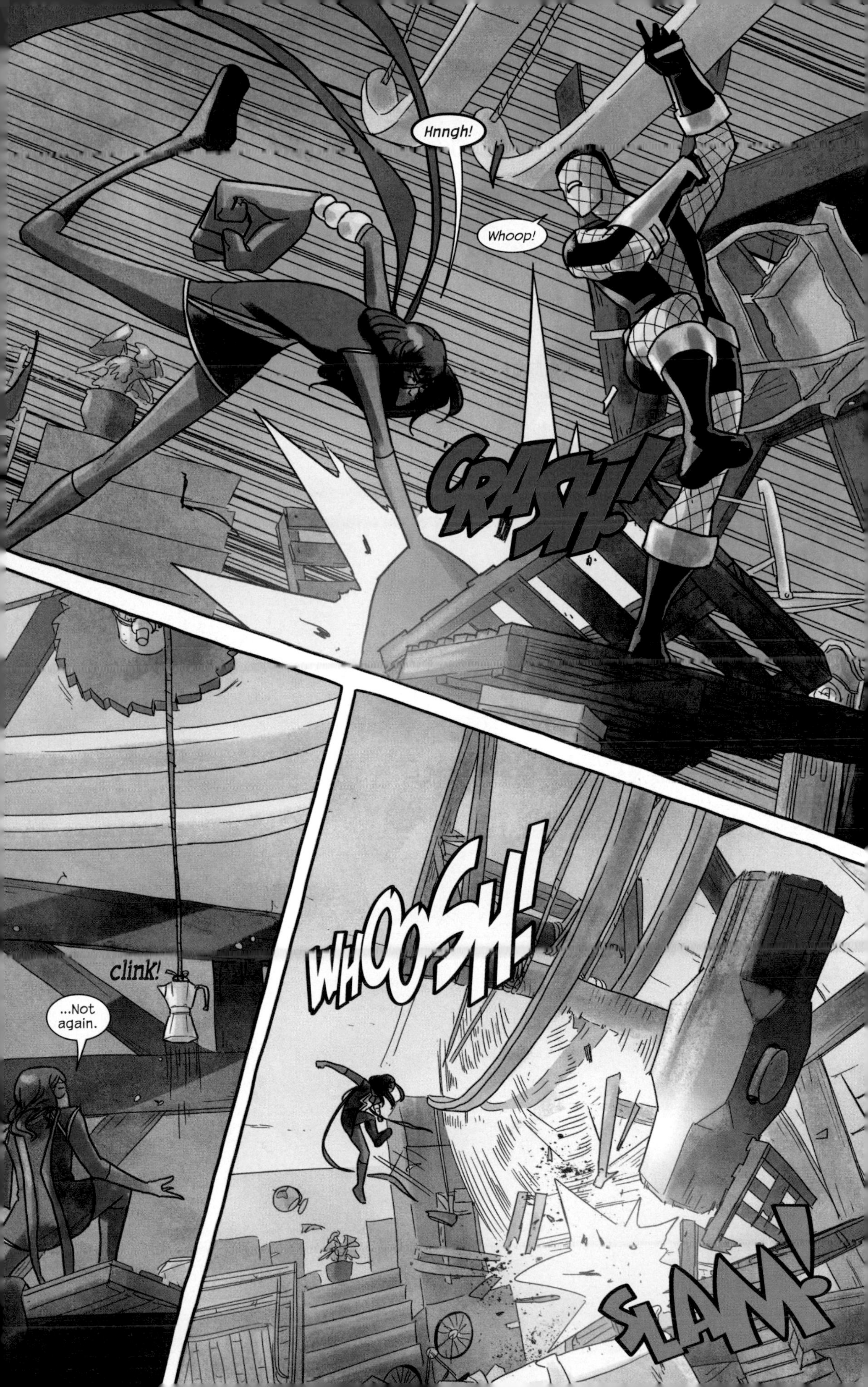
Hnngh!
Whoop!
CRASH!
clink!
...Not again.
WHOOSH!
SLAM!

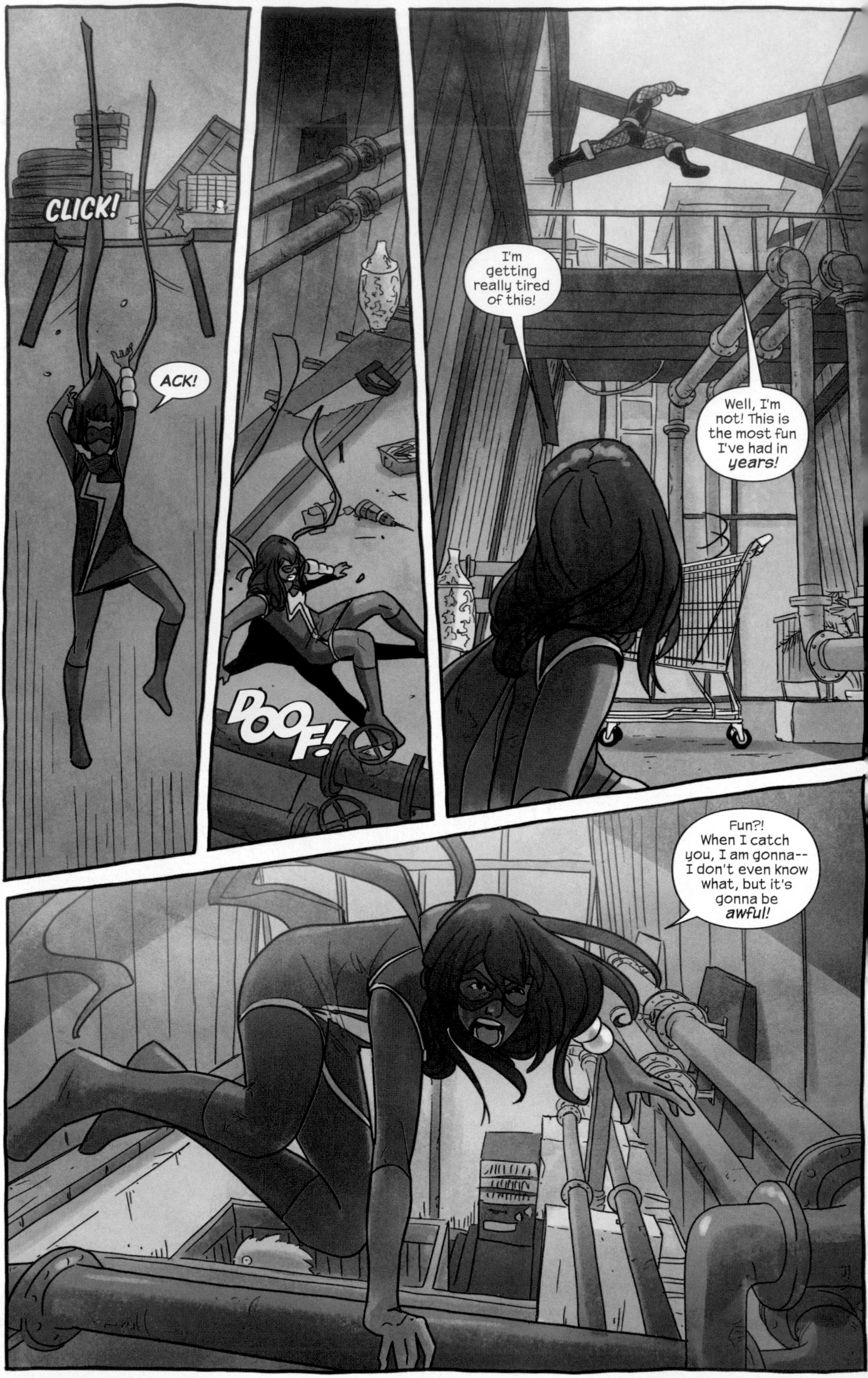
CLICK!
ACK!
DOOF!
I'm getting really tired of this!
Well, I'm not! This is the most fun I've had in *years!*
Fun?! When I catch you, I am gonna-- I don't even know what, but it's gonna be *awful!*

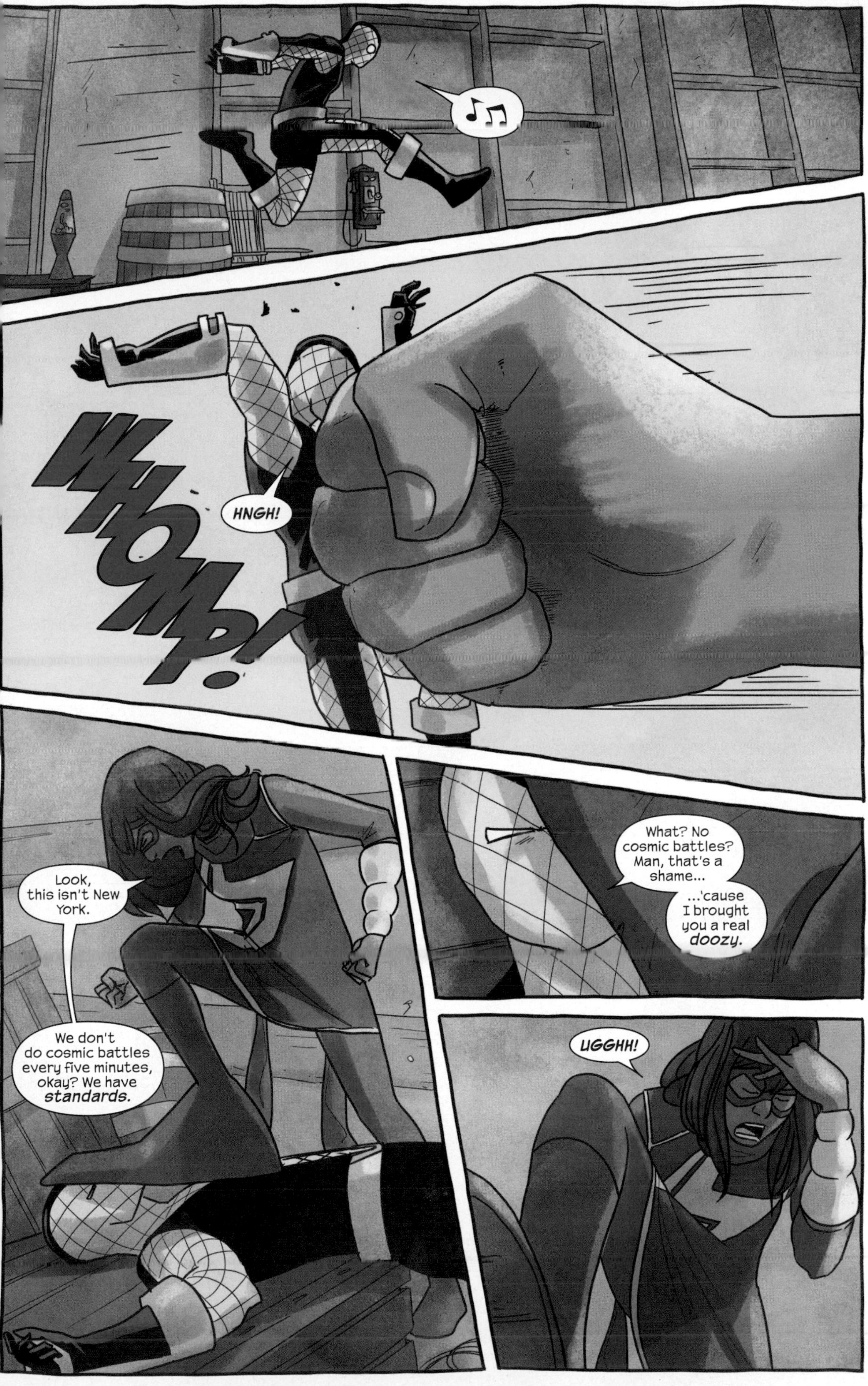
♫
HNGH!
WHOMP!
What? No cosmic battles? Man, that's a shame...
...'cause I brought you a real doozy.
Look, this isn't New York.
We don't do cosmic battles every five minutes, okay? We have standards.
UGGHH!

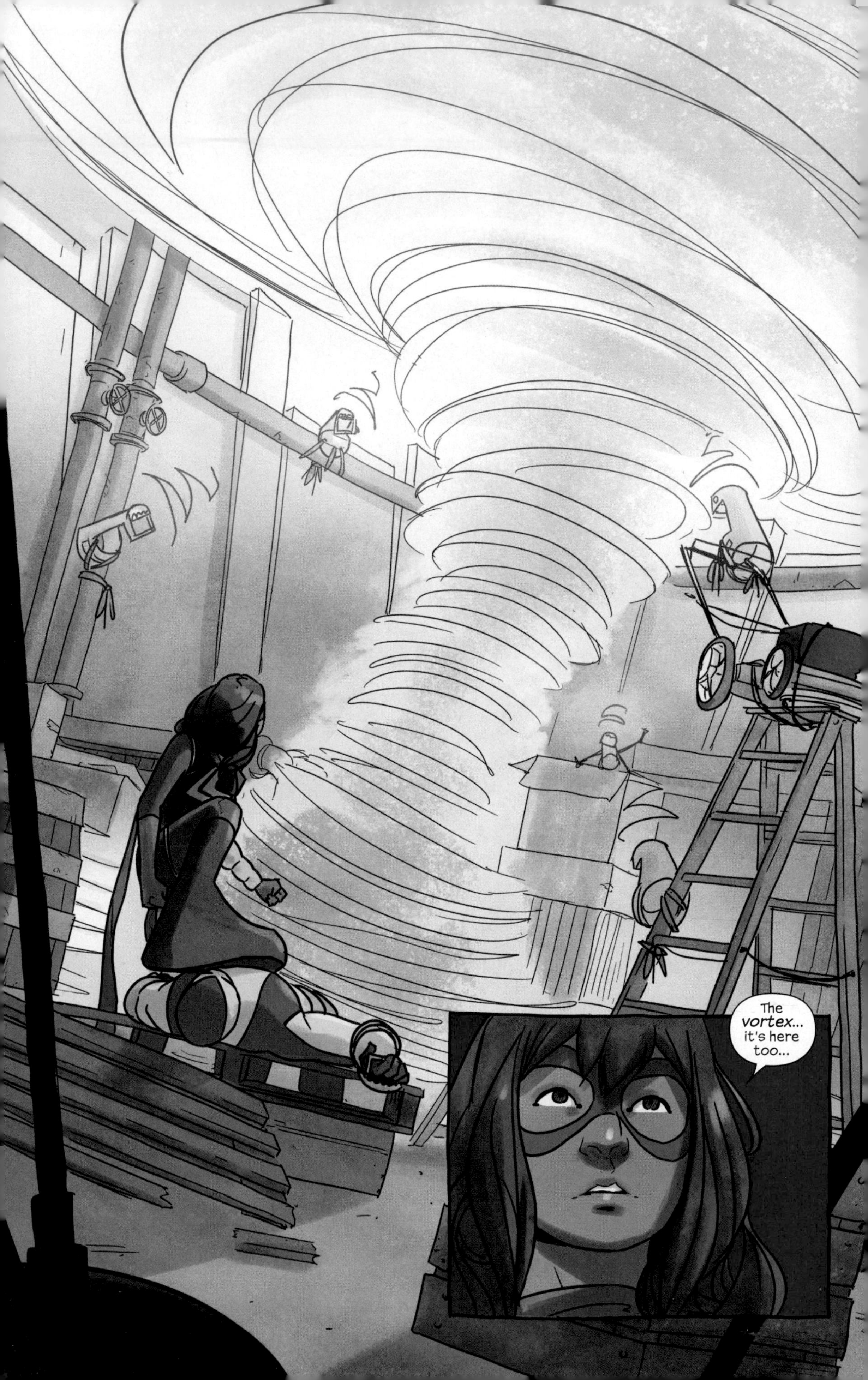
The *vortex*... it's here too...

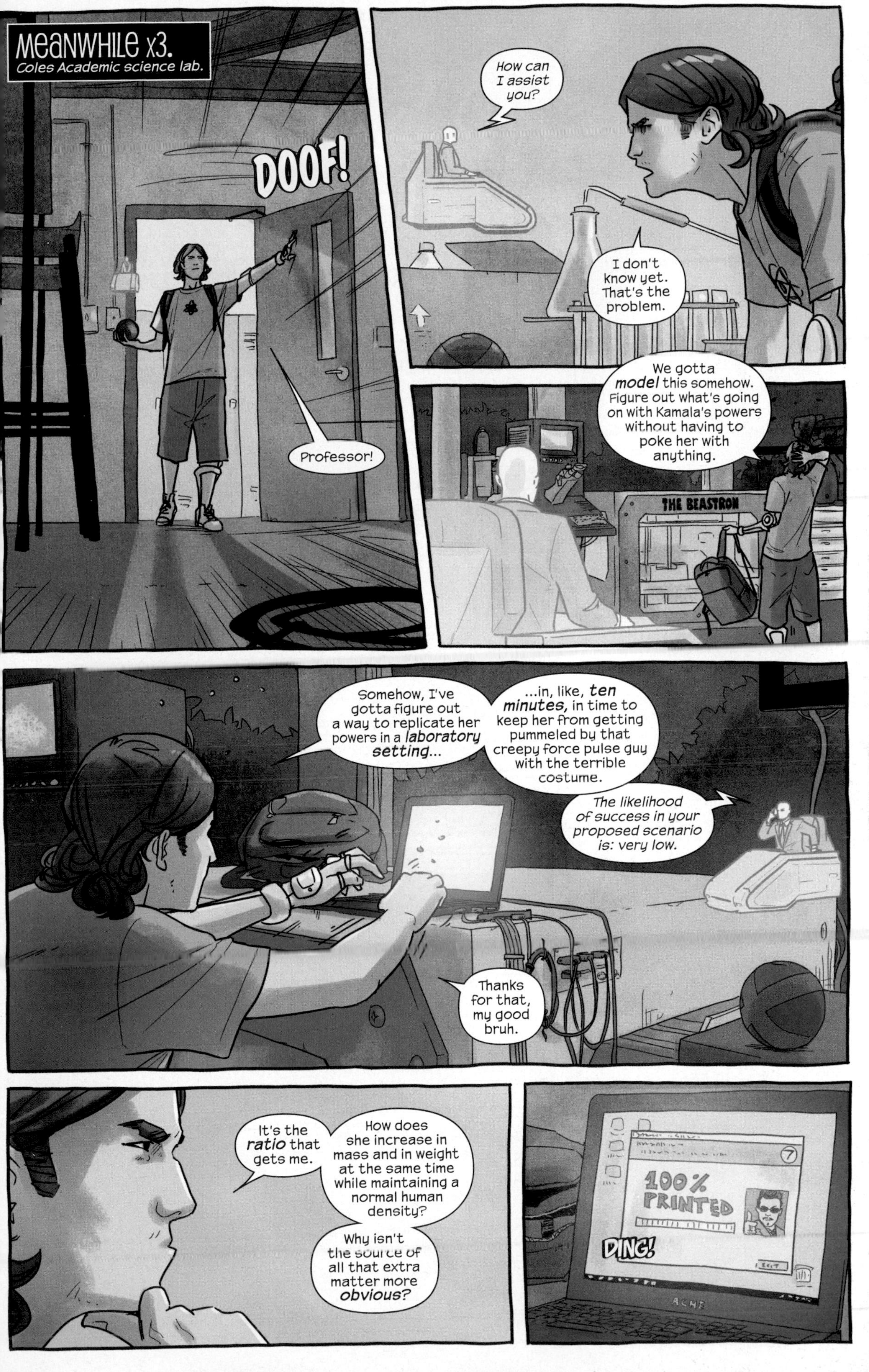
MEANWHILE x3.
Coles Academic science lab.
DOOF!
Professor!
How can I assist you?
I don't know yet. That's the problem.
We gotta *model* this somehow. Figure out what's going on with Kamala's powers without having to poke her with anything.
THE BEASTRON
Somehow, I've gotta figure out a way to replicate her powers in a *laboratory setting*...
...in, like, *ten minutes,* in time to keep her from getting pummeled by that creepy force pulse guy with the terrible costume.
The likelihood of success in your proposed scenario is: very low.
Thanks for that, my good bruh.
It's the *ratio* that gets me.
How does she increase in mass and in weight at the same time while maintaining a normal human density?
Why isn't the source of all that extra matter more *obvious?*
100% PRINTED
DING!
ACME

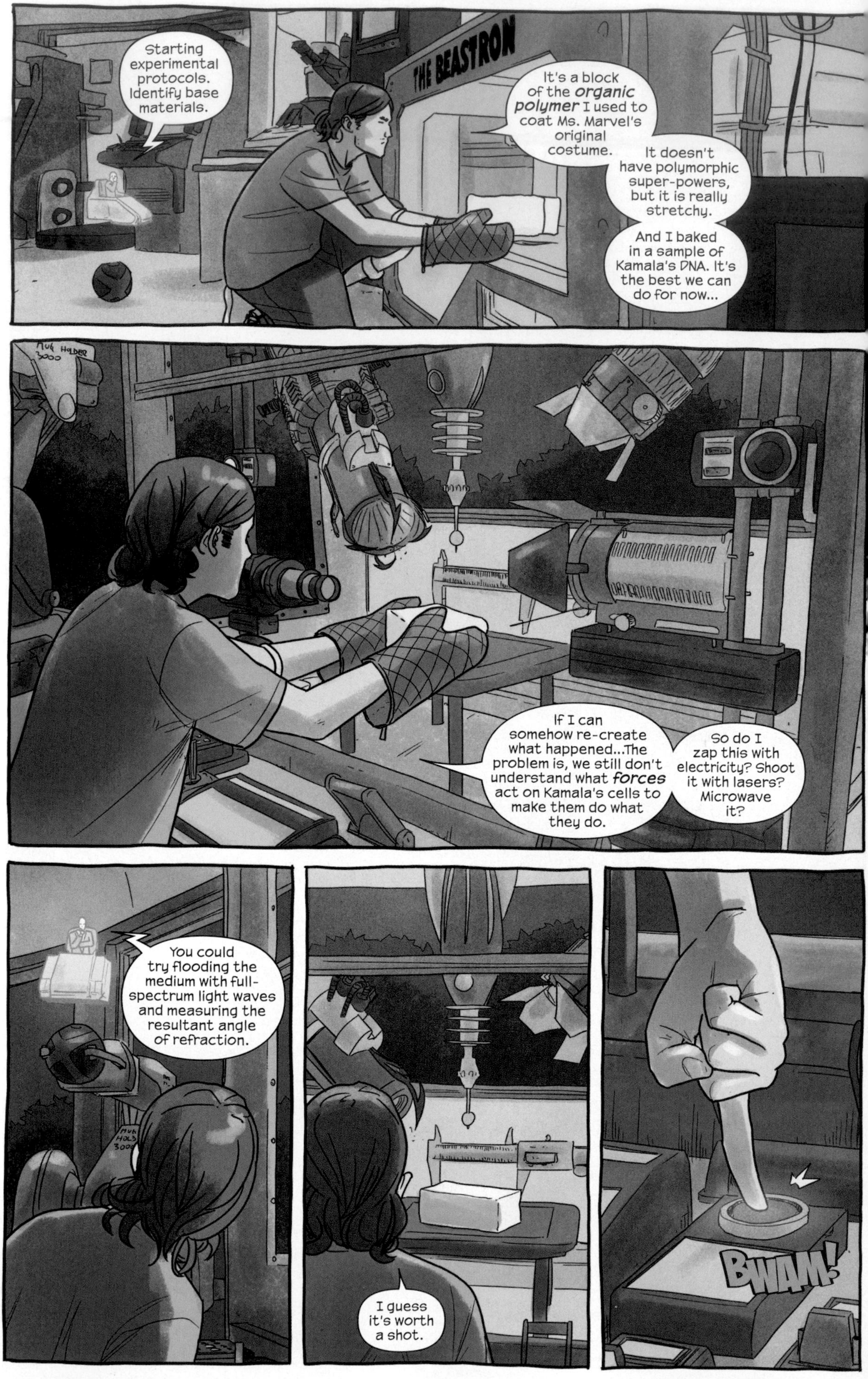
THE BEASTRON
Starting experimental protocols. Identify base materials.
It's a block of the *organic polymer* I used to coat Ms. Marvel's original costume.
It doesn't have polymorphic super-powers, but it is really stretchy.
And I baked in a sample of Kamala's DNA. It's the best we can do for now...
MUG HOLDER 3000
If I can somehow re-create what happened...The problem is, we still don't understand what *forces* act on Kamala's cells to make them do what they do.
So do I zap this with electricity? Shoot it with lasers? Microwave it?
You could try flooding the medium with full-spectrum light waves and measuring the resultant angle of refraction.
I guess it's worth a shot.
BWAM!

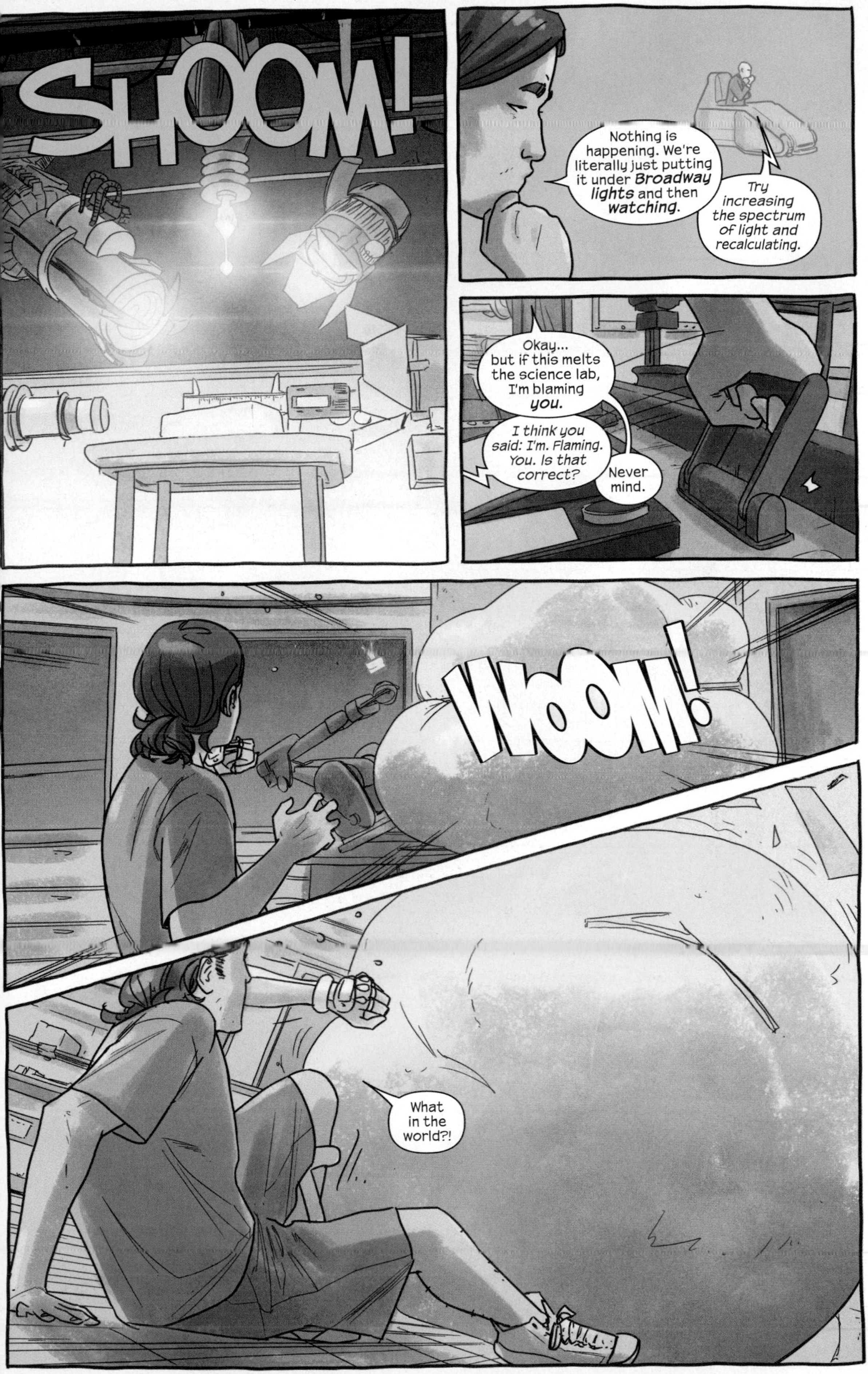
SHOOM!
Nothing is happening. We're literally just putting it under Broadway lights and then watching.
Try increasing the spectrum of light and recalculating.
Okay... but if this melts the science lab, I'm blaming you.
I think you said: I'm. Flaming. You. Is that correct?
Never mind.
WOOM!
What in the world?!

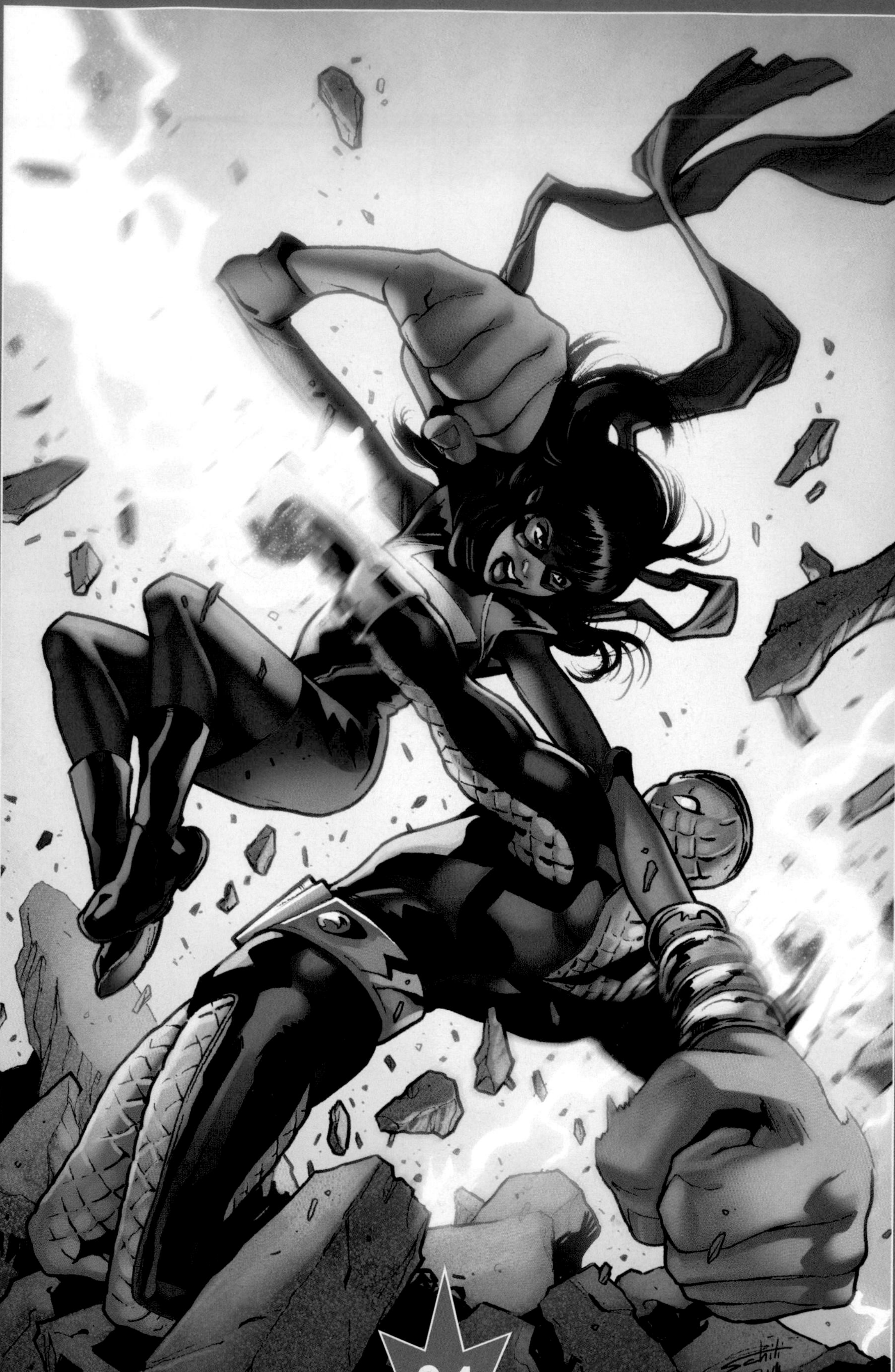

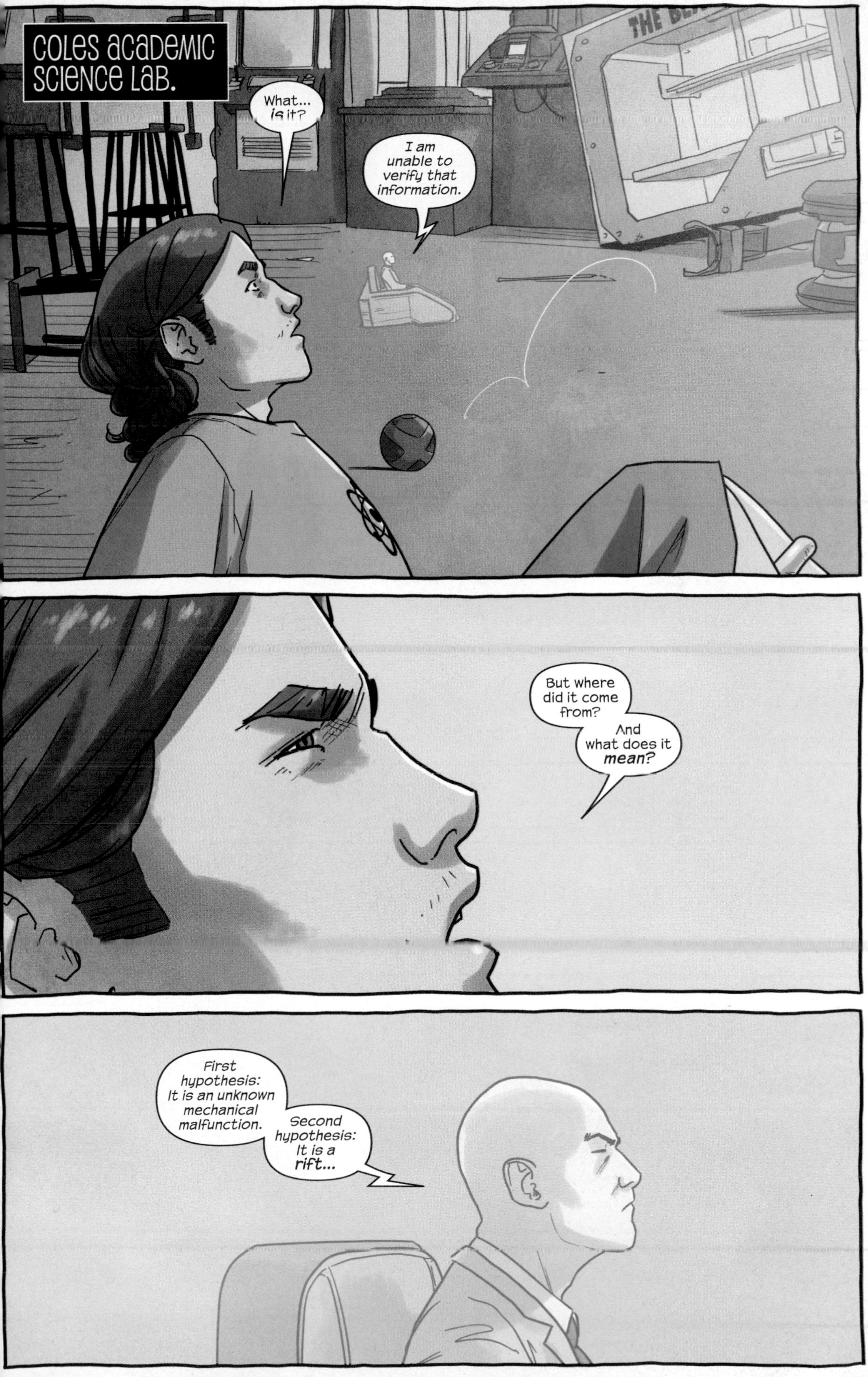
COLES ACADEMIC SCIENCE LAB.
What... is it?
I am unable to verify that information.
But where did it come from?
And what does it mean?
First hypothesis: It is an unknown mechanical malfunction.
Second hypothesis: It is a rift...

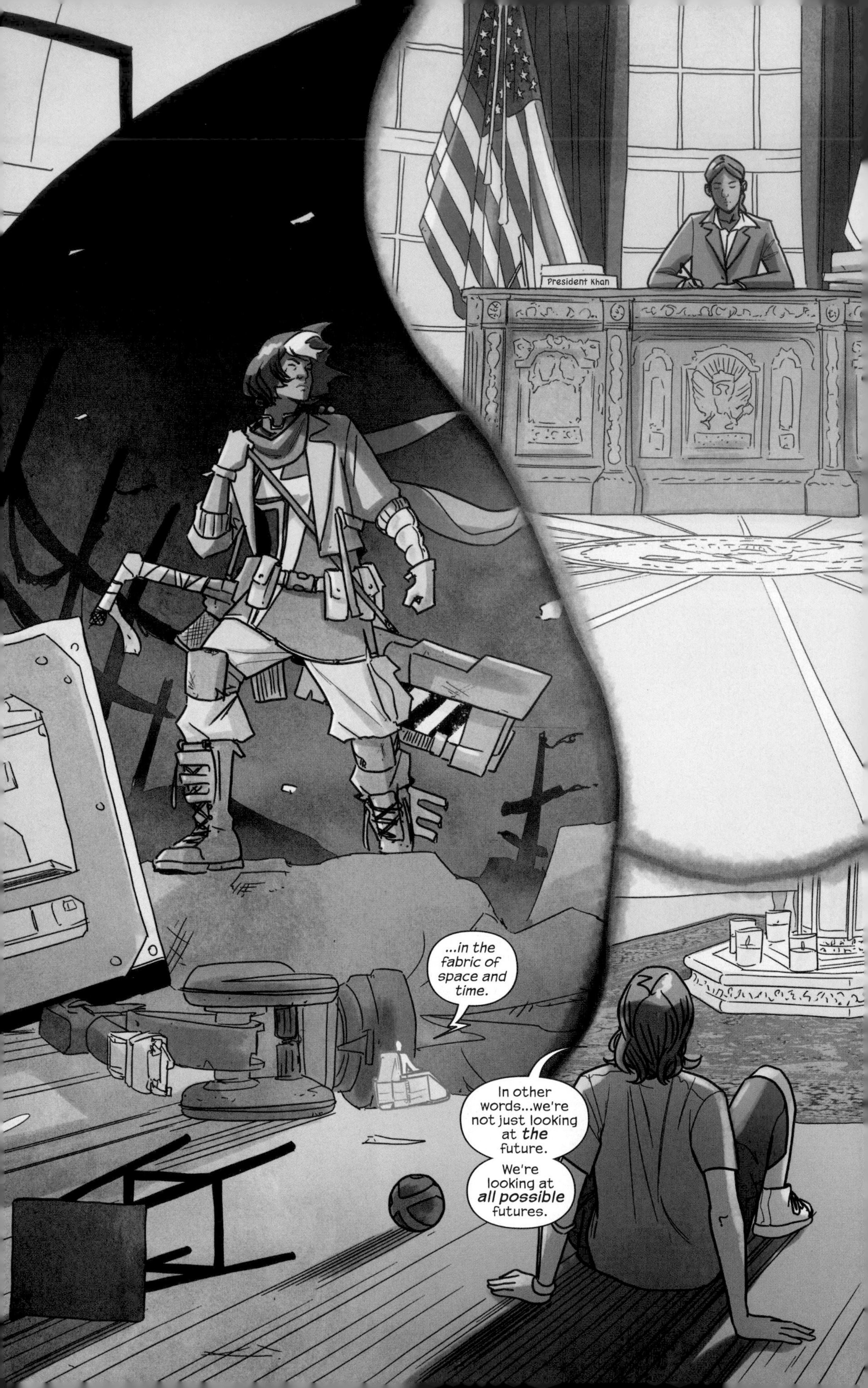
President Khan
...in the fabric of space and time.
In other words...we're not just looking at *the* future.
We're looking at ***all possible*** futures.

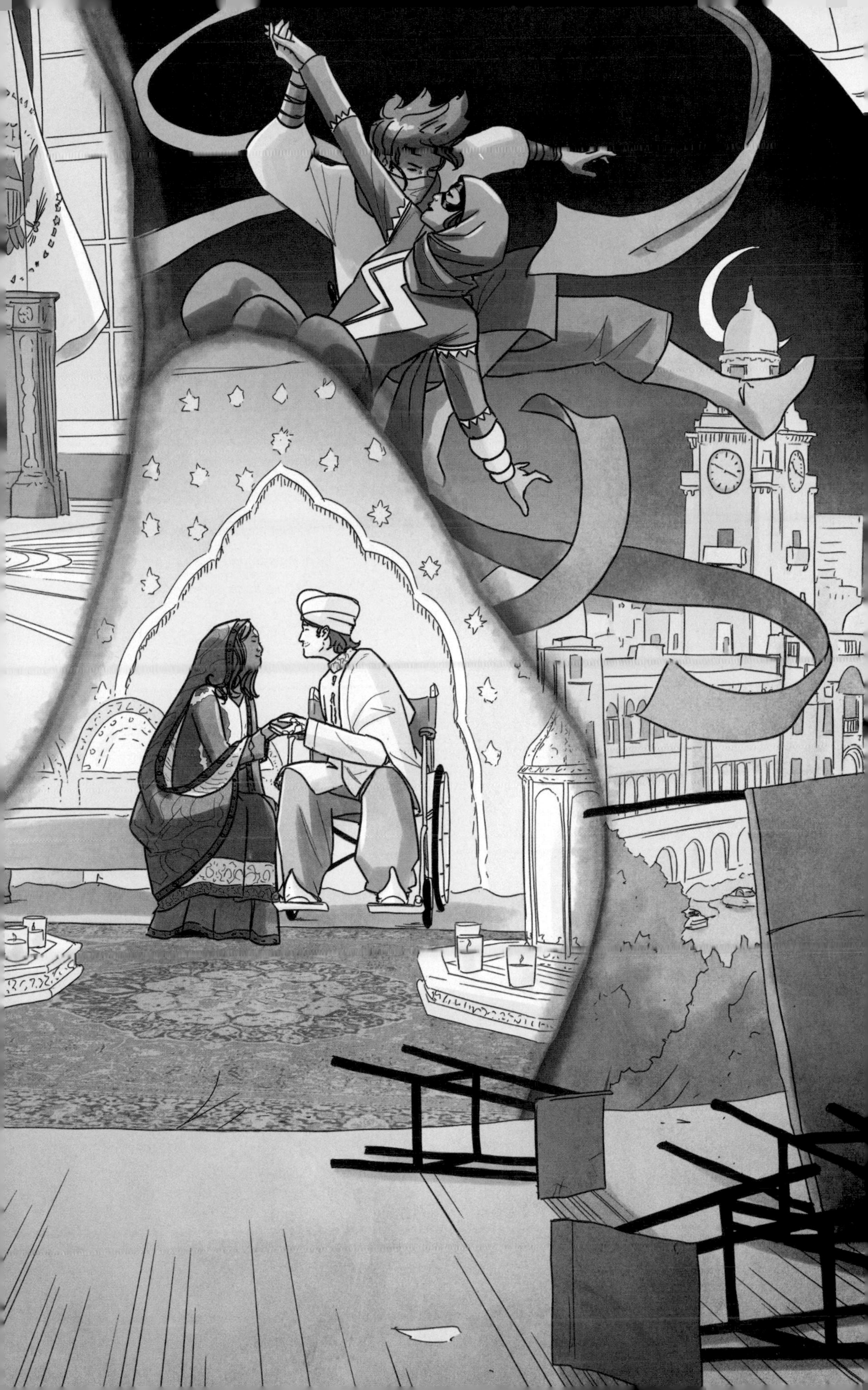

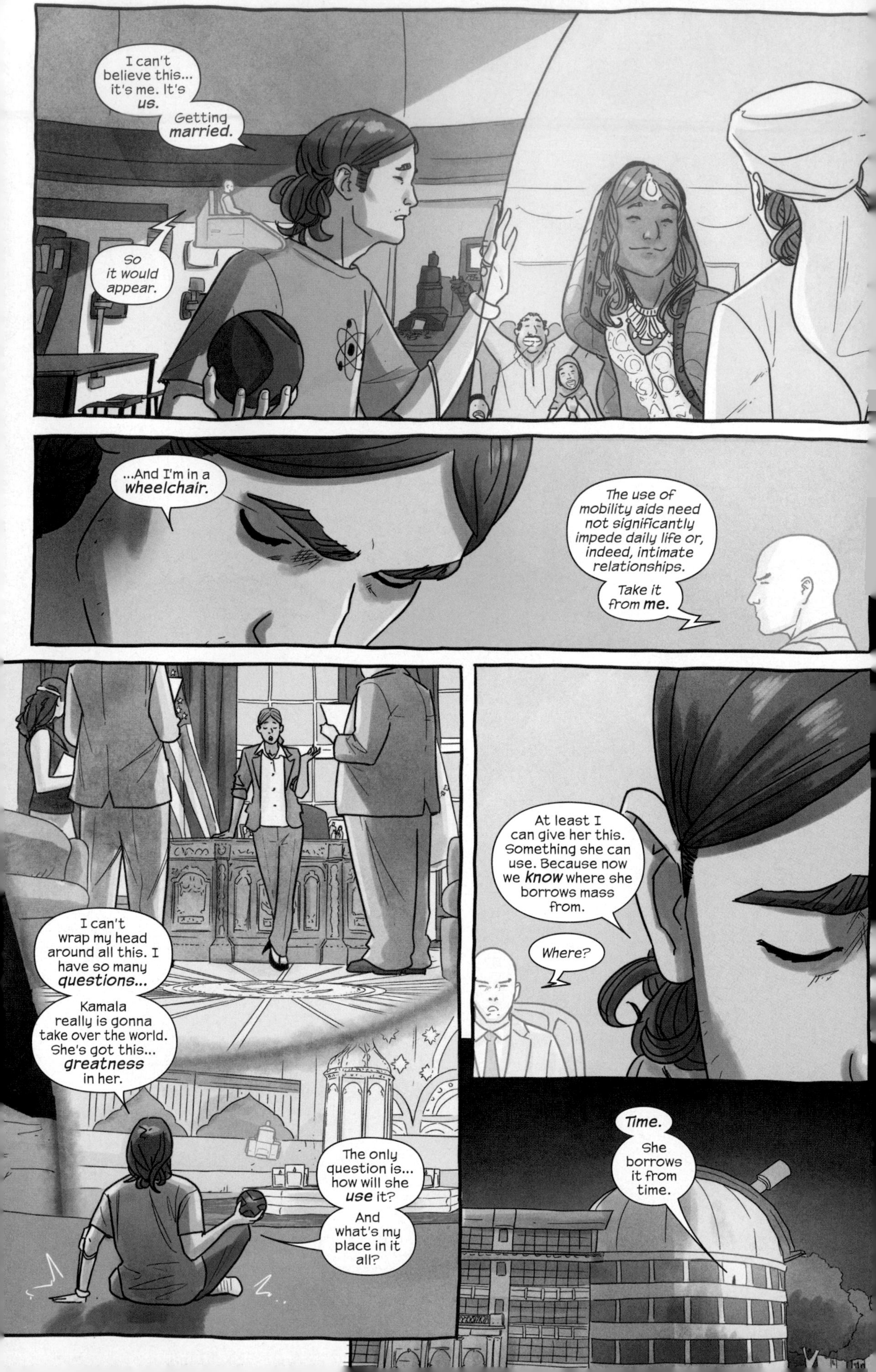
I can't believe this... it's me. It's us.
Getting married.
So it would appear.
...And I'm in a wheelchair.
The use of mobility aids need not significantly impede daily life or, indeed, intimate relationships.
Take it from me.
I can't wrap my head around all this. I have so many questions...
Kamala really is gonna take over the world. She's got this... greatness in her.
The only question is... how will she use it?
And what's my place in it all?
At least I can give her this. Something she can use. Because now we know where she borrows mass from.
Where?
Time.
She borrows it from time.

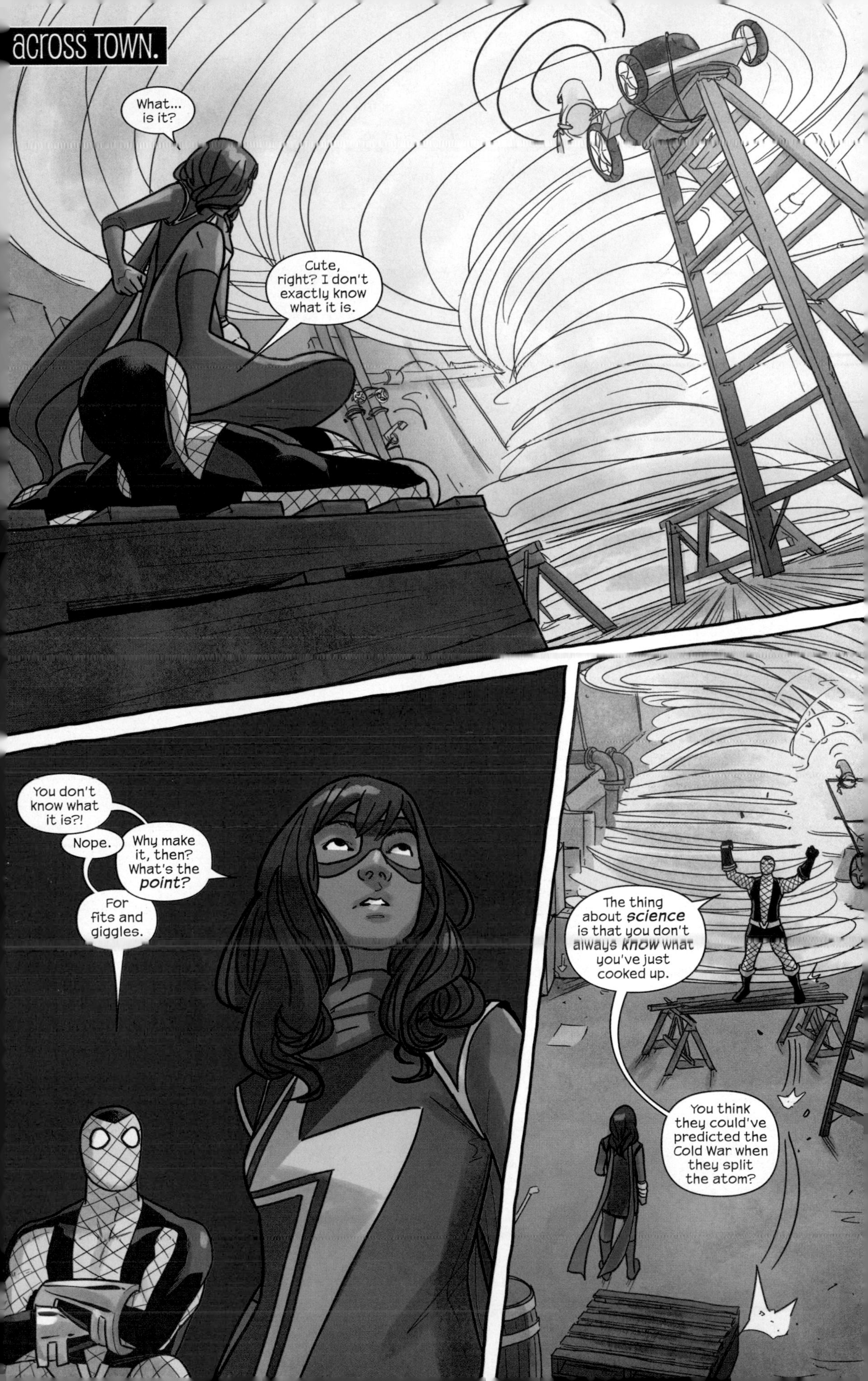
across TOWN.
What... is it?
Cute, right? I don't exactly know what it is.
You don't know what it is?!
Nope.
Why make it, then? What's the point?
For fits and giggles.
The thing about science is that you don't always know what you've just cooked up.
You think they could've predicted the Cold War when they split the atom?

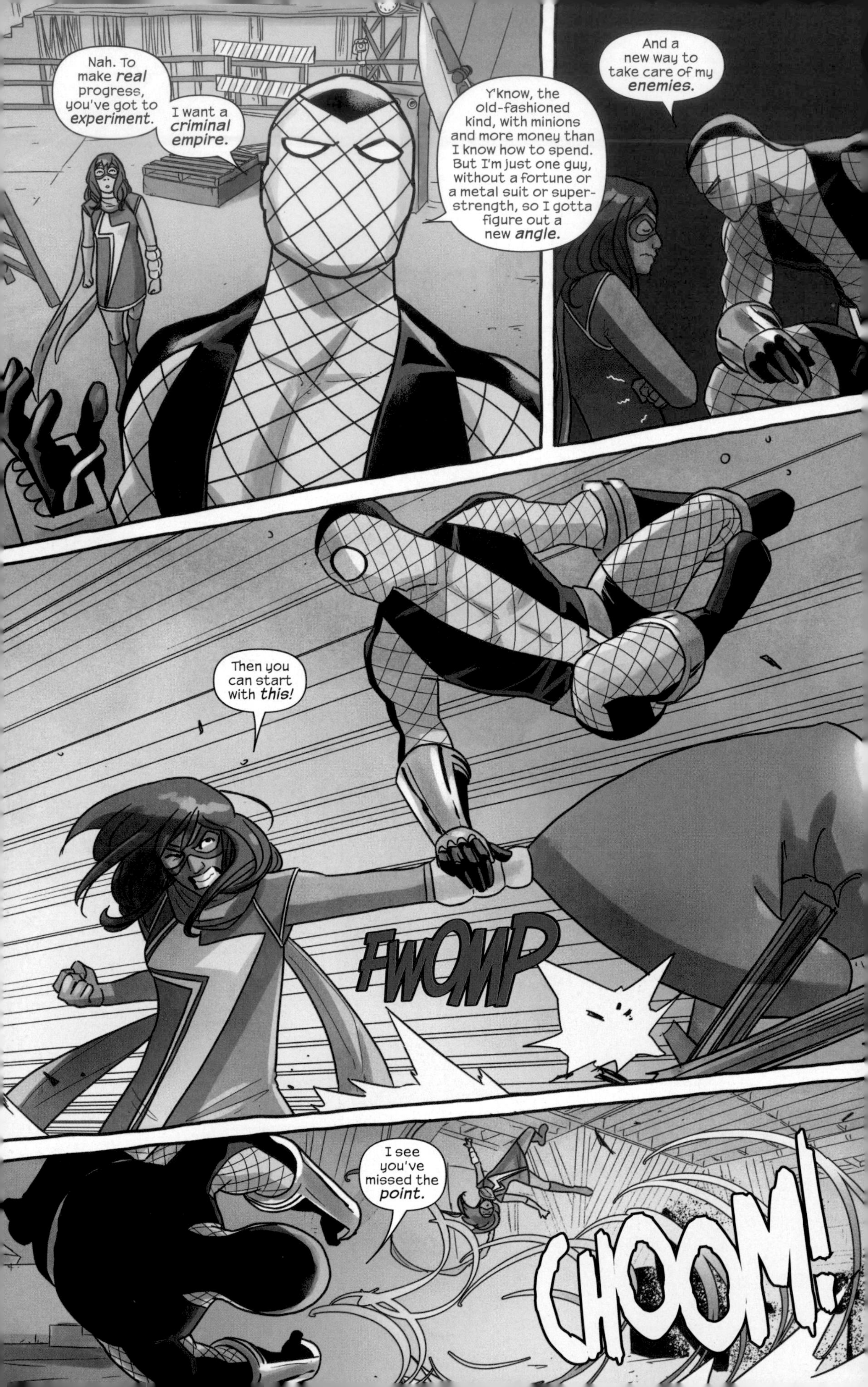
Nah. To make *real* progress, you've got to *experiment*.
I want a *criminal empire*.
Y'know, the old-fashioned kind, with minions and more money than I know how to spend. But I'm just one guy, without a fortune or a metal suit or super-strength, so I gotta figure out a new *angle*.
And a new way to take care of my *enemies*.
Then you can start with *this!*
FWOMP
I see you've missed the *point*.
CHOOM!

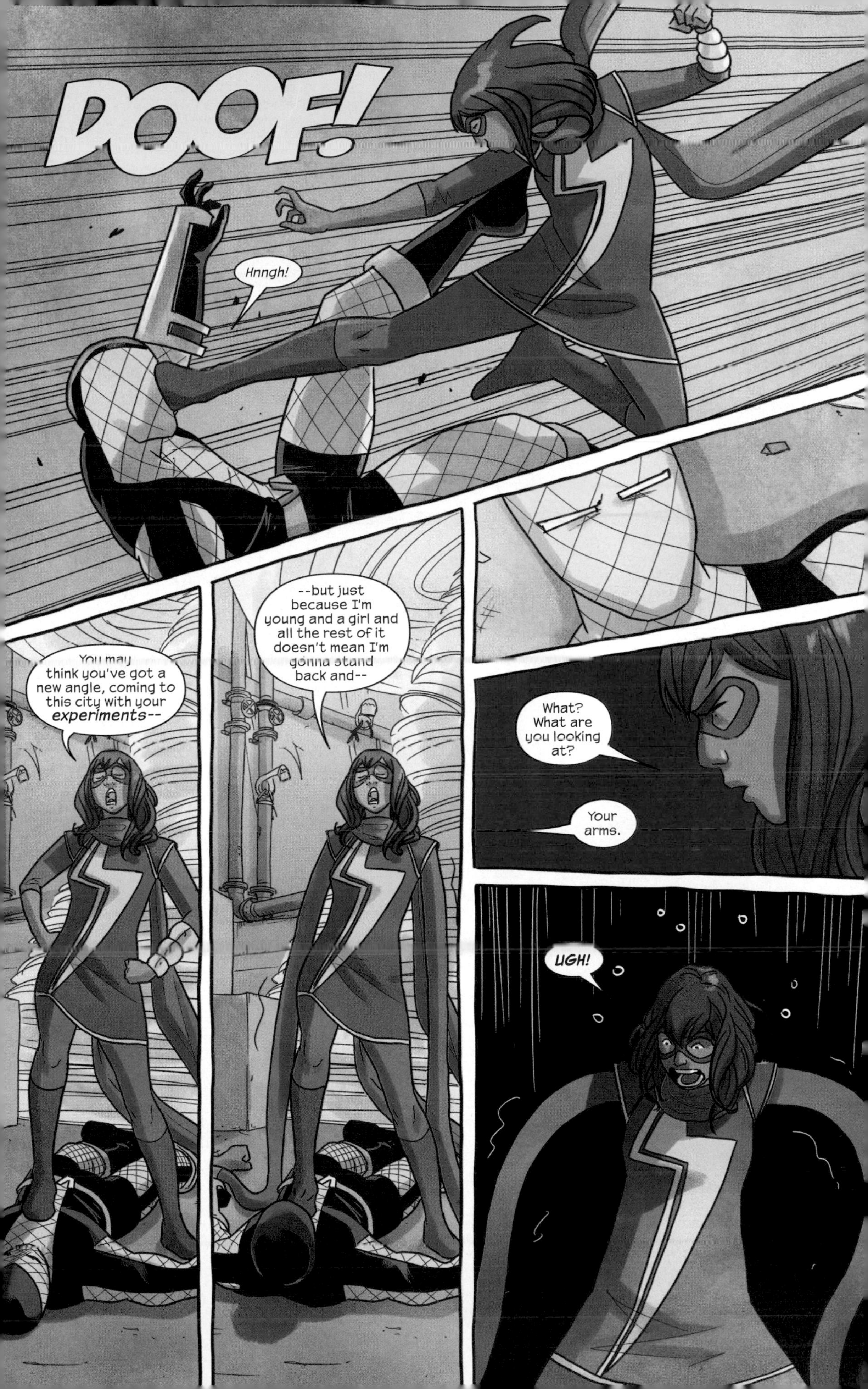
DOOF!
Hnngh!
You may think you've got a new angle, coming to this city with your experiments--
--but just because I'm young and a girl and all the rest of it doesn't mean I'm gonna stand back and--
What? What are you looking at?
Your arms.
UGH!

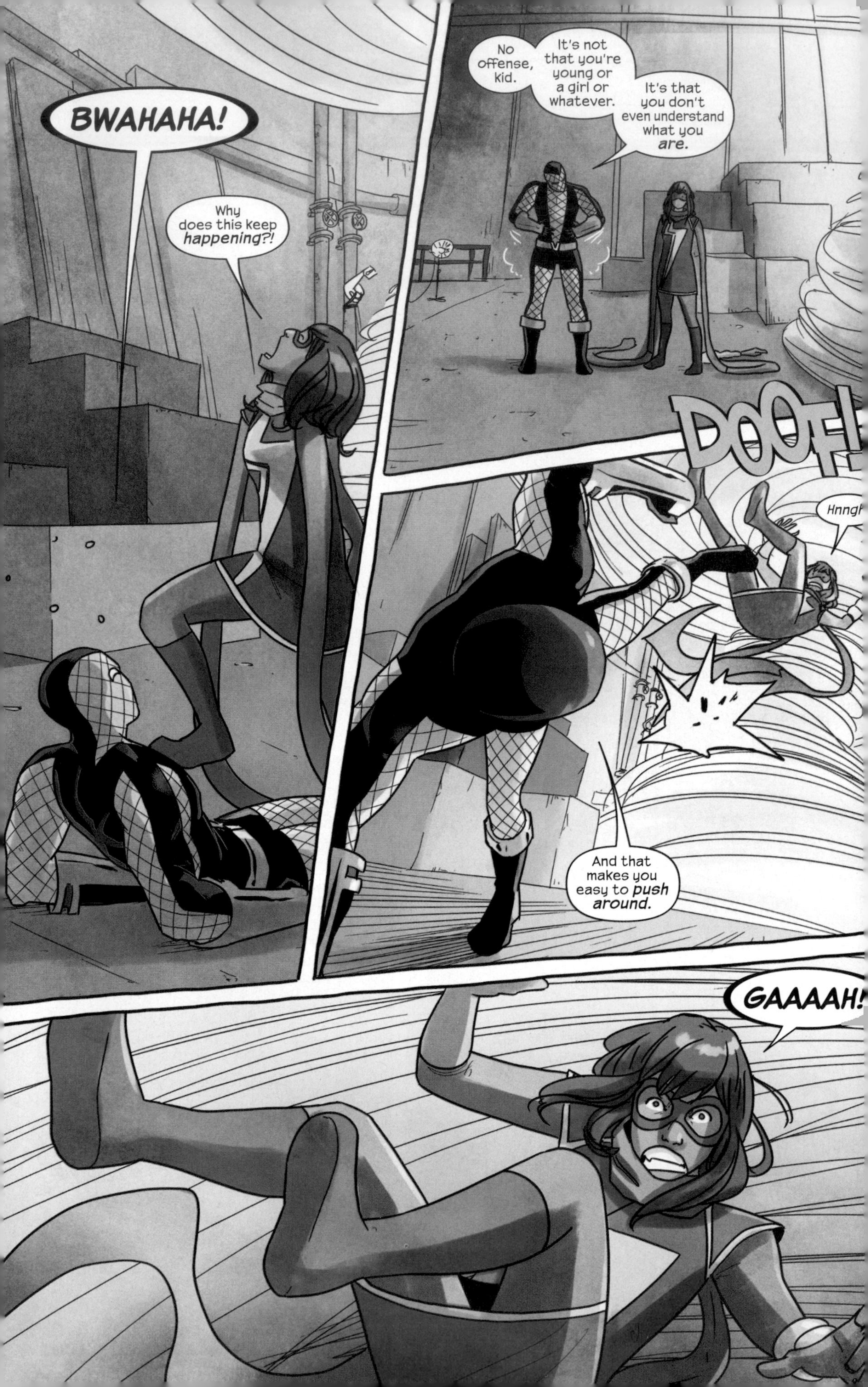
BWAHAHA!
Why does this keep happening?!
No offense, kid.
It's not that you're young or a girl or whatever.
It's that you don't even understand what you are.
DOOF!
Hnngh
And that makes you easy to push around.
GAAAAH!

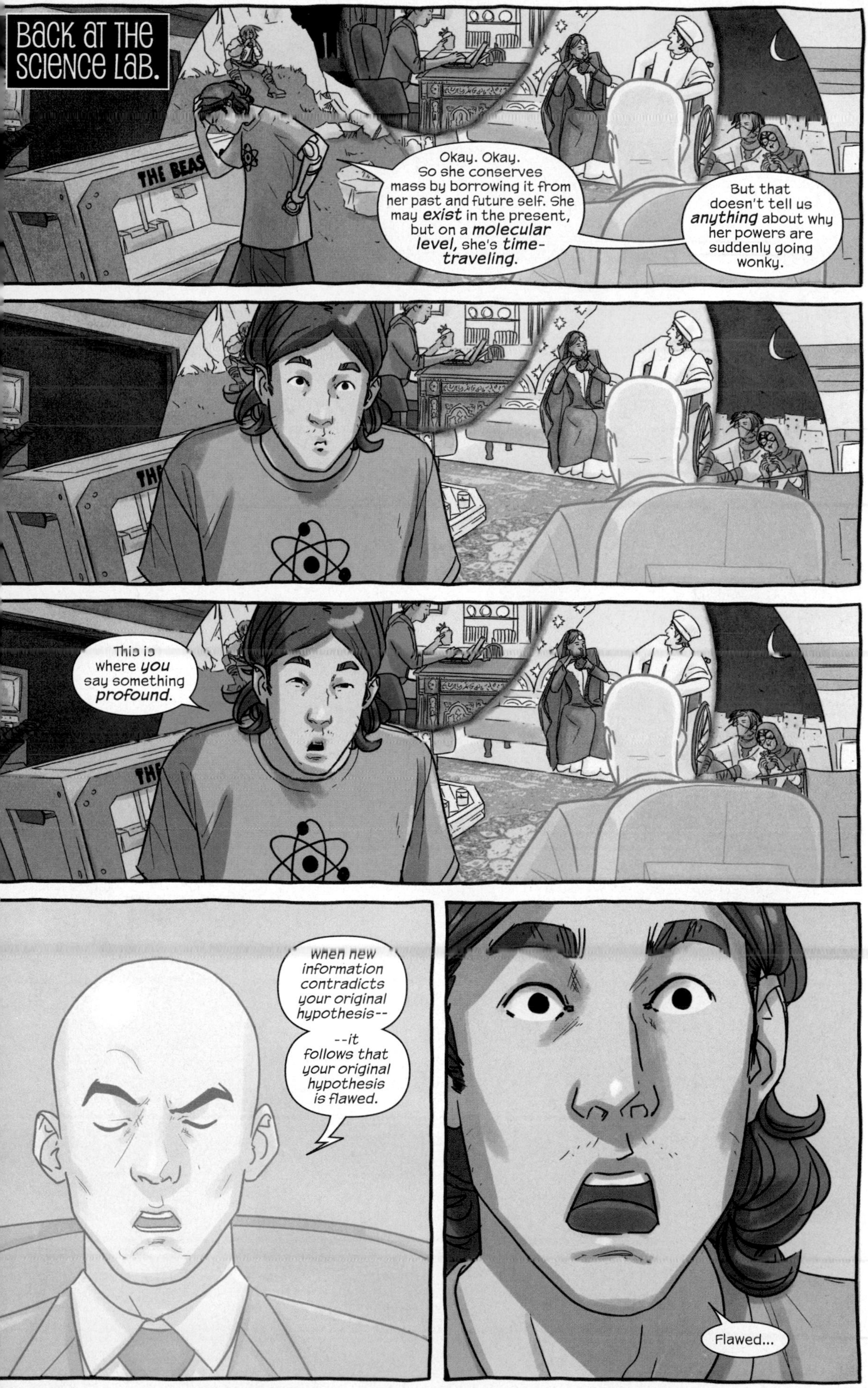
Back at the Science Lab.
THE BEAS
Okay. Okay. So she conserves mass by borrowing it from her past and future self. She may exist in the present, but on a molecular level, she's time-traveling.
But that doesn't tell us anything about why her powers are suddenly going wonky.
This is where you say something profound.
When new information contradicts your original hypothesis--
--it follows that your original hypothesis is flawed.
Flawed...

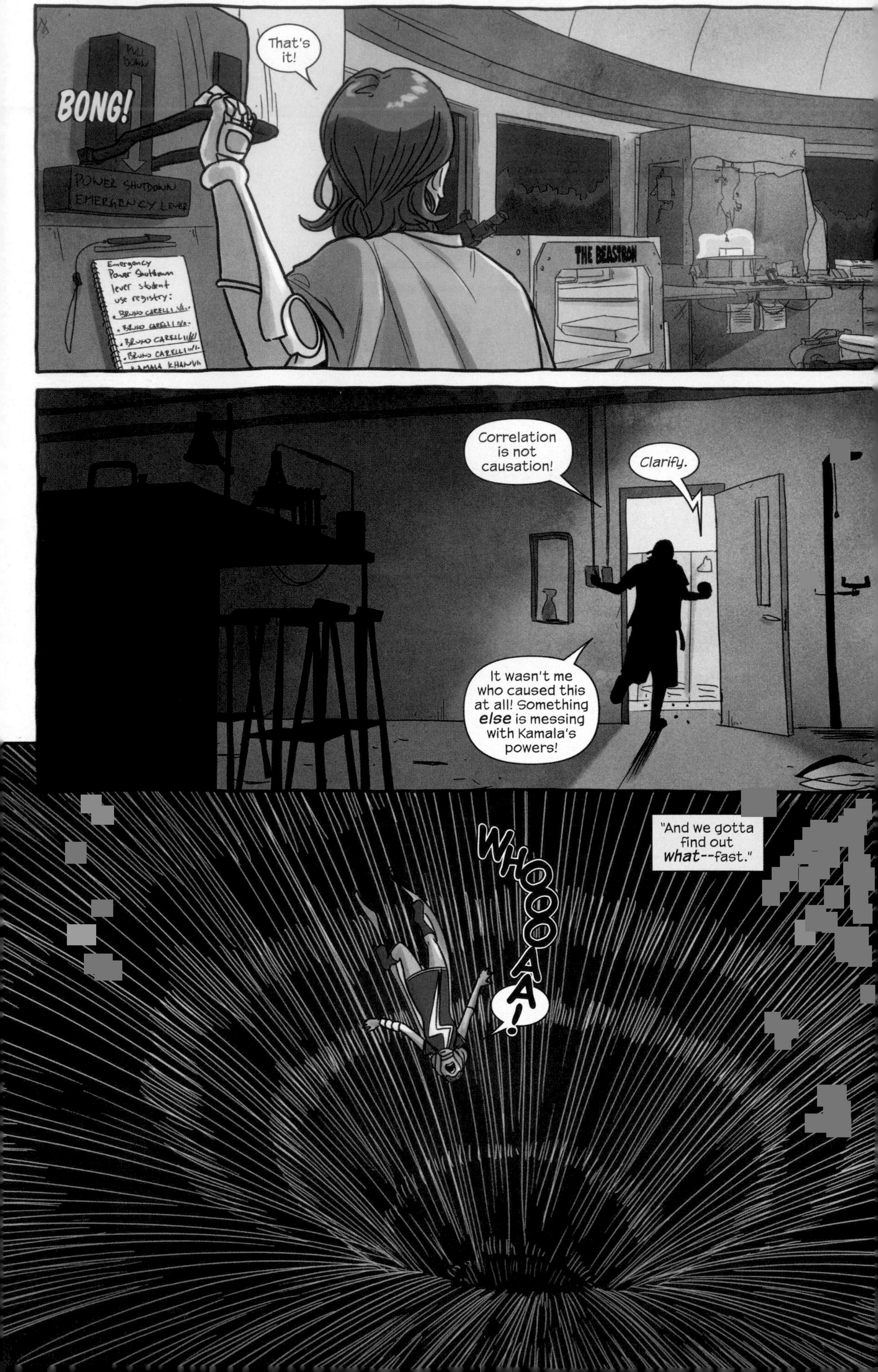
BONG!
PULL DOWN
POWER SHUTDOWN EMERGENCY LEVER
Emergency Power Shutdown lever student use registry:
BRUNO CARELLI
BRUNO CARELLI
BRUNO CARELLI
BRUNO CARELLI
That's it!
THE BEASTRON
Correlation is not causation!
Clarify.
It wasn't me who caused this at all! Something *else* is messing with Kamala's powers!
"And we gotta find out *what*--fast."
WHOOOAA!

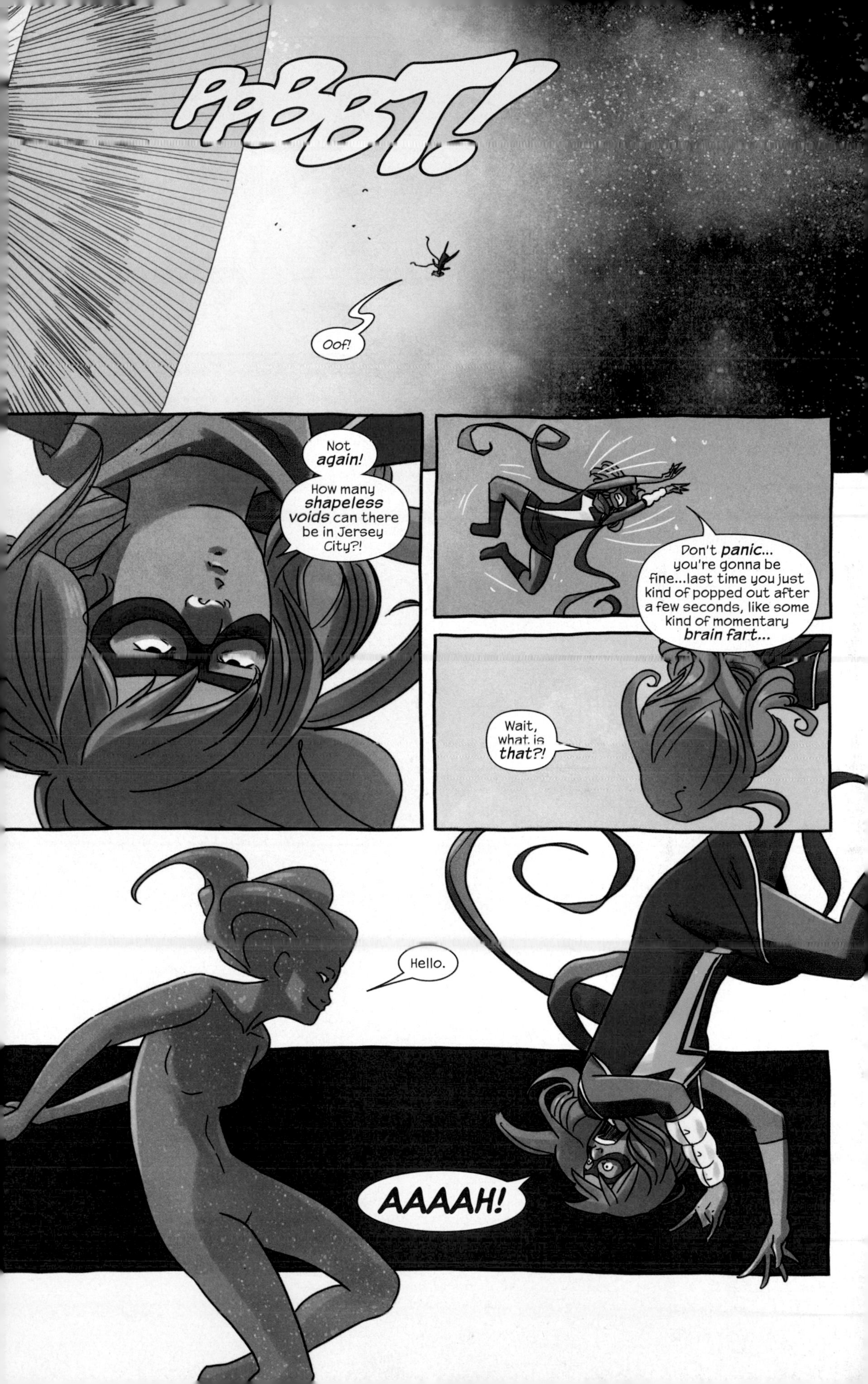
PPBBBT!
Oof!
Not again!
How many shapeless voids can there be in Jersey City?!
Don't panic... you're gonna be fine...last time you just kind of popped out after a few seconds, like some kind of momentary brain fart...
Wait, what is that?!
Hello.
AAAAH!

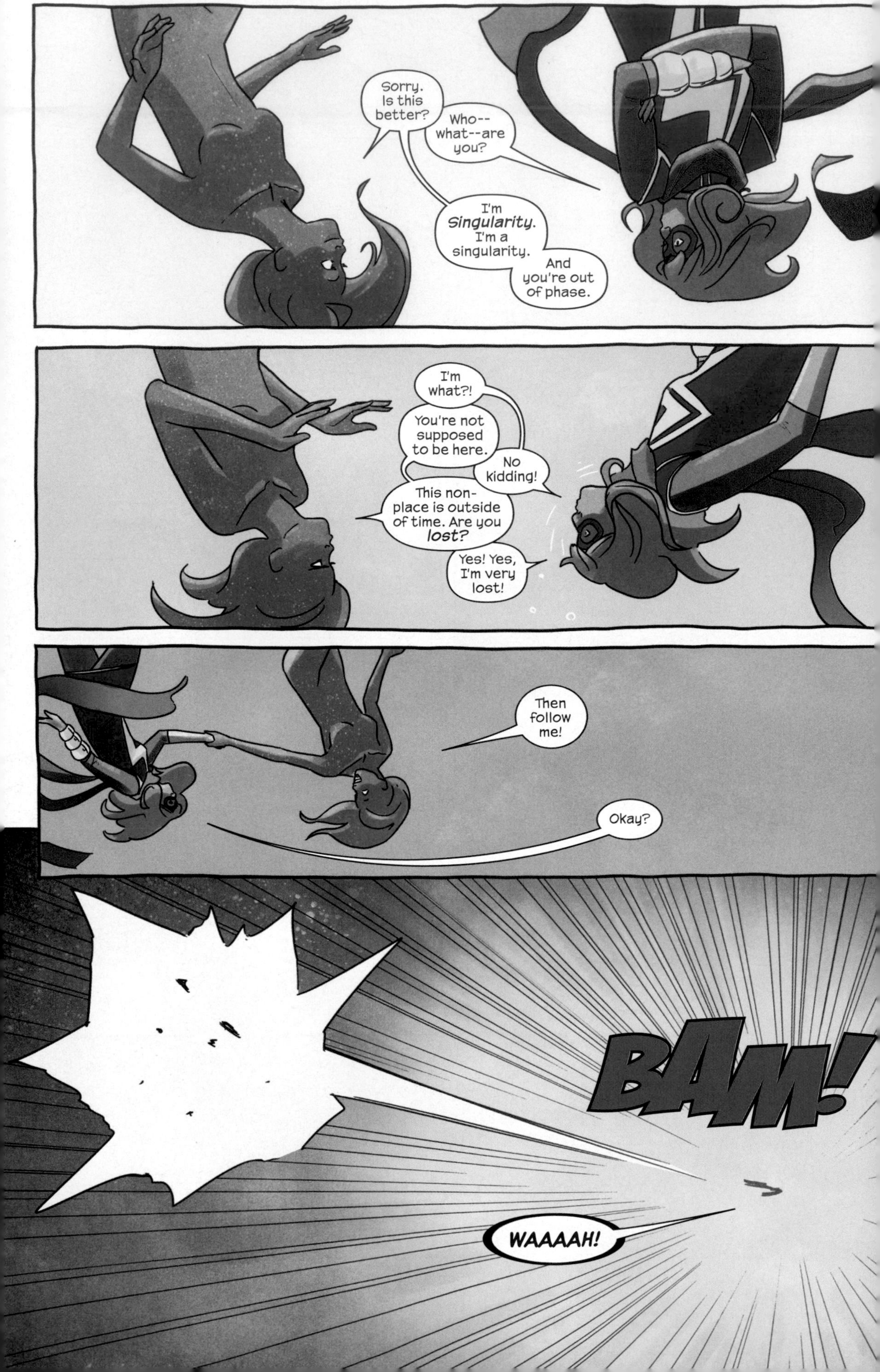

Sorry. Is this better?
Who--what--are you?
I'm *Singularity*. I'm a singularity.
And you're out of phase.
I'm what?!
You're not supposed to be here.
No kidding!
This non-place is outside of time. Are you *lost?*
Yes! Yes, I'm very lost!
Then follow me!
Okay?
BAM!
WAAAAH!

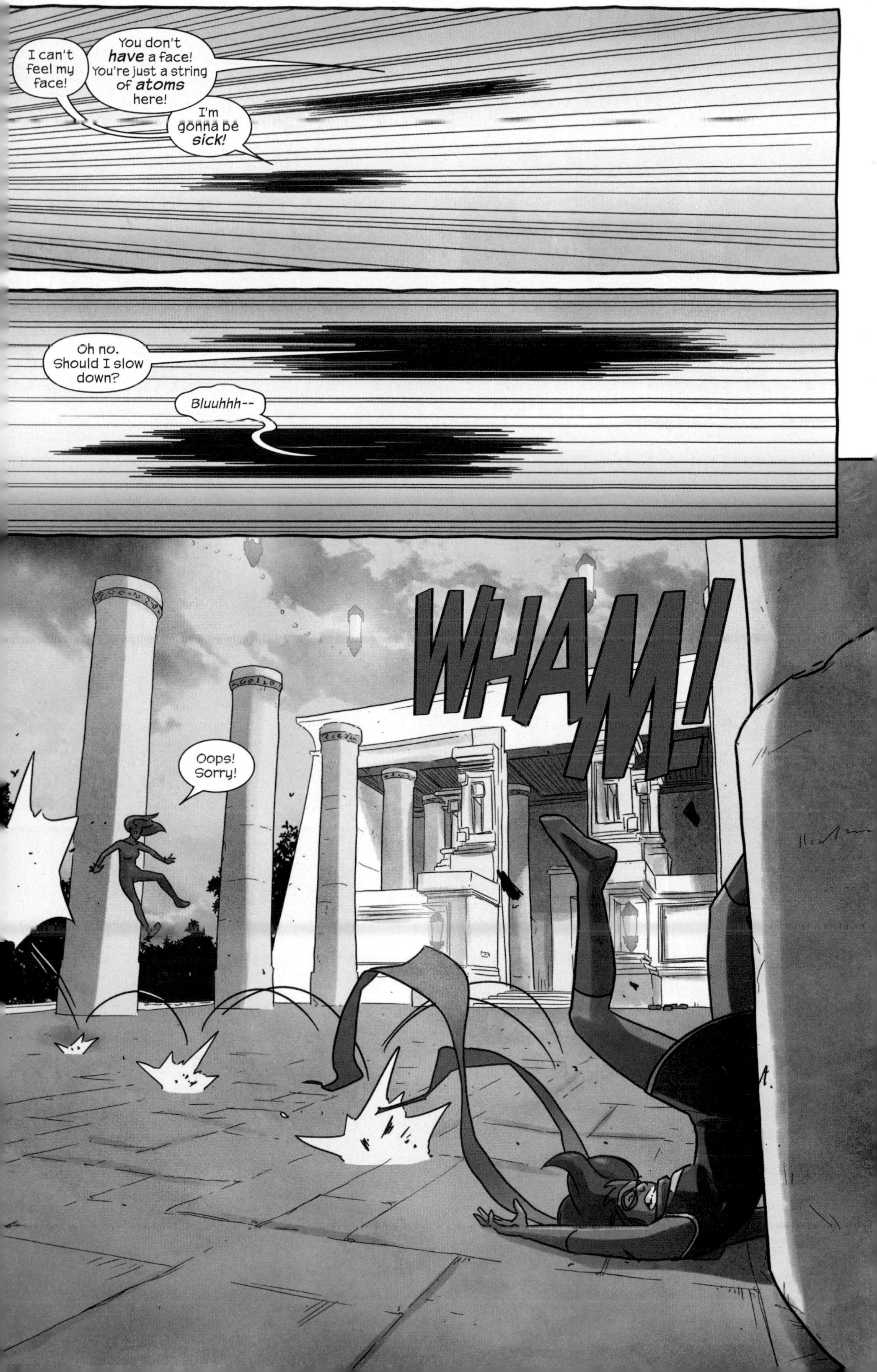
I can't feel my face!
You don't *have* a face! You're just a string of *atoms* here!
I'm gonna be *sick!*
Oh no. Should I slow down?
Bluuhhh--
WHAM!
Oops! Sorry!

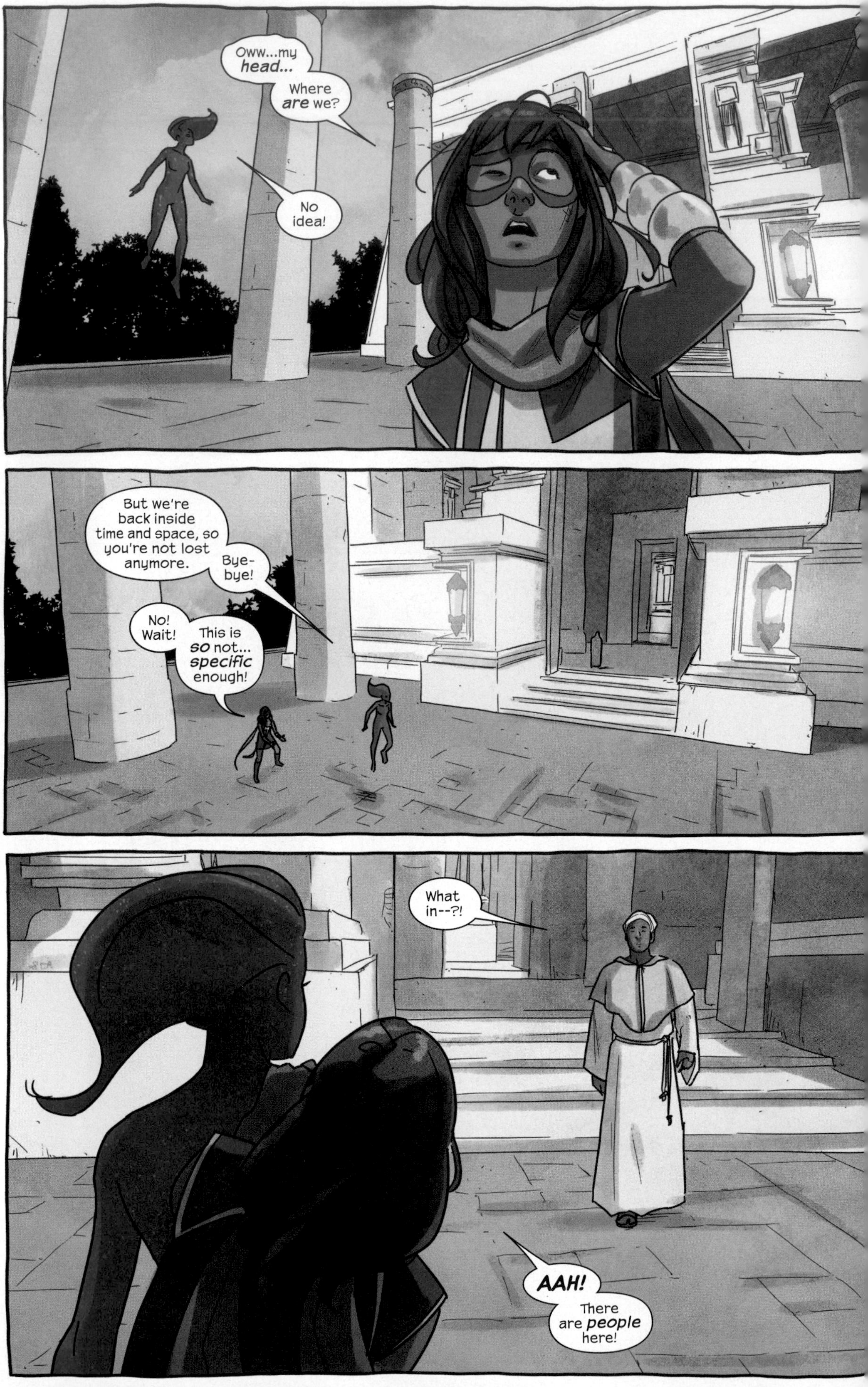
Oww...my head...
Where are we?
No idea!
But we're back inside time and space, so you're not lost anymore.
Bye-bye!
No! Wait!
This is so not... specific enough!
What in--?!
AAH!
There are people here!

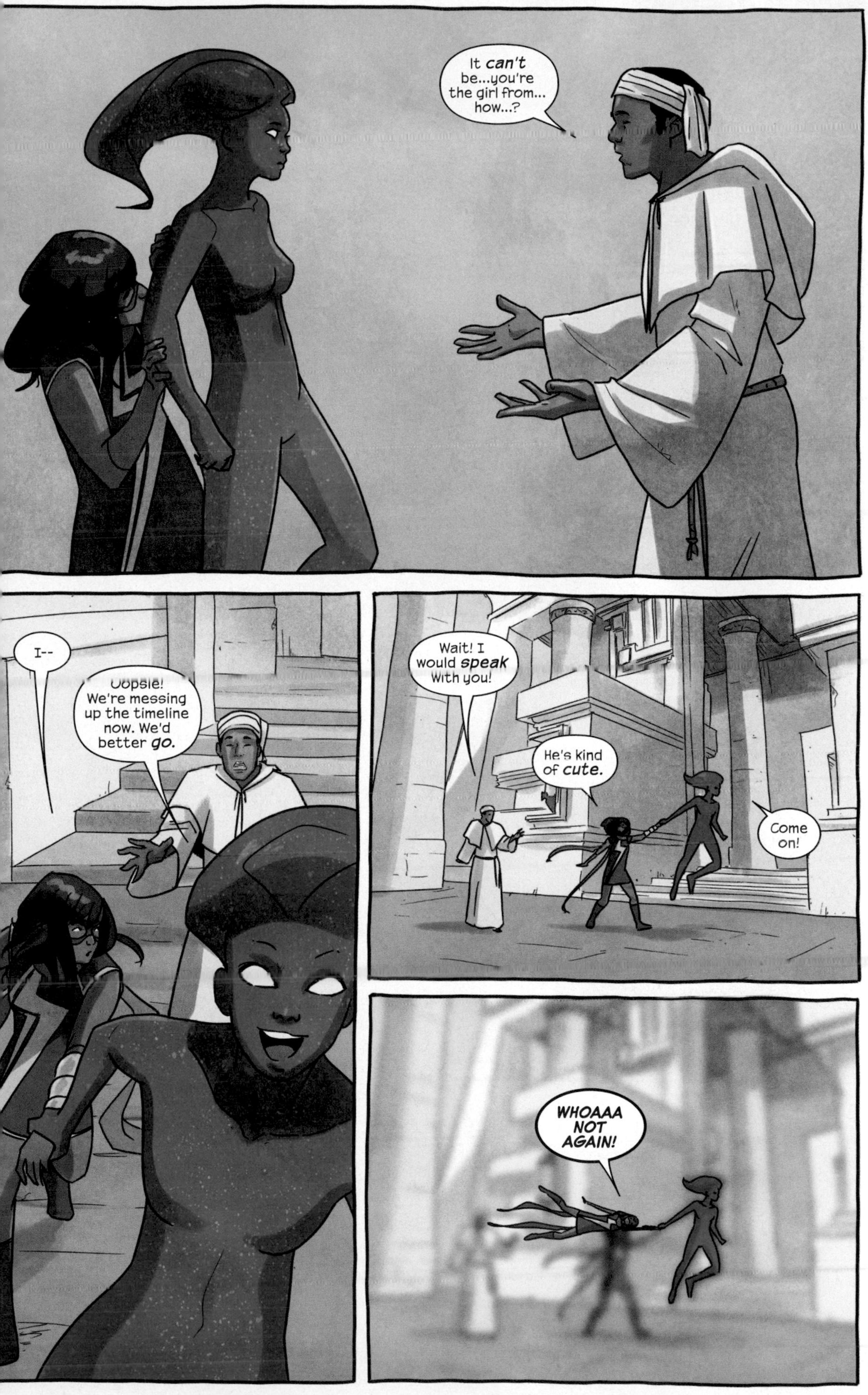
It can't be...you're the girl from... how...?
I--
Oopsie! We're messing up the timeline now. We'd better go.
Wait! I would speak with you!
He's kind of cute.
Come on!
WHOAAA NOT AGAIN!

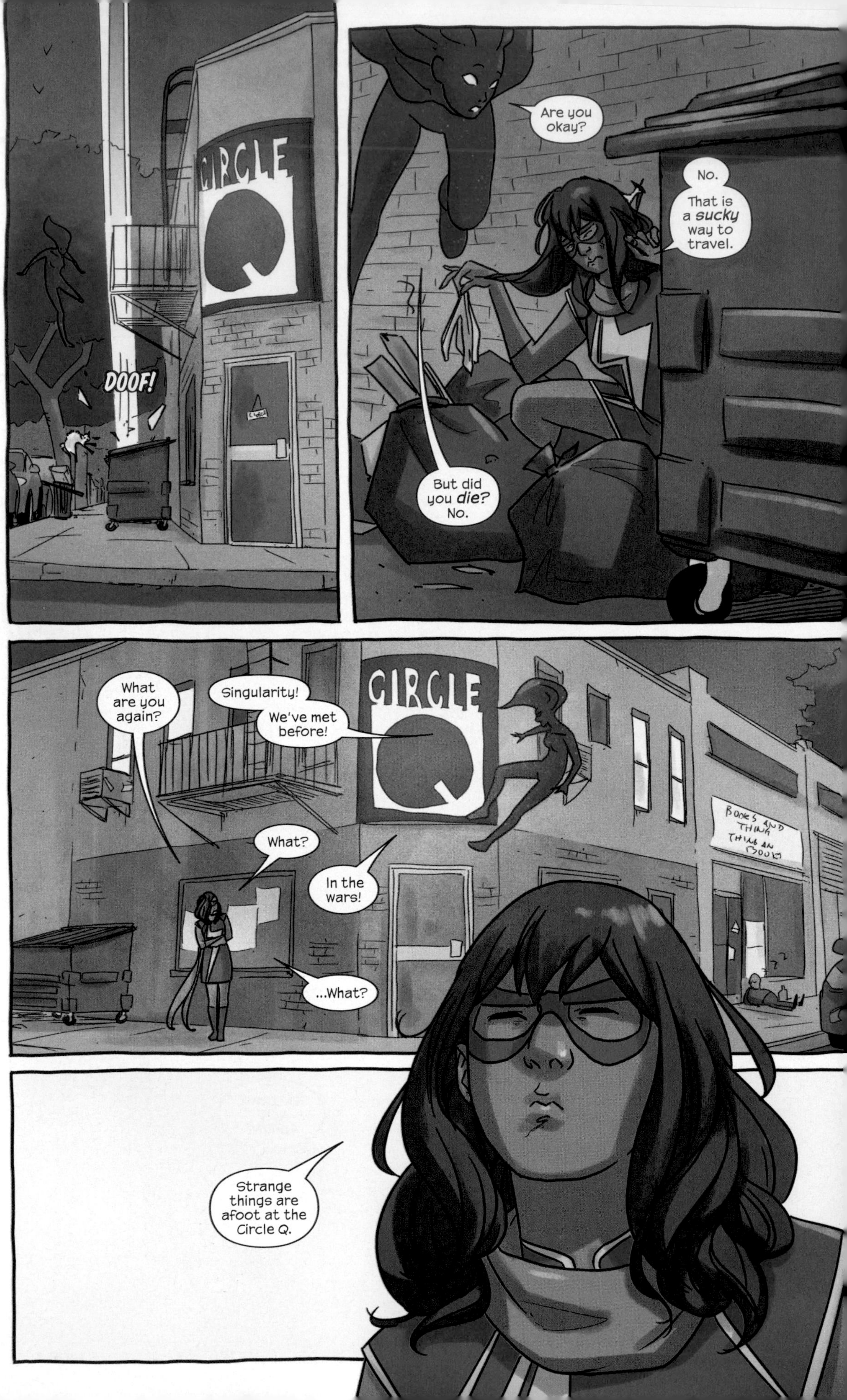
CIRCLE Q
DOOF!
Are you okay?
No.
That is a sucky way to travel.
But did you die? No.
CIRCLE Q
What are you again?
Singularity!
We've met before!
What?
In the wars!
...What?
Strange things are afoot at the Circle Q.

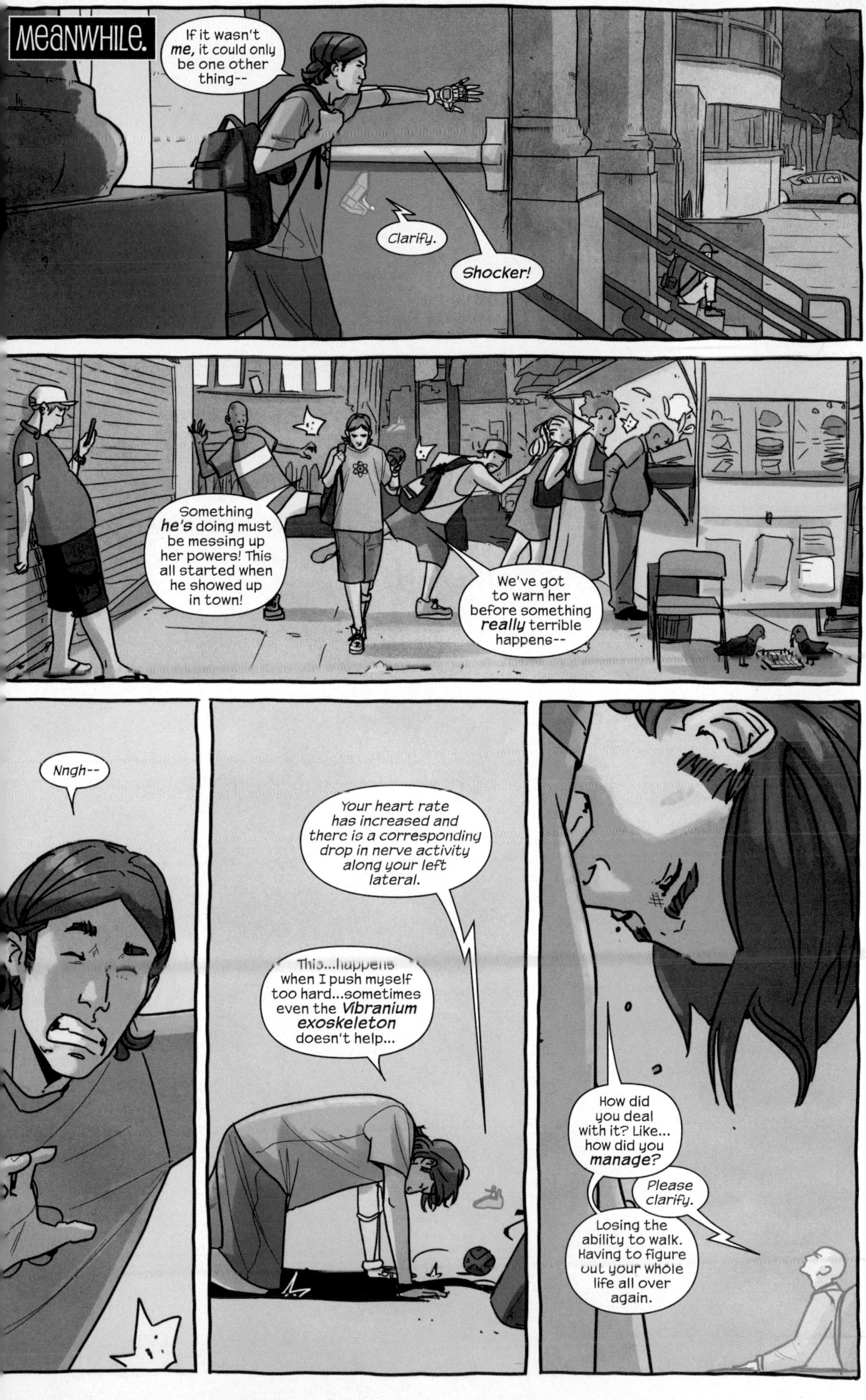
MEANWHILE.
If it wasn't me, it could only be one other thing--
Clarify.
Shocker!
Something he's doing must be messing up her powers! This all started when he showed up in town!
We've got to warn her before something really terrible happens--
Nngh--
Your heart rate has increased and there is a corresponding drop in nerve activity along your left lateral.
This...happens when I push myself too hard...sometimes even the Vibranium exoskeleton doesn't help...
How did you deal with it? Like... how did you manage?
Please clarify.
Losing the ability to walk. Having to figure out your whole life all over again.

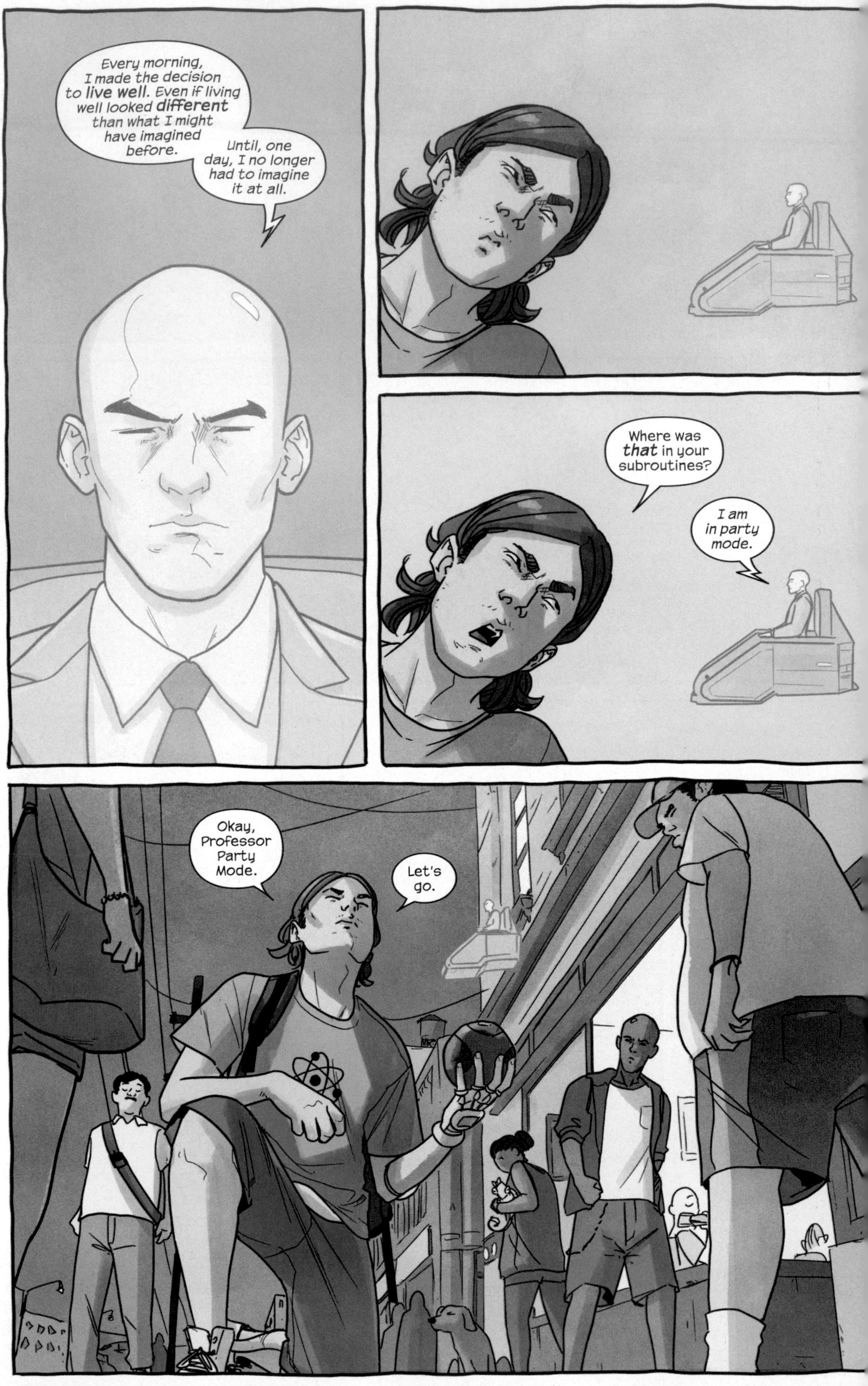
Every morning, I made the decision to live well. Even if living well looked different than what I might have imagined before.
Until, one day, I no longer had to imagine it at all.
Where was that in your subroutines?
I am in party mode.
Okay, Professor Party Mode.
Let's go.

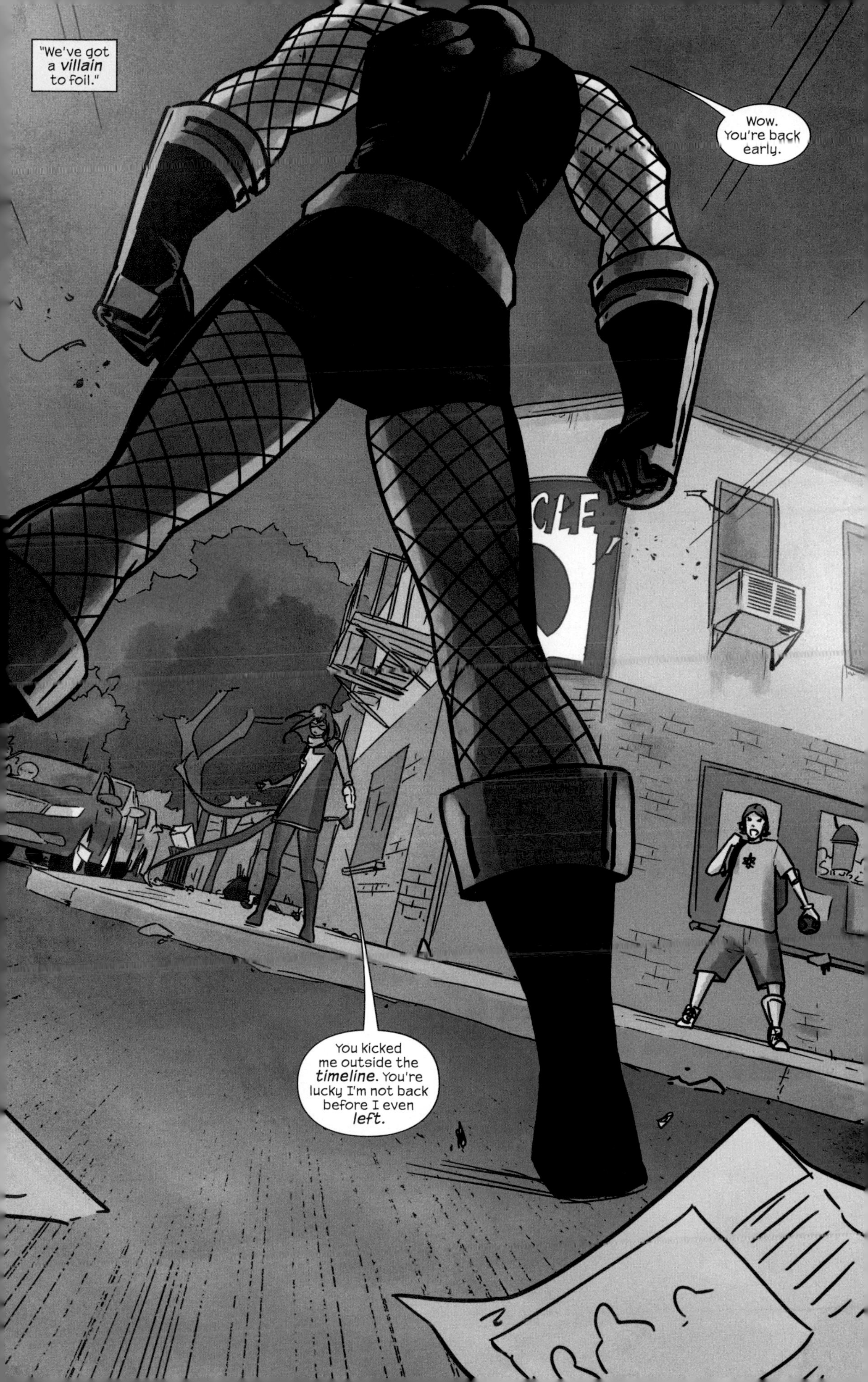
"We've got a *villain* to foil."
Wow. You're back early.
You kicked me outside the *timeline*. You're lucky I'm not back before I even *left*.

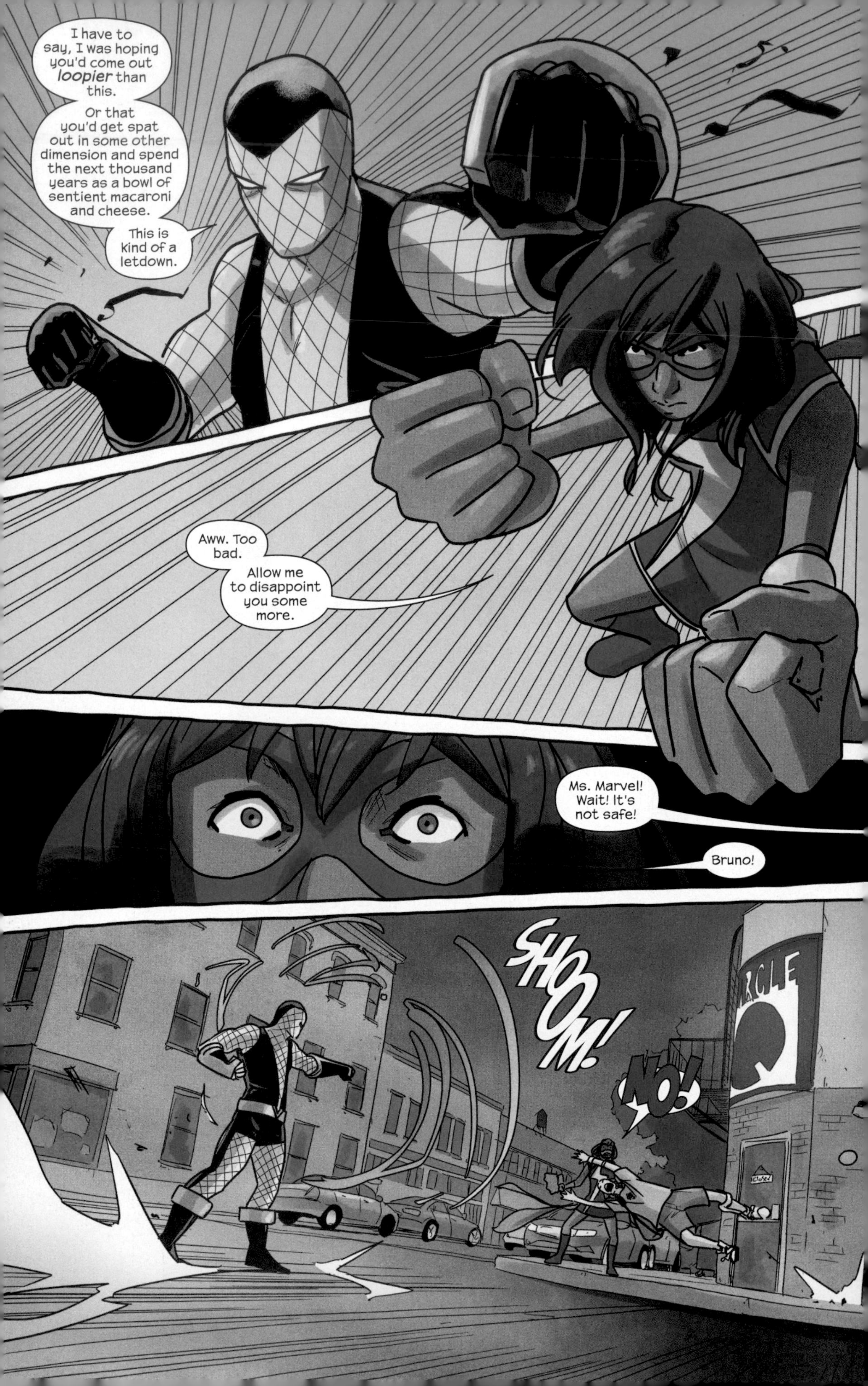
I have to say, I was hoping you'd come out *loopier* than this.
Or that you'd get spat out in some other dimension and spend the next thousand years as a bowl of sentient macaroni and cheese.
This is kind of a letdown.
Aww. Too bad.
Allow me to disappoint you some more.
Ms. Marvel! Wait! It's not safe!
Bruno!
SHOOM!
NO!
CLOSED

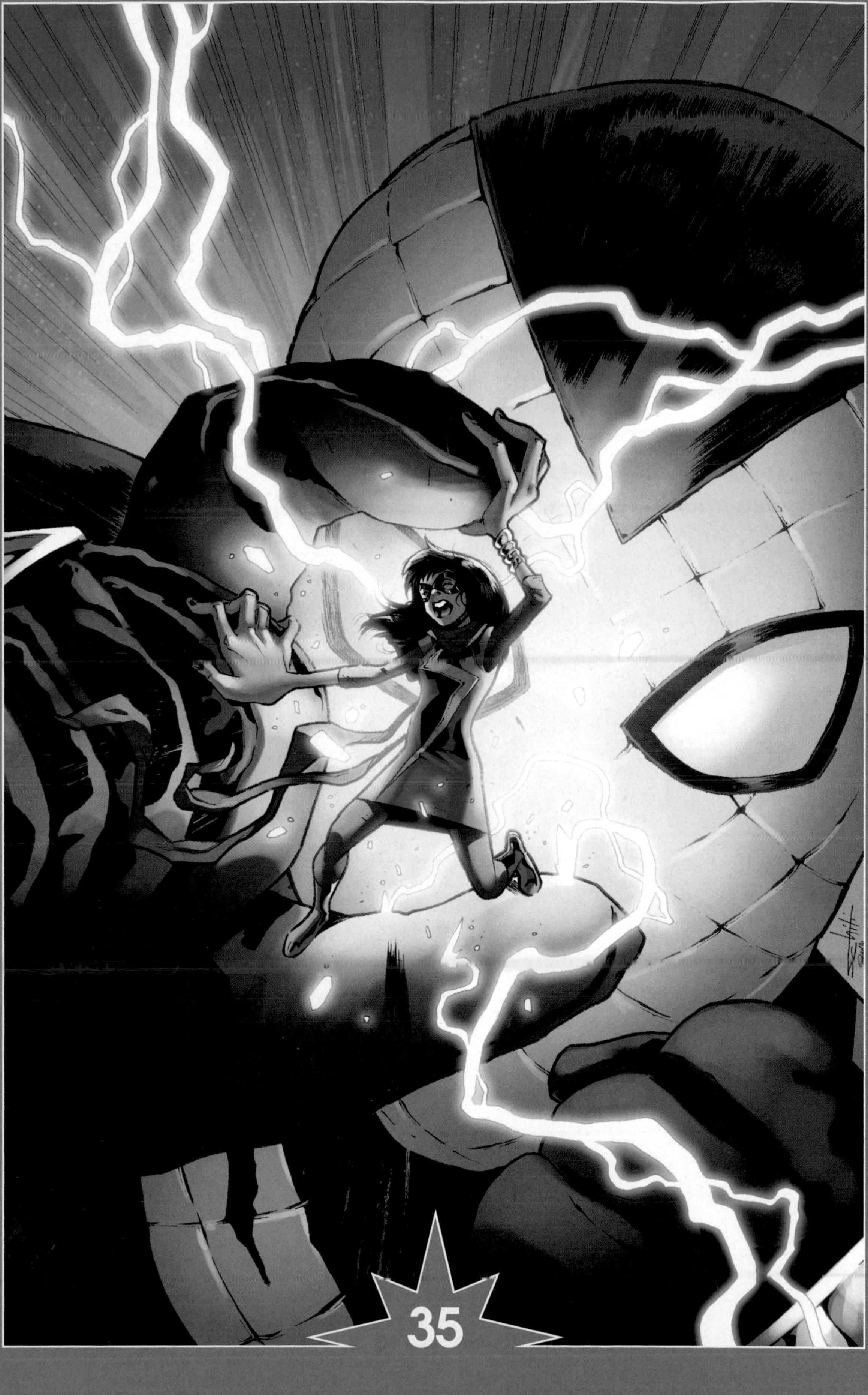
35

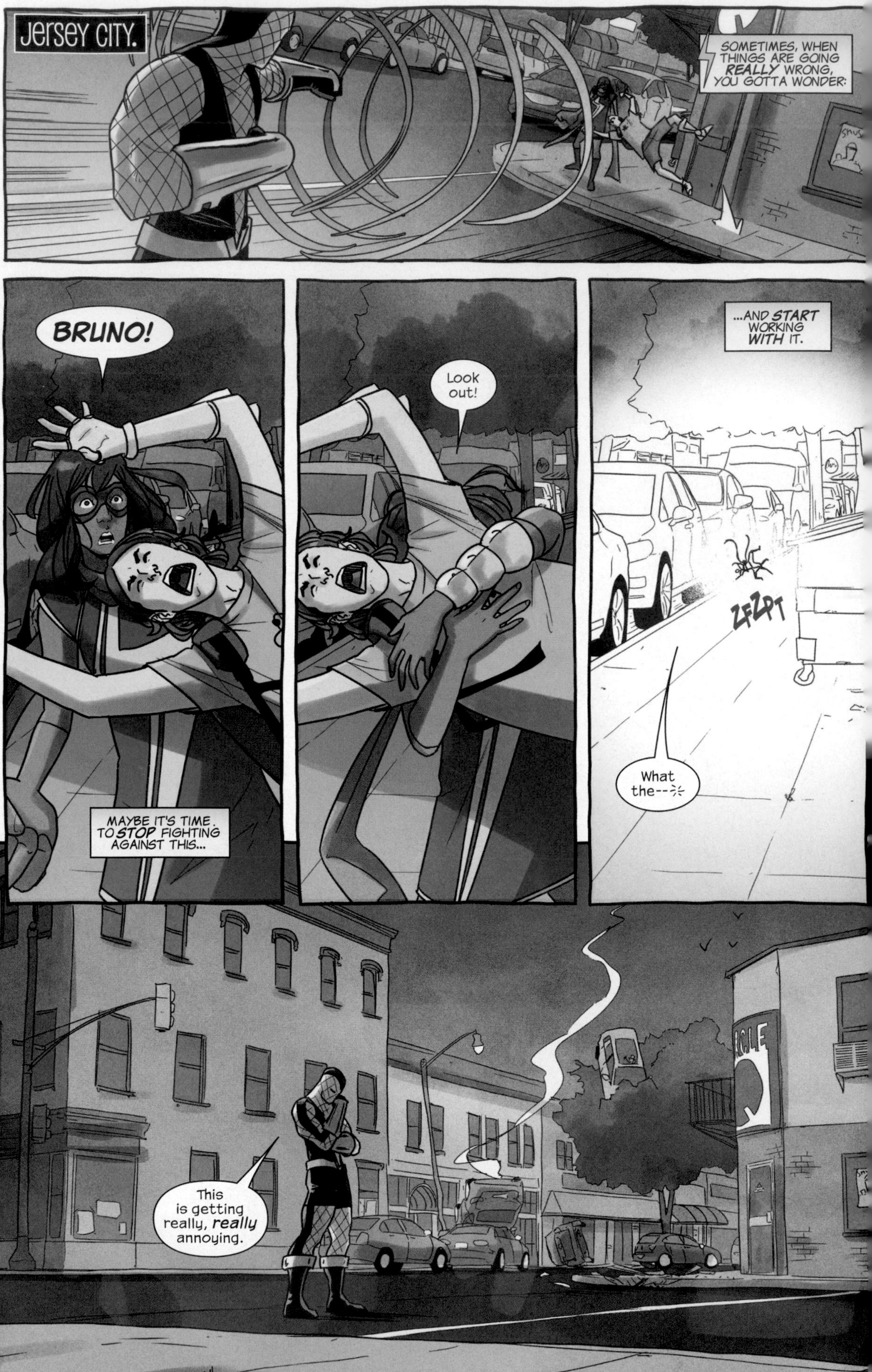
JERSEY CITY.
SOMETIMES, WHEN THINGS ARE GOING REALLY WRONG, YOU GOTTA WONDER:
BRUNO!
MAYBE IT'S TIME TO STOP FIGHTING AGAINST THIS...
Look out!
...AND START WORKING WITH IT.
ZZZPT
What the--
This is getting really, really annoying.

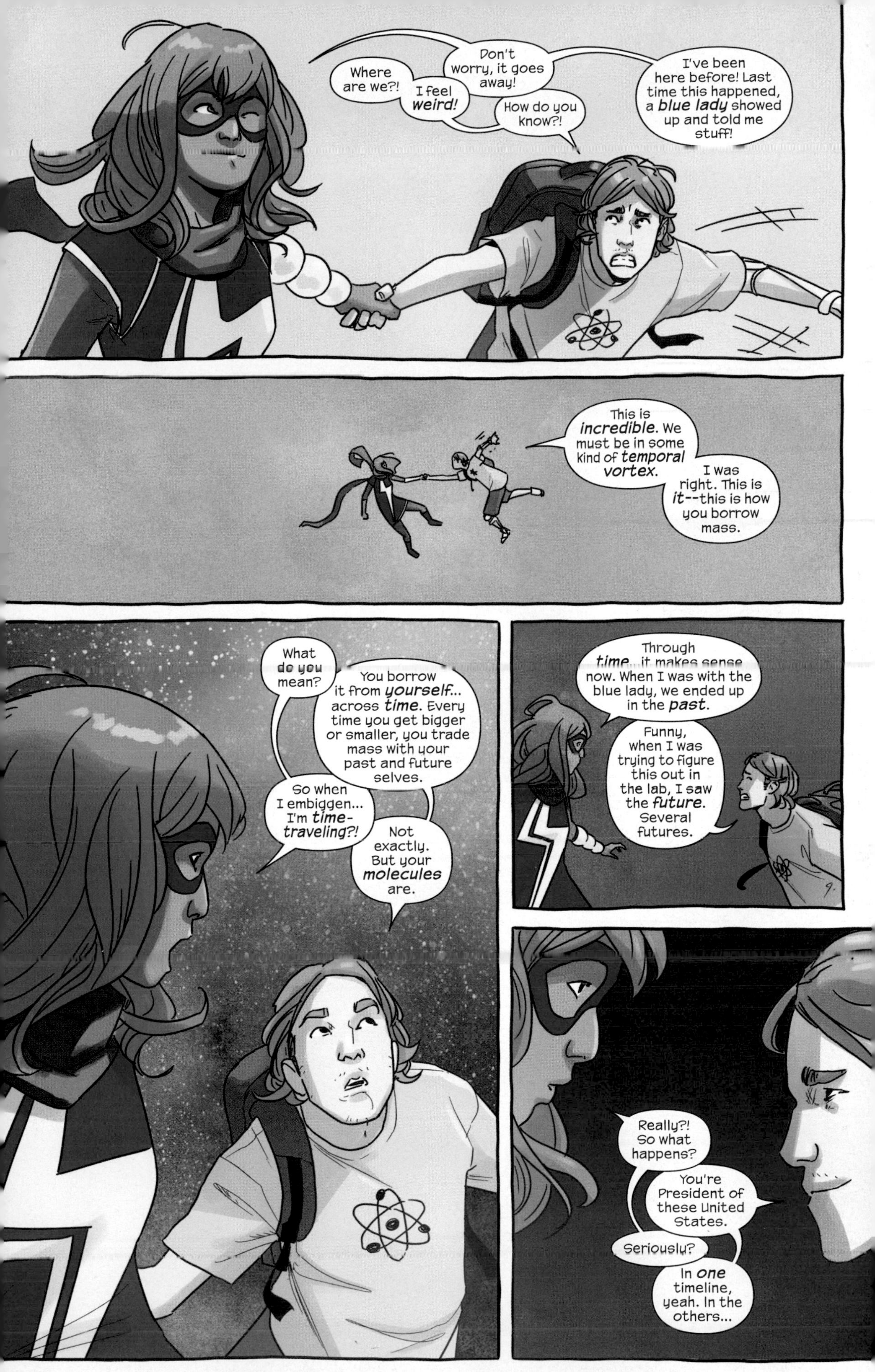
Where are we?!
I feel weird!
Don't worry, it goes away!
How do you know?!
I've been here before! Last time this happened, a blue lady showed up and told me stuff!
This is incredible. We must be in some kind of temporal vortex.
I was right. This is it--this is how you borrow mass.
What do you mean?
You borrow it from yourself... across time. Every time you get bigger or smaller, you trade mass with your past and future selves.
So when I embiggen... I'm time-traveling?!
Not exactly. But your molecules are.
Through time...it makes sense now. When I was with the blue lady, we ended up in the past.
Funny, when I was trying to figure this out in the lab, I saw the future. Several futures.
Really?! So what happens?
You're President of these United States.
Seriously?
In one timeline, yeah. In the others...

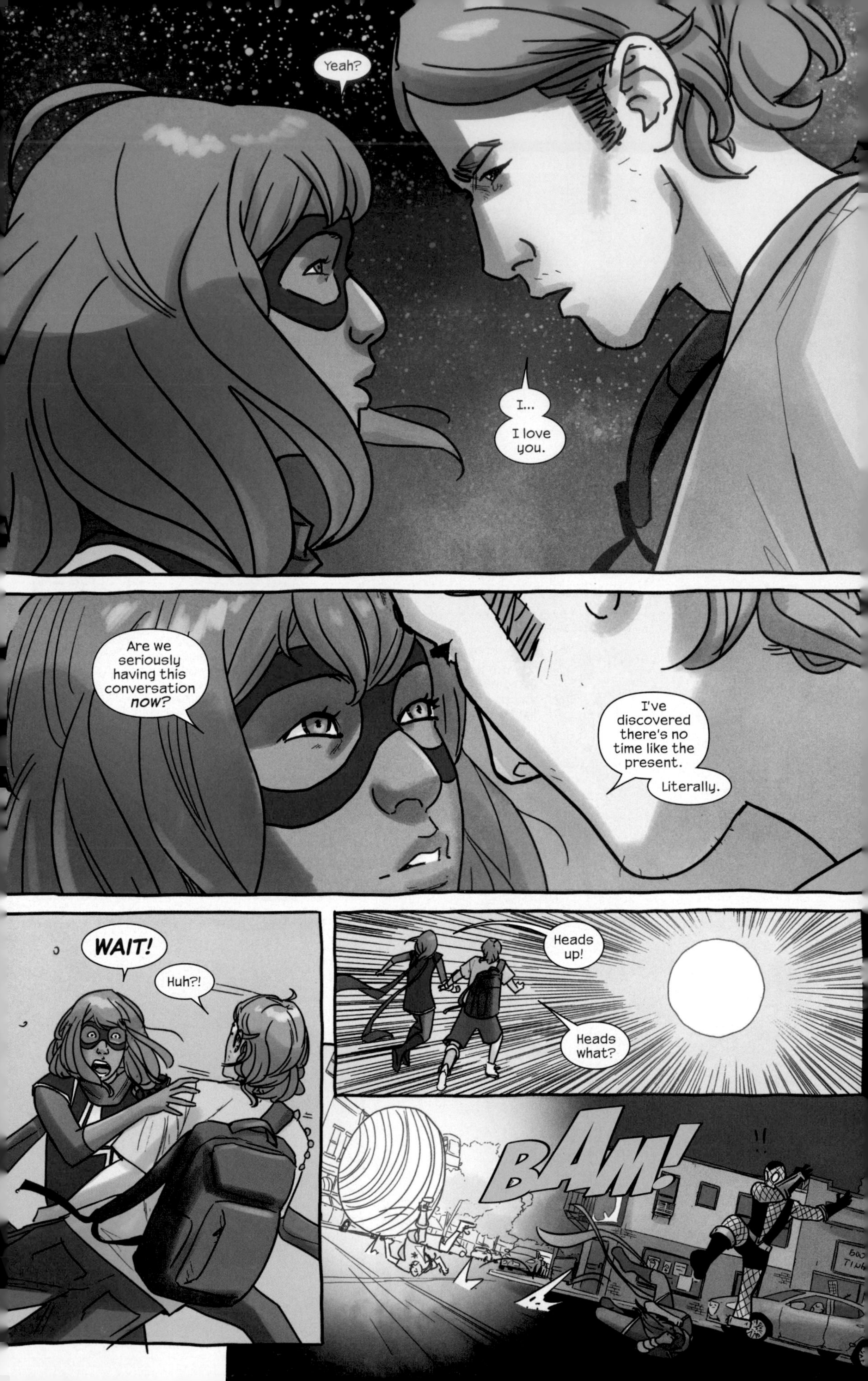

Yeah?
I...
I love you.
Are we seriously having this conversation *now*?
I've discovered there's no time like the present.
Literally.
WAIT!
Huh?!
Heads up!
Heads what?
BAM!

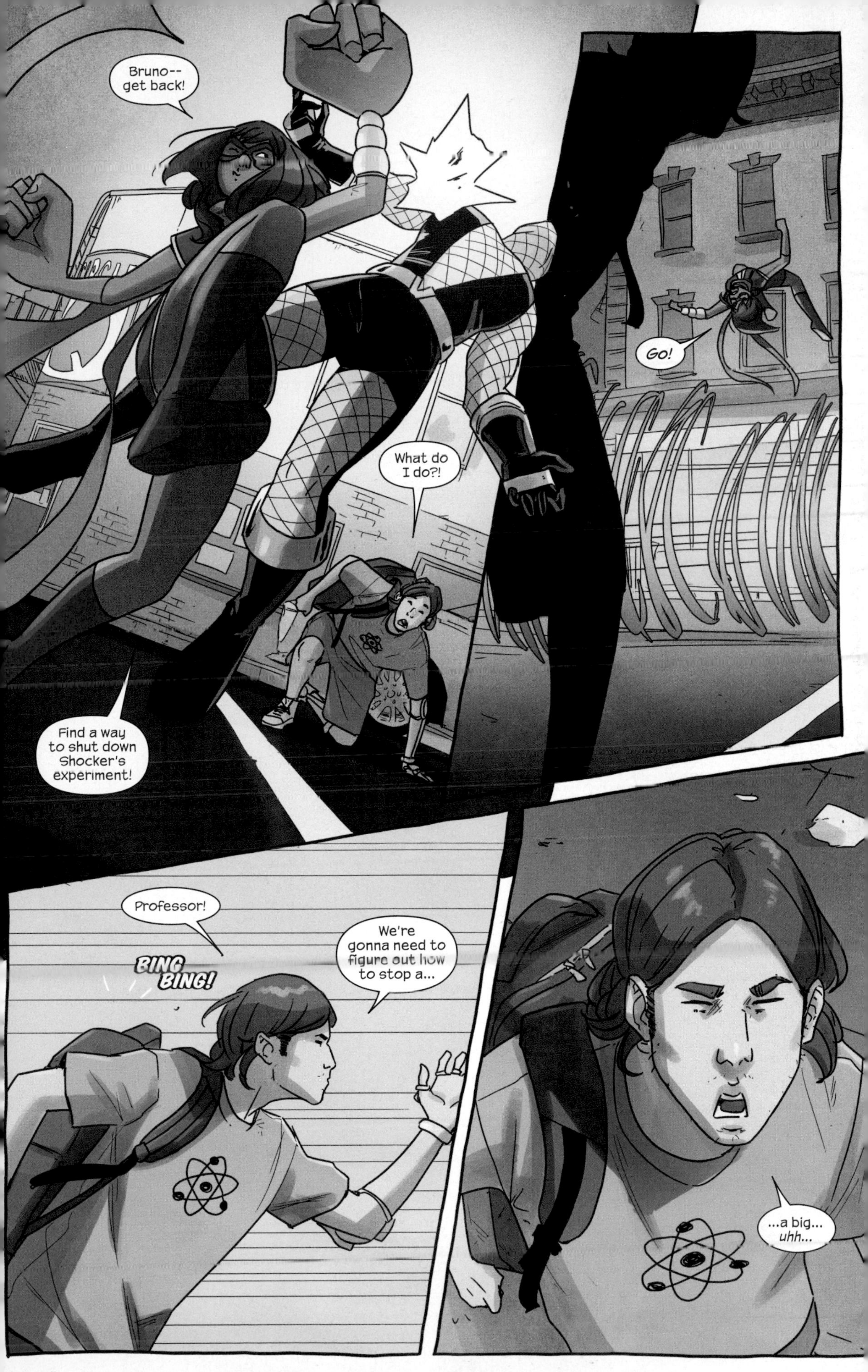
Bruno--
get back!
Go!
What do
I do?!
Find a way
to shut down
Shocker's
experiment!
Professor!
BING
BING!
We're
gonna need to
figure out how
to stop a...
...a big...
uhh...

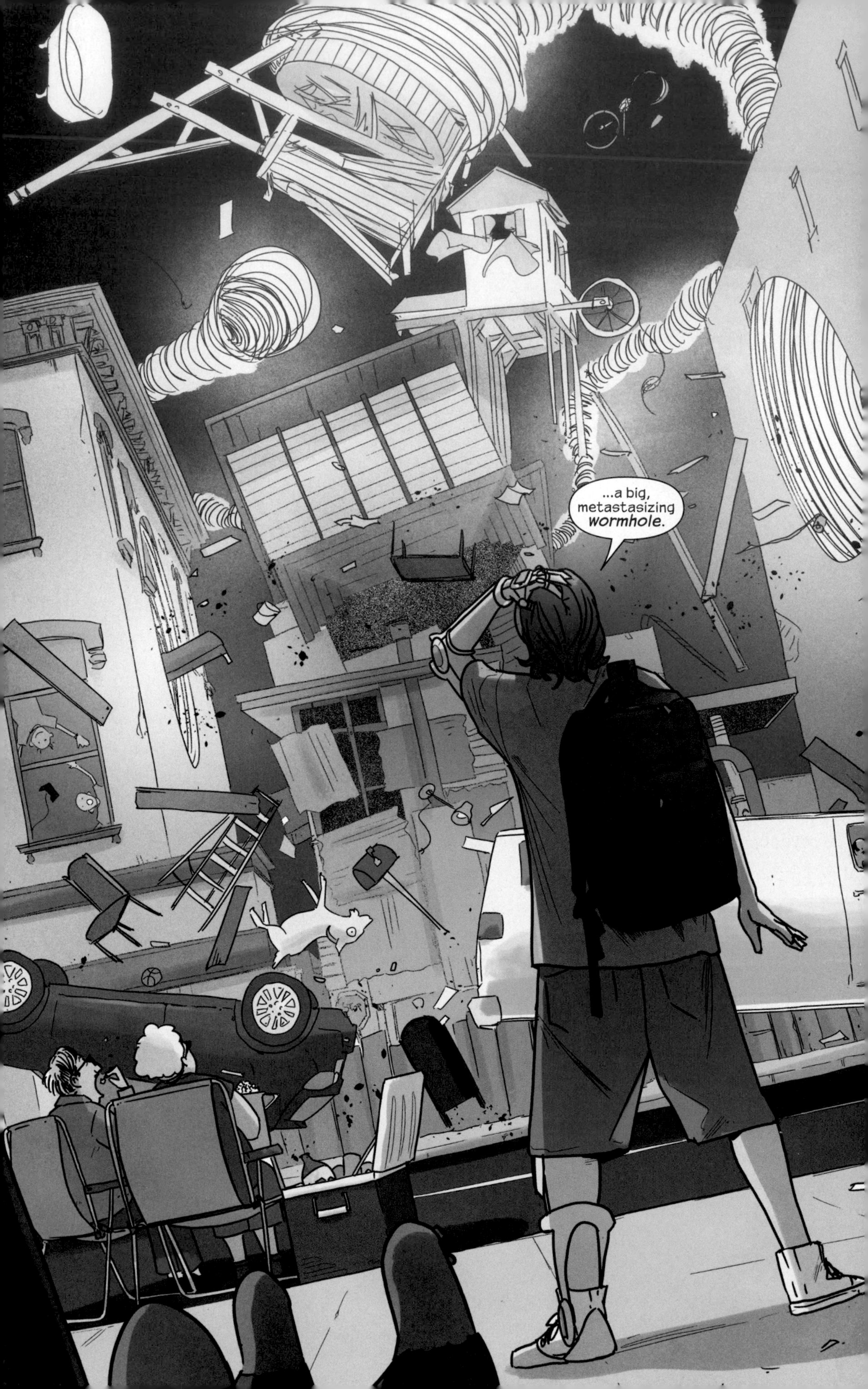
...a big, metastasizing *wormhole*.

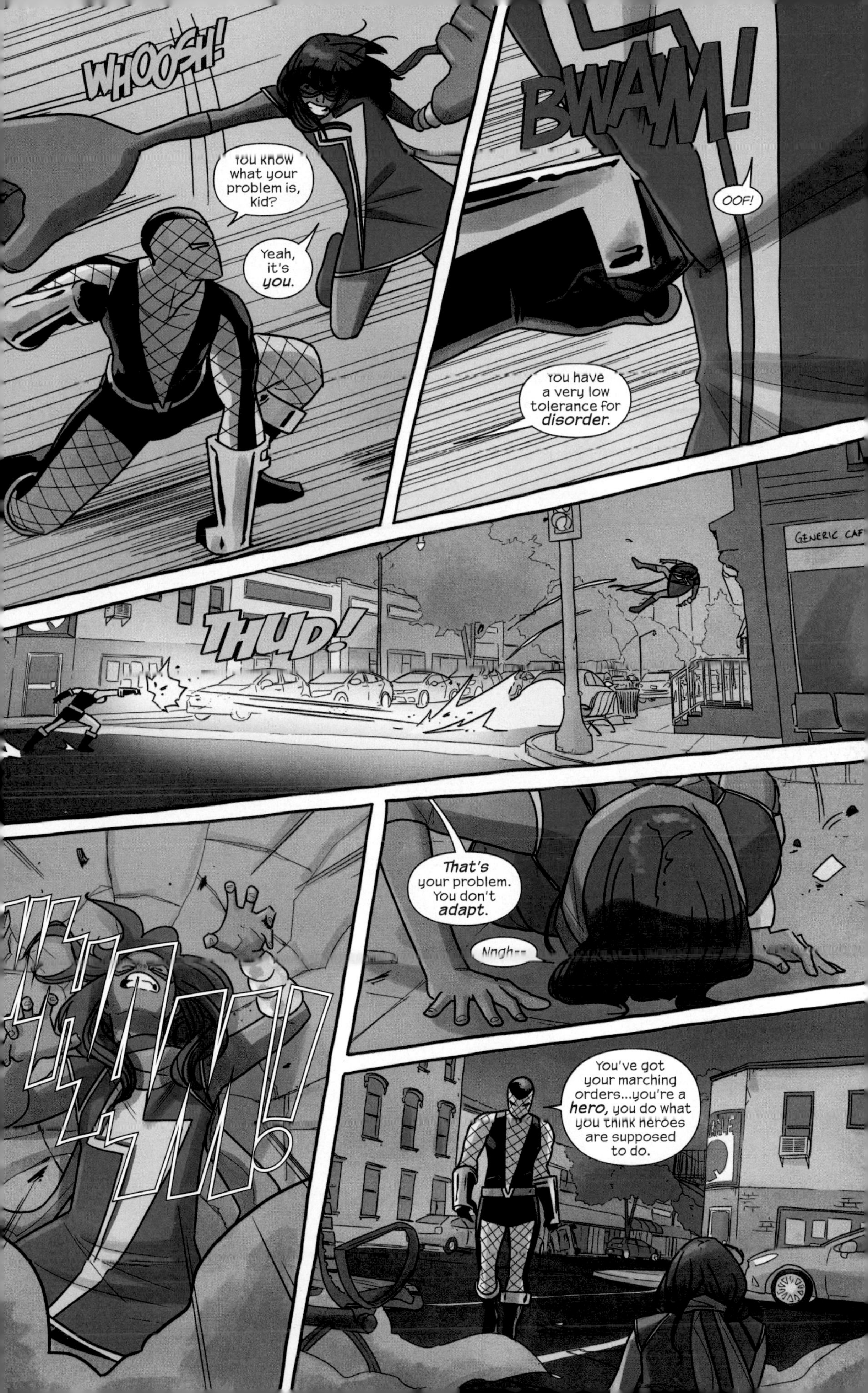
WHOOSH!
You know what your problem is, kid?
Yeah, it's *you*.
BWAM!
OOF!
You have a very low tolerance for *disorder*.
GENERIC CAF
THUD!
That's your problem. You don't *adapt*.
Nngh--
You've got your marching orders...you're a *hero*, you do what you think heroes are supposed to do.

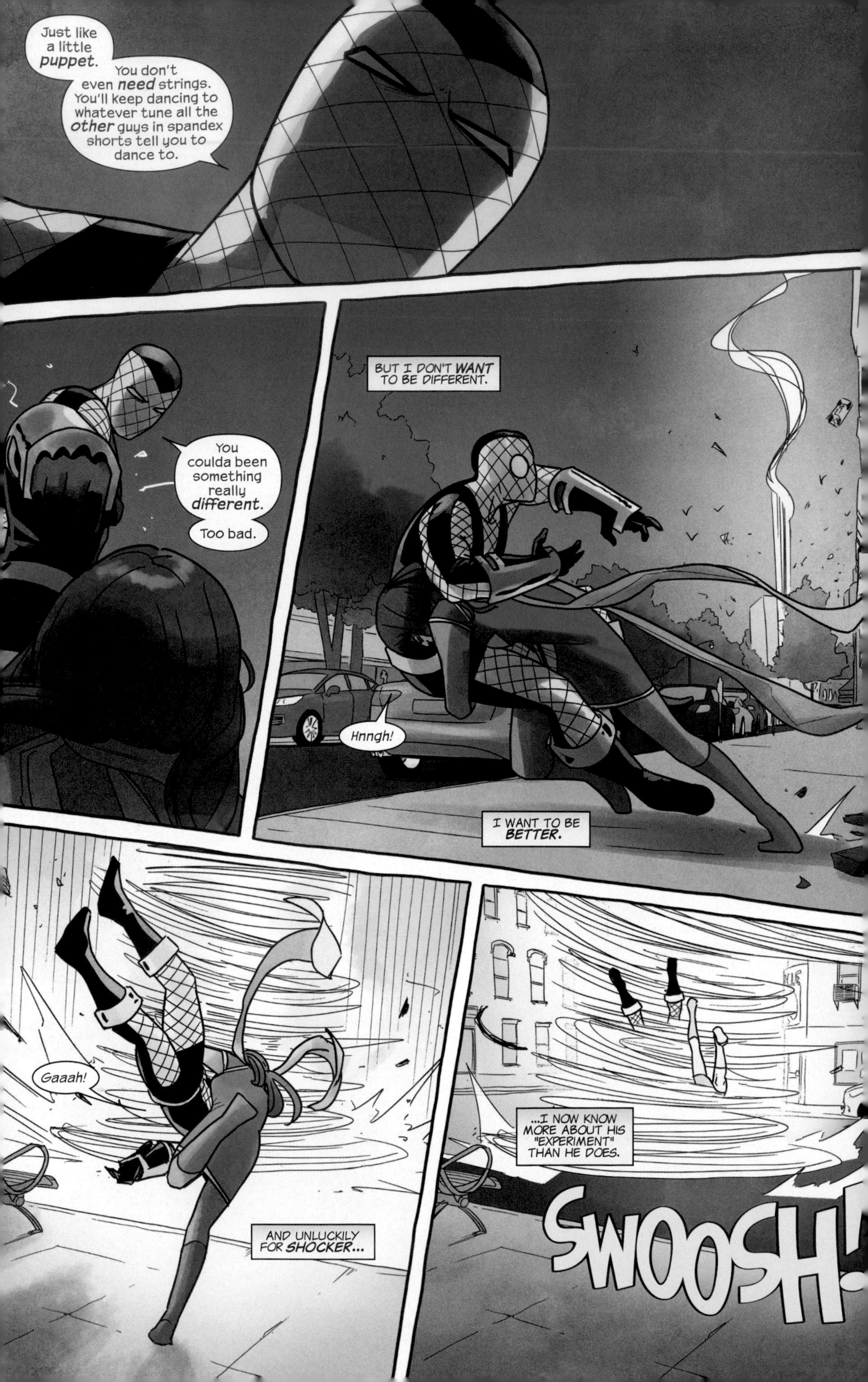
Just like a little *puppet*.
You don't even *need* strings. You'll keep dancing to whatever tune all the *other* guys in spandex shorts tell you to dance to.
You coulda been something really *different*.
Too bad.
BUT I DON'T *WANT* TO BE DIFFERENT.
Hnngh!
I WANT TO BE *BETTER*.
Gaaah!
AND UNLUCKILY FOR *SHOCKER*...
...I NOW KNOW MORE ABOUT HIS "EXPERIMENT" THAN HE DOES.
SWOOSH!

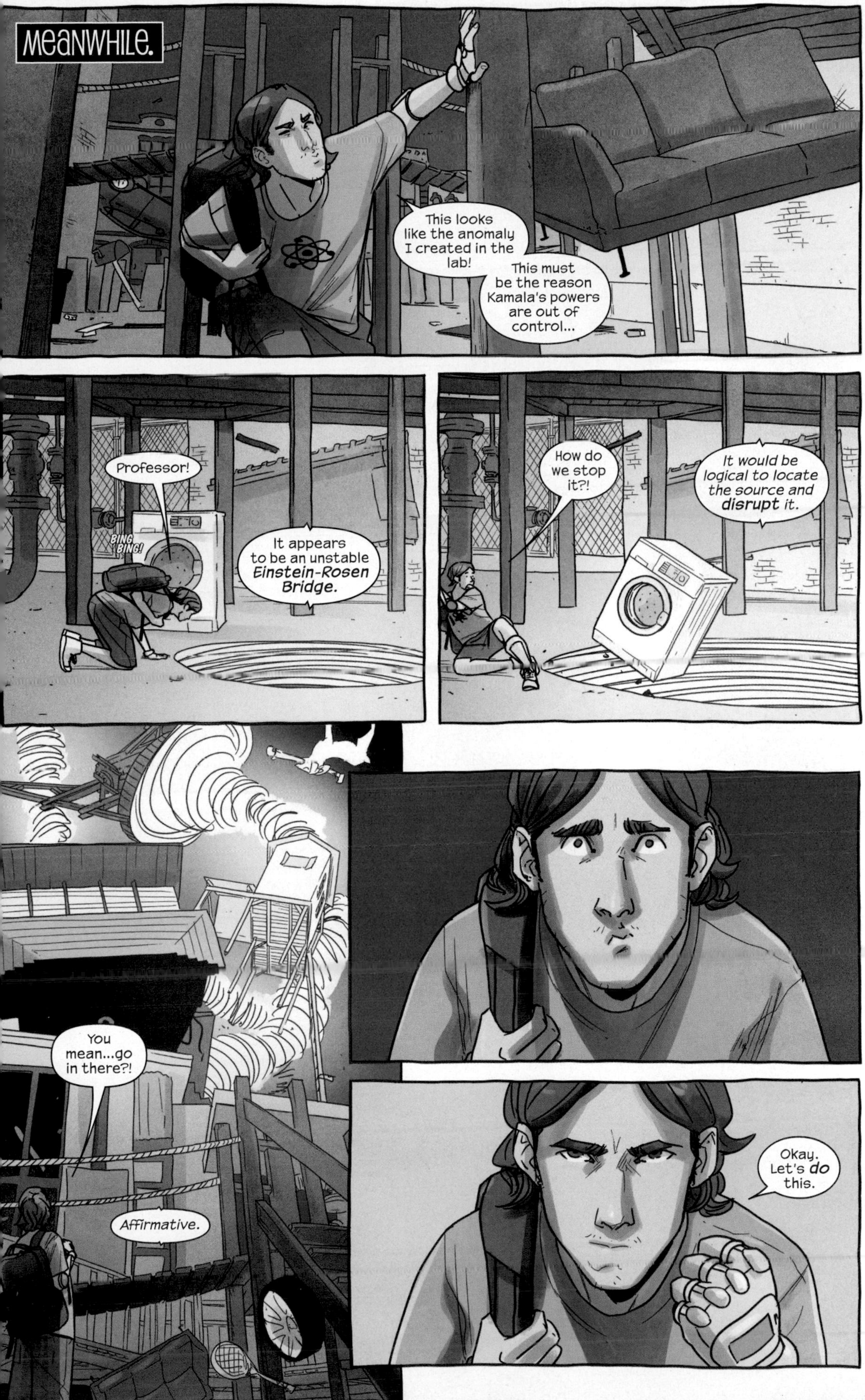
MEANWHILE.
This looks like the anomaly I created in the lab!
This must be the reason Kamala's powers are out of control...
Professor!
BING BING!
It appears to be an unstable *Einstein-Rosen Bridge.*
How do we stop it?!
It would be logical to locate the source and **disrupt** it.
You mean...go in there?!
Affirmative.
Okay. Let's **do** this.

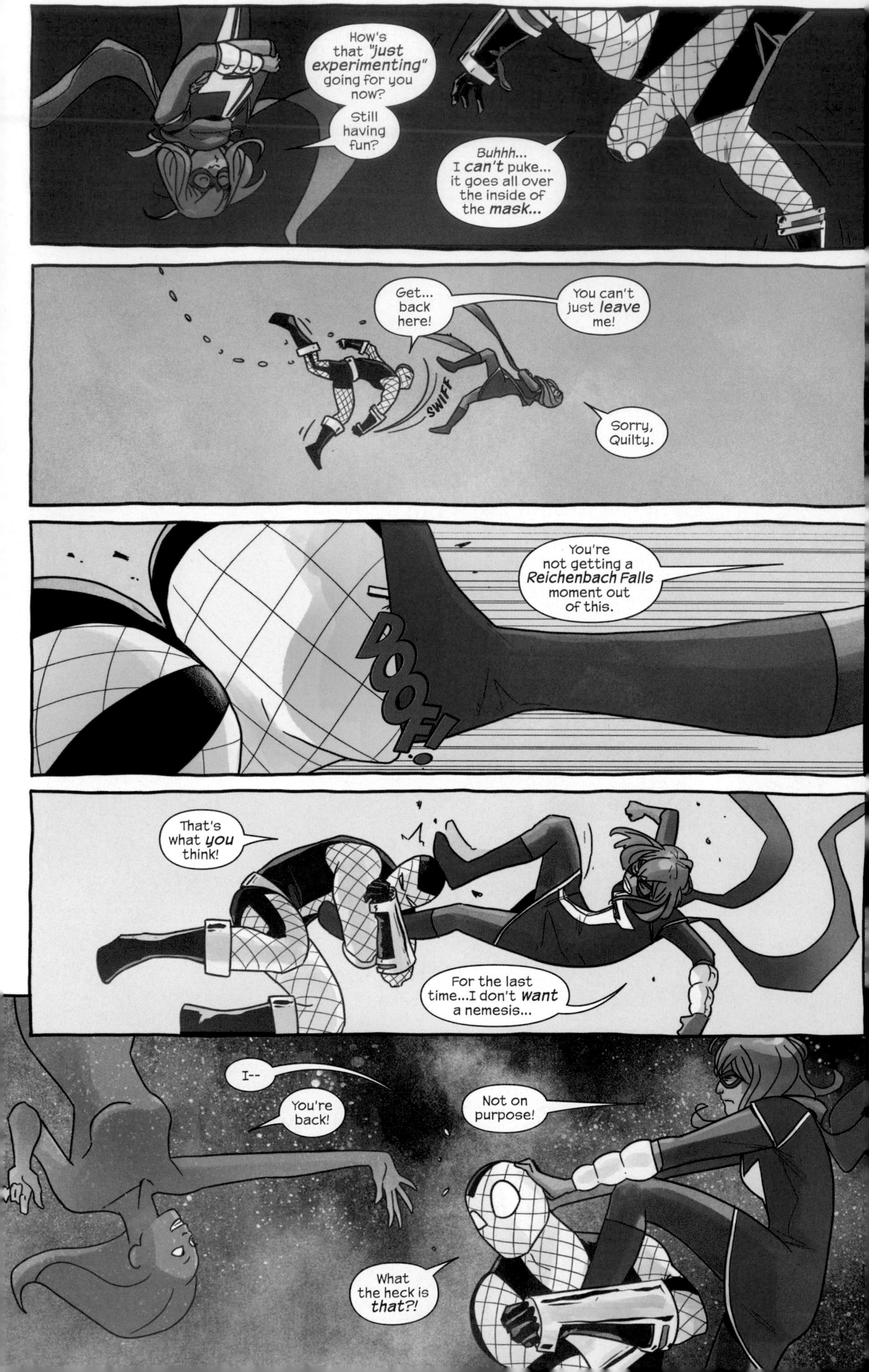
How's that "just experimenting" going for you now?
Still having fun?
Buhhh... I can't puke... it goes all over the inside of the mask...
Get... back here!
You can't just leave me!
SWIFF
Sorry, Quilty.
You're not getting a Reichenbach Falls moment out of this.
DOOF!
That's what you think!
For the last time...I don't want a nemesis...
I--
You're back!
Not on purpose!
What the heck is that?!

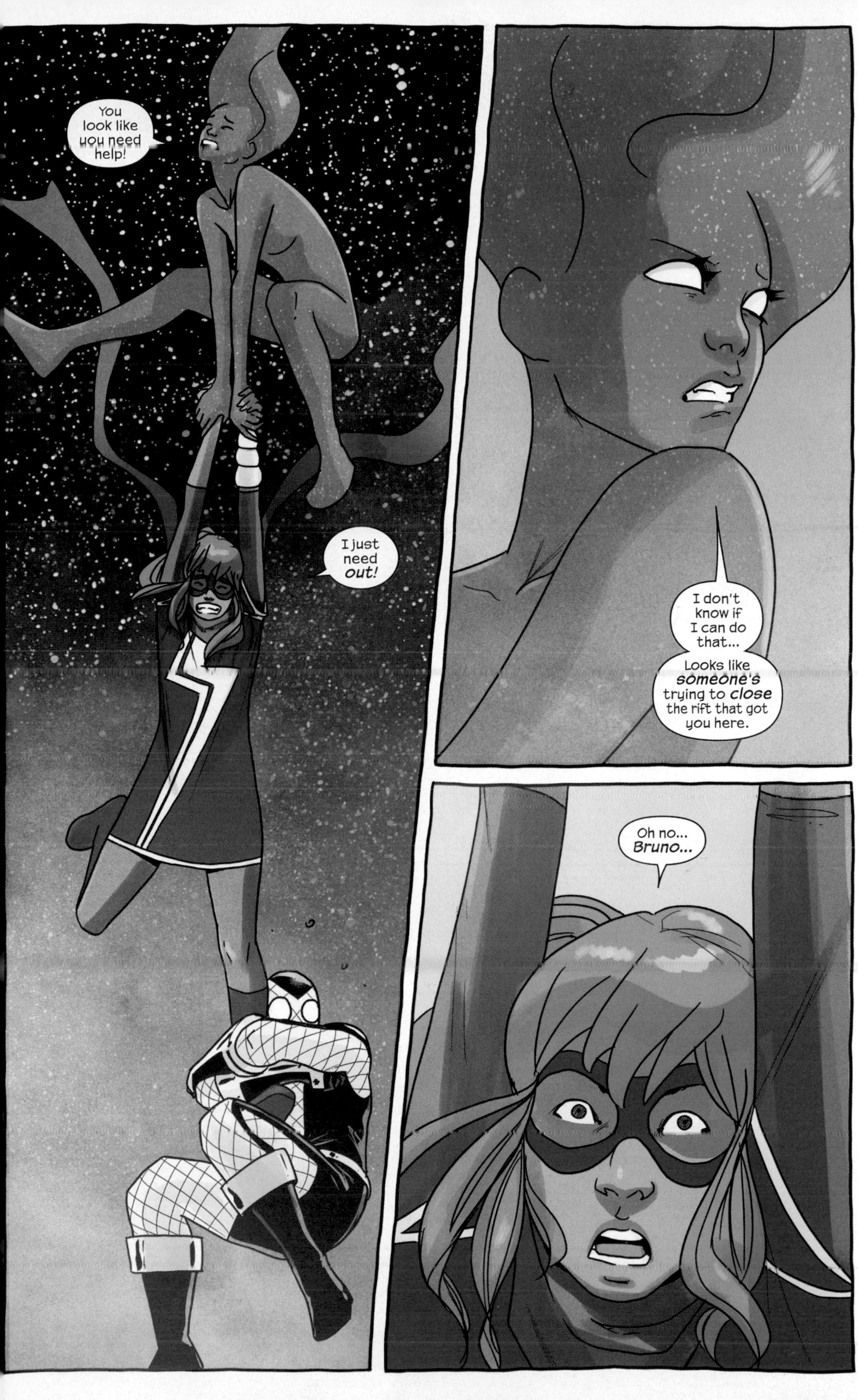
You look like you need help!
I just need *out!*
I don't know if I can do that...
Looks like ***someone's*** trying to ***close*** the rift that got you here.
Oh no... *Bruno...*

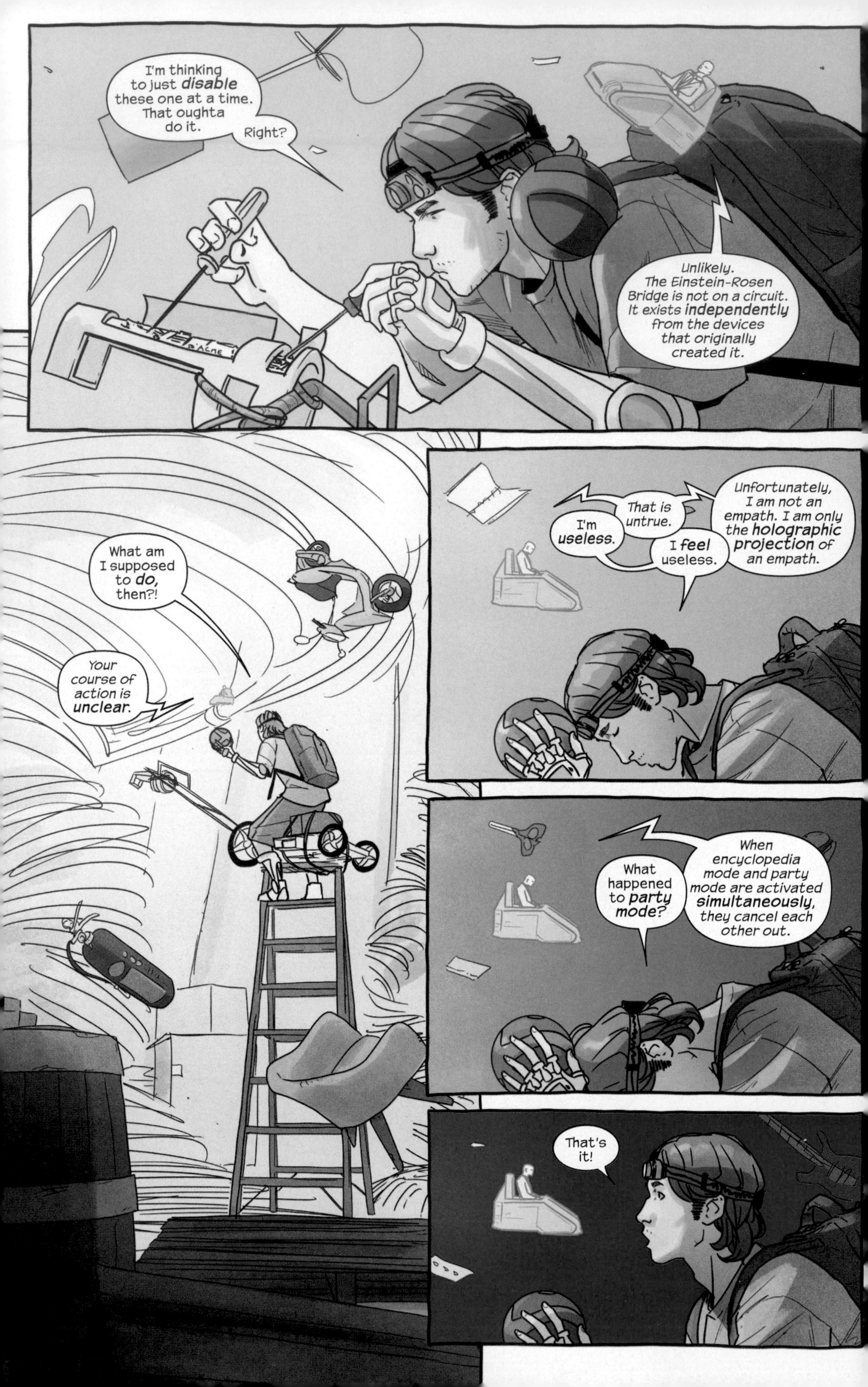
I'm thinking to just *disable* these one at a time. That oughta do it.
Right?
Unlikely. The Einstein-Rosen Bridge is not on a circuit. It exists **independently** from the devices that originally created it.
What am I supposed to *do,* then?!
Your course of action is **unclear**.
I'm *useless*.
That is untrue.
I *feel* useless.
Unfortunately, I am not an empath. I am only the **holographic projection** of an empath.
What happened to *party mode?*
When encyclopedia mode and party mode are activated **simultaneously,** they cancel each other out.
That's it!

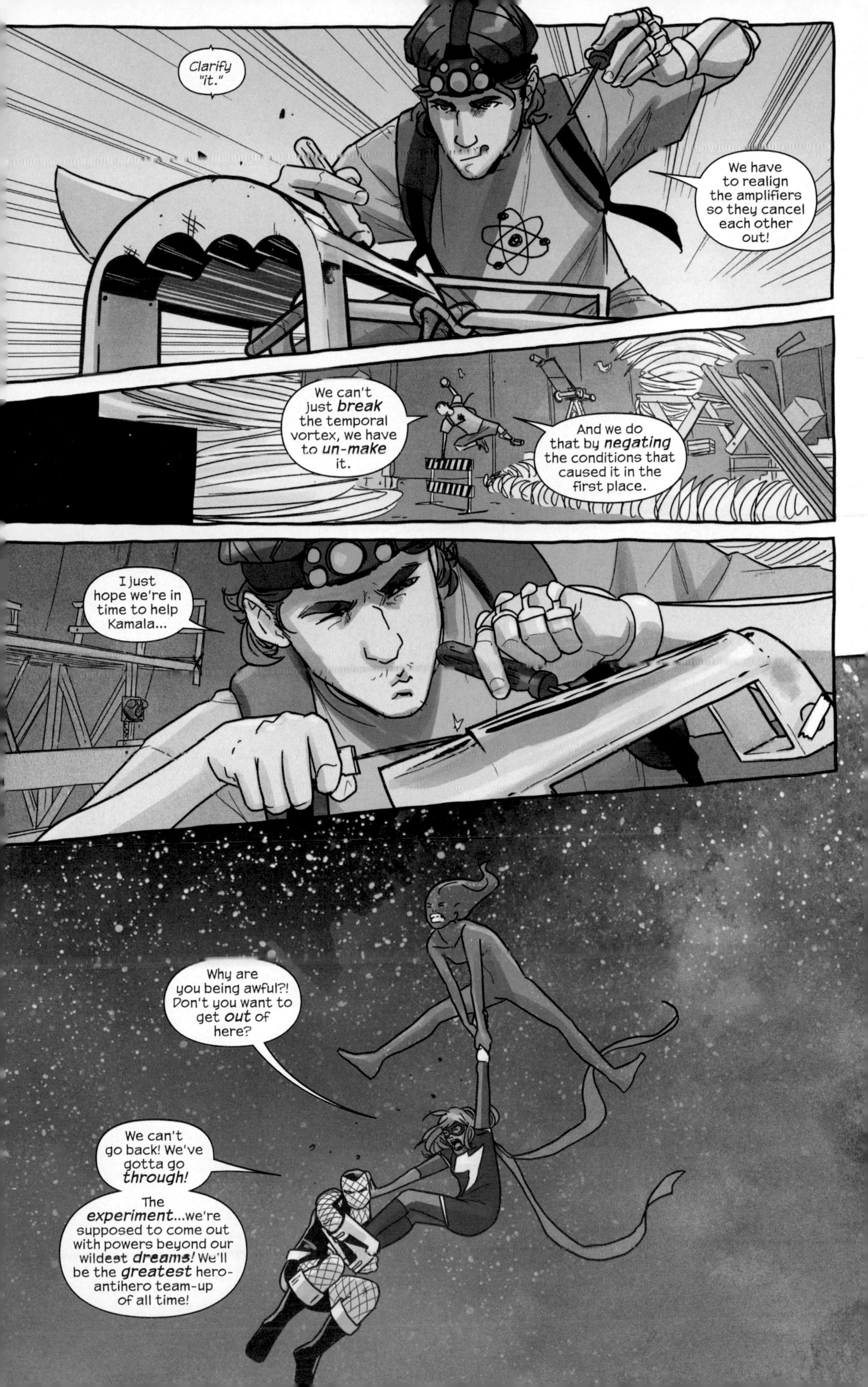
Clarify "it."
We have to realign the amplifiers so they cancel each other out!
We can't just *break* the temporal vortex, we have to *un-make* it.
And we do that by *negating* the conditions that caused it in the first place.
I just hope we're in time to help Kamala...
Why are you being awful?! Don't you want to get *out* of here?
We can't go back! We've gotta go *through!*
The *experiment*...we're supposed to come out with powers beyond our wildest *dreams!* We'll be the *greatest* hero-antihero team-up of all time!

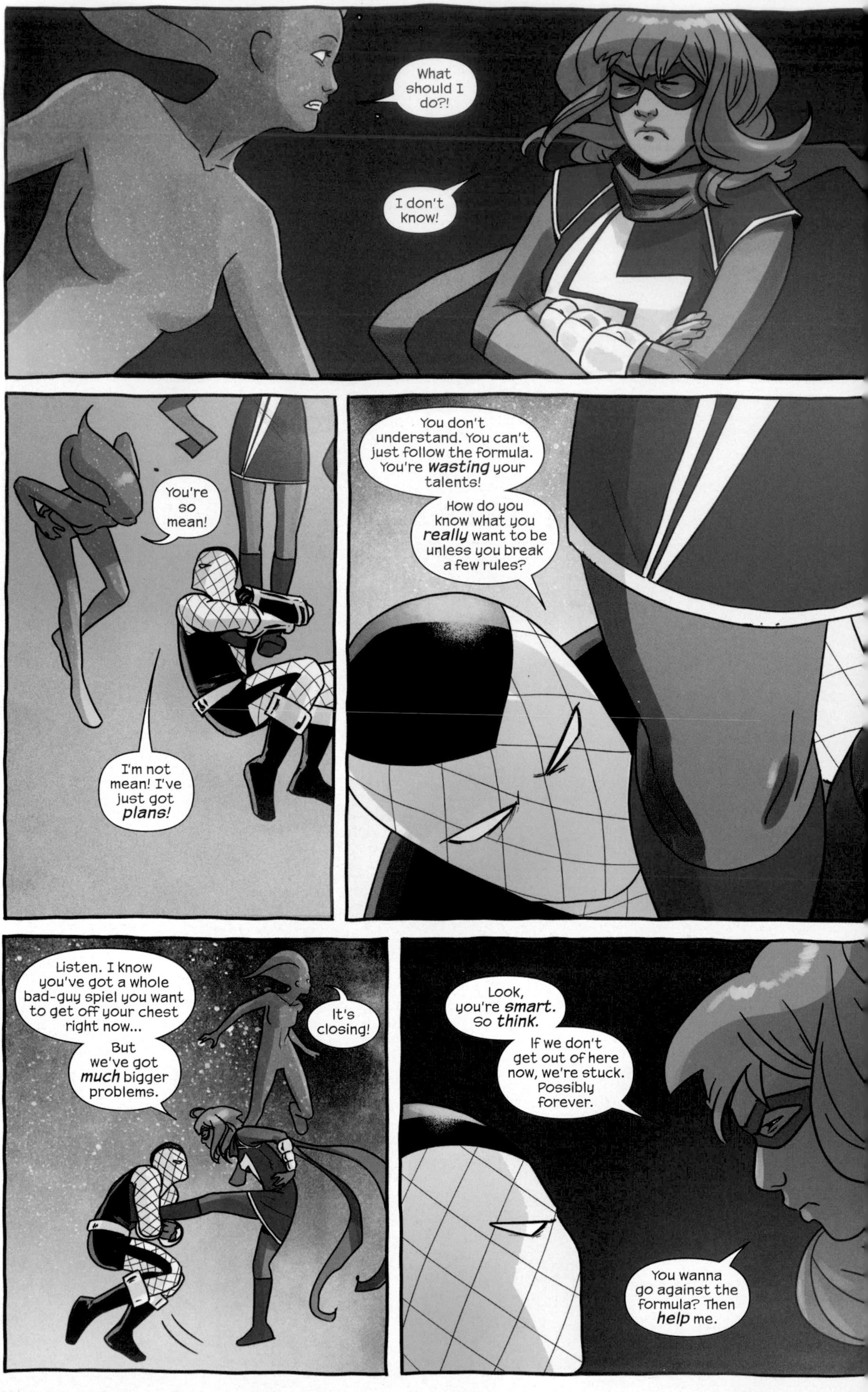
What should I do?!
I don't know!
You're so mean!
I'm not mean! I've just got *plans!*
You don't understand. You can't just follow the formula. You're *wasting* your talents!
How do you know what you *really* want to be unless you break a few rules?
Listen. I know you've got a whole bad-guy spiel you want to get off your chest right now...
But we've got *much* bigger problems.
It's closing!
Look, you're *smart.* So *think.*
If we don't get out of here now, we're stuck. Possibly forever.
You wanna go against the formula? Then *help* me.

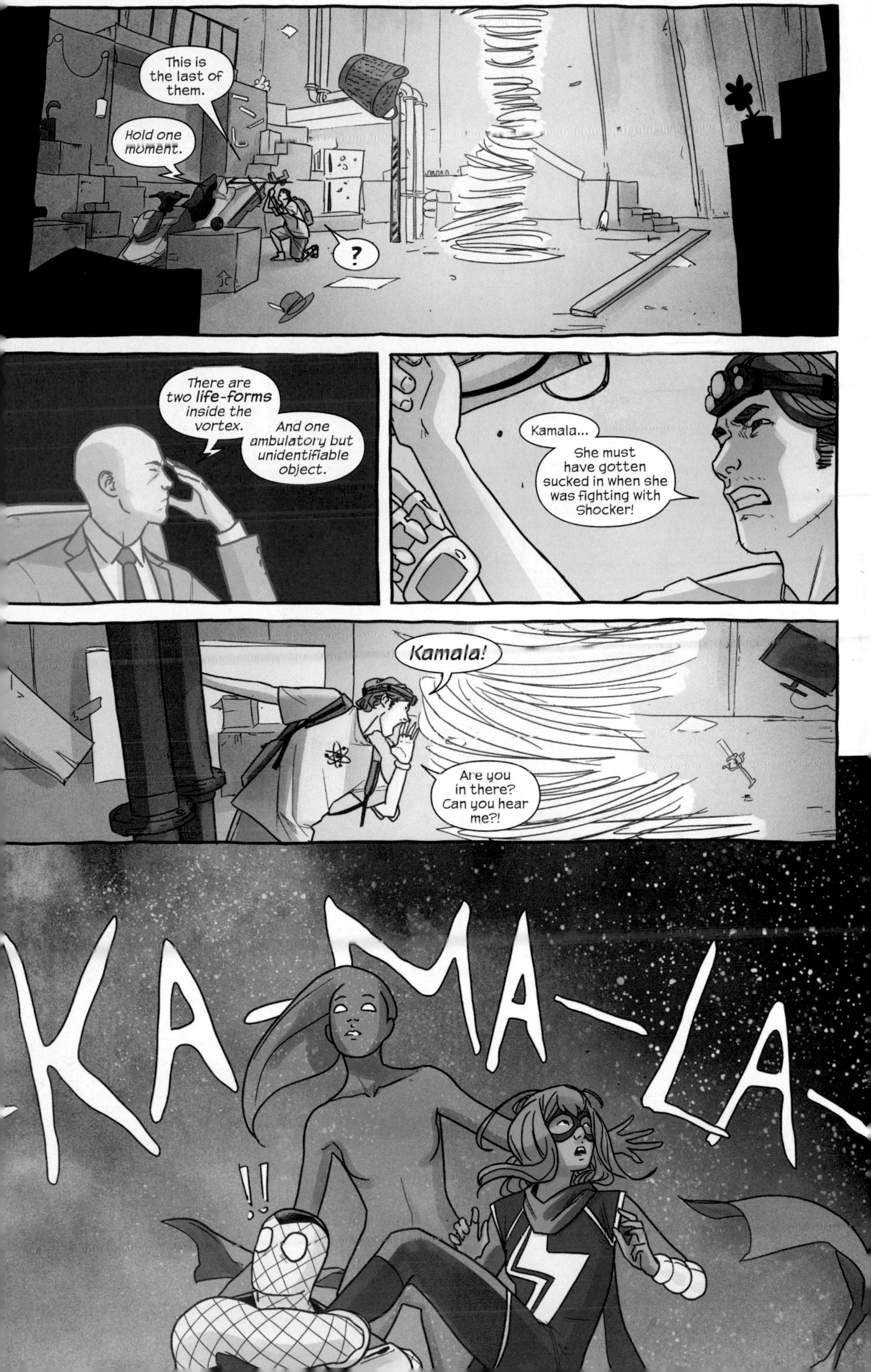

This is the last of them.
Hold one moment.
?
There are two life-forms inside the vortex.
And one ambulatory but unidentifiable object.
Kamala...
She must have gotten sucked in when she was fighting with Shocker!
Kamala!
Are you in there? Can you hear me?!
KA-MA-LA-
!!

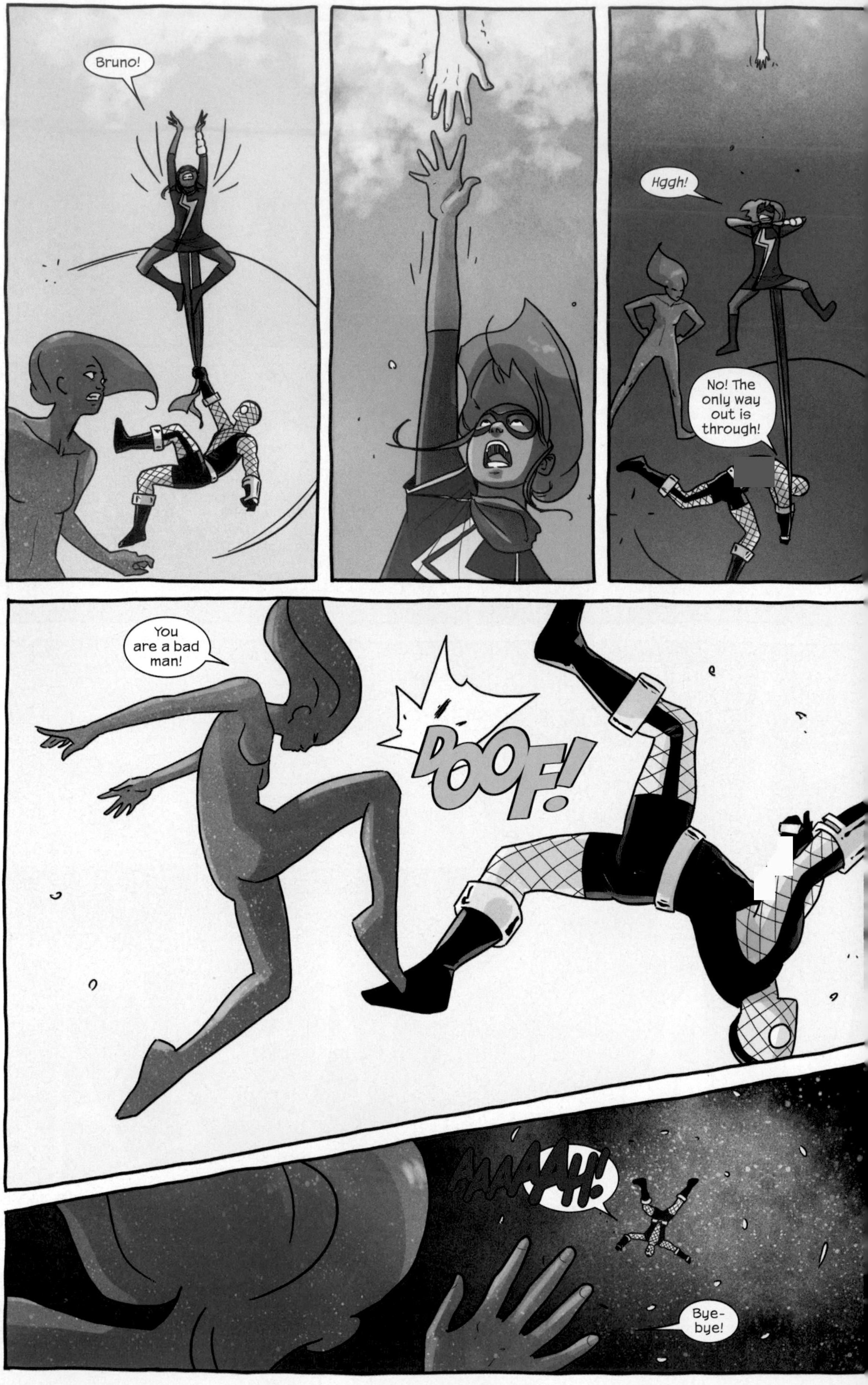
Bruno!
Hggh!
No! The only way out is through!
You are a bad man!
DOOF!
AAAAAH!
Bye-bye!

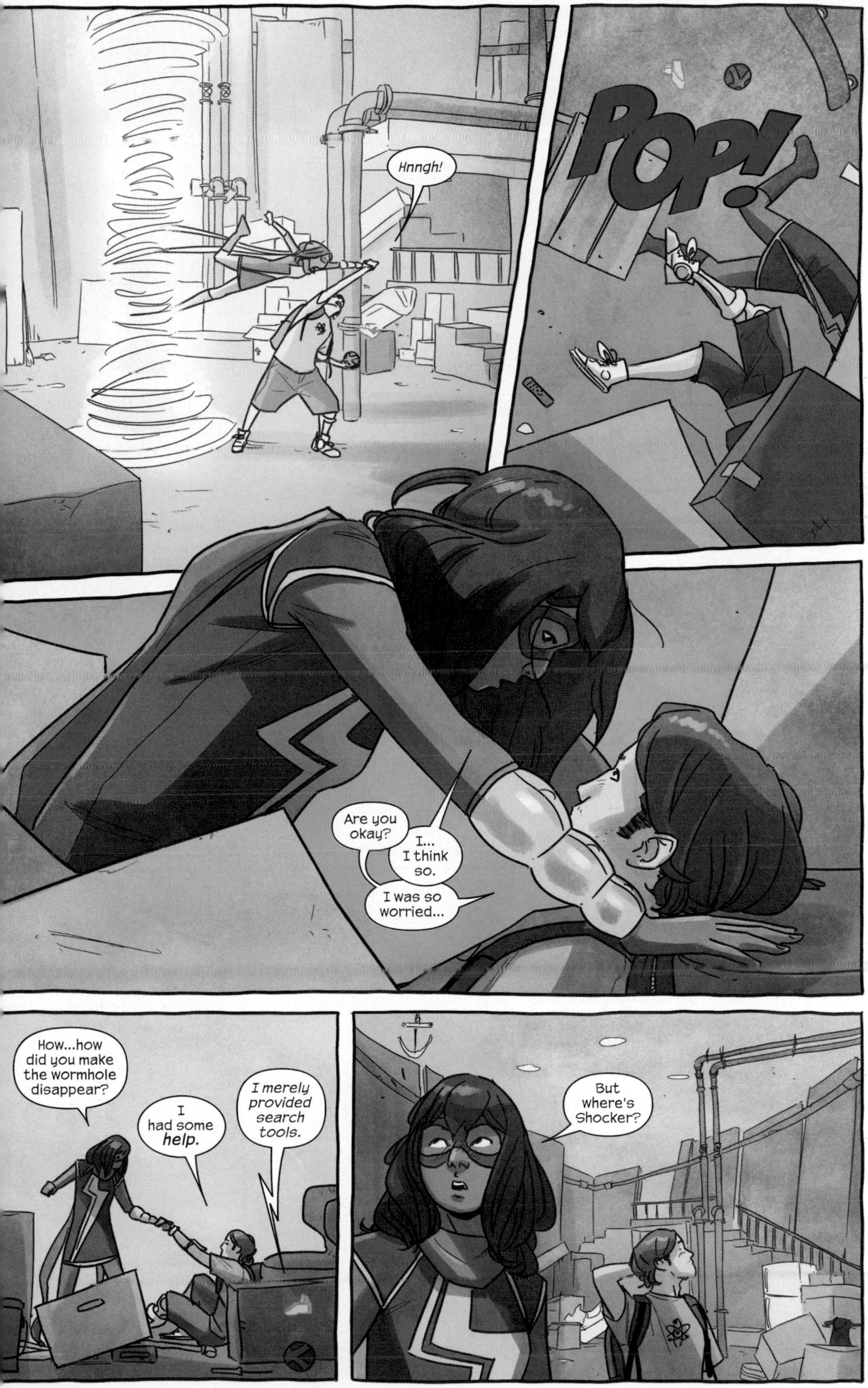

Hnngh!
POP!
Are you okay?
I... I think so.
I was so worried...
How...how did you make the wormhole disappear?
I had some *help.*
I merely provided search tools.
But where's Shocker?

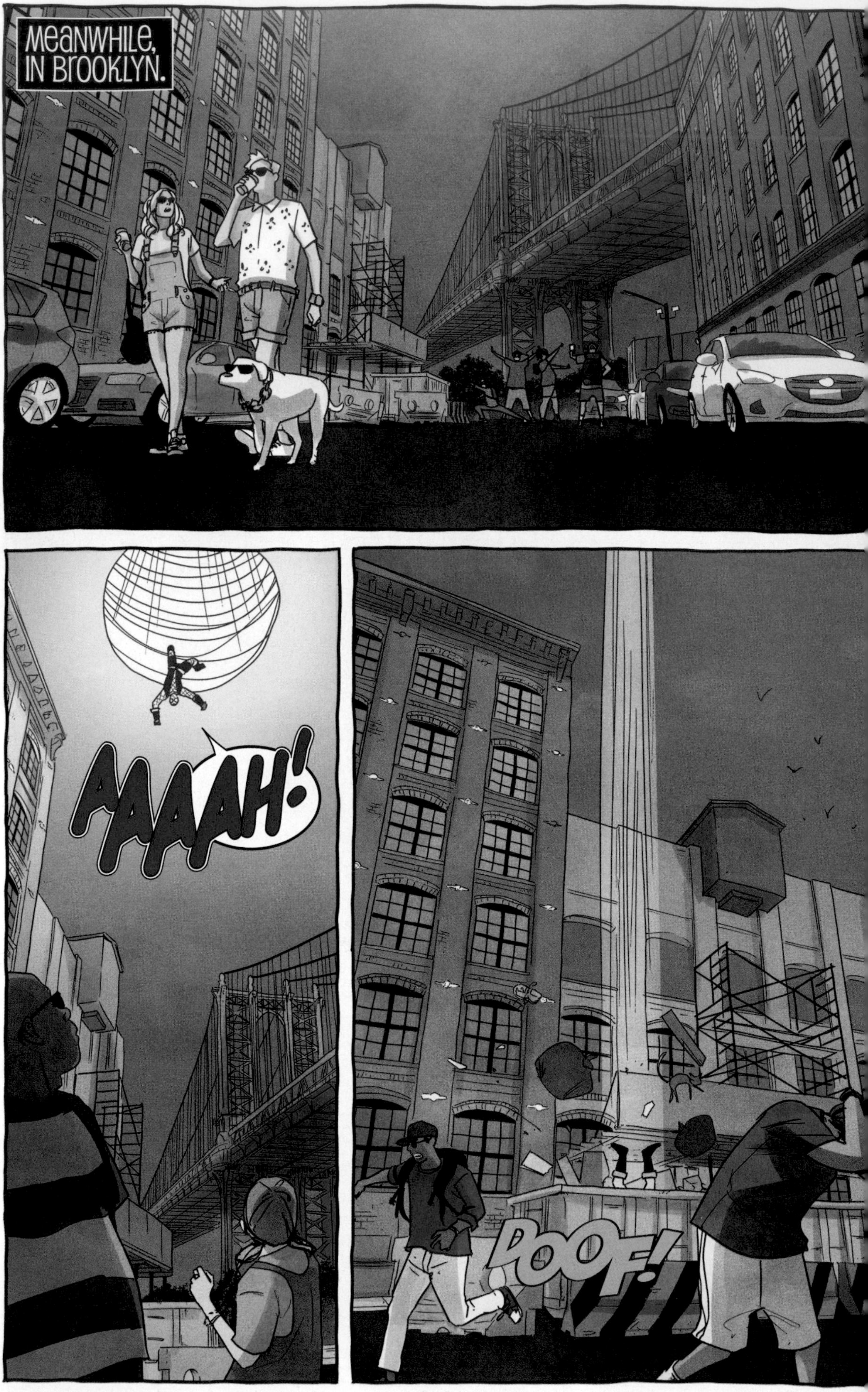
MEANWHILE, IN BROOKLYN.
AAAAH!
DOOF!

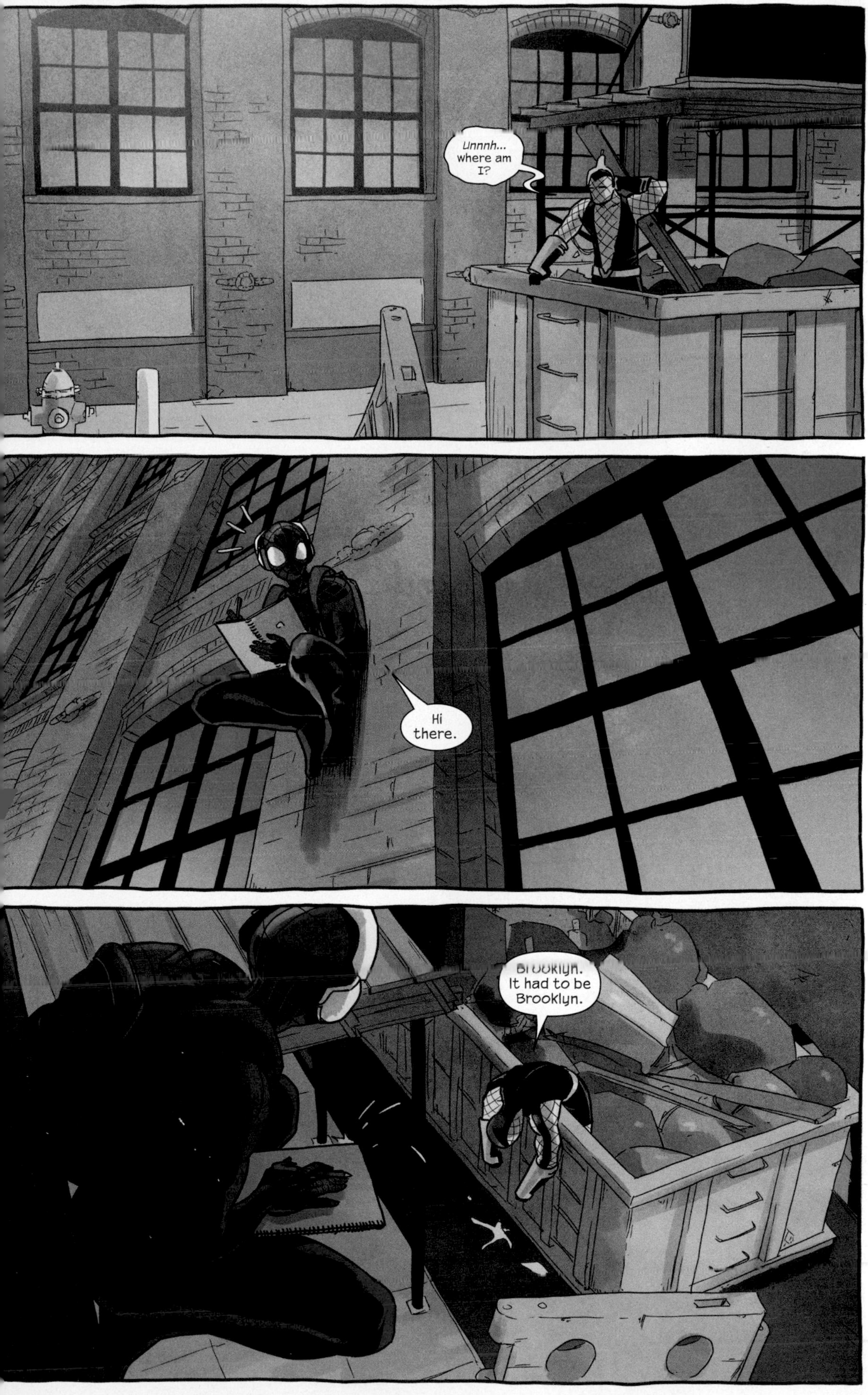
Unnnh... where am I?
Hi there.
Brooklyn. It had to be Brooklyn.

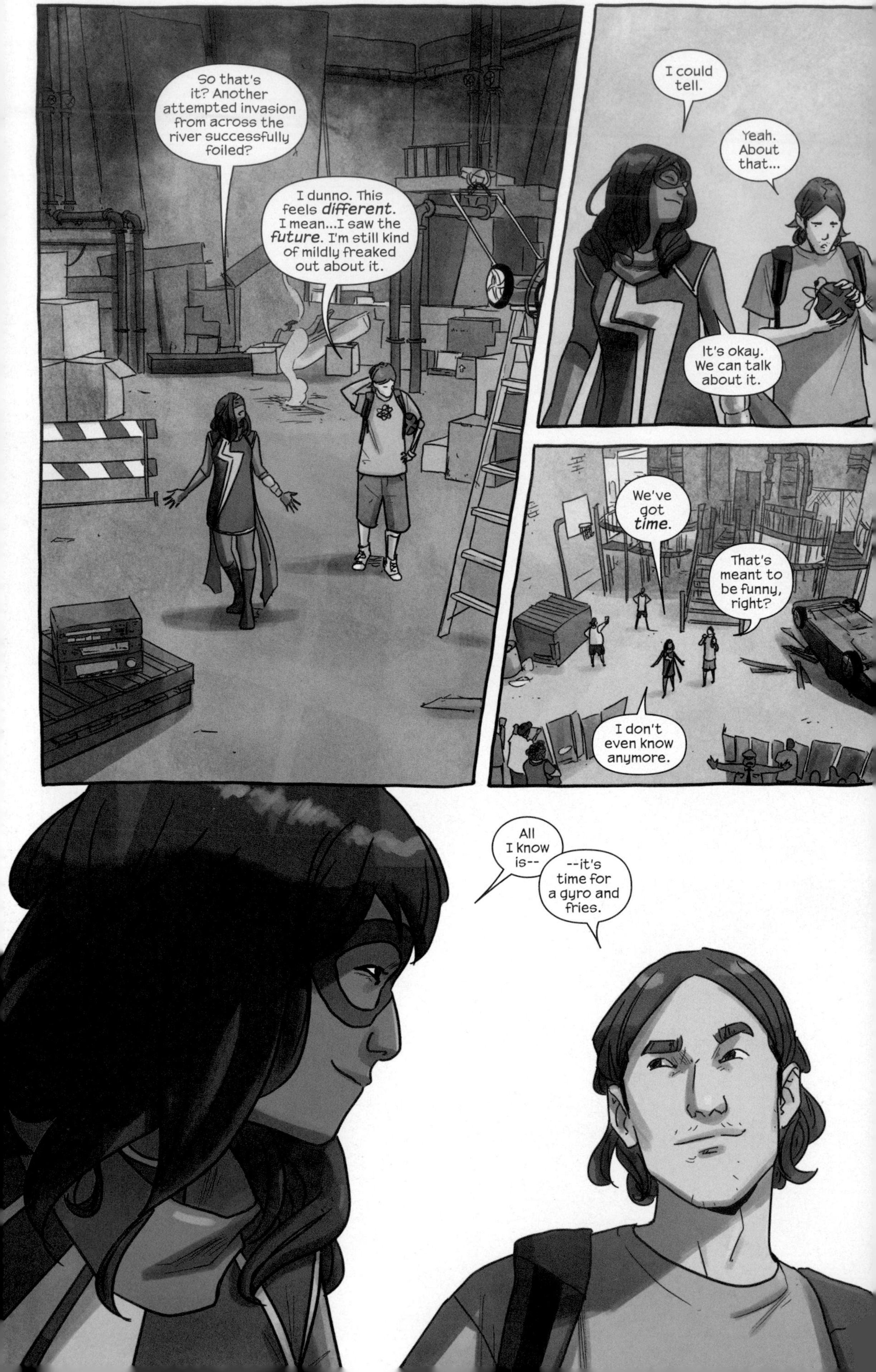
So that's it? Another attempted invasion from across the river successfully foiled?
I dunno. This feels *different*. I mean...I saw the *future*. I'm still kind of mildly freaked out about it.
I could tell.
Yeah. About that...
It's okay. We can talk about it.
We've got *time*.
That's meant to be funny, right?
I don't even know anymore.
All I know is--
--it's time for a gyro and fries.

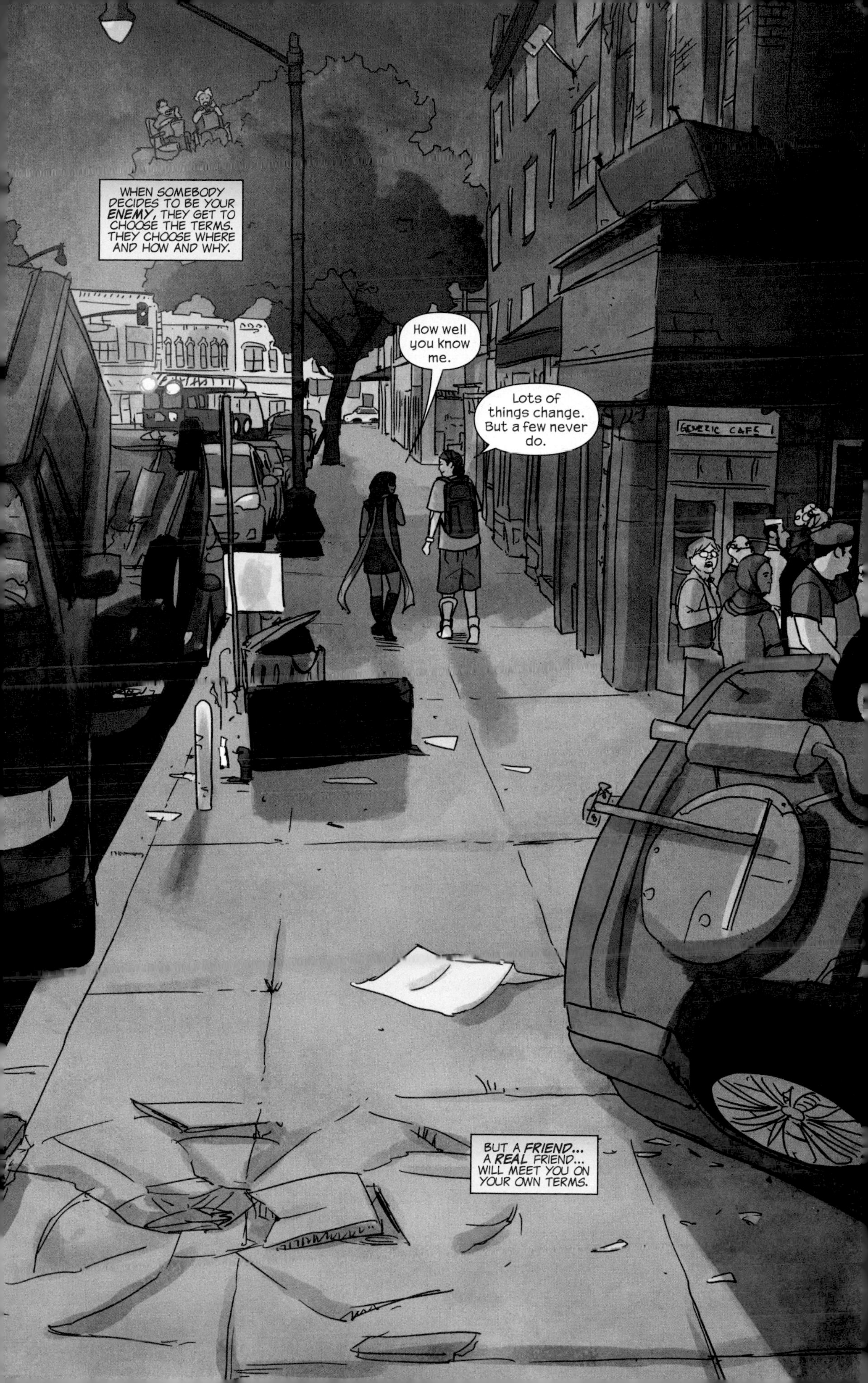
WHEN SOMEBODY DECIDES TO BE YOUR ENEMY, THEY GET TO CHOOSE THE TERMS. THEY CHOOSE WHERE AND HOW AND WHY.
How well you know me.
Lots of things change. But a few never do.
GENERIC CAFE
BUT A FRIEND... A REAL FRIEND... WILL MEET YOU ON YOUR OWN TERMS.

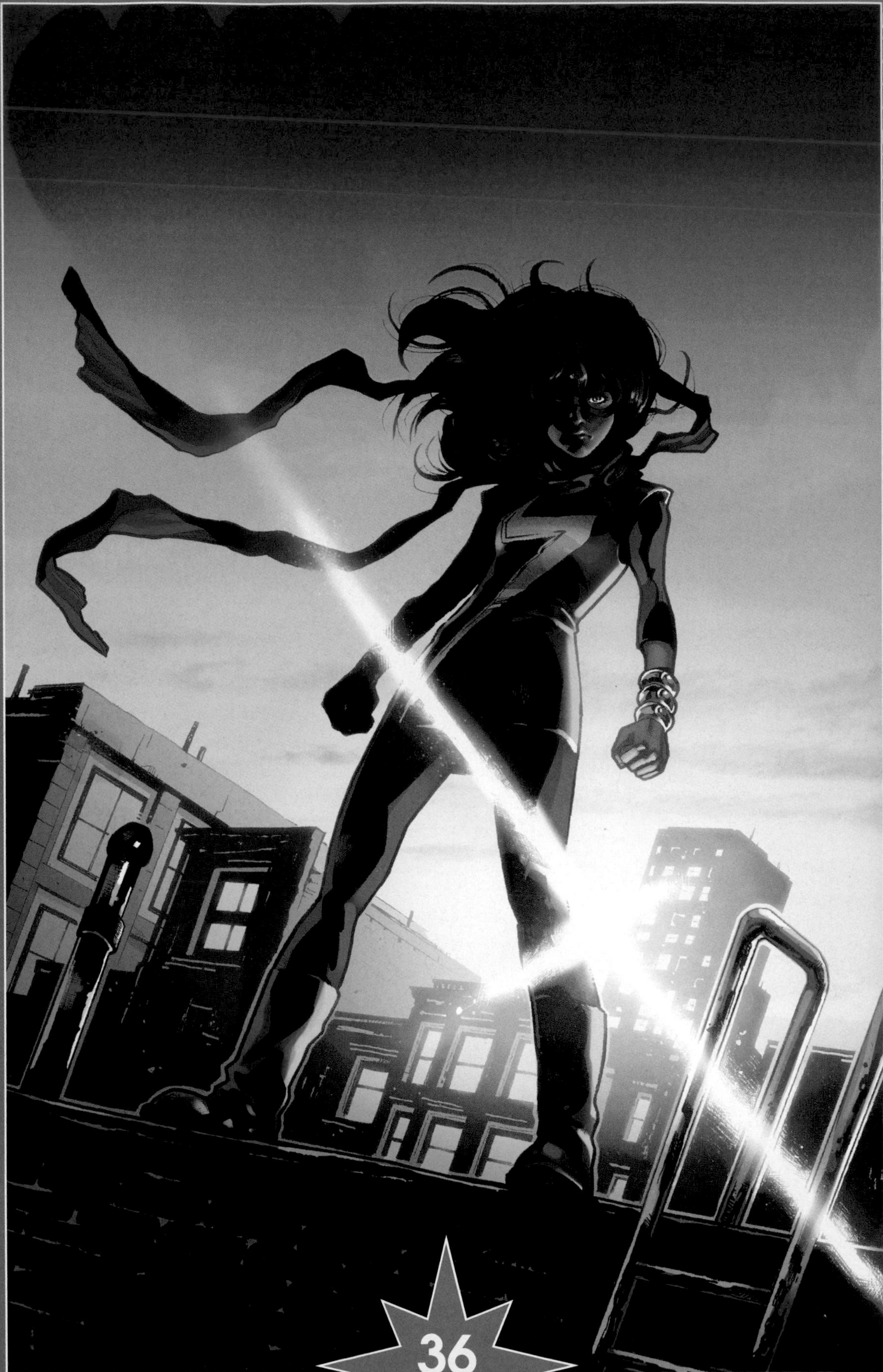
36

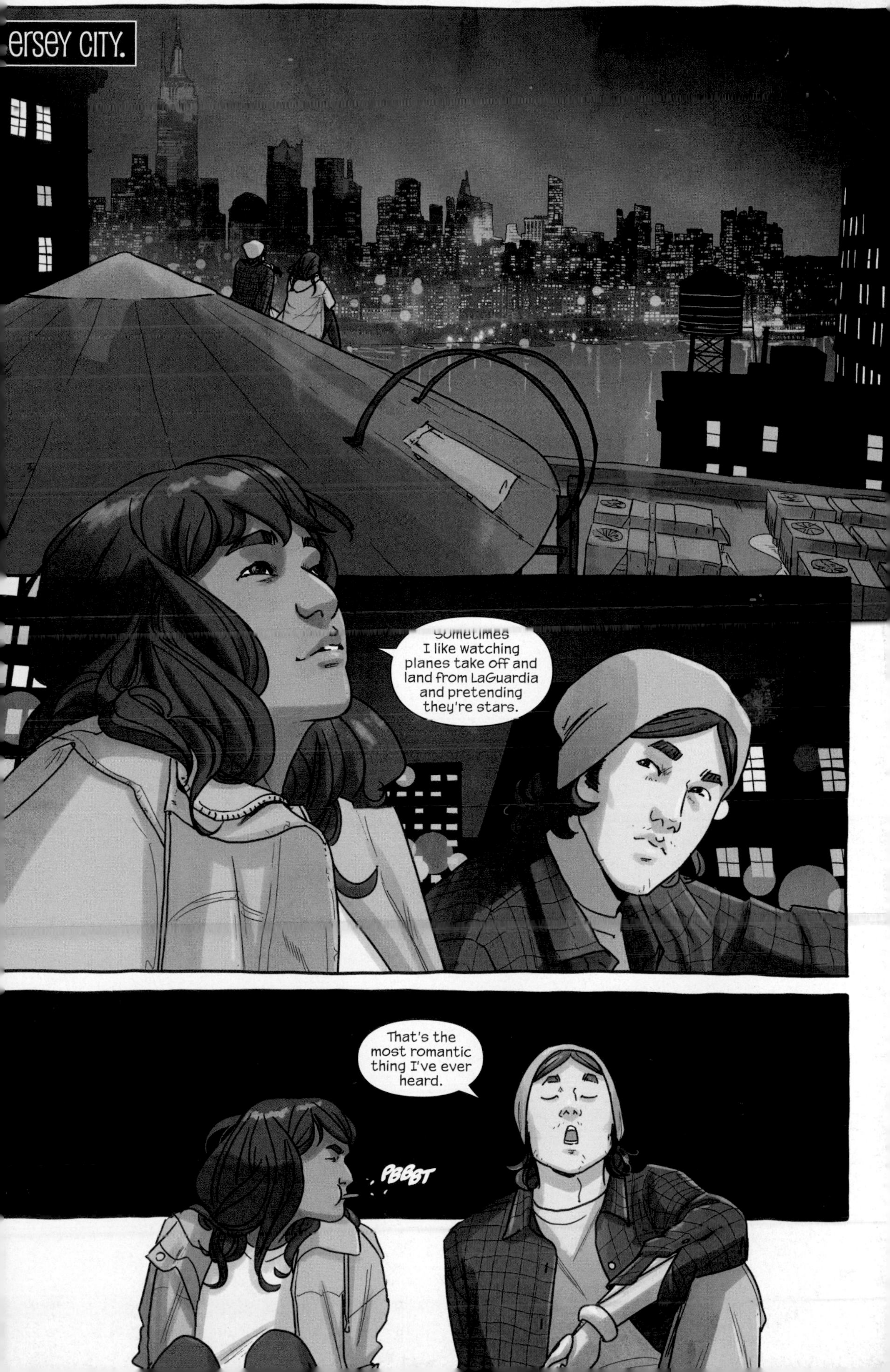
ersey CITY.
Sometimes I like watching planes take off and land from LaGuardia and pretending they're stars.
That's the most romantic thing I've ever heard.
PBBBT

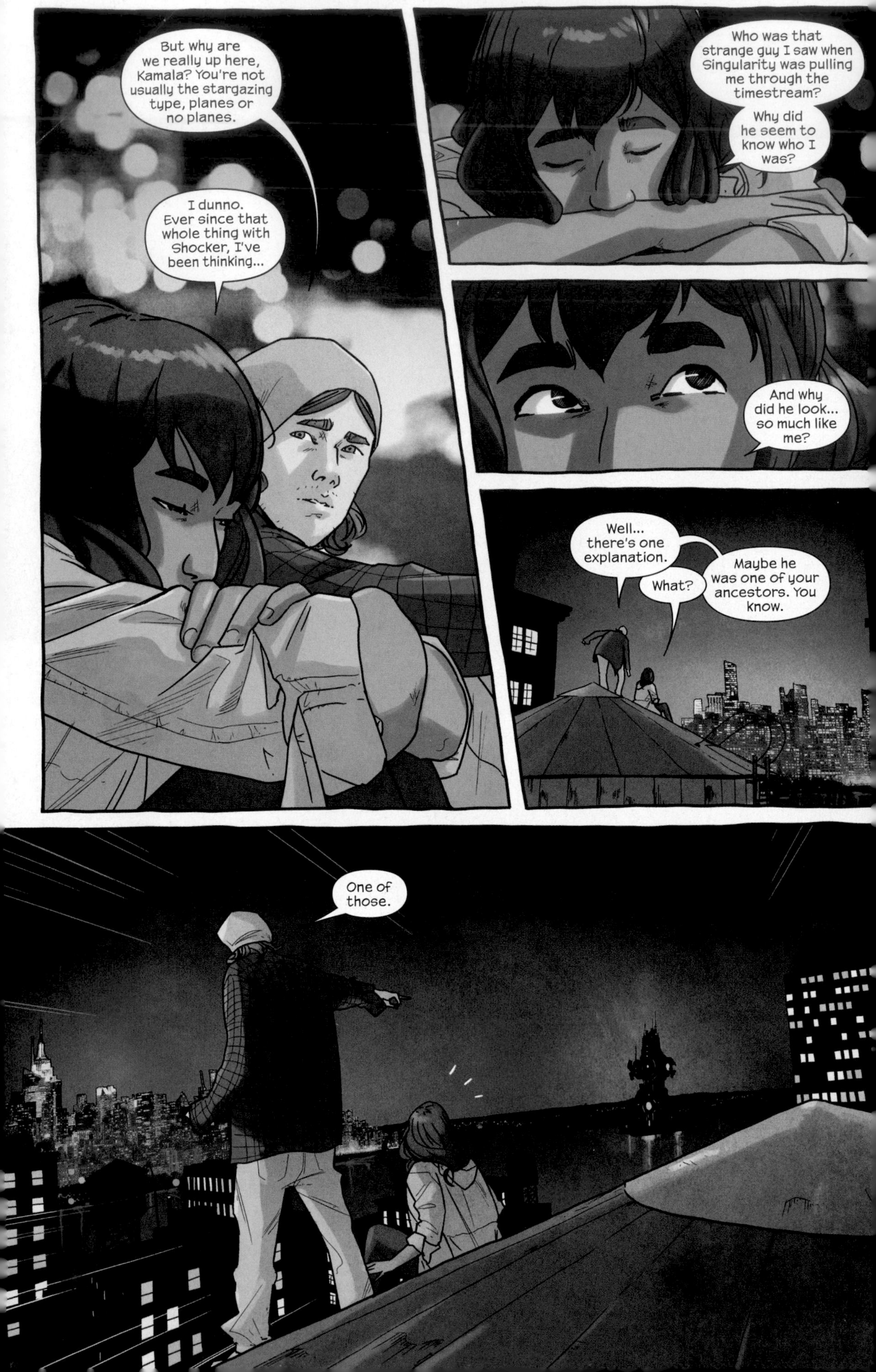
But why are we really up here, Kamala? You're not usually the stargazing type, planes or no planes.
I dunno. Ever since that whole thing with Shocker, I've been thinking...
Who was that strange guy I saw when Singularity was pulling me through the timestream?
Why did he seem to know who I was?
And why did he look... so much like me?
Well... there's one explanation.
What?
Maybe he was one of your ancestors. You know.
One of those.

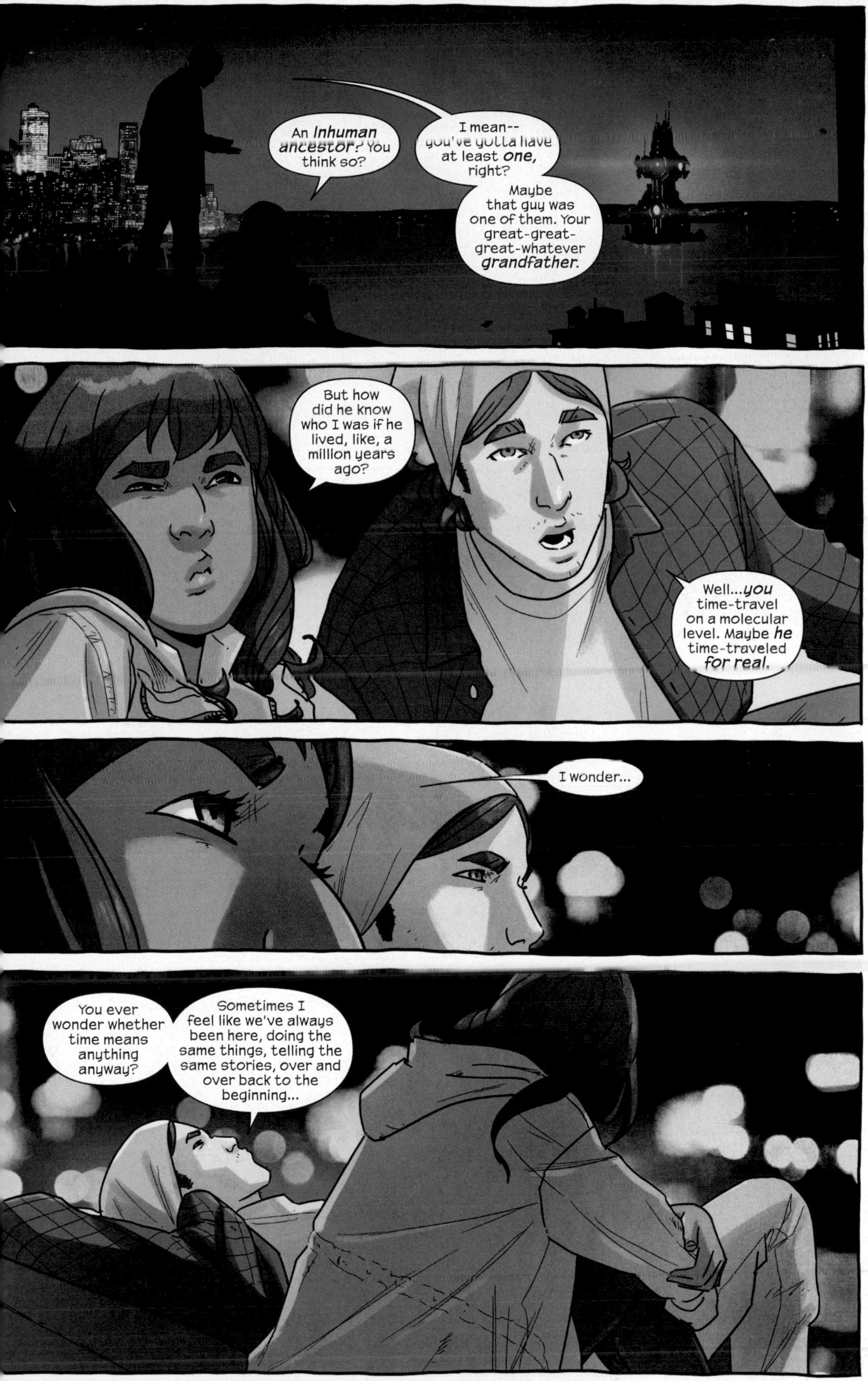
An Inhuman ancestor? You think so?
I mean-- you've gotta have at least one, right?
Maybe that guy was one of them. Your great-great-great-whatever grandfather.
But how did he know who I was if he lived, like, a million years ago?
Well...you time-travel on a molecular level. Maybe he time-traveled for real.
I wonder...
You ever wonder whether time means anything anyway?
Sometimes I feel like we've always been here, doing the same things, telling the same stories, over and over back to the beginning...

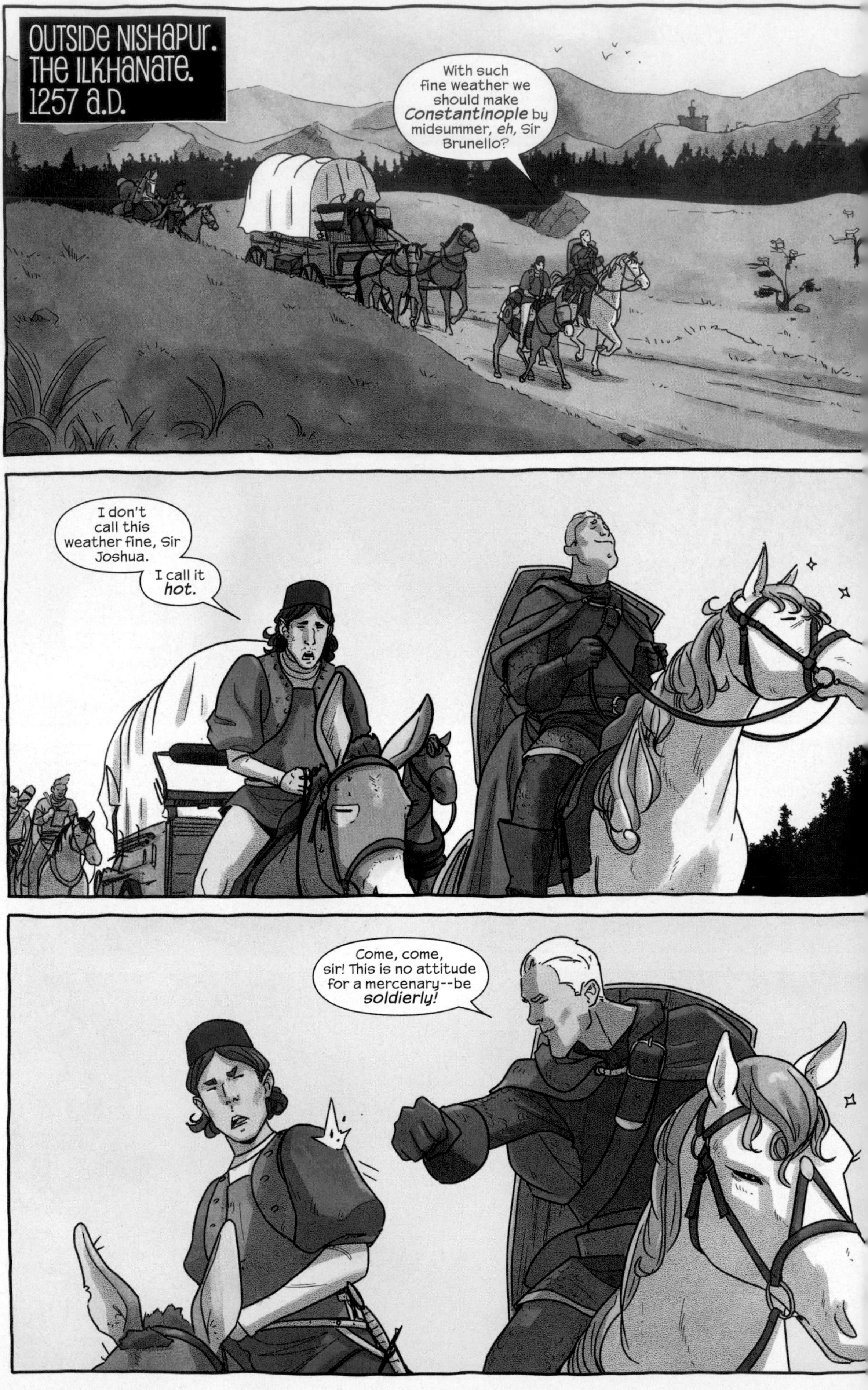
OUTSIDE NISHAPUR. THE ILKHANATE. 1257 A.D.
With such fine weather we should make *Constantinople* by midsummer, *eh,* Sir Brunello?
I don't call this weather fine, Sir Joshua.
I call it *hot.*
Come, come, sir! This is no attitude for a mercenary--be *soldierly!*

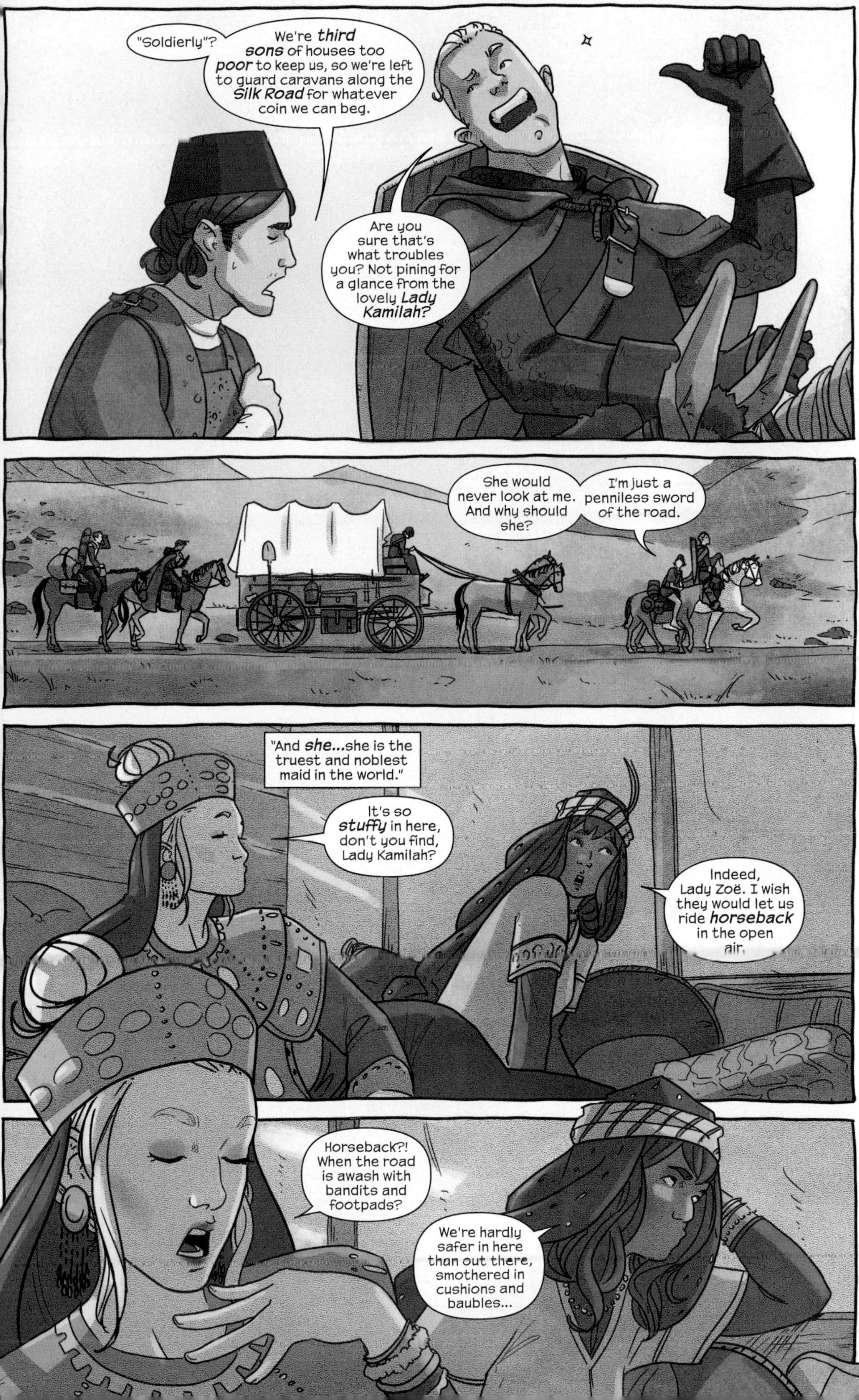
"Soldierly"?
We're third sons of houses too poor to keep us, so we're left to guard caravans along the Silk Road for whatever coin we can beg.
Are you sure that's what troubles you? Not pining for a glance from the lovely Lady Kamilah?
She would never look at me. And why should she?
I'm just a penniless sword of the road.
"And she...she is the truest and noblest maid in the world."
It's so stuffy in here, don't you find, Lady Kamilah?
Indeed, Lady Zoë. I wish they would let us ride horseback in the open air.
Horseback?! When the road is awash with bandits and footpads?
We're hardly safer in here than out there, smothered in cushions and baubles...

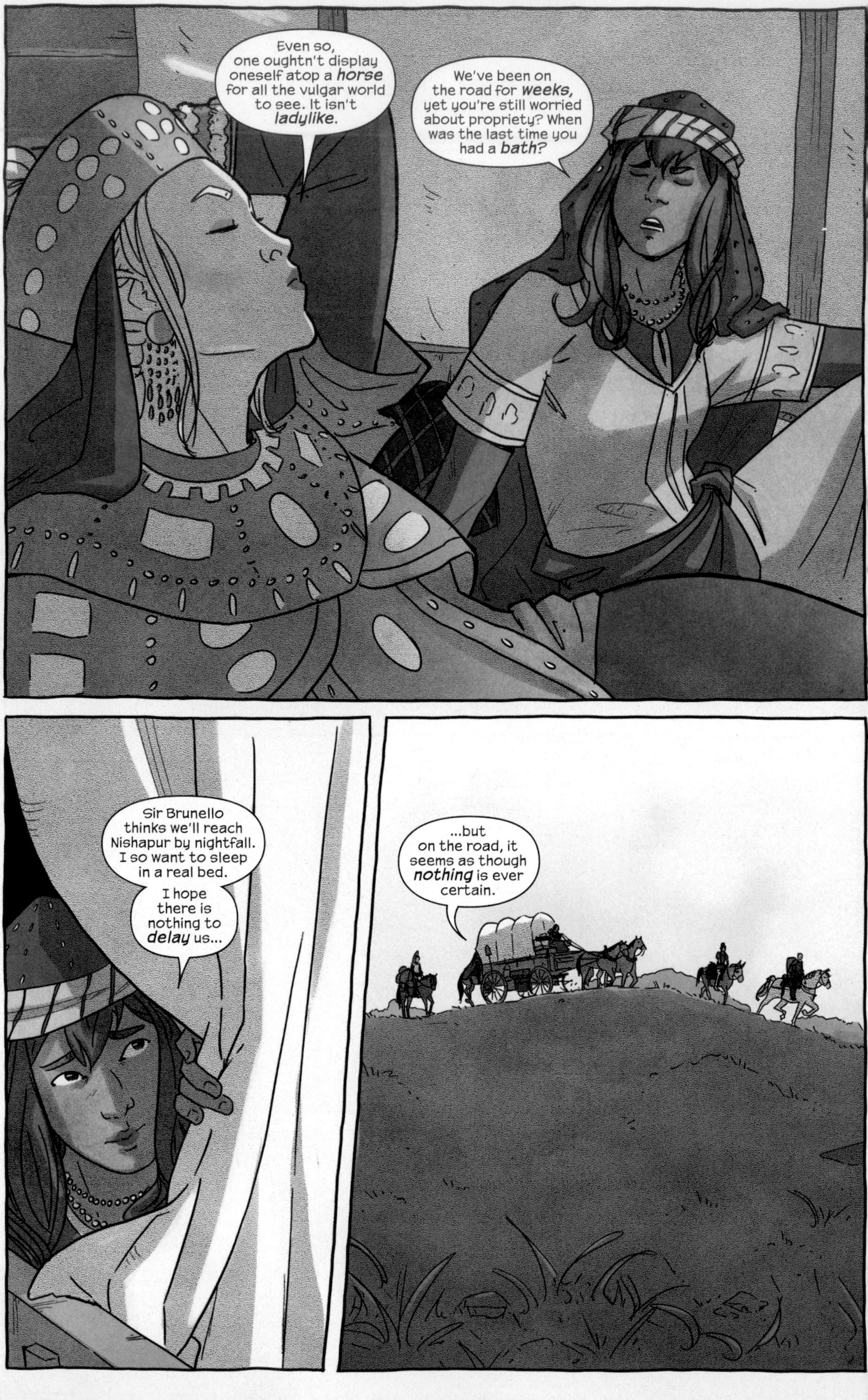
Even so, one oughtn't display oneself atop a *horse* for all the vulgar world to see. It isn't *ladylike*.
We've been on the road for *weeks*, yet you're still worried about propriety? When was the last time you had a *bath*?
Sir Brunello thinks we'll reach Nishapur by nightfall. I so want to sleep in a real bed.
I hope there is nothing to *delay* us...
...but on the road, it seems as though *nothing* is ever certain.

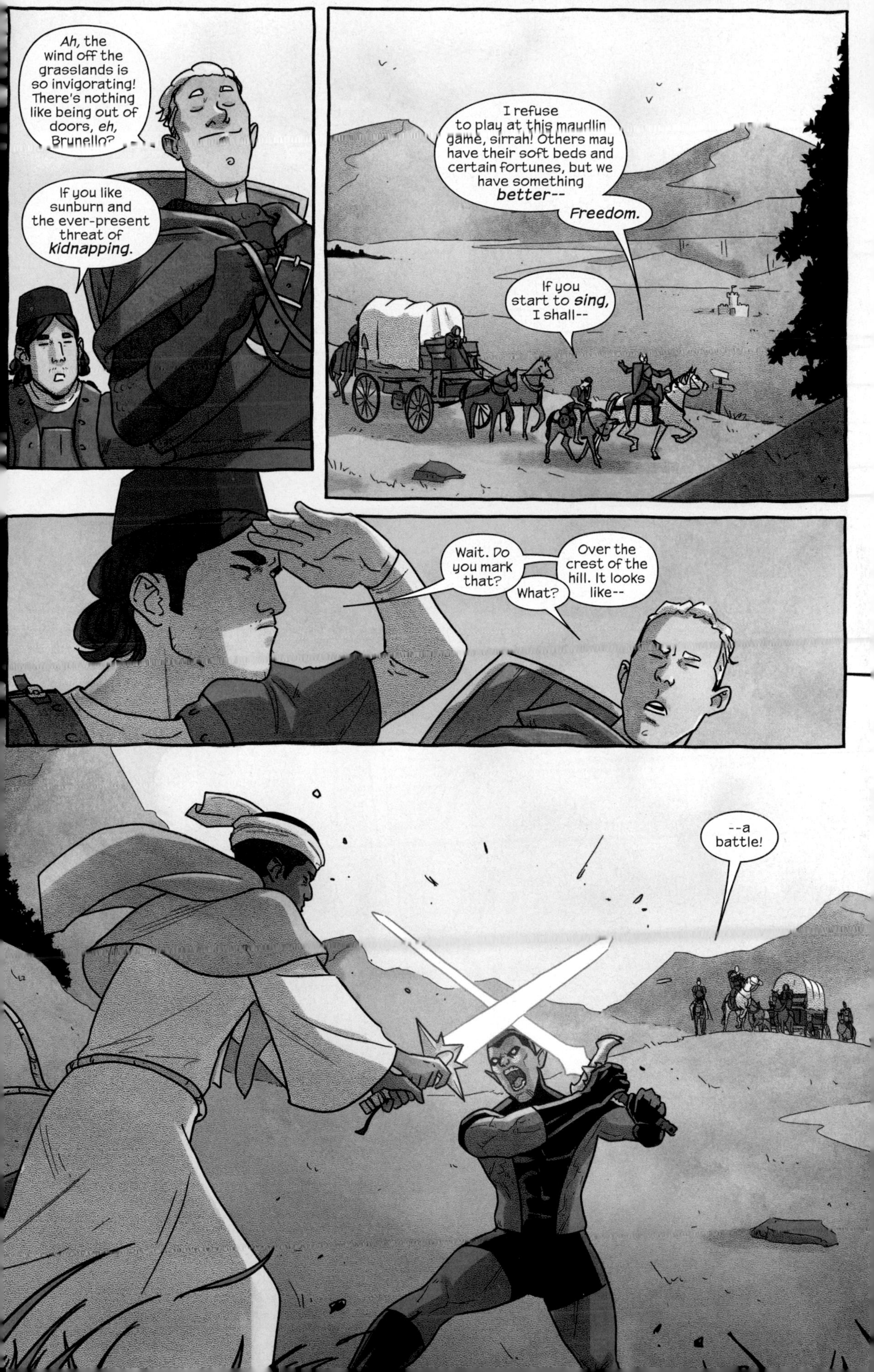

Ah, the wind off the grasslands is so invigorating! There's nothing like being out of doors, eh, Brunello?
If you like sunburn and the ever-present threat of kidnapping.
I refuse to play at this maudlin game, sirrah! Others may have their soft beds and certain fortunes, but we have something better--
Freedom.
If you start to sing, I shall--
Wait. Do you mark that?
What?
Over the crest of the hill. It looks like--
--a battle!

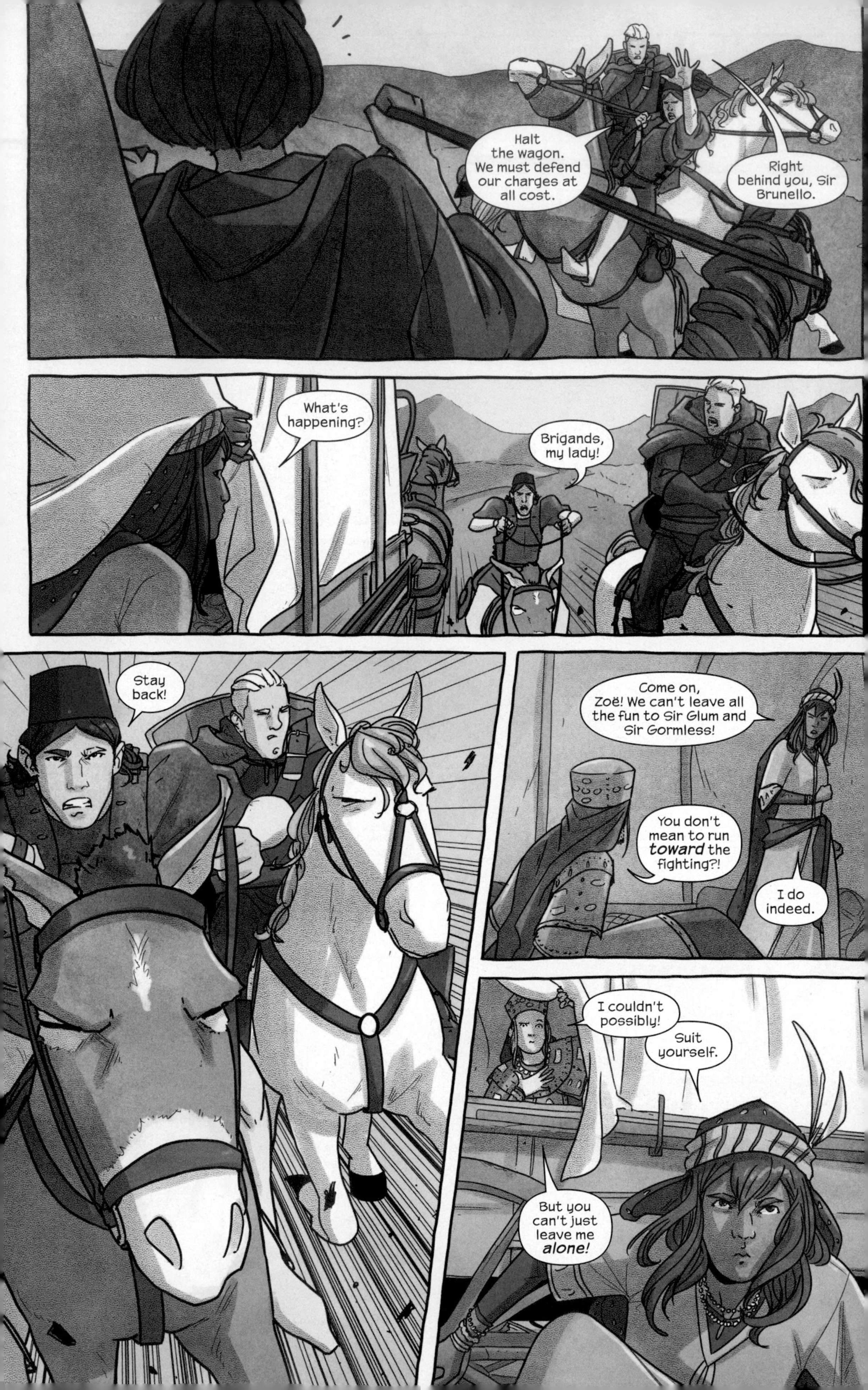
Halt the wagon. We must defend our charges at all cost.
Right behind you, Sir Brunello.
What's happening?
Brigands, my lady!
Stay back!
Come on, Zoë! We can't leave all the fun to Sir Glum and Sir Gormless!
You don't mean to run *toward* the fighting?!
I do indeed.
I couldn't possibly!
Suit yourself.
But you can't just leave me *alone!*

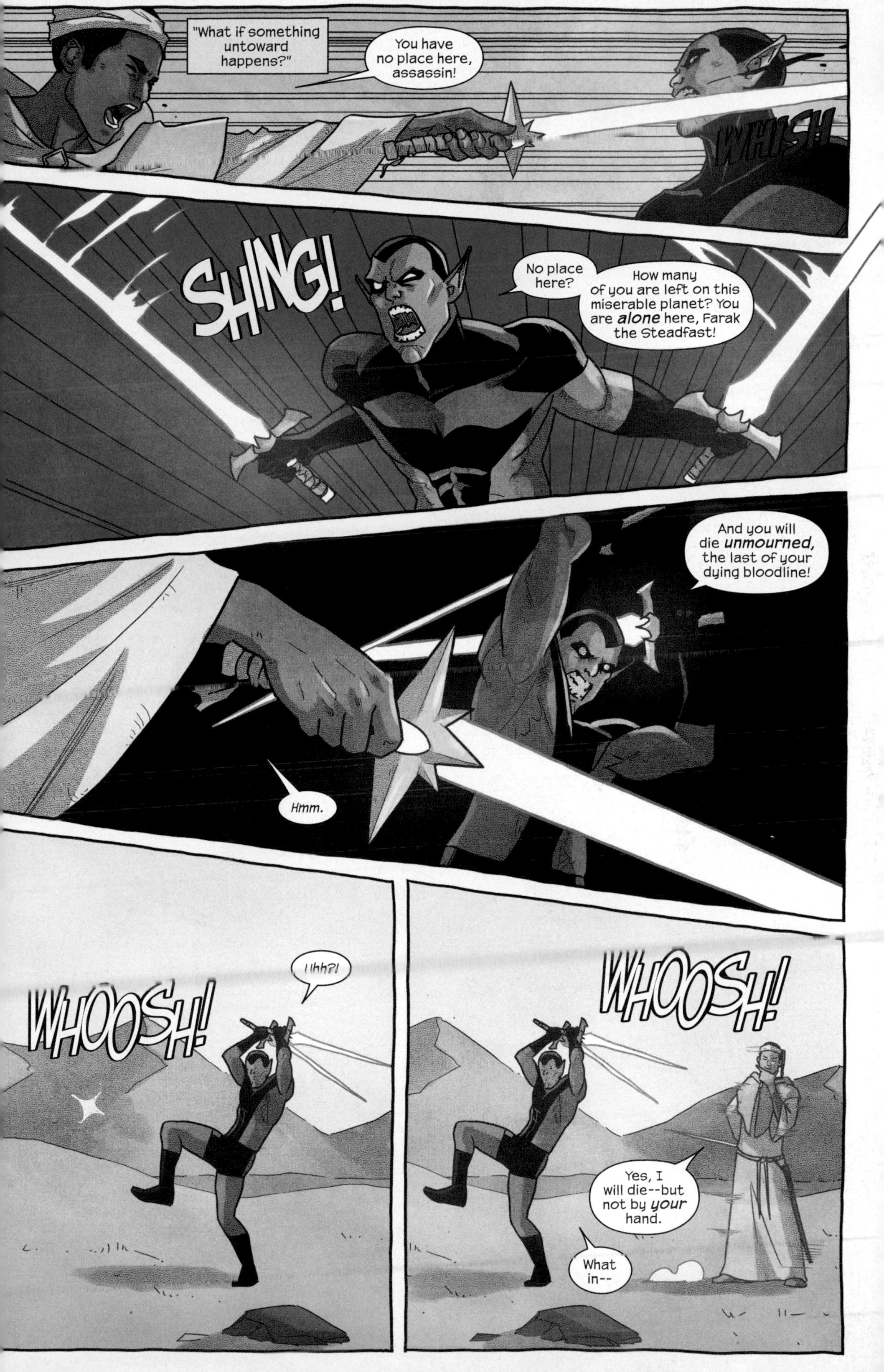
"What if something untoward happens?"
You have no place here, assassin!
WHISH
SHING!
No place here?
How many of you are left on this miserable planet? You are *alone* here, Farak the Steadfast!
And you will die *unmourned,* the last of your dying bloodline!
Hmm.
WHOOSH!
Uhh?!
WHOOSH!
Yes, I will die--but not by *your* hand.
What in--

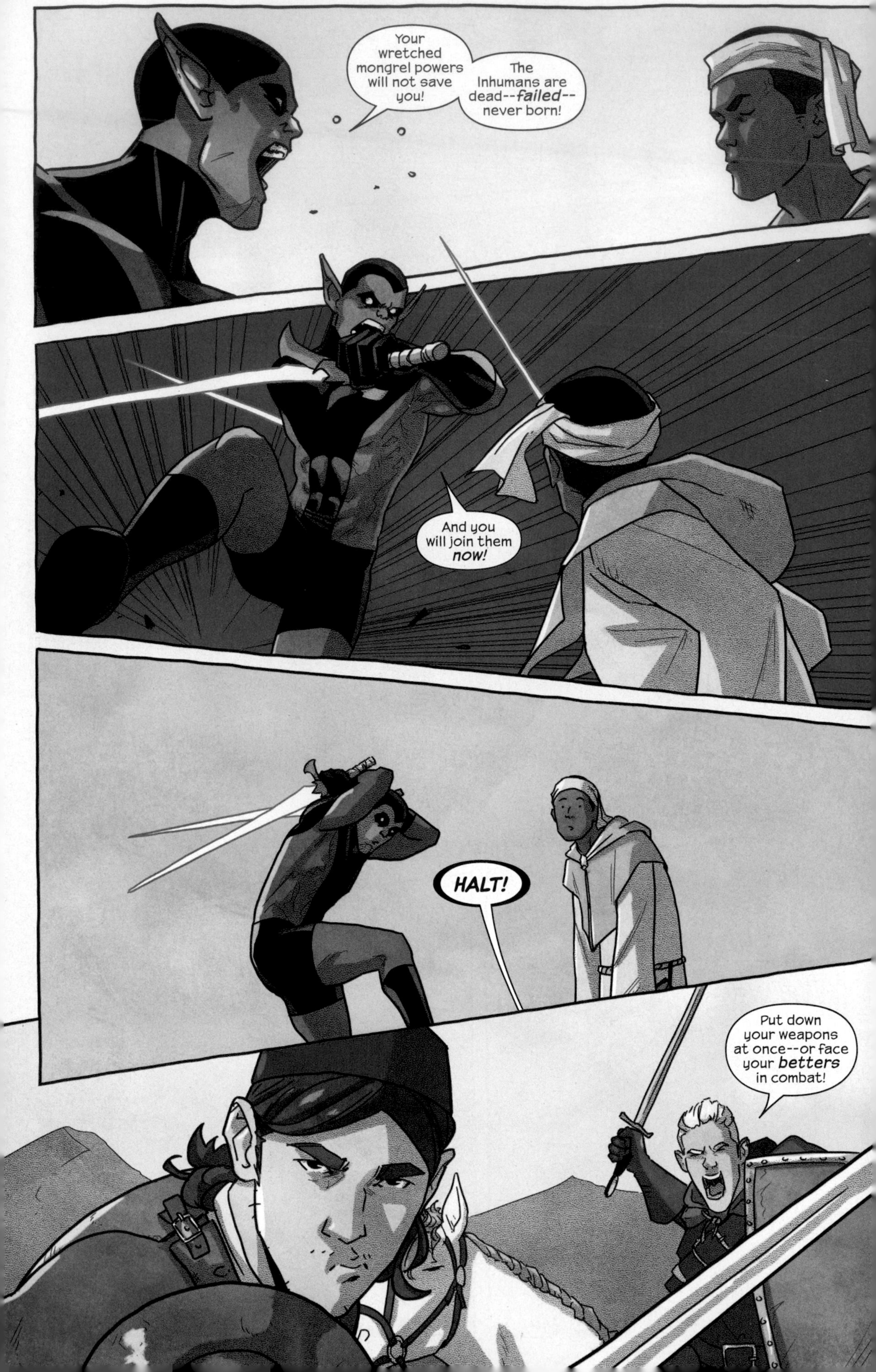
Your wretched mongrel powers will not save you!
The Inhumans are dead--failed--never born!
And you will join them now!
HALT!
Put down your weapons at once--or face your betters in combat!

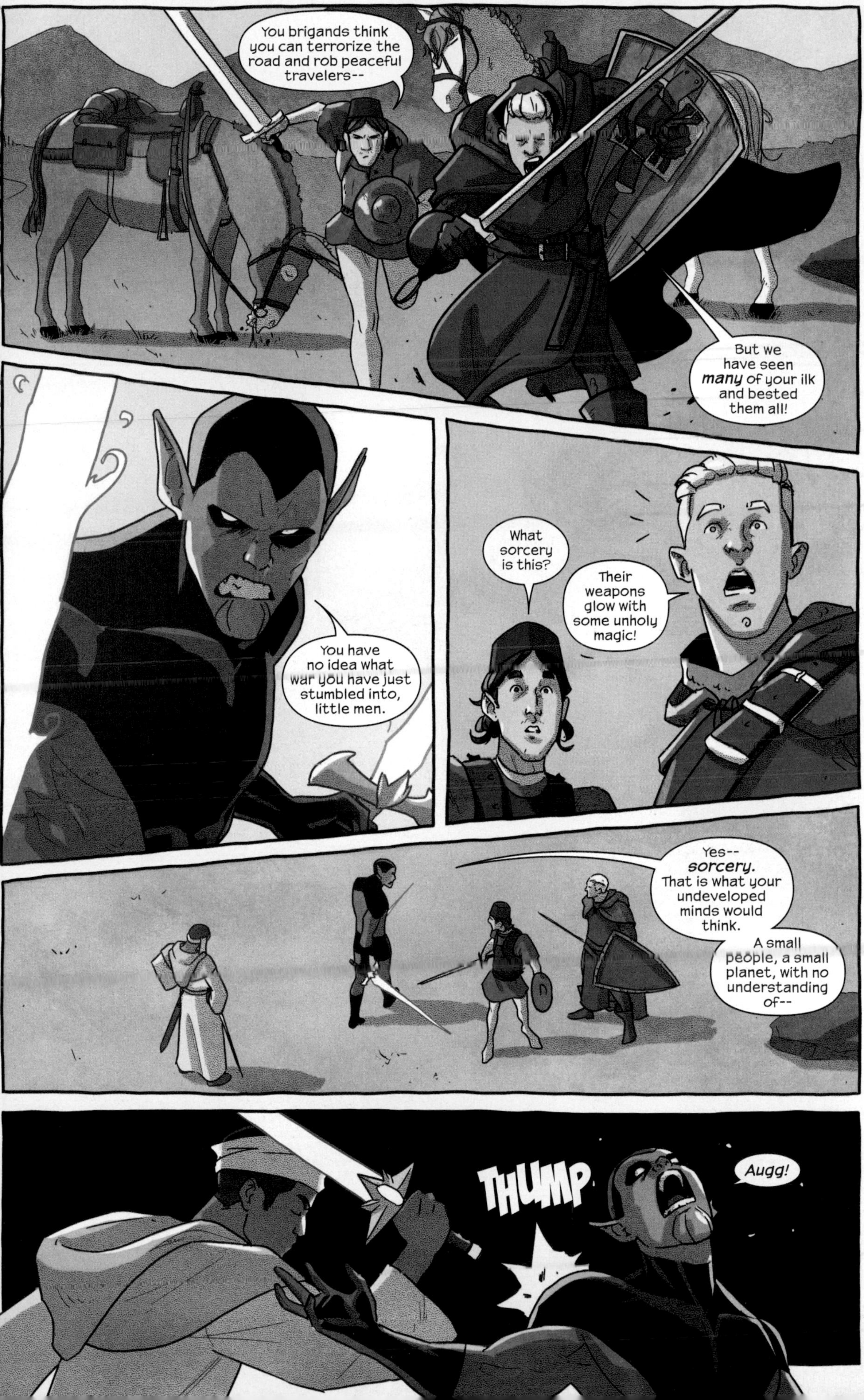
You brigands think you can terrorize the road and rob peaceful travelers--
But we have seen *many* of your ilk and bested them all!
You have no idea what war you have just stumbled into, little men.
What sorcery is this?
Their weapons glow with some unholy magic!
Yes-- *sorcery.* That is what your undeveloped minds would think.
A small people, a small planet, with no understanding of--
THUMP
Augg!

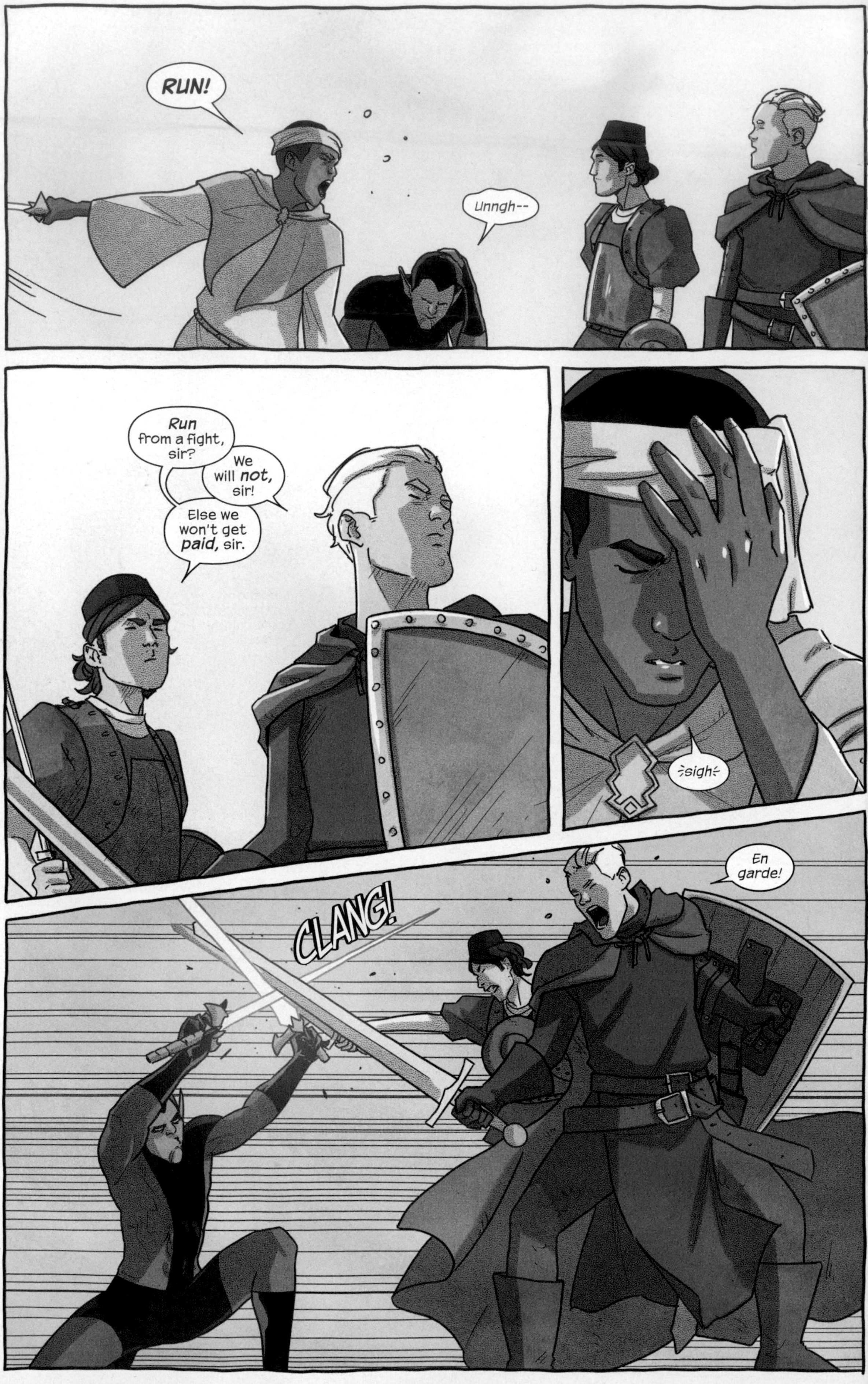
RUN!
Unngh--
Run from a fight, sir?
We will not, sir!
Else we won't get paid, sir.
sigh
En garde!
CLANG!

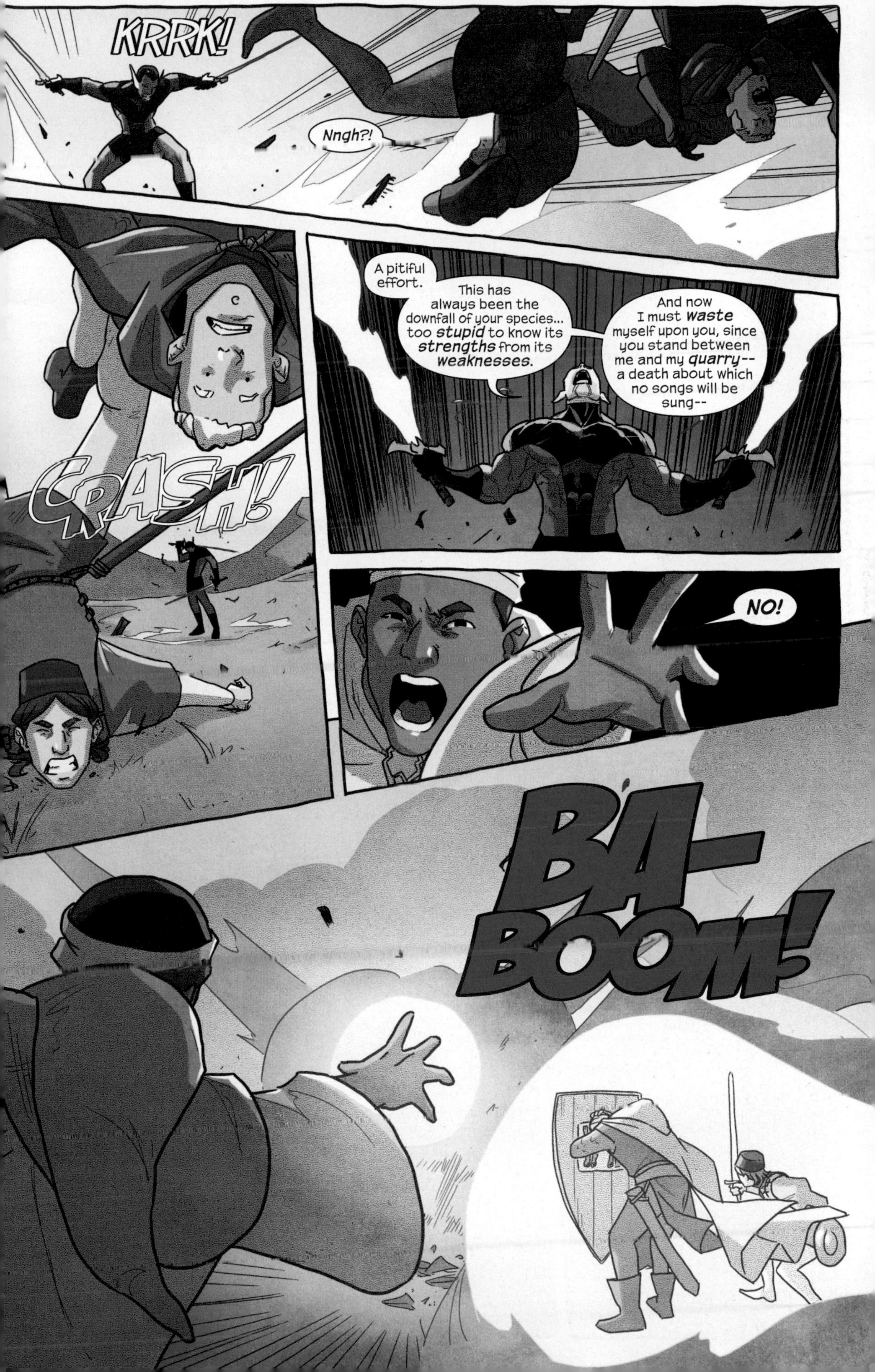
KRRK!
Nngh?!
CRASH!
A pitiful effort.
This has always been the downfall of your species... too stupid to know its strengths from its weaknesses.
And now I must waste myself upon you, since you stand between me and my quarry-- a death about which no songs will be sung--
NO!
BA-BOOM!

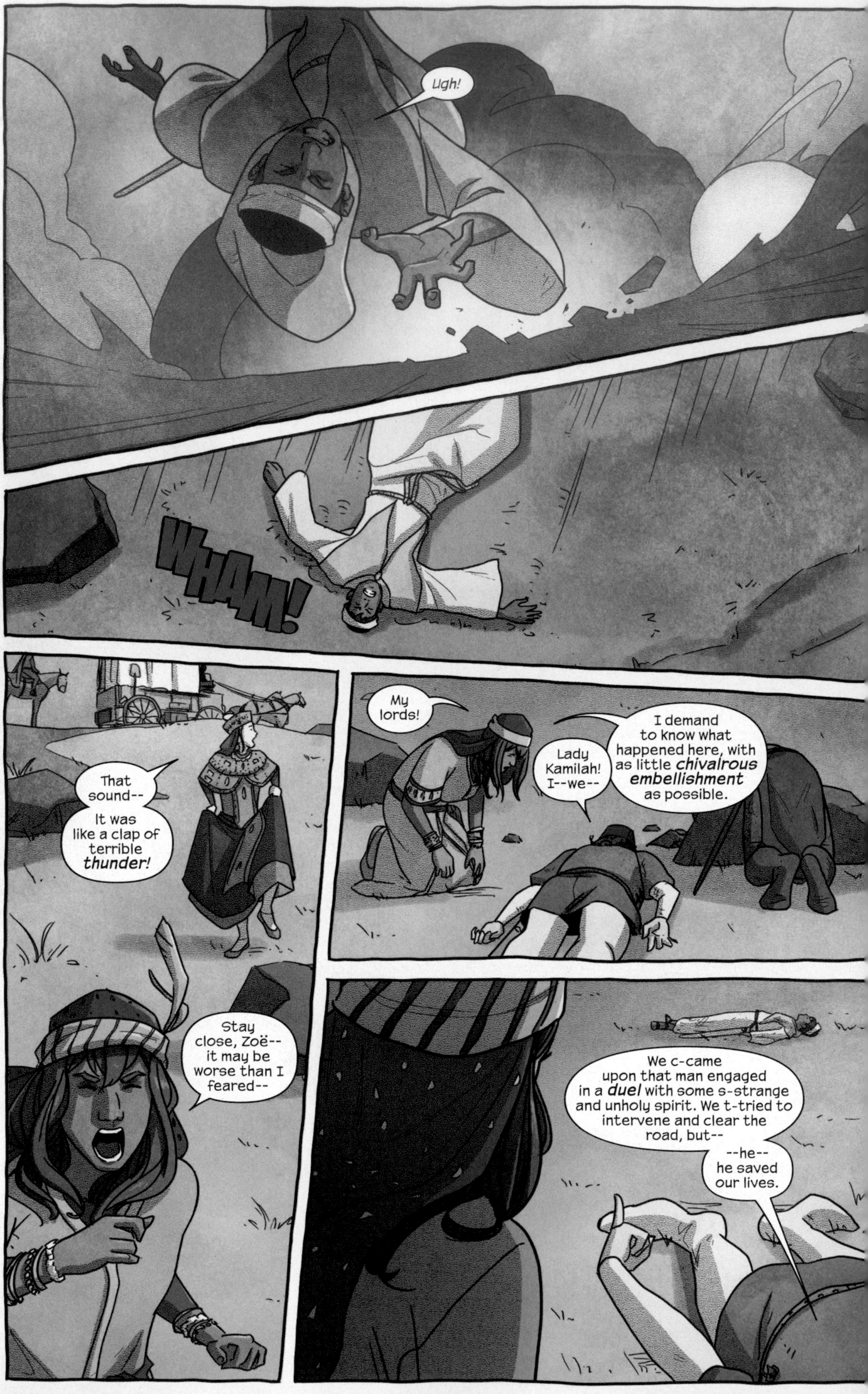
Ugh!
WHAM!
That sound-- It was like a clap of terrible *thunder!*
My lords!
Lady Kamilah! I--we--
I demand to know what happened here, with as little *chivalrous embellishment* as possible.
Stay close, Zoë-- it may be worse than I feared--
We c-came upon that man engaged in a *duel* with some s-strange and unholy spirit. We t-tried to intervene and clear the road, but--
--he-- he saved our lives.

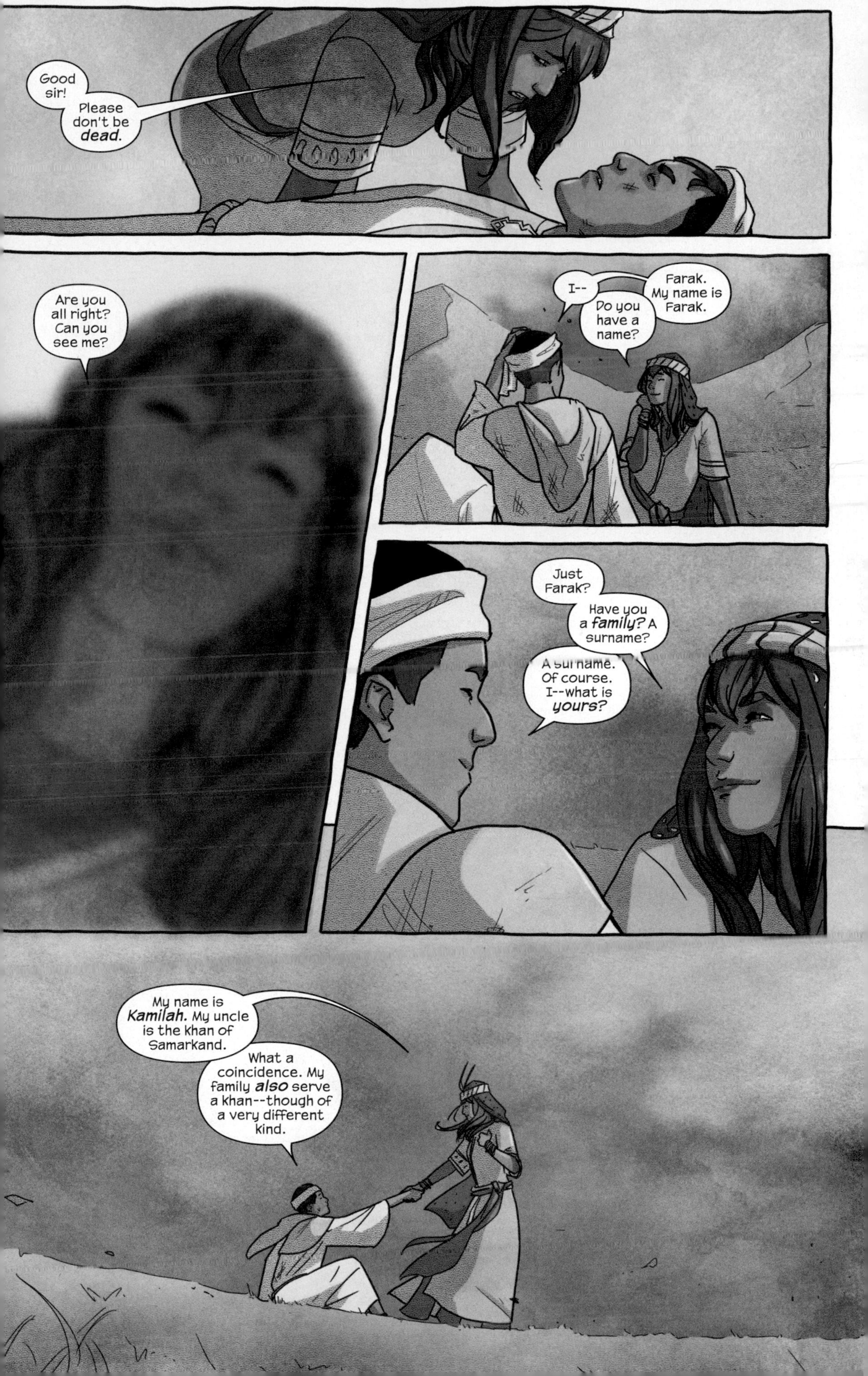
Good sir!
Please don't be dead.
Are you all right? Can you see me?
I--
Do you have a name?
Farak. My name is Farak.
Just Farak?
Have you a family? A surname?
A surname. Of course. I--what is yours?
My name is Kamilah. My uncle is the khan of Samarkand.
What a coincidence. My family also serve a khan--though of a very different kind.

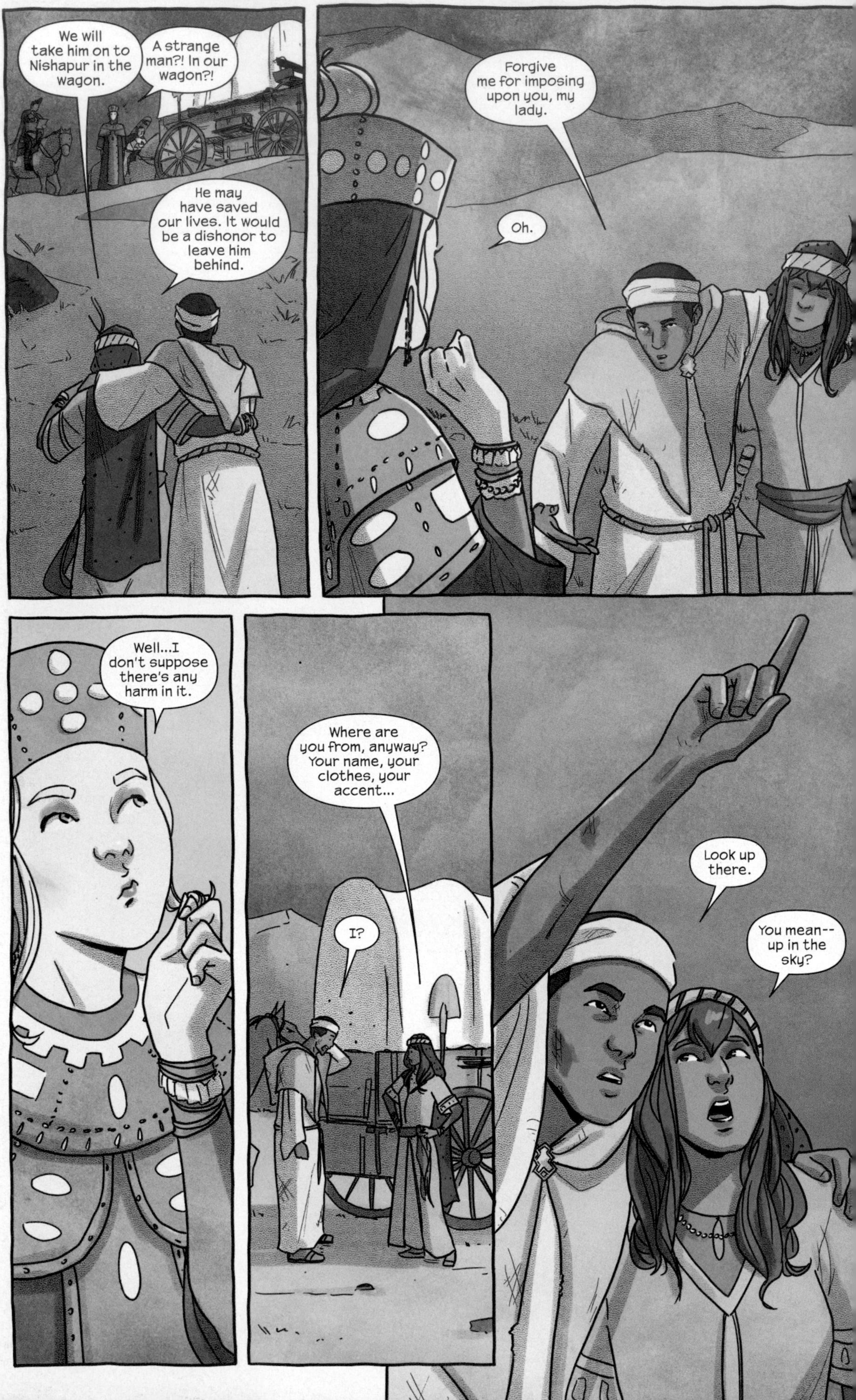
We will take him on to Nishapur in the wagon.
A strange man?! In our wagon?!
He may have saved our lives. It would be a dishonor to leave him behind.
Forgive me for imposing upon you, my lady.
Oh.
Well...I don't suppose there's any harm in it.
Where are you from, anyway? Your name, your clothes, your accent...
I?
Look up there.
You mean--up in the sky?

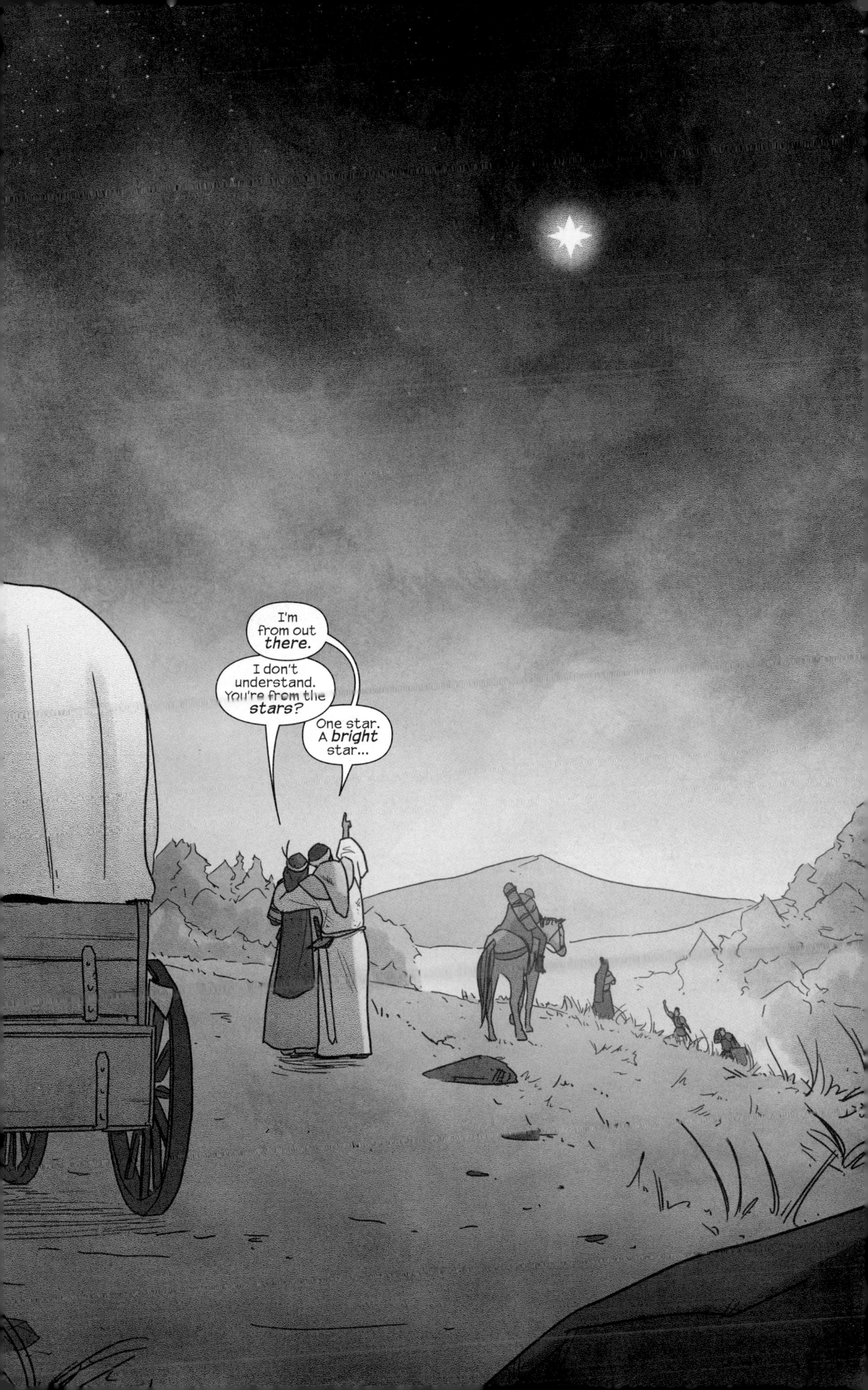
I'm from out *there.*
I don't understand. You're from the *stars?*
One star. A *bright* star...

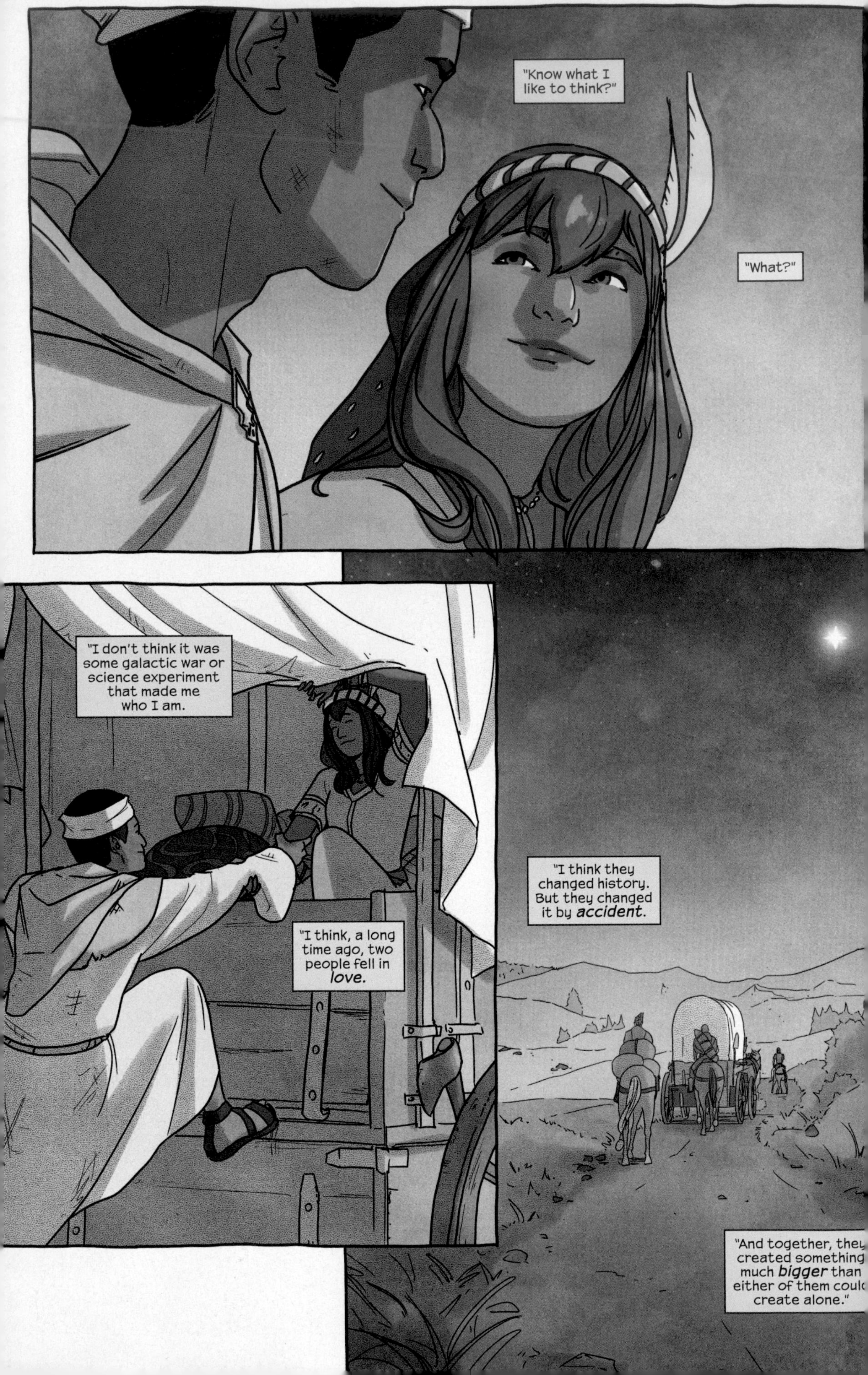
"Know what I like to think?"
"What?"
"I don't think it was some galactic war or science experiment that made me who I am.
"I think, a long time ago, two people fell in *love.*
"I think they changed history. But they changed it by *accident*.
"And together, they created something much *bigger* than either of them could create alone."

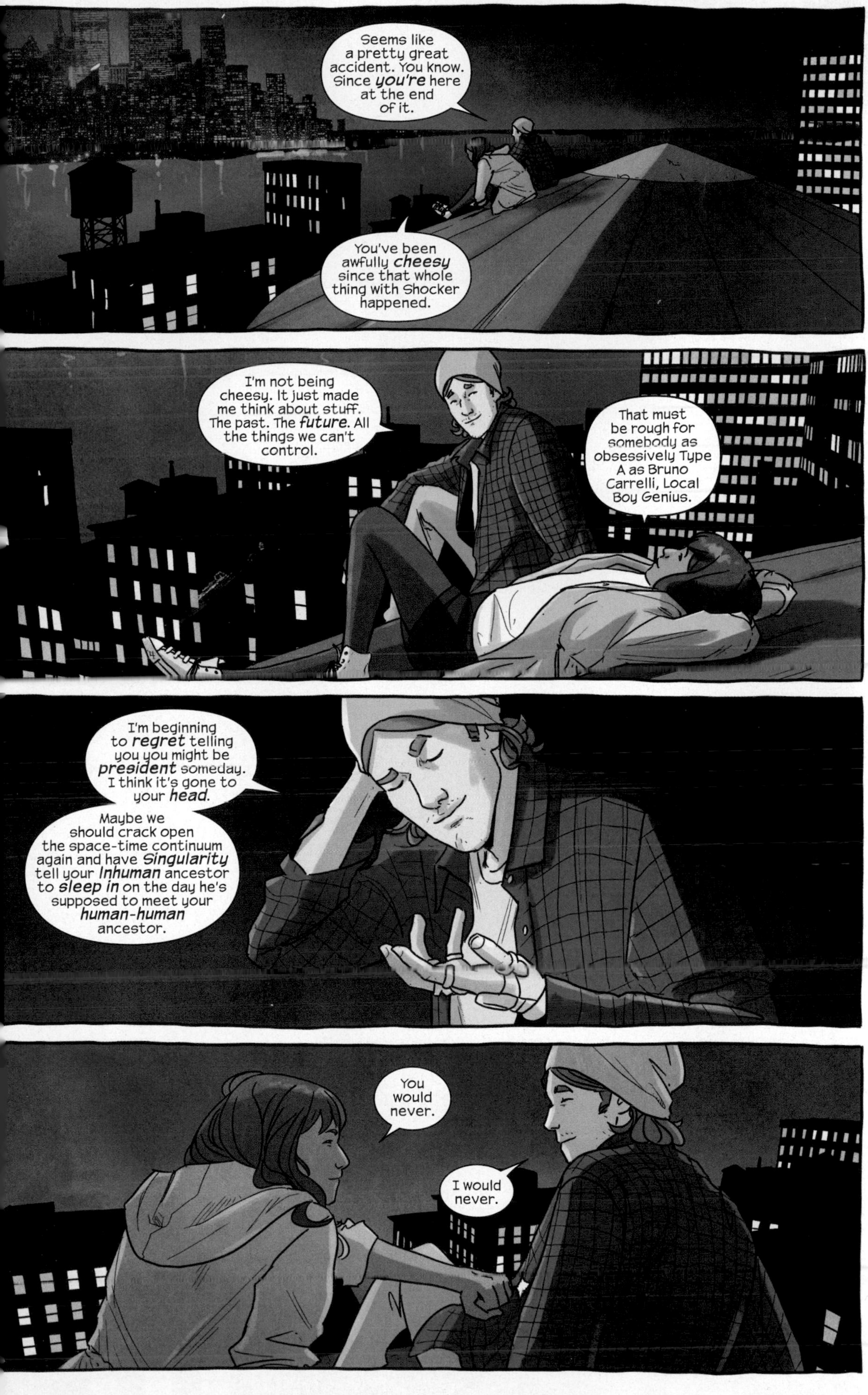
Seems like a pretty great accident. You know. Since *you're* here at the end of it.
You've been awfully *cheesy* since that whole thing with Shocker happened.
I'm not being cheesy. It just made me think about stuff. The past. The *future*. All the things we can't control.
That must be rough for somebody as obsessively Type A as Bruno Carrelli, Local Boy Genius.
I'm beginning to *regret* telling you you might be *president* someday. I think it's gone to your *head*.
Maybe we should crack open the space-time continuum again and have *Singularity* tell your *Inhuman* ancestor to *sleep in* on the day he's supposed to meet your *human-human* ancestor.
You would never.
I would never.

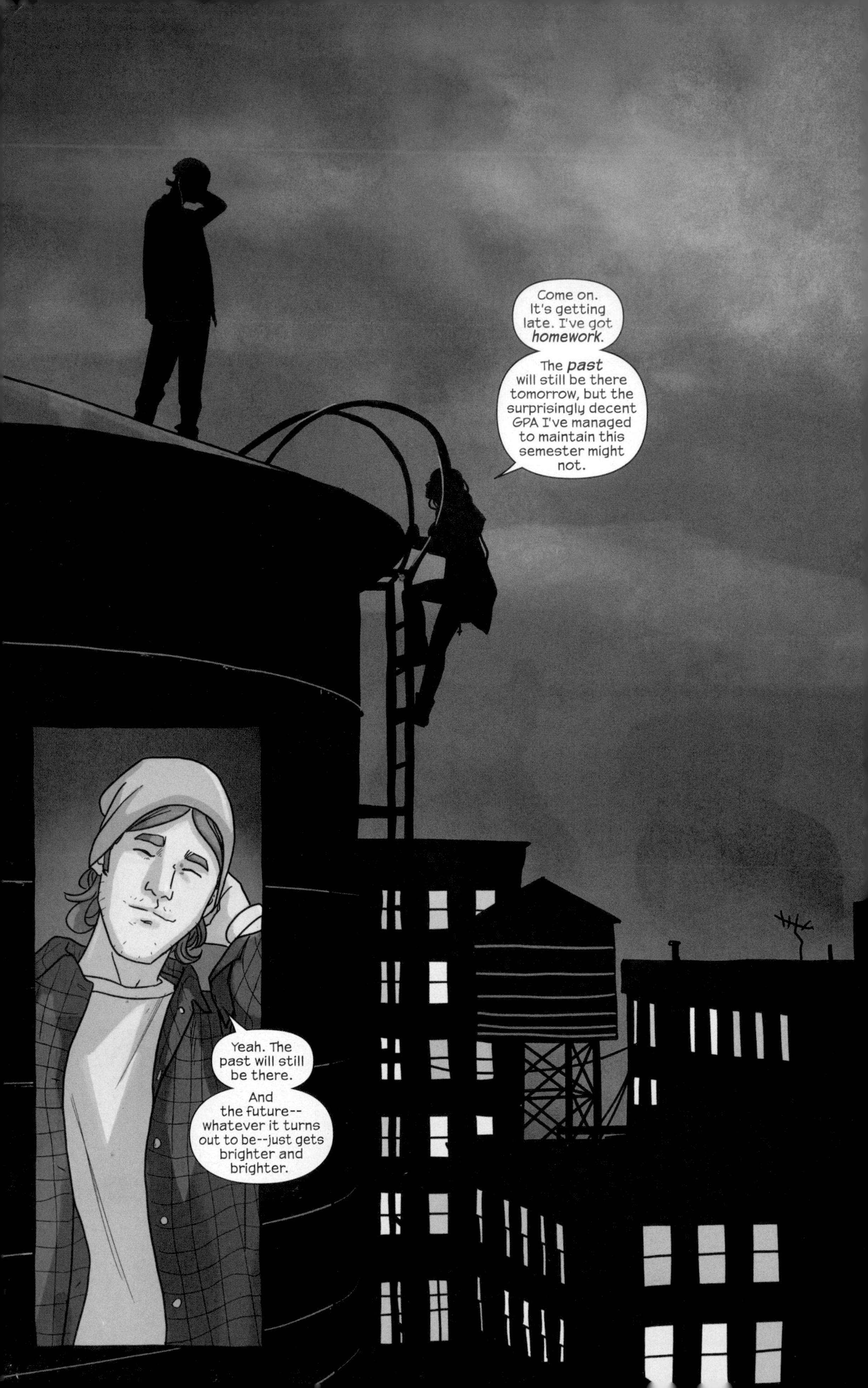
Come on. It's getting late. I've got *homework*.
The *past* will still be there tomorrow, but the surprisingly decent GPA I've managed to maintain this semester might not.
Yeah. The past will still be there.
And the future--whatever it turns out to be--just gets brighter and brighter.

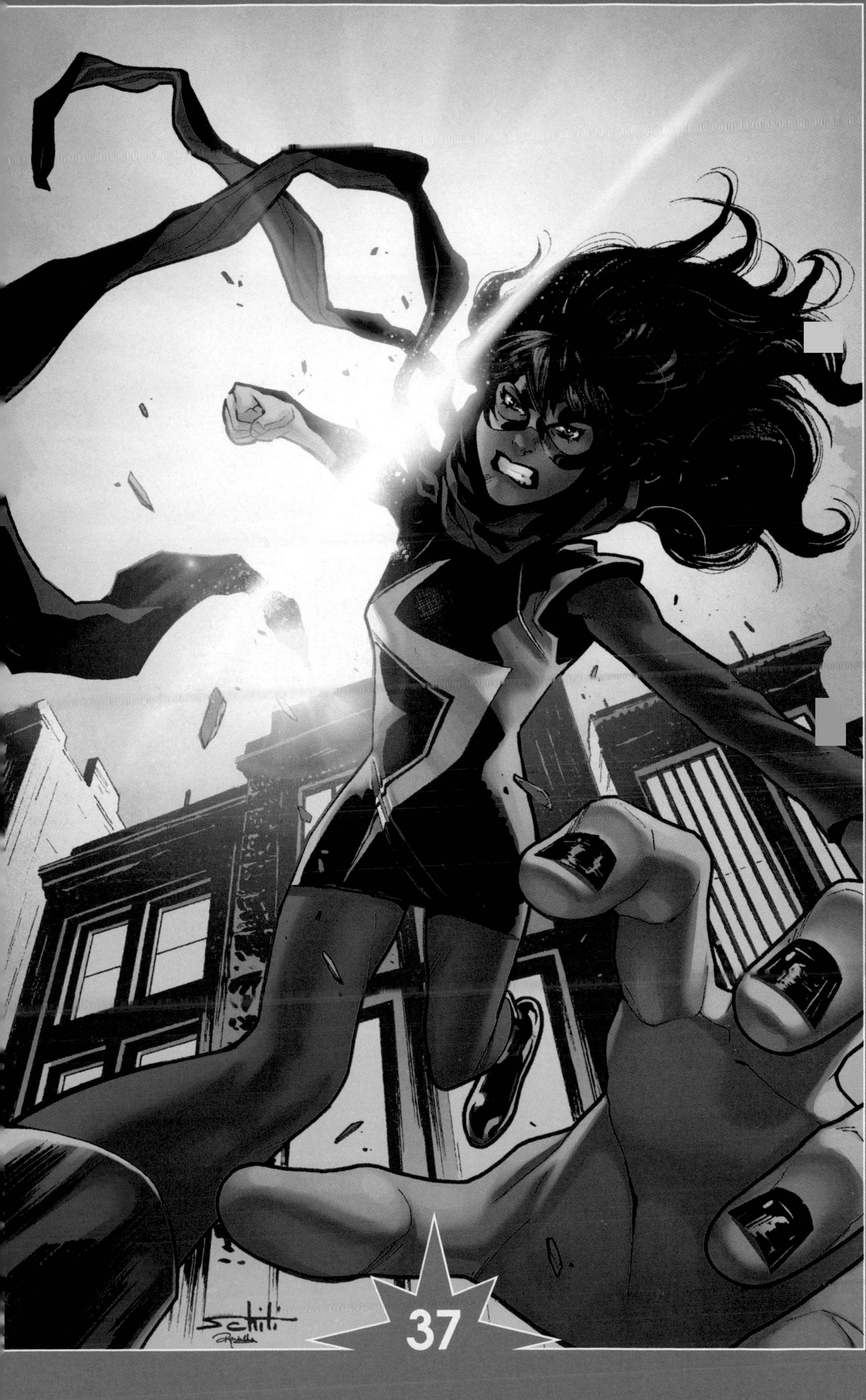
37

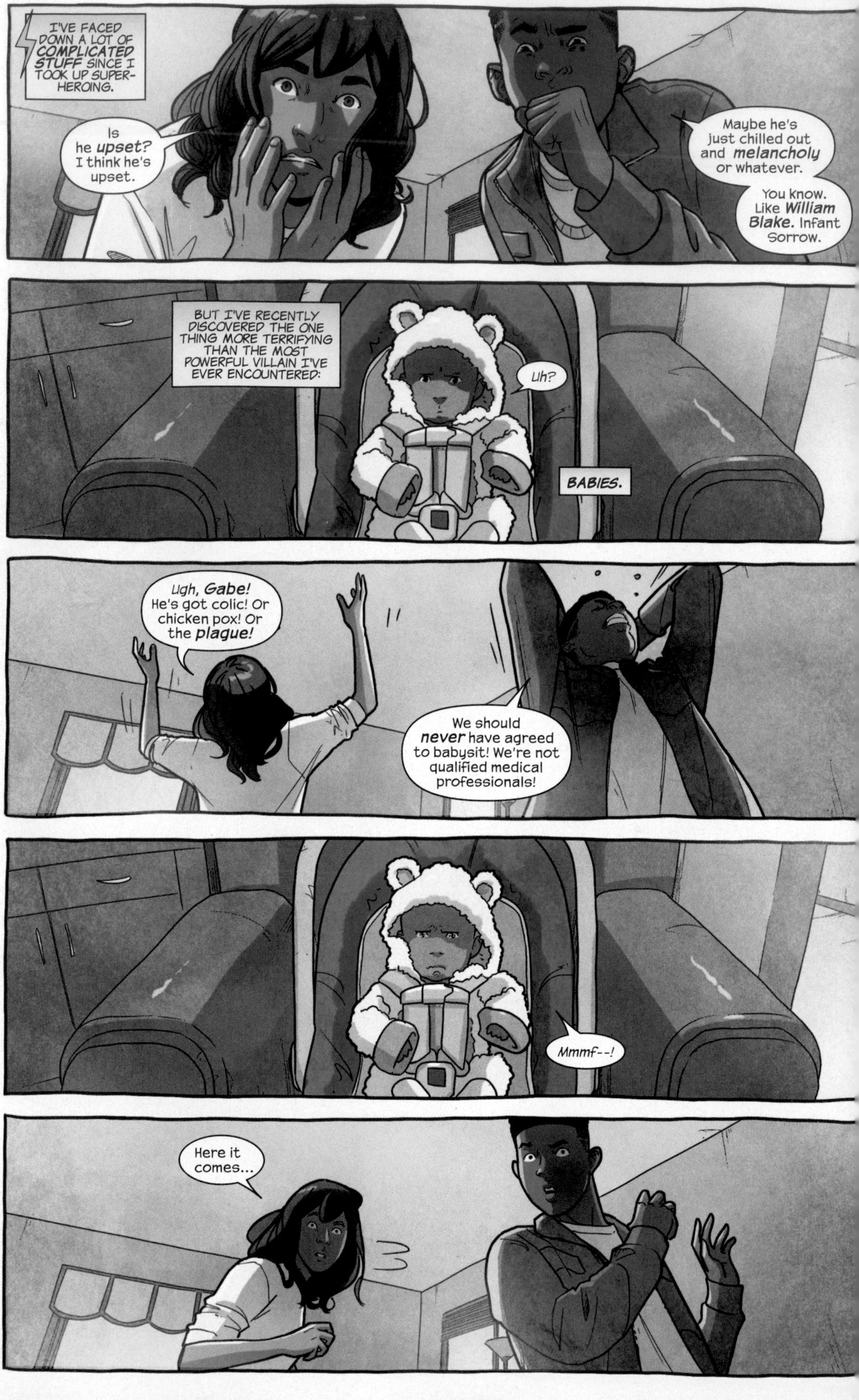
I'VE FACED DOWN A LOT OF COMPLICATED STUFF SINCE I TOOK UP SUPER-HEROING.
Is he upset? I think he's upset.
Maybe he's just chilled out and melancholy or whatever.
You know. Like William Blake. Infant Sorrow.
BUT I'VE RECENTLY DISCOVERED THE ONE THING MORE TERRIFYING THAN THE MOST POWERFUL VILLAIN I'VE EVER ENCOUNTERED:
Uh?
BABIES.
Ugh, Gabe! He's got colic! Or chicken pox! Or the plague!
We should never have agreed to babysit! We're not qualified medical professionals!
Mmmf--!
Here it comes...

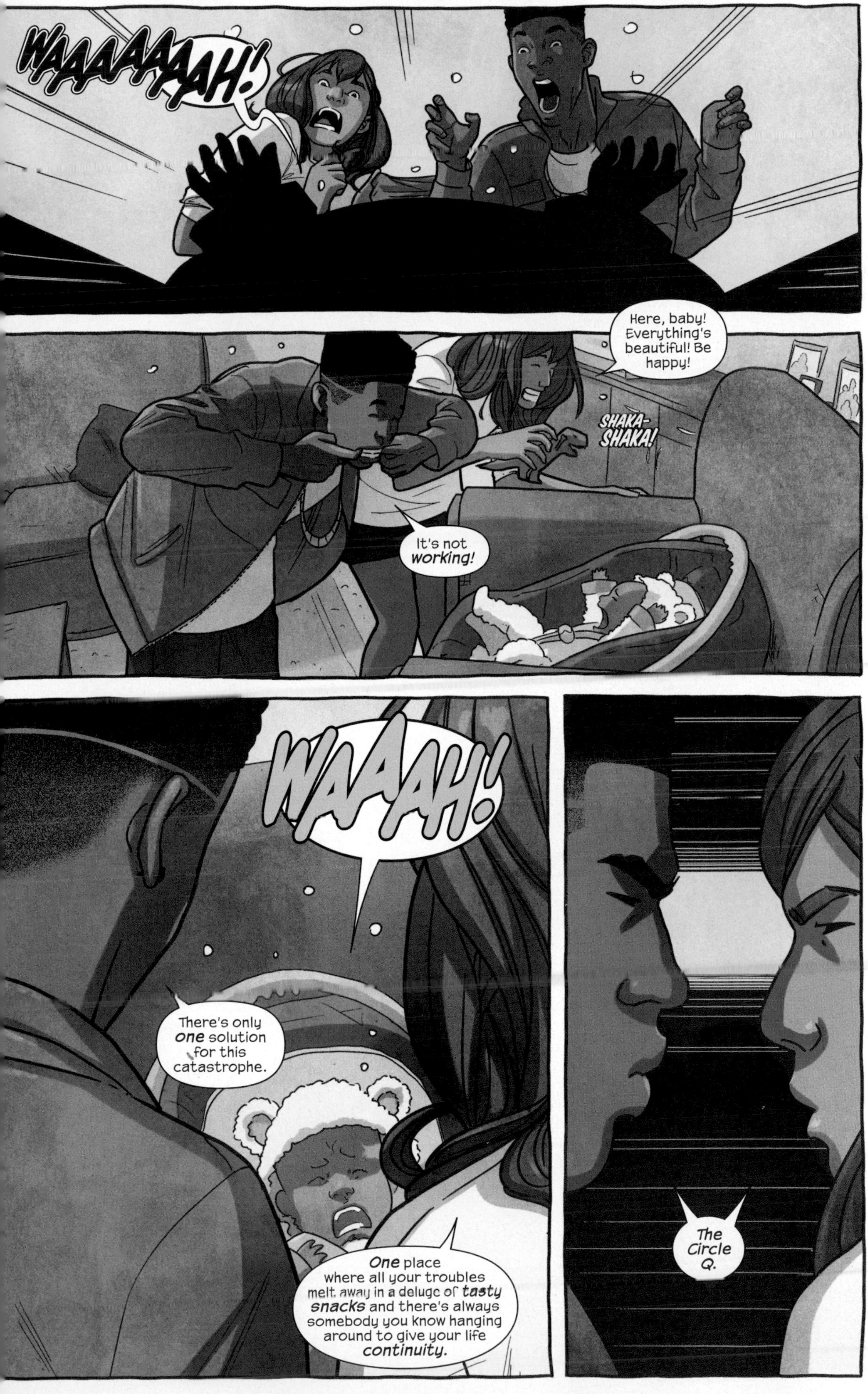
WAAAAAAAH!
Here, baby! Everything's beautiful! Be happy!
SHAKA-SHAKA!
It's not working!
WAAAH!
There's only one solution for this catastrophe.
One place where all your troubles melt away in a deluge of tasty snacks and there's always somebody you know hanging around to give your life continuity.
The Circle Q.

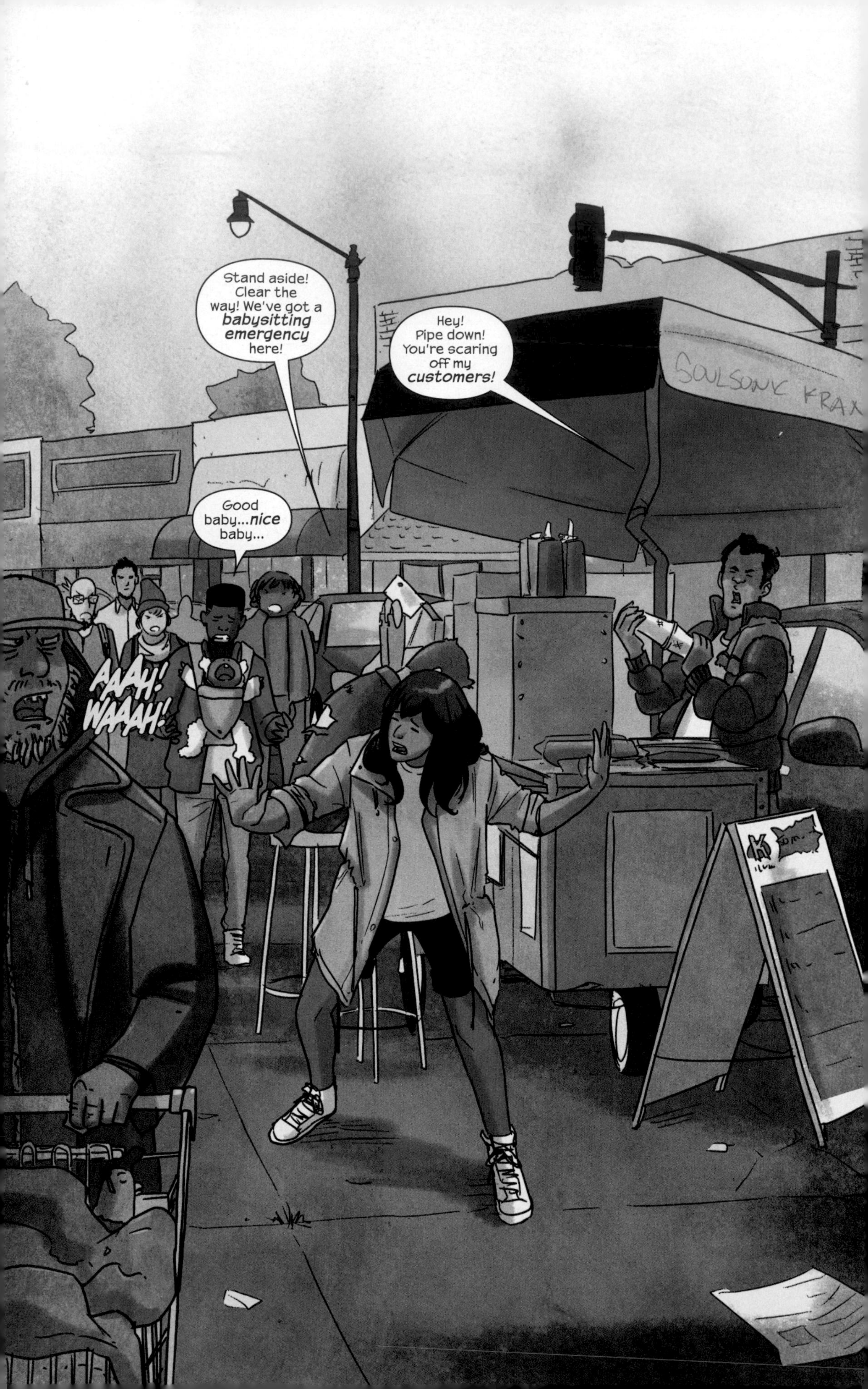
Stand aside! Clear the way! We've got a *babysitting emergency* here!
Hey! Pipe down! You're scaring off my *customers!*
Good baby...*nice* baby...
AAAH! WAAAH!
SOULSONIC KRAX

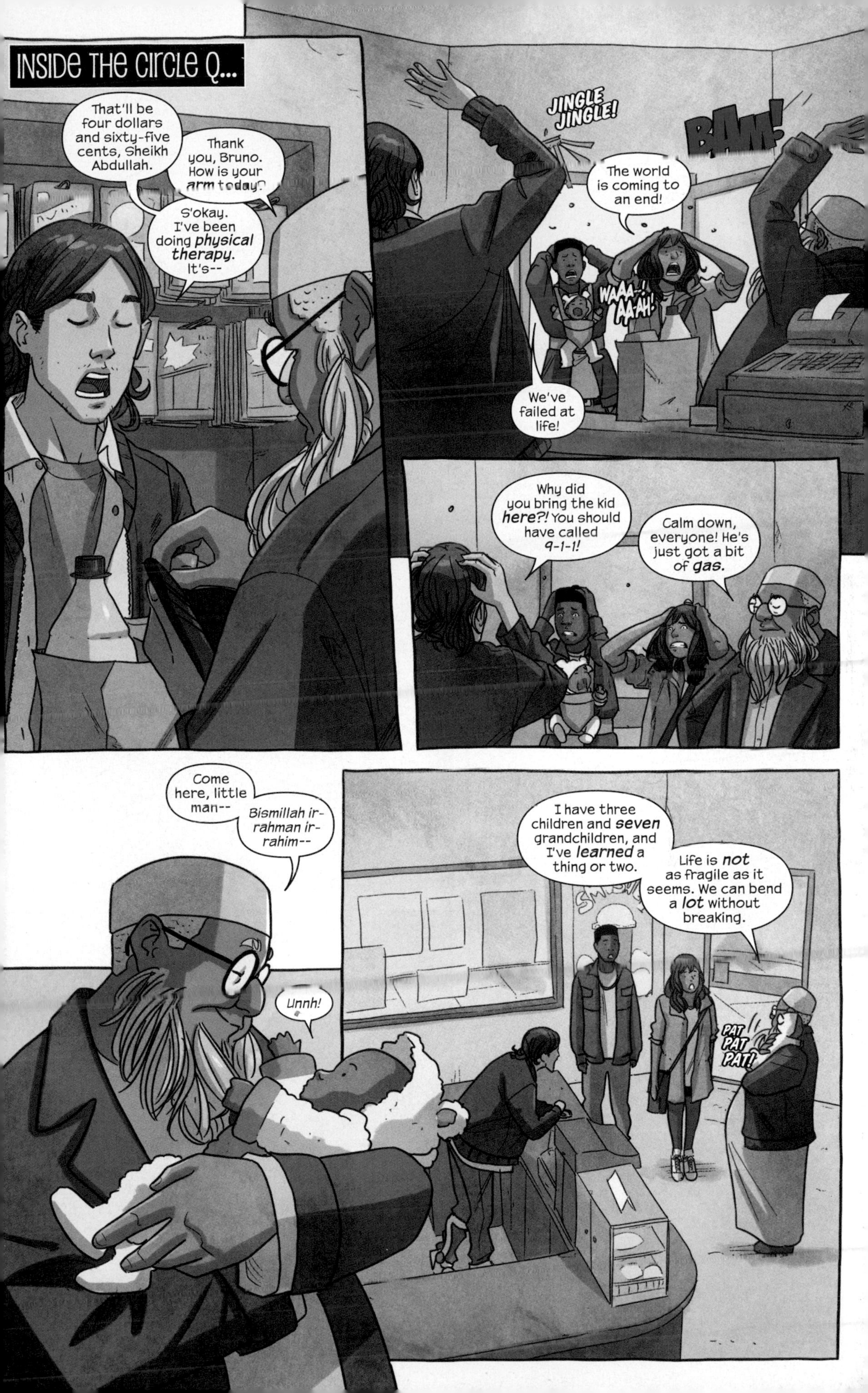
INSIDE THE CIRCLE Q...
That'll be four dollars and sixty-five cents, Sheikh Abdullah.
Thank you, Bruno. How is your arm today?
S'okay. I've been doing physical therapy. It's--
JINGLE JINGLE!
BAM!
The world is coming to an end!
WAAA--! AA-AH!
We've failed at life!
Why did you bring the kid here?! You should have called 9-1-1!
Calm down, everyone! He's just got a bit of gas.
Come here, little man--
Bismillah ir-rahman ir-rahim--
Unnh!
I have three children and seven grandchildren, and I've learned a thing or two.
Life is not as fragile as it seems. We can bend a lot without breaking.
PAT PAT PAT!

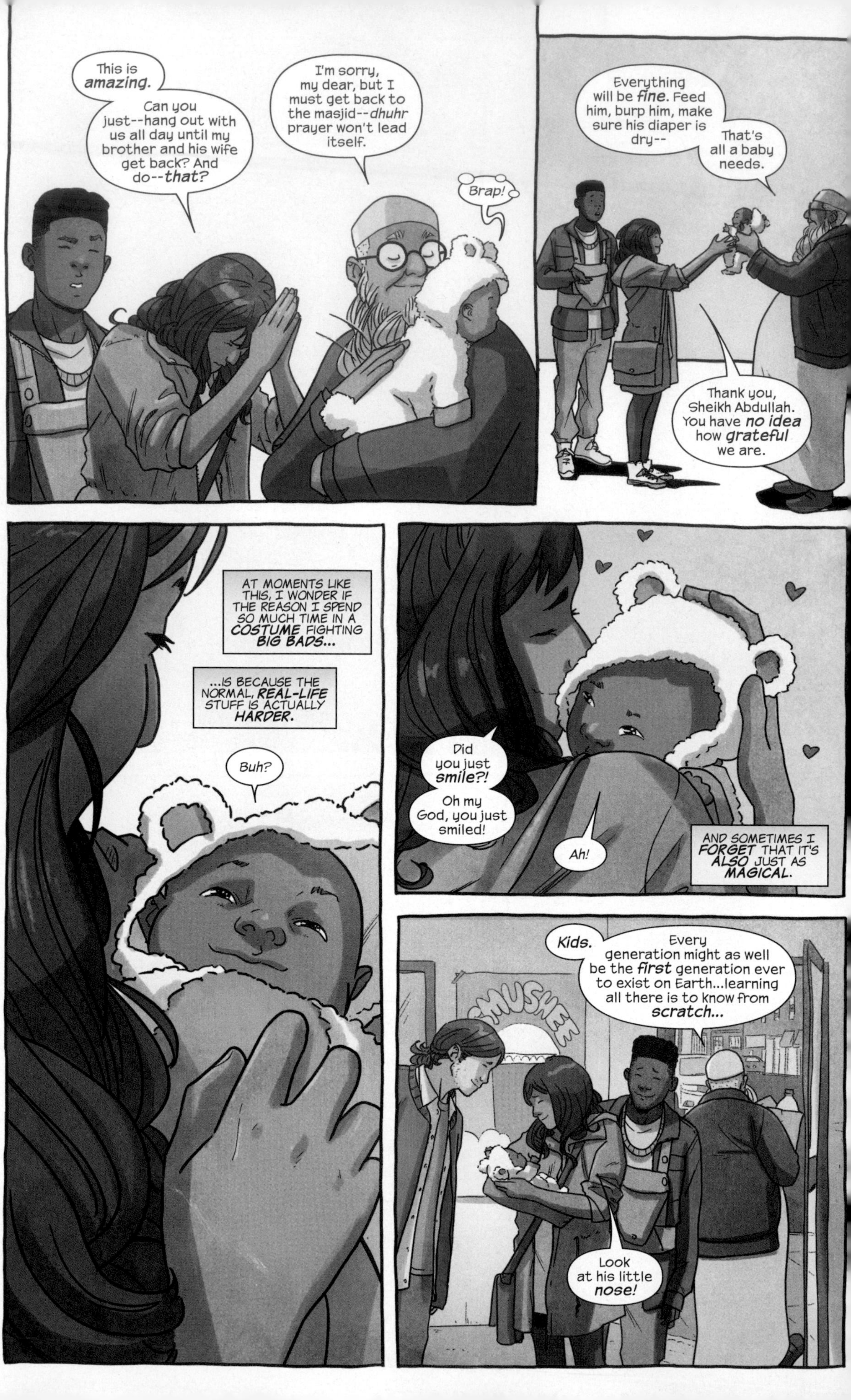
This is amazing.
Can you just--hang out with us all day until my brother and his wife get back? And do--that?
I'm sorry, my dear, but I must get back to the masjid--dhuhr prayer won't lead itself.
Brap!
Everything will be fine. Feed him, burp him, make sure his diaper is dry--
That's all a baby needs.
Thank you, Sheikh Abdullah. You have no idea how grateful we are.
AT MOMENTS LIKE THIS, I WONDER IF THE REASON I SPEND SO MUCH TIME IN A COSTUME FIGHTING BIG BADS...
...IS BECAUSE THE NORMAL, REAL-LIFE STUFF IS ACTUALLY HARDER.
Buh?
Did you just smile?!
Oh my God, you just smiled!
Ah!
AND SOMETIMES I FORGET THAT IT'S ALSO JUST AS MAGICAL.
Kids.
Every generation might as well be the first generation ever to exist on Earth...learning all there is to know from scratch...
Look at his little nose!

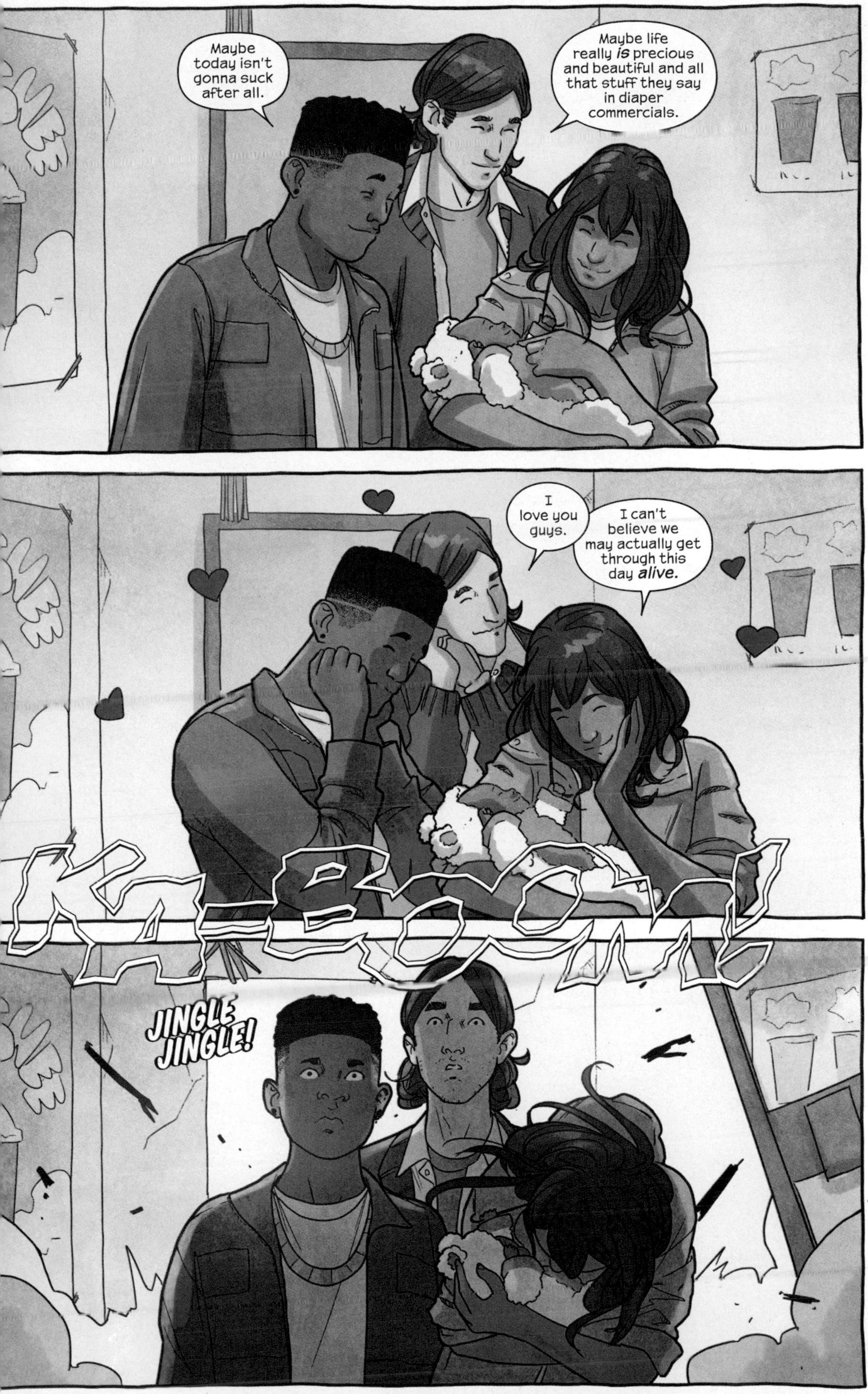
Maybe today isn't gonna suck after all.
Maybe life really *is* precious and beautiful and all that stuff they say in diaper commercials.
I love you guys.
I can't believe we may actually get through this day ***alive.***
JINGLE JINGLE!

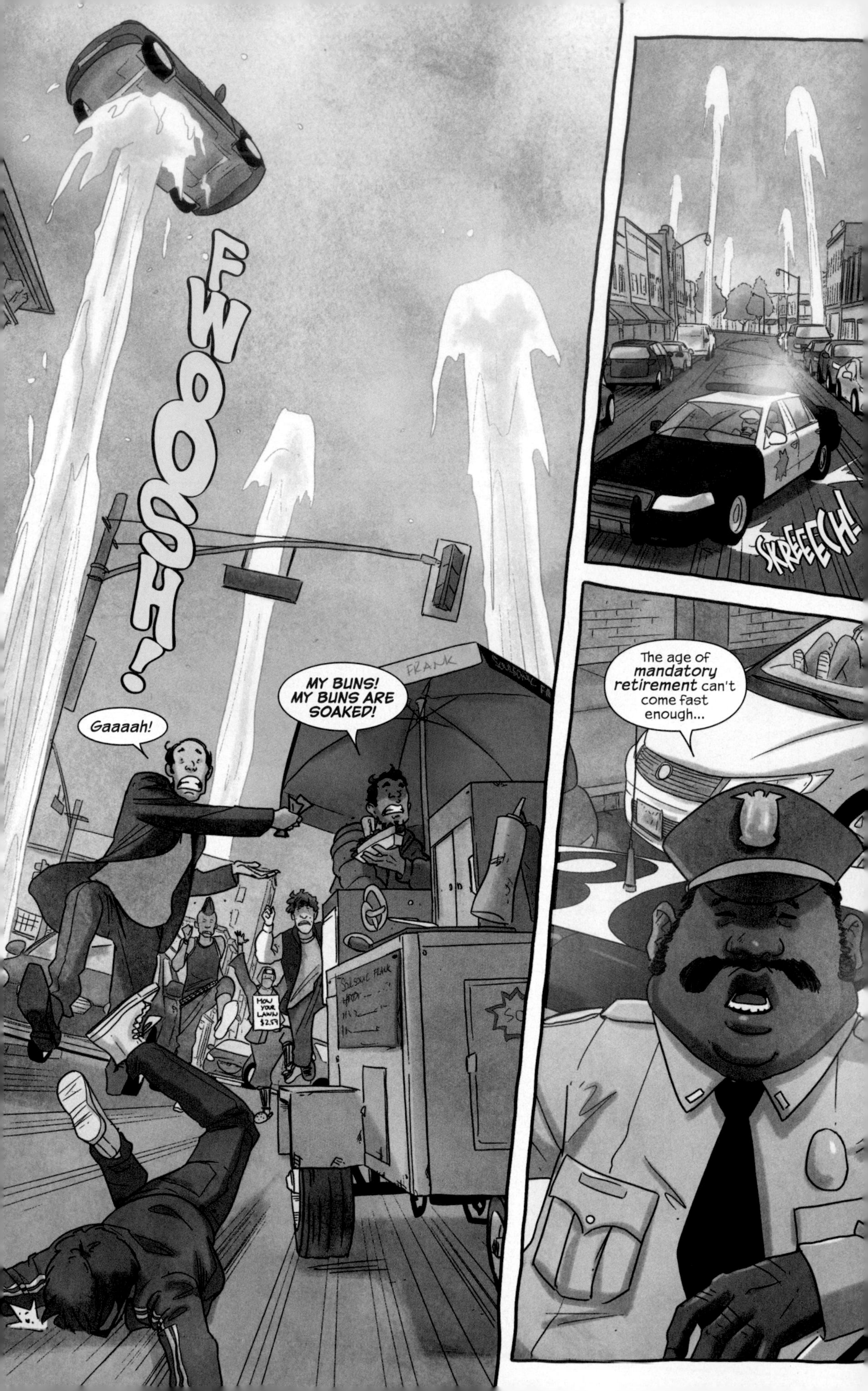
FWOOSH!
Gaaaah!
MY BUNS! MY BUNS ARE SOAKED!
SKREEECH!
The age of mandatory retirement can't come fast enough...

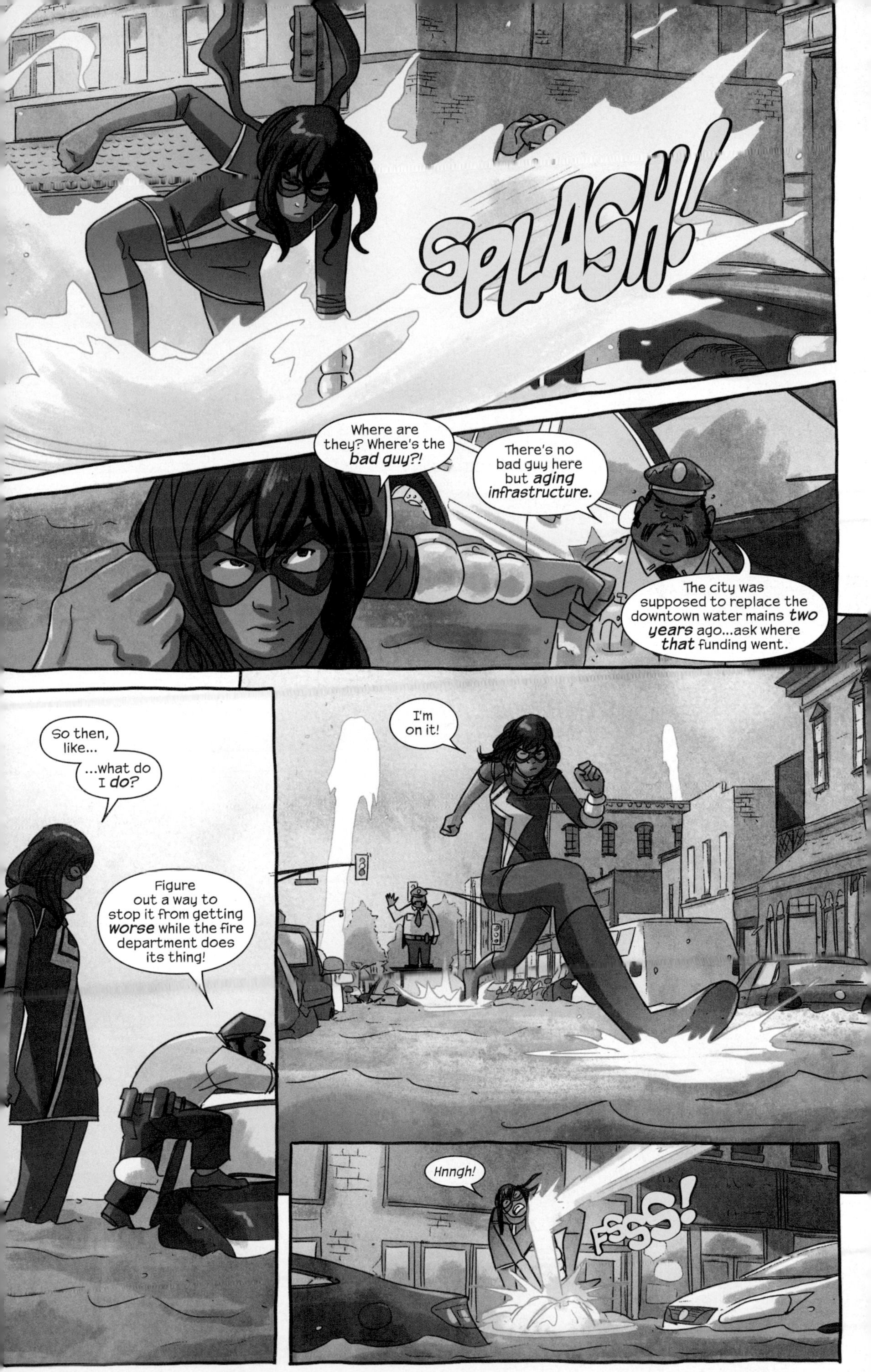
SPLASH!
Where are they? Where's the *bad guy?!*
There's no bad guy here but *aging infrastructure.*
The city was supposed to replace the downtown water mains *two years* ago...ask where *that* funding went.
So then, like...
...what do I *do?*
Figure out a way to stop it from getting *worse* while the fire department does its thing!
I'm on it!
Hnngh!
FSSS!

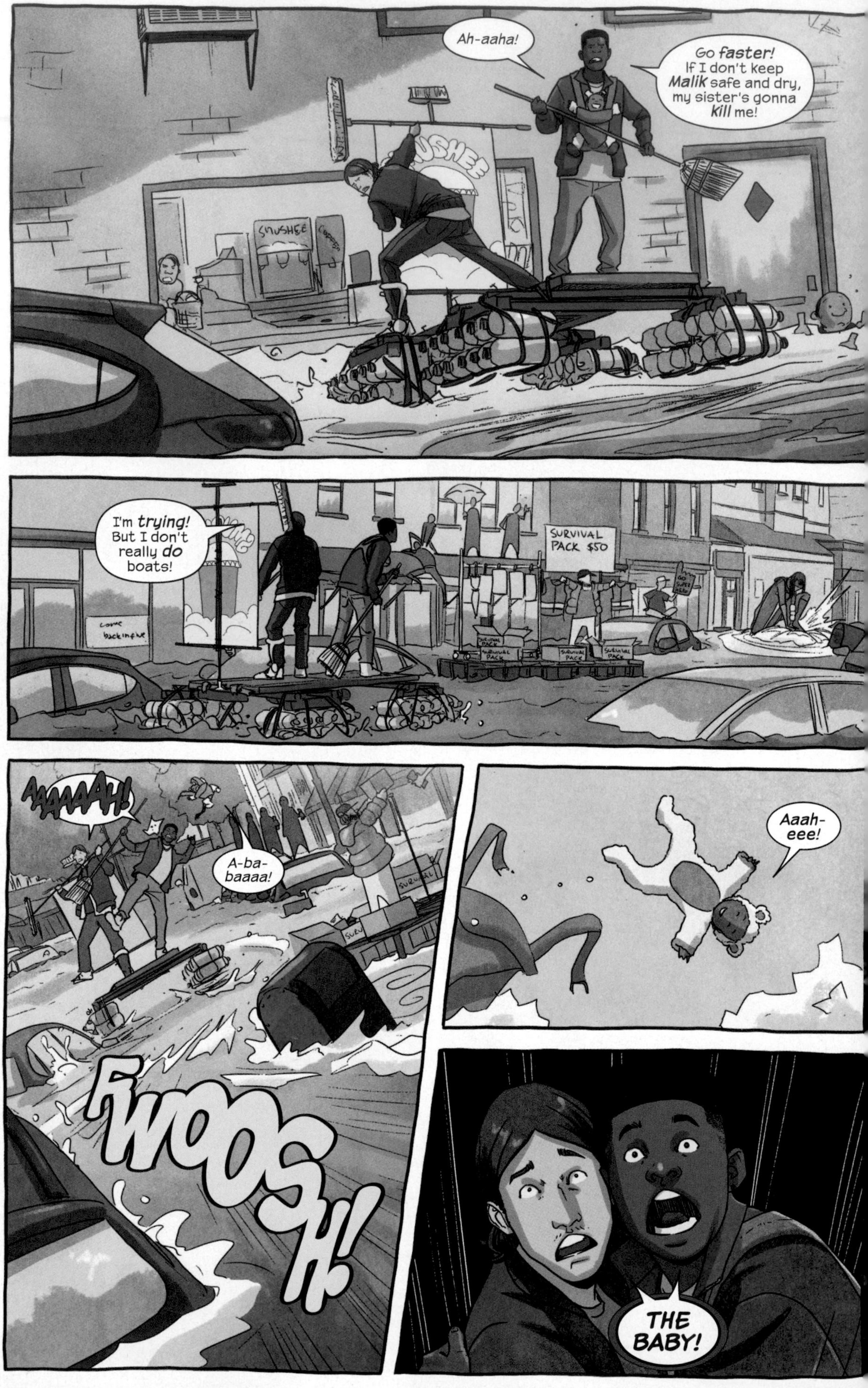
Ah-aaha!
Go faster! If I don't keep Malik safe and dry, my sister's gonna kill me!
SMUSHEE
I'm trying! But I don't really do boats!
SURVIVAL PACK $50
AAAAAH!
A-ba-baaaa!
FWOOSH!
Aaah-eee!
THE BABY!

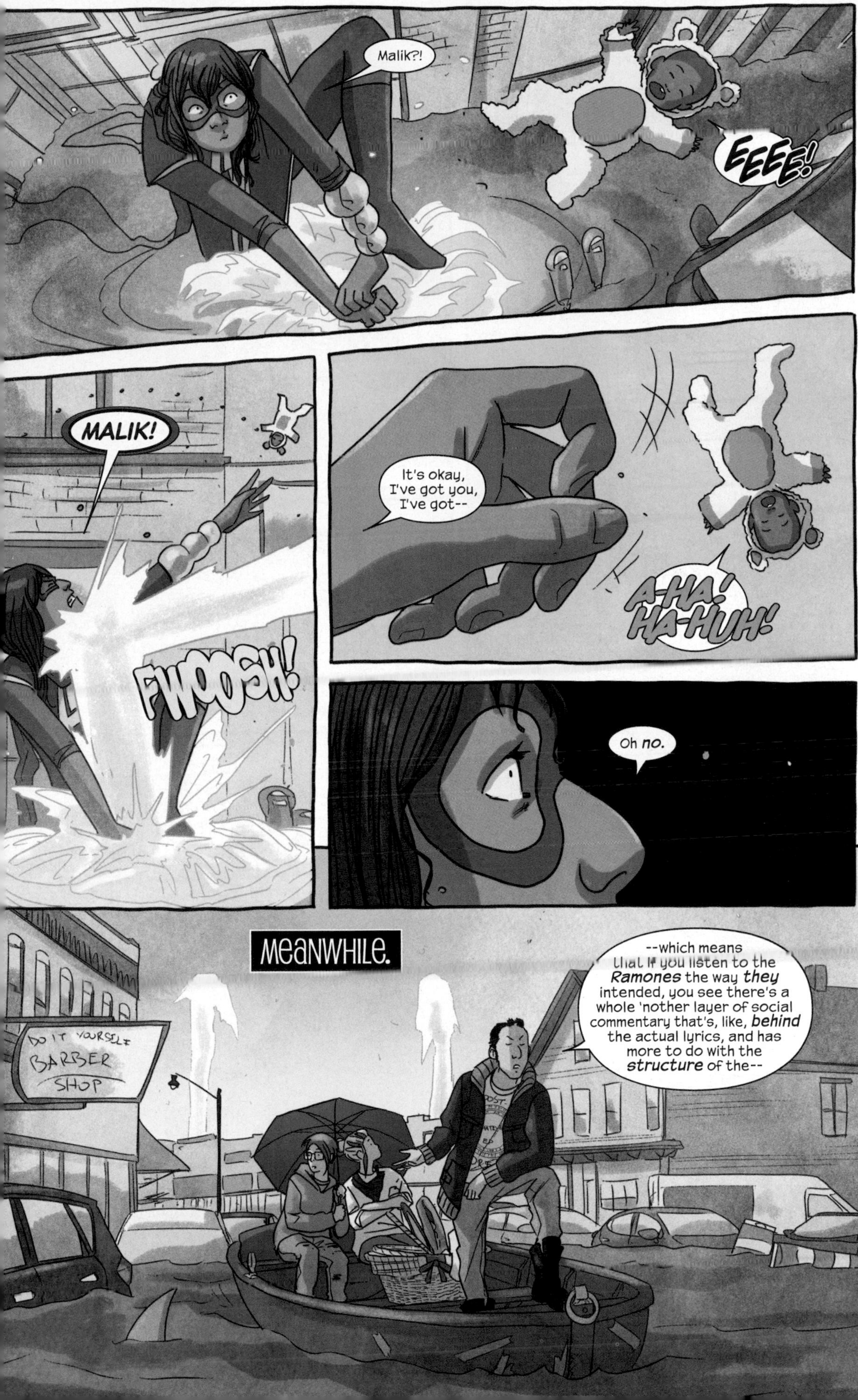
Malik?!
EEEE!
MALIK!
FWOOSH!
It's okay, I've got you, I've got--
A-HA! HA-HUH!
Oh no.
MEANWHILE.
--which means that if you listen to the Ramones the way they intended, you see there's a whole 'nother layer of social commentary that's, like, behind the actual lyrics, and has more to do with the structure of the--
DO IT YOURSELF BARBER SHOP

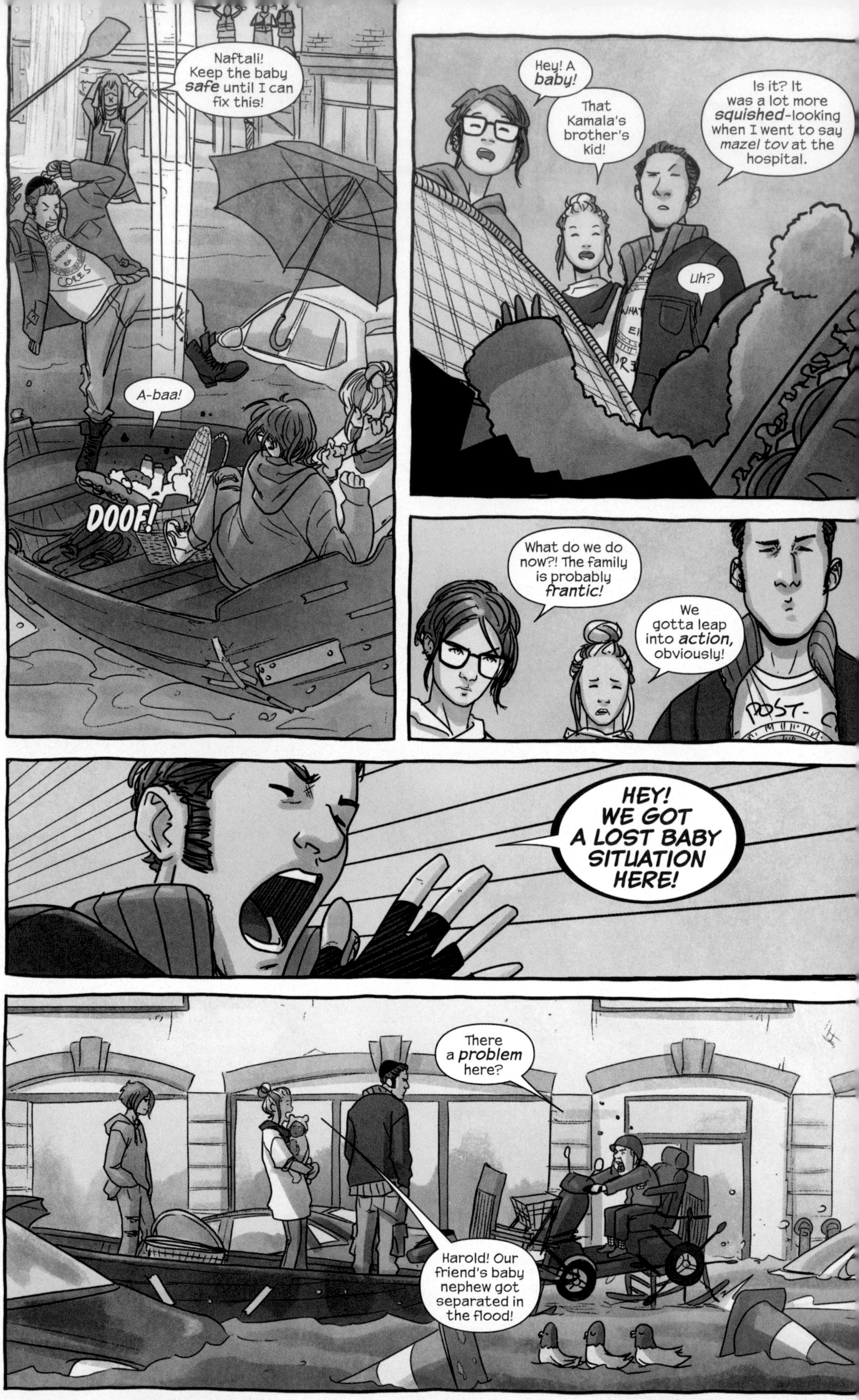

Naftali! Keep the baby safe until I can fix this!
A-baa!
DOOF!
Hey! A baby!
That Kamala's brother's kid!
Is it? It was a lot more squished-looking when I went to say mazel tov at the hospital.
Uh?
What do we do now?! The family is probably frantic!
We gotta leap into action, obviously!
HEY! WE GOT A LOST BABY SITUATION HERE!
There a problem here?
Harold! Our friend's baby nephew got separated in the flood!

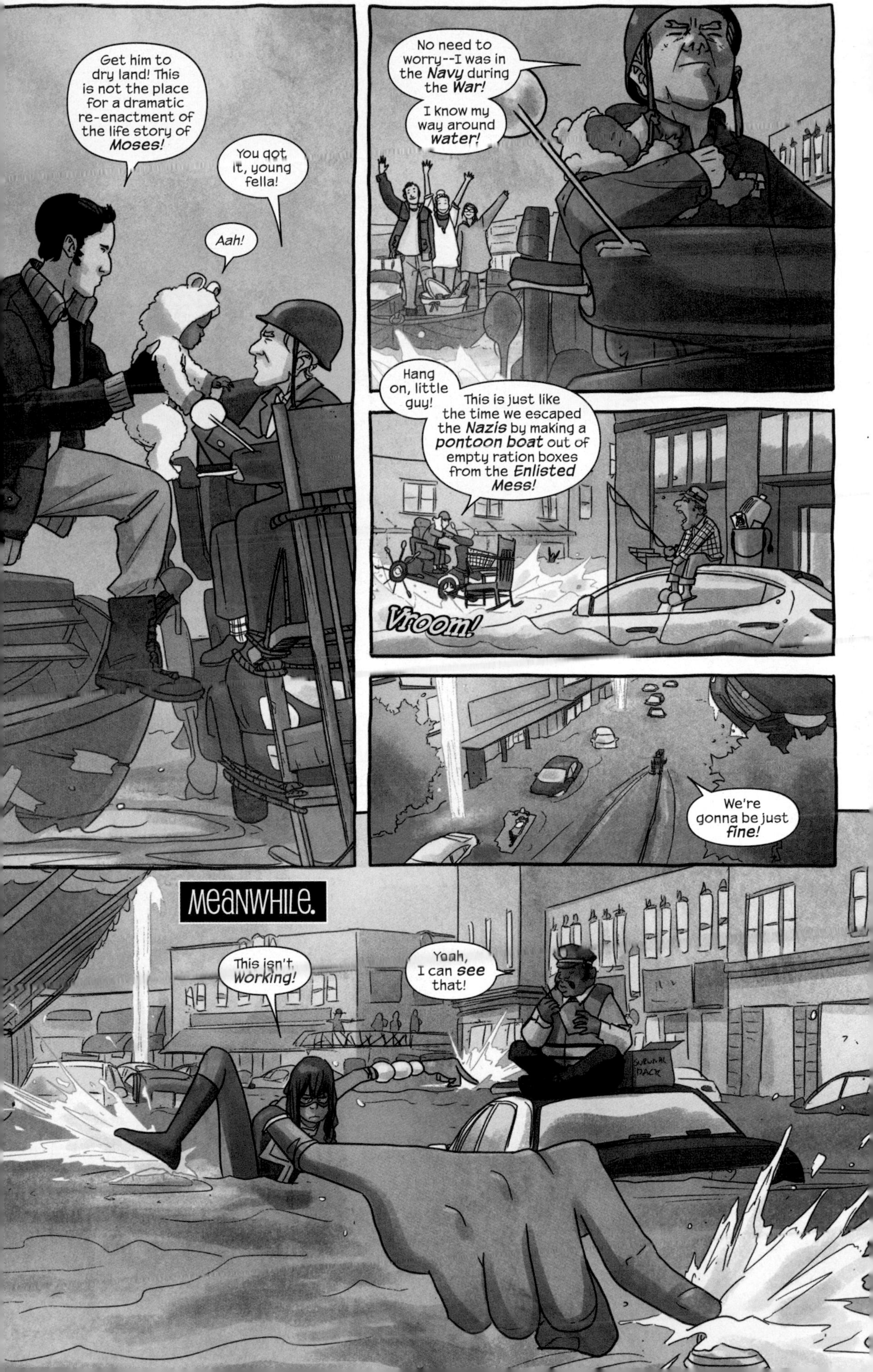
Get him to dry land! This is not the place for a dramatic re-enactment of the life story of Moses!
You got it, young fella!
Aah!
No need to worry--I was in the Navy during the War!
I know my way around water!
Hang on, little guy!
This is just like the time we escaped the Nazis by making a pontoon boat out of empty ration boxes from the Enlisted Mess!
Vroom!
We're gonna be just fine!
MEANWHILE.
This isn't working!
Yeah, I can see that!
SURVIVAL PACK

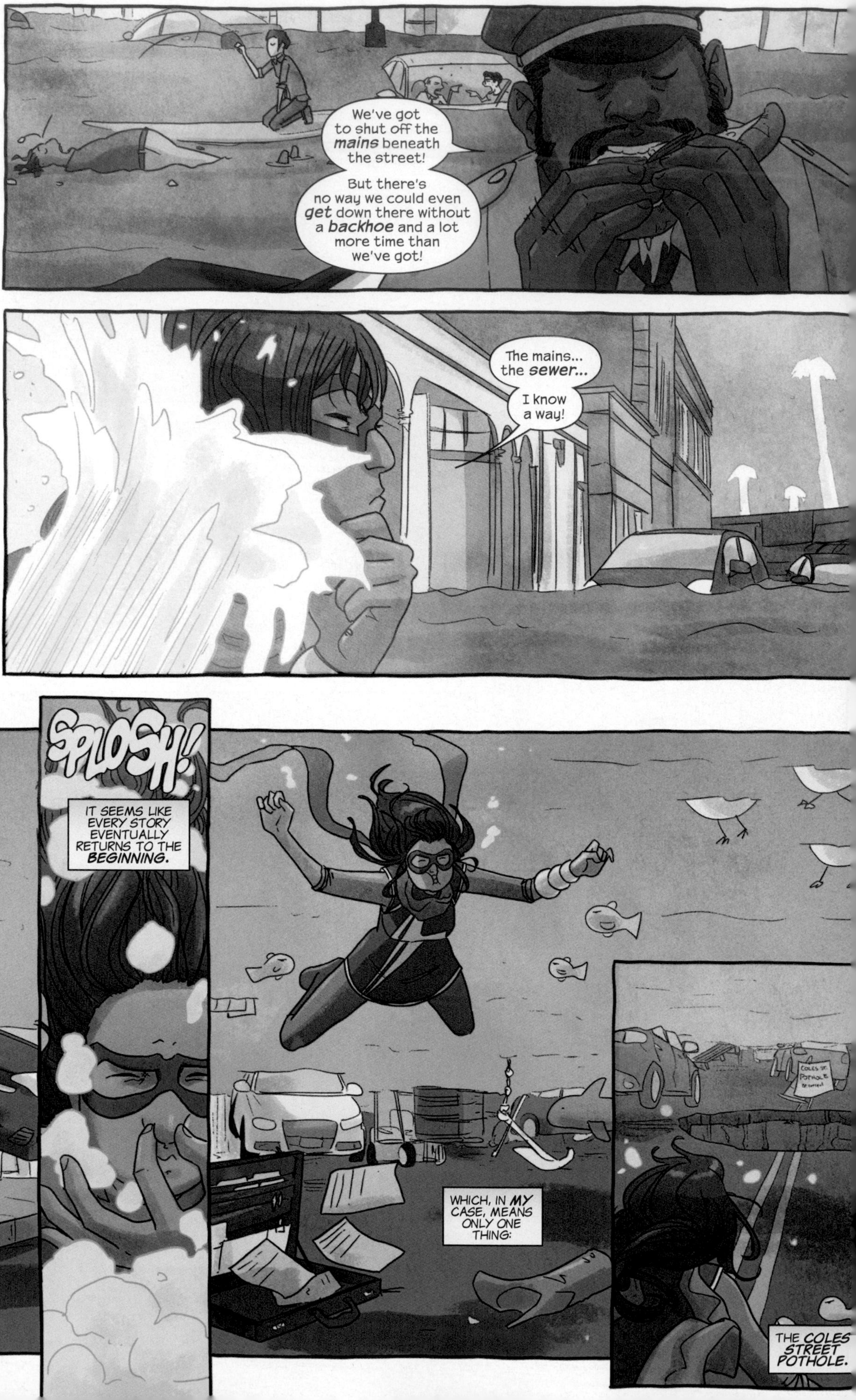
We've got to shut off the mains beneath the street!
But there's no way we could even get down there without a backhoe and a lot more time than we've got!
The mains... the sewer...
I know a way!
SPLOSH!
IT SEEMS LIKE EVERY STORY EVENTUALLY RETURNS TO THE BEGINNING.
WHICH, IN MY CASE, MEANS ONLY ONE THING:
THE COLES STREET POTHOLE.

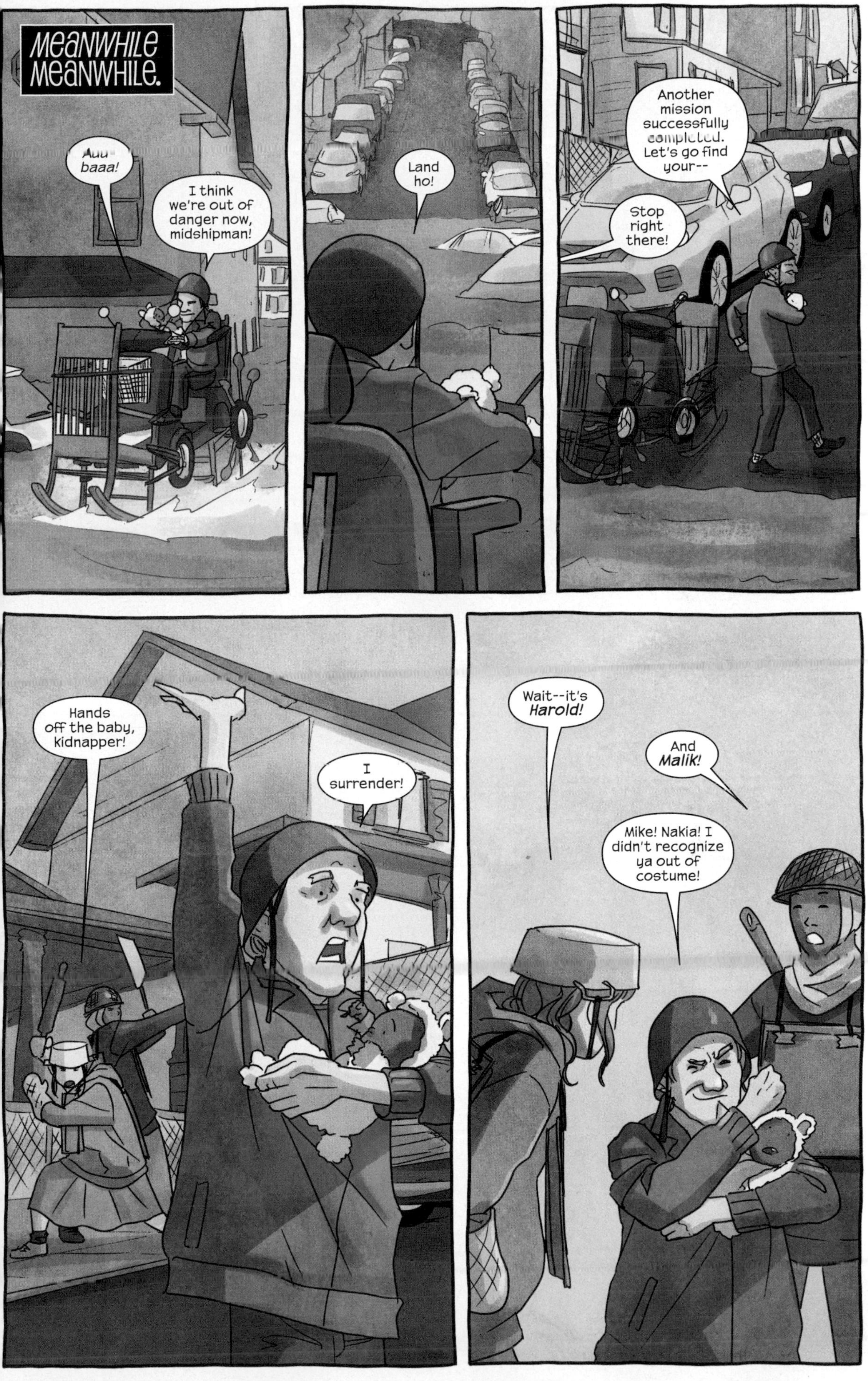

MEANWHILE MEANWHILE.
Auu baaa!
I think we're out of danger now, midshipman!
Land ho!
Another mission successfully completed. Let's go find your--
Stop right there!
Hands off the baby, kidnapper!
I surrender!
Wait--it's *Harold!*
And *Malik!*
Mike! Nakia! I didn't recognize ya out of costume!

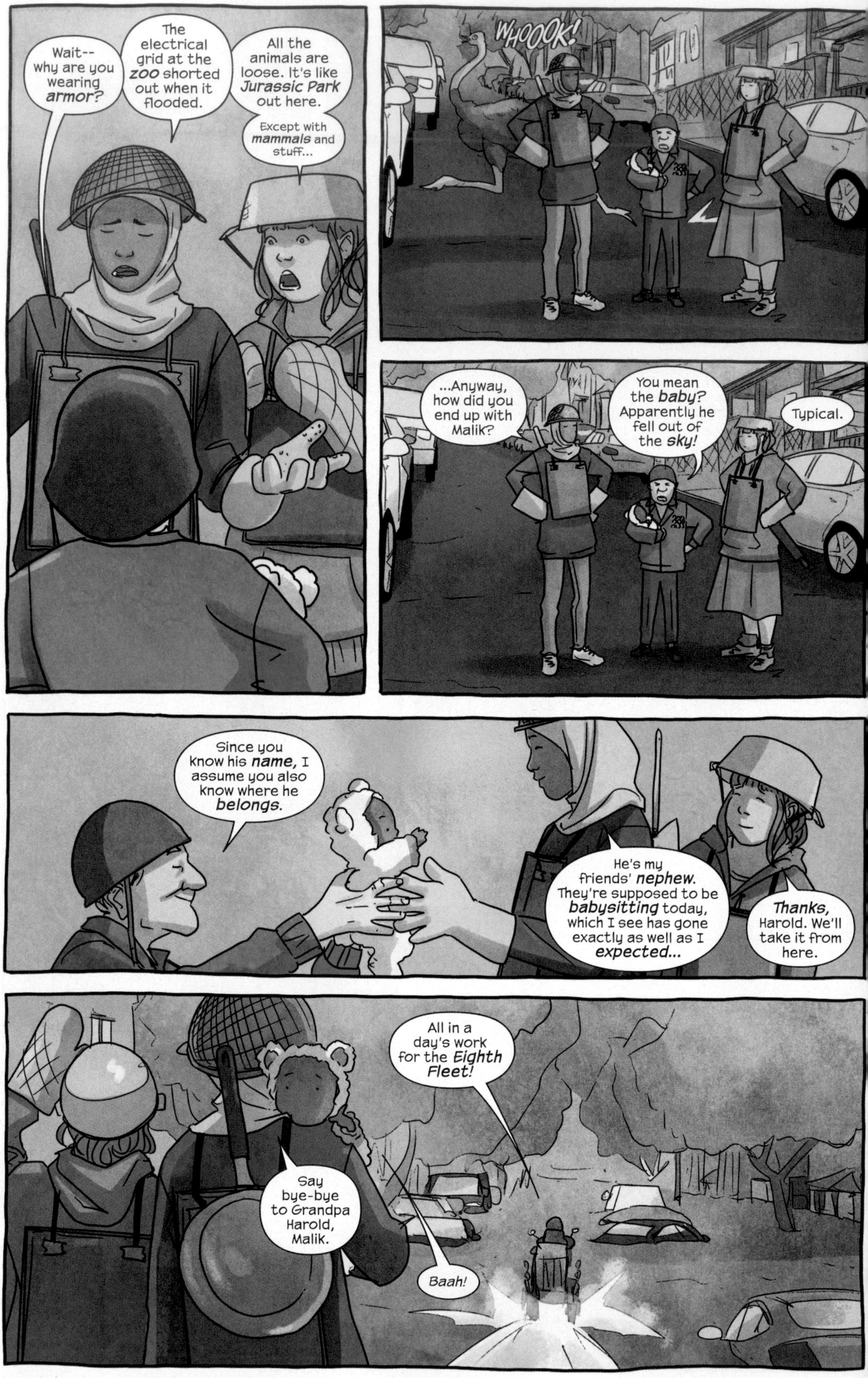
Wait-- why are you wearing armor?
The electrical grid at the zoo shorted out when it flooded.
All the animals are loose. It's like Jurassic Park out here.
Except with mammals and stuff...
WHOOOK!
...Anyway, how did you end up with Malik?
You mean the baby? Apparently he fell out of the sky!
Typical.
Since you know his name, I assume you also know where he belongs.
He's my friends' nephew. They're supposed to be babysitting today, which I see has gone exactly as well as I expected...
Thanks, Harold. We'll take it from here.
All in a day's work for the Eighth Fleet!
Say bye-bye to Grandpa Harold, Malik.
Baah!

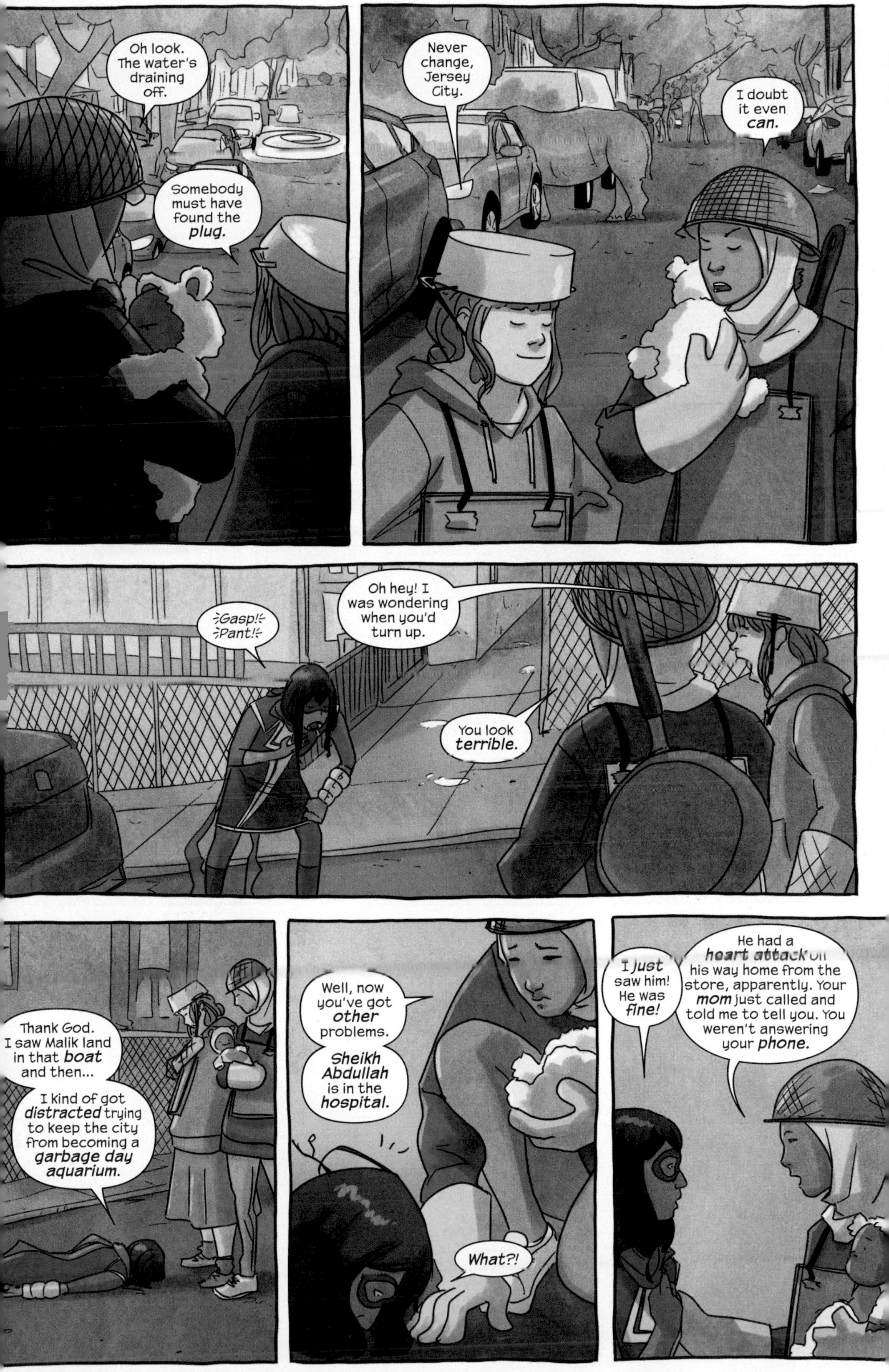
Oh look. The water's draining off.
Somebody must have found the *plug.*
Never change, Jersey City.
I doubt it even *can.*
Gasp! Pant!
Oh hey! I was wondering when you'd turn up.
You look *terrible.*
Thank God. I saw Malik land in that *boat* and then...
I kind of got *distracted* trying to keep the city from becoming a *garbage day aquarium.*
Well, now you've got *other* problems.
Sheikh Abdullah is in the *hospital.*
What?!
He had a *heart attack* on his way home from the store, apparently. Your *mom* just called and told me to tell you. You weren't answering your *phone.*
I *just* saw him! He was *fine!*

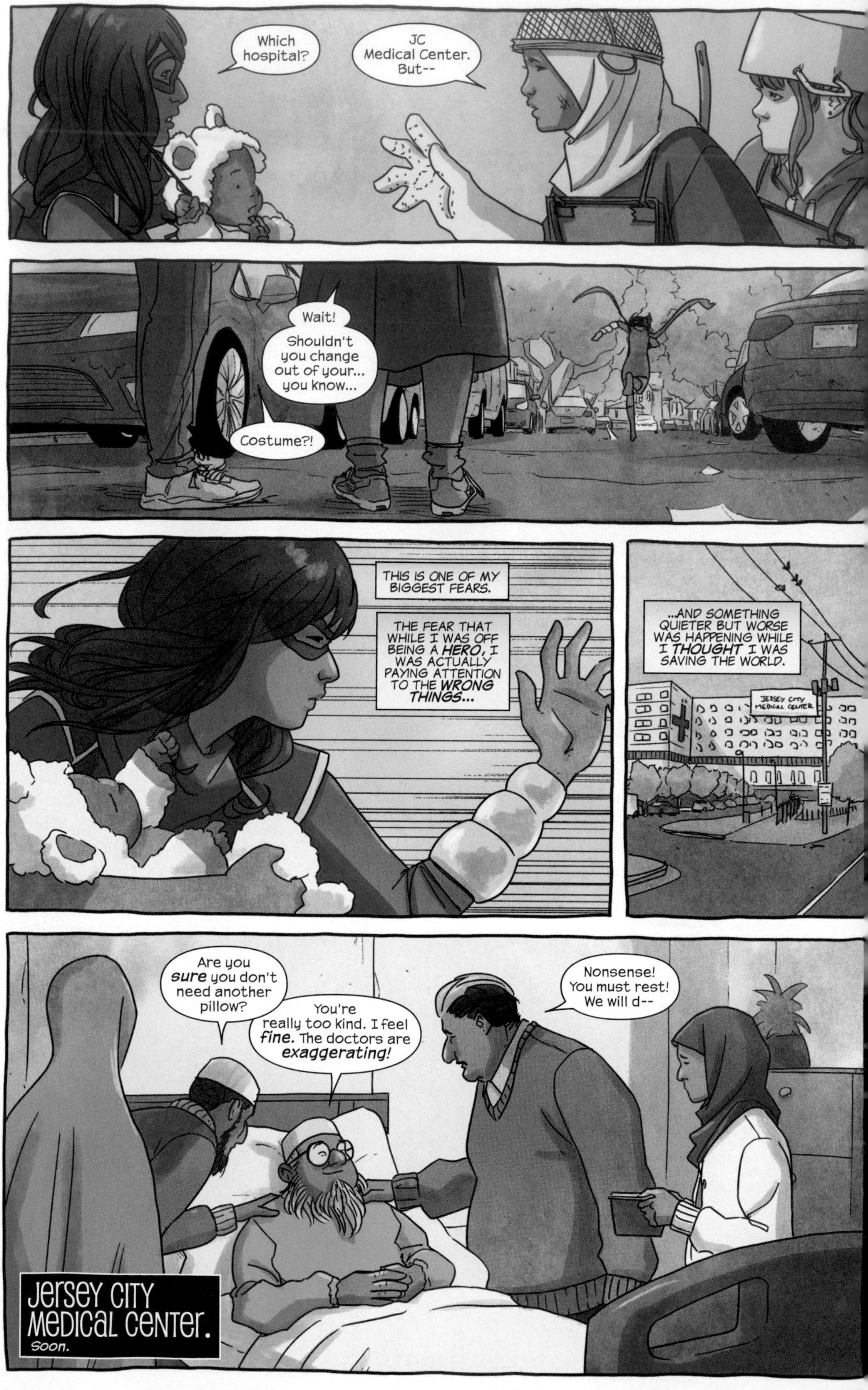
Which hospital?
JC Medical Center. But--
Wait! Shouldn't you change out of your... you know...
Costume?!
THIS IS ONE OF MY BIGGEST FEARS.
THE FEAR THAT WHILE I WAS OFF BEING A HERO, I WAS ACTUALLY PAYING ATTENTION TO THE WRONG THINGS...
...AND SOMETHING QUIETER BUT WORSE WAS HAPPENING WHILE I THOUGHT I WAS SAVING THE WORLD.
JERSEY CITY MEDICAL CENTER
Are you sure you don't need another pillow?
You're really too kind. I feel fine. The doctors are exaggerating!
Nonsense! You must rest! We will d--
Jersey City Medical Center.
Soon.

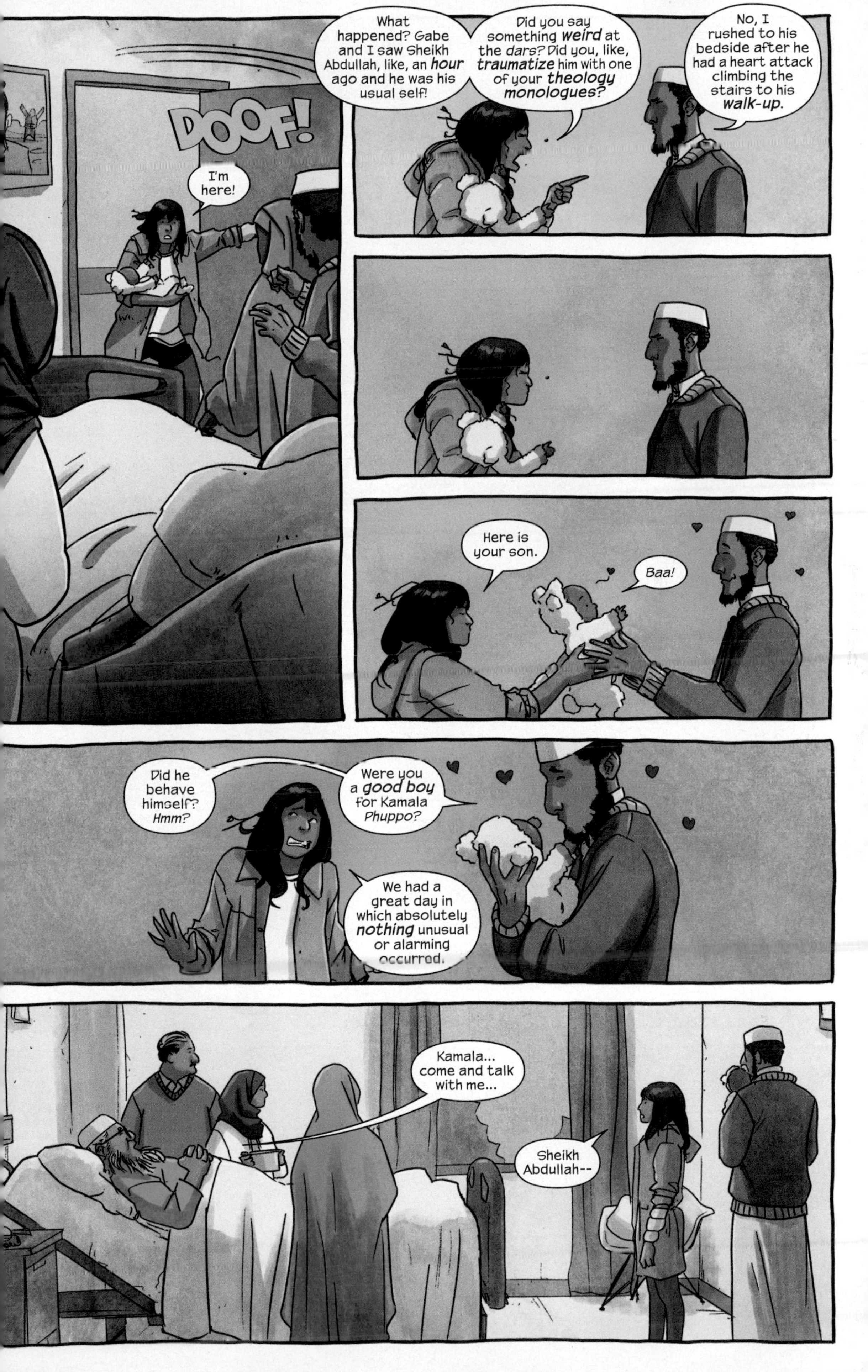
DOOF!
I'm here!
What happened? Gabe and I saw Sheikh Abdullah, like, an hour ago and he was his usual self!
Did you say something weird at the dars? Did you, like, traumatize him with one of your theology monologues?
No, I rushed to his bedside after he had a heart attack climbing the stairs to his walk-up.
Here is your son.
Baa!
Did he behave himself? Hmm?
Were you a good boy for Kamala Phuppo?
We had a great day in which absolutely nothing unusual or alarming occurred.
Kamala... come and talk with me...
Sheikh Abdullah--

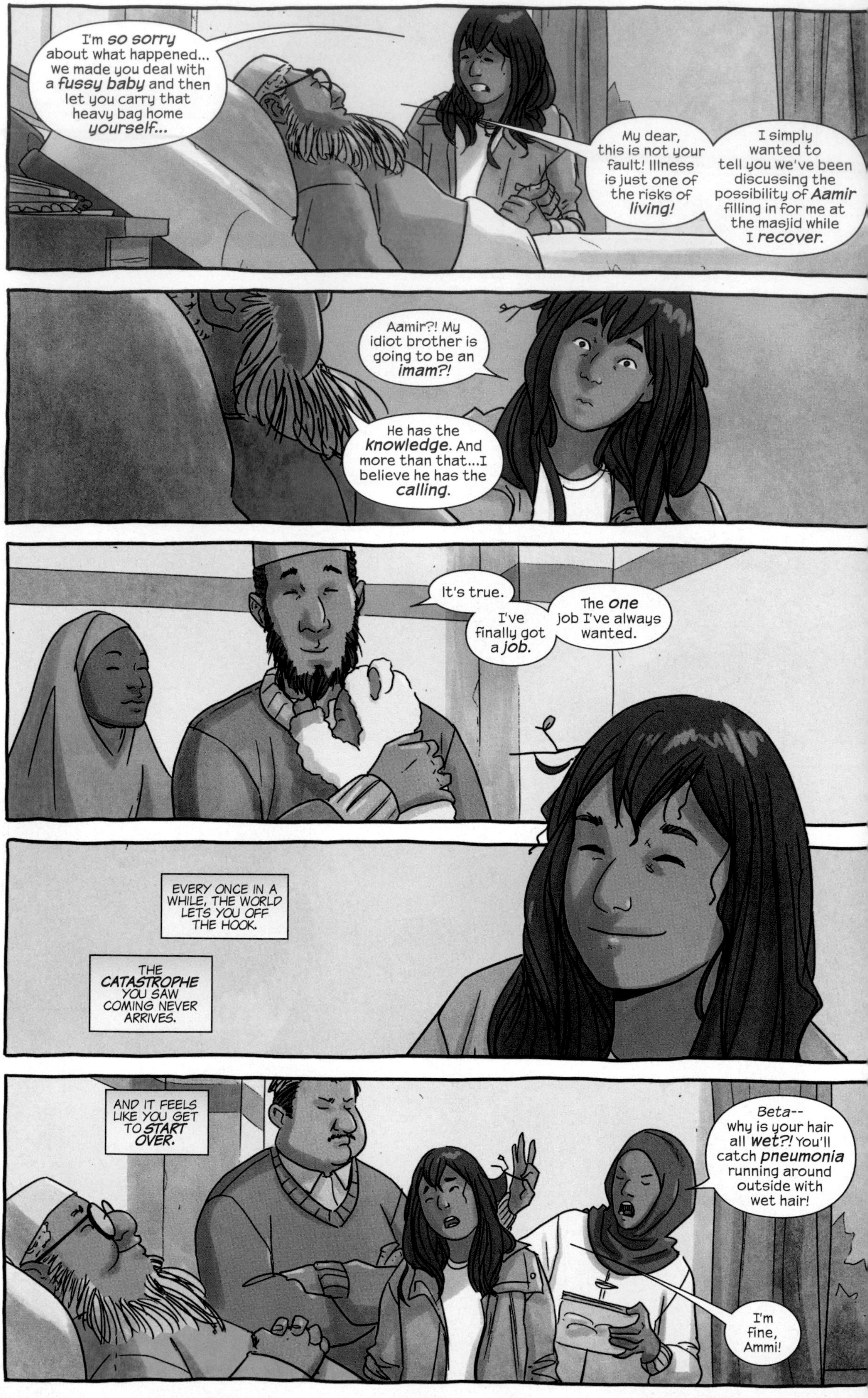
I'm so sorry about what happened... we made you deal with a fussy baby and then let you carry that heavy bag home yourself...
My dear, this is not your fault! Illness is just one of the risks of living!
I simply wanted to tell you we've been discussing the possibility of Aamir filling in for me at the masjid while I recover.
Aamir?! My idiot brother is going to be an imam?!
He has the knowledge. And more than that...I believe he has the calling.
It's true.
I've finally got a job.
The one job I've always wanted.
EVERY ONCE IN A WHILE, THE WORLD LETS YOU OFF THE HOOK.
THE CATASTROPHE YOU SAW COMING NEVER ARRIVES.
AND IT FEELS LIKE YOU GET TO START OVER.
Beta-- why is your hair all wet?! You'll catch pneumonia running around outside with wet hair!
I'm fine, Ammi!

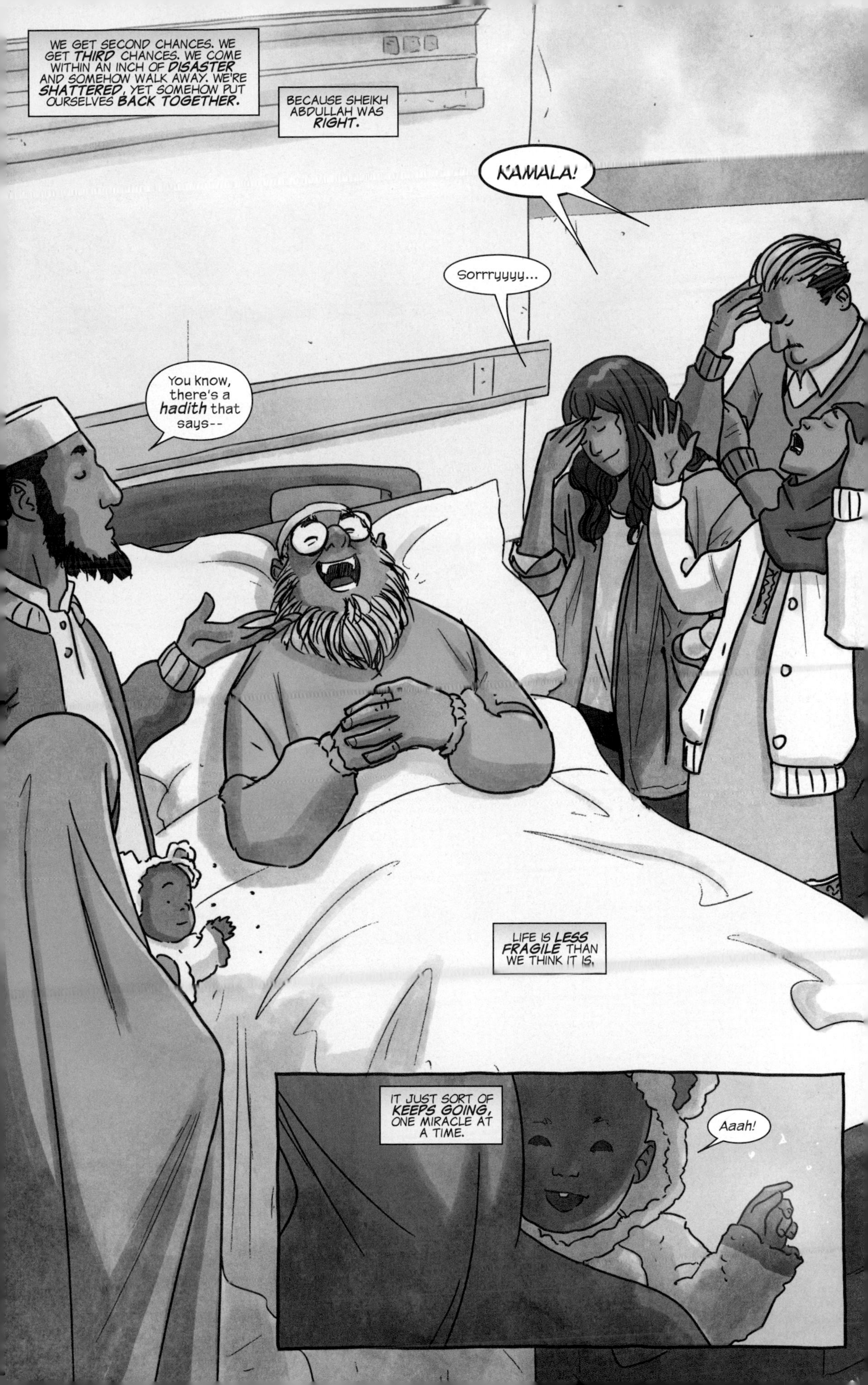
WE GET SECOND CHANCES. WE GET THIRD CHANCES. WE COME WITHIN AN INCH OF DISASTER AND SOMEHOW WALK AWAY. WE'RE SHATTERED, YET SOMEHOW PUT OURSELVES BACK TOGETHER.
BECAUSE SHEIKH ABDULLAH WAS RIGHT.
KAMALA!
Sorrryyyy...
You know, there's a hadith that says--
LIFE IS LESS FRAGILE THAN WE THINK IT IS.
IT JUST SORT OF KEEPS GOING, ONE MIRACLE AT A TIME.
Aaah!

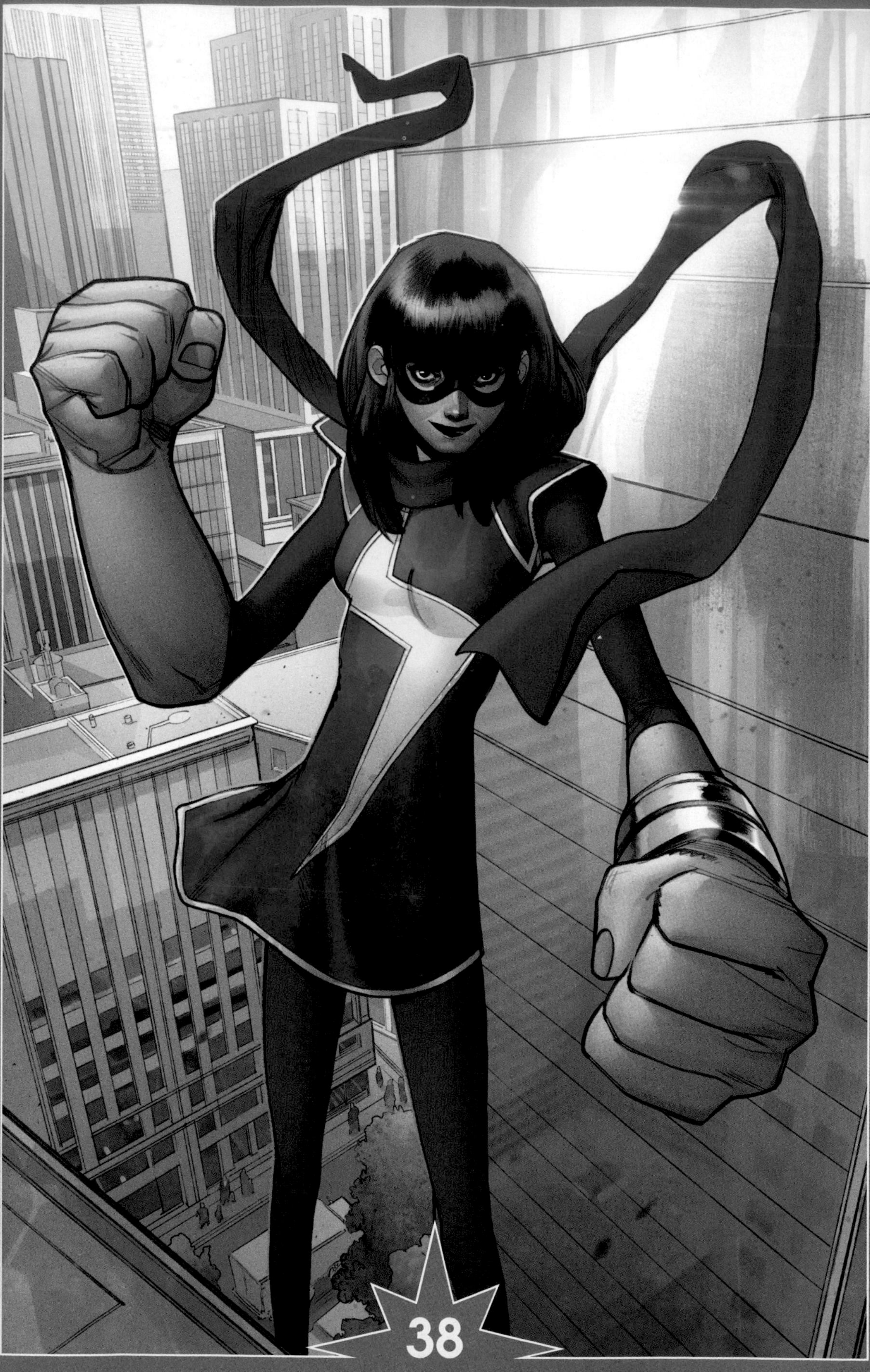
38

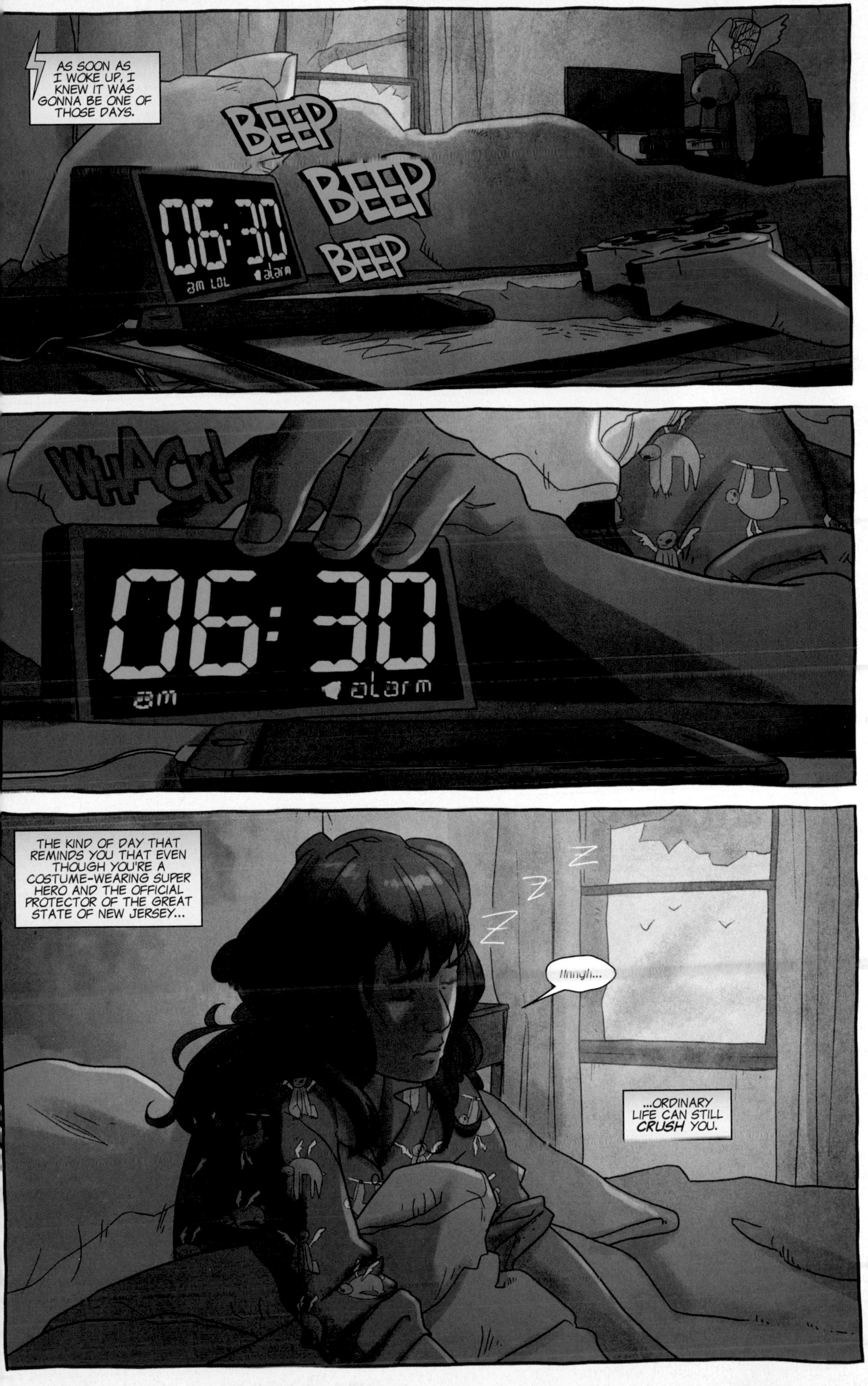
AS SOON AS I WOKE UP, I KNEW IT WAS GONNA BE ONE OF THOSE DAYS.
BEEP
BEEP
BEEP
06:30
am LOL
alarm
WHACK!
06:30
am
alarm
THE KIND OF DAY THAT REMINDS YOU THAT EVEN THOUGH YOU'RE A COSTUME-WEARING SUPER HERO AND THE OFFICIAL PROTECTOR OF THE GREAT STATE OF NEW JERSEY...
Z
Z
Z
Nnngh...
...ORDINARY LIFE CAN STILL CRUSH YOU.

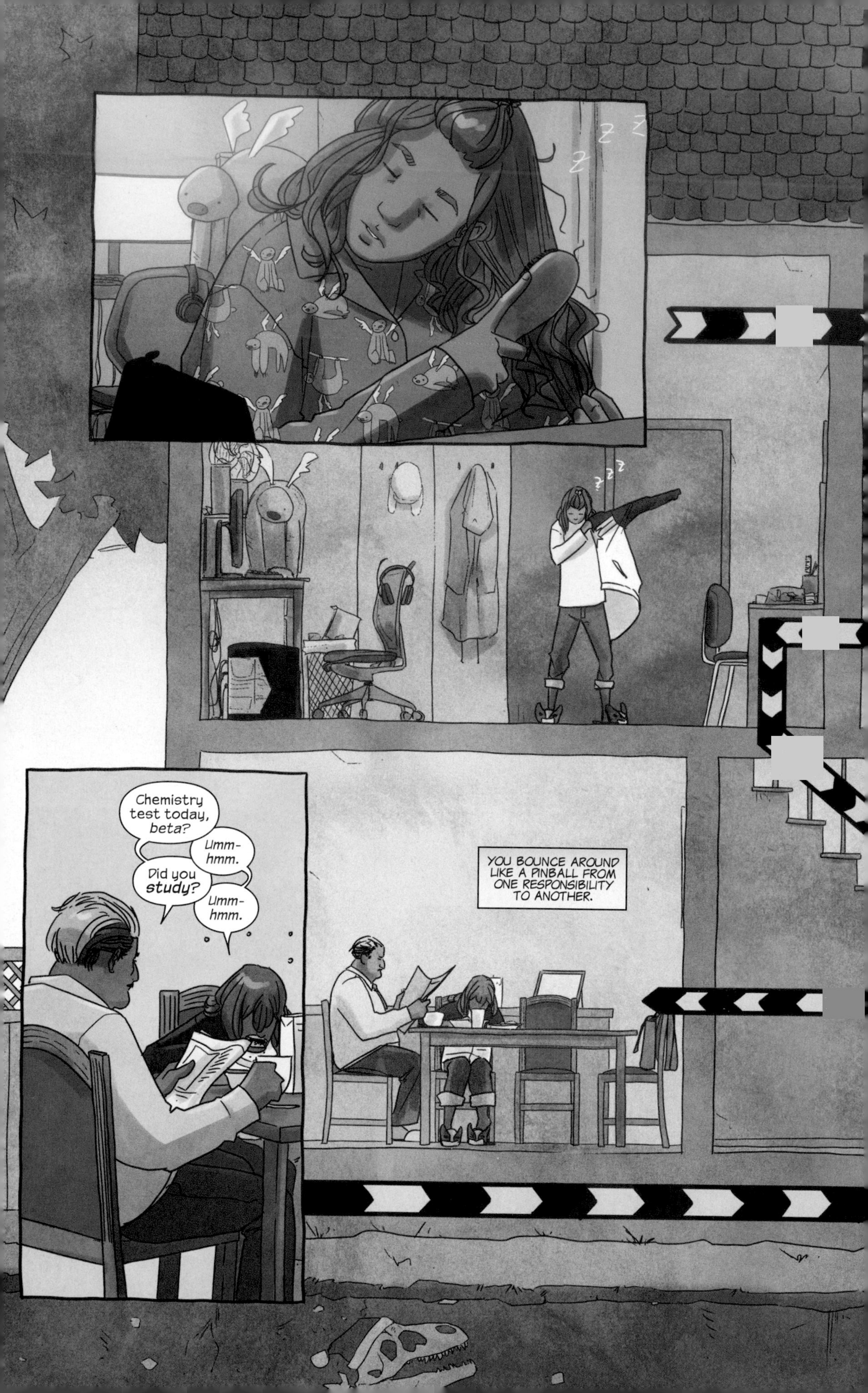

Chemistry test today, beta?
Umm-hmm.
Did you study?
Umm-hmm.
YOU BOUNCE AROUND LIKE A PINBALL FROM ONE RESPONSIBILITY TO ANOTHER.

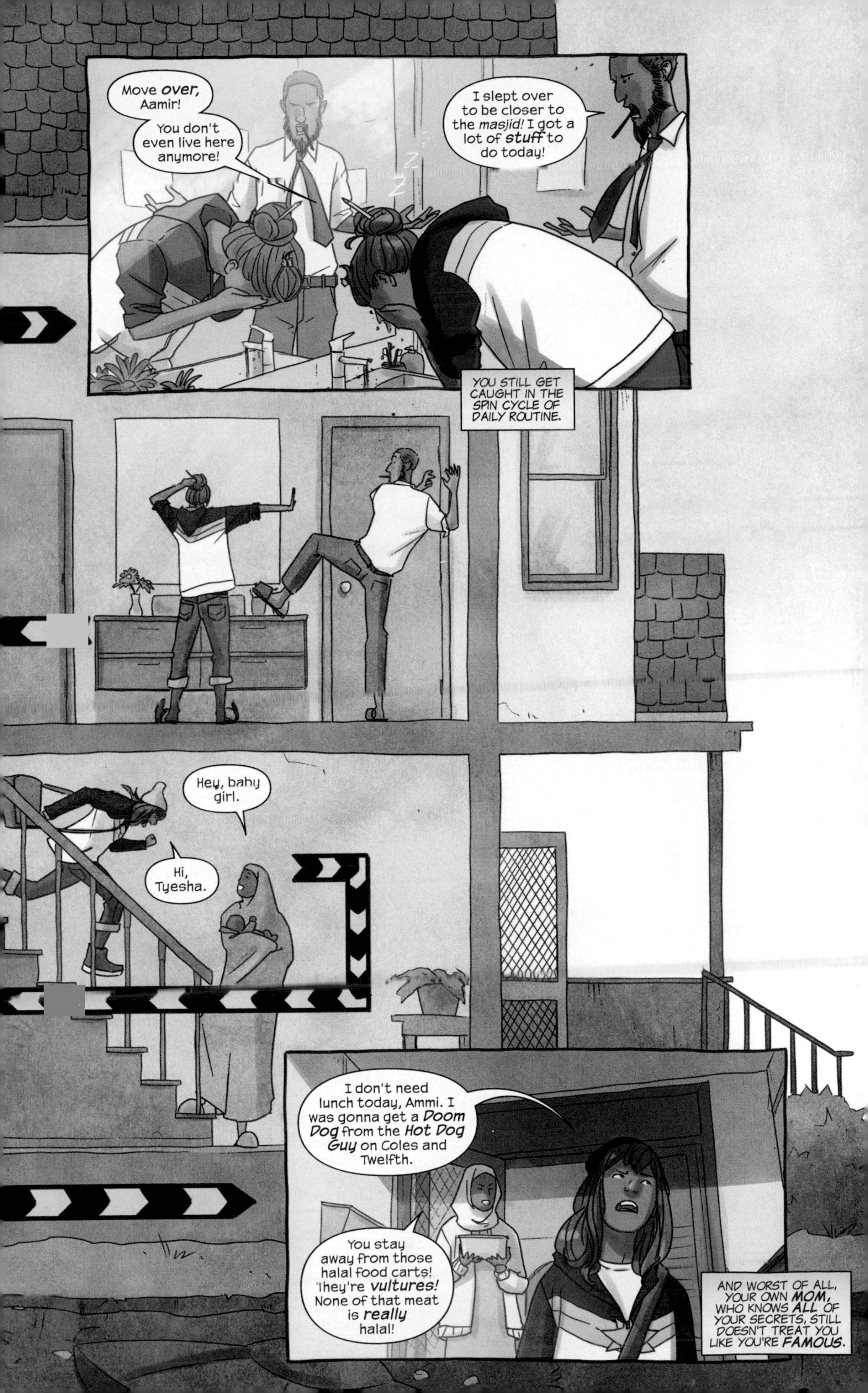
Move over, Aamir!
You don't even live here anymore!
I slept over to be closer to the masjid! I got a lot of stuff to do today!
YOU STILL GET CAUGHT IN THE SPIN CYCLE OF DAILY ROUTINE.
Hey, baby girl.
Hi, Tyesha.
I don't need lunch today, Ammi. I was gonna get a Doom Dog from the Hot Dog Guy on Coles and Twelfth.
You stay away from those halal food carts! They're vultures! None of that meat is really halal!
AND WORST OF ALL, YOUR OWN MOM, WHO KNOWS ALL OF YOUR SECRETS, STILL DOESN'T TREAT YOU LIKE YOU'RE FAMOUS.

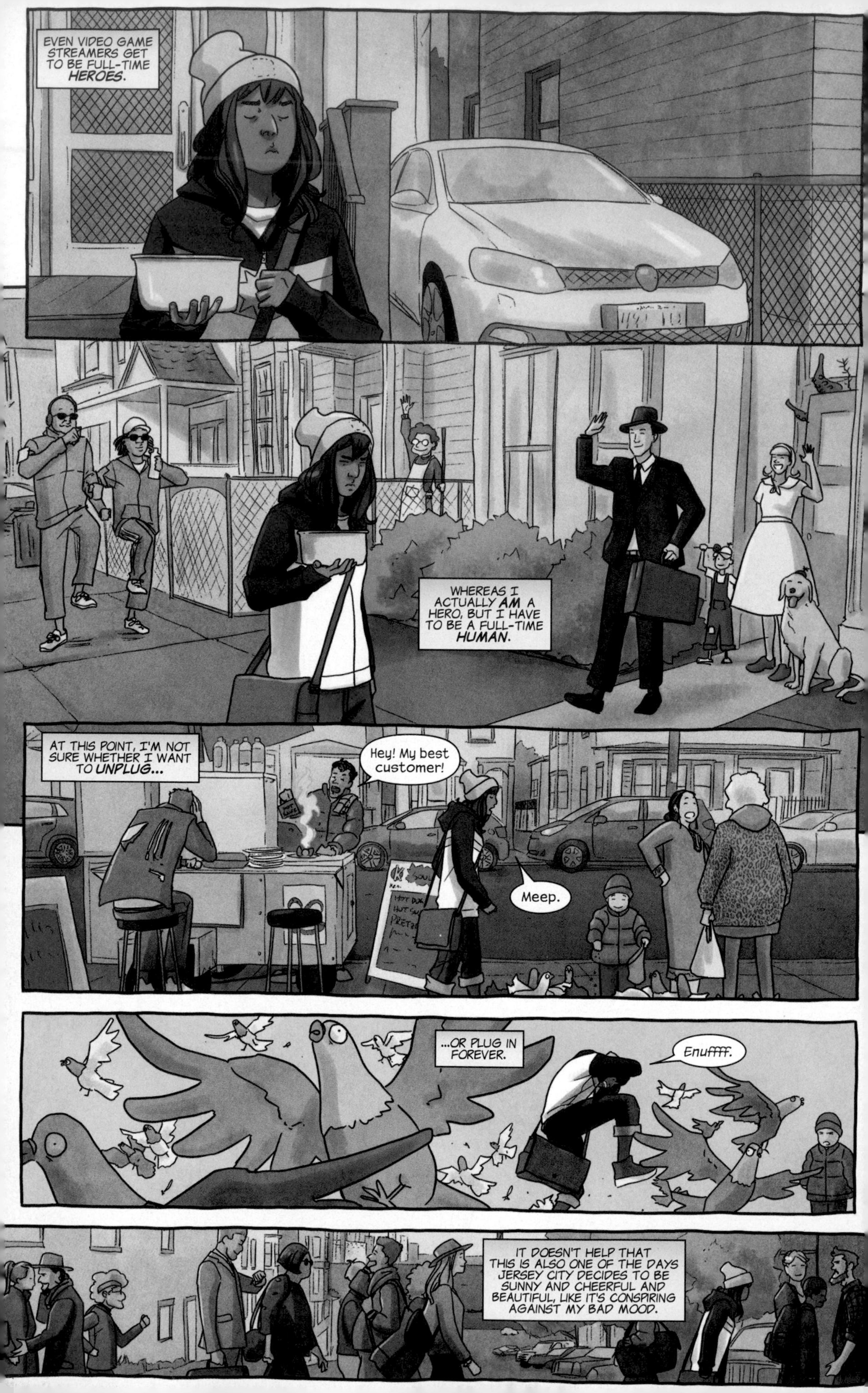
EVEN VIDEO GAME STREAMERS GET TO BE FULL-TIME HEROES.
WHEREAS I ACTUALLY AM A HERO, BUT I HAVE TO BE A FULL-TIME HUMAN.
AT THIS POINT, I'M NOT SURE WHETHER I WANT TO UNPLUG...
Hey! My best customer!
Meep.
...OR PLUG IN FOREVER.
Enuffff.
IT DOESN'T HELP THAT THIS IS ALSO ONE OF THE DAYS JERSEY CITY DECIDES TO BE SUNNY AND CHEERFUL AND BEAUTIFUL, LIKE IT'S CONSPIRING AGAINST MY BAD MOOD.

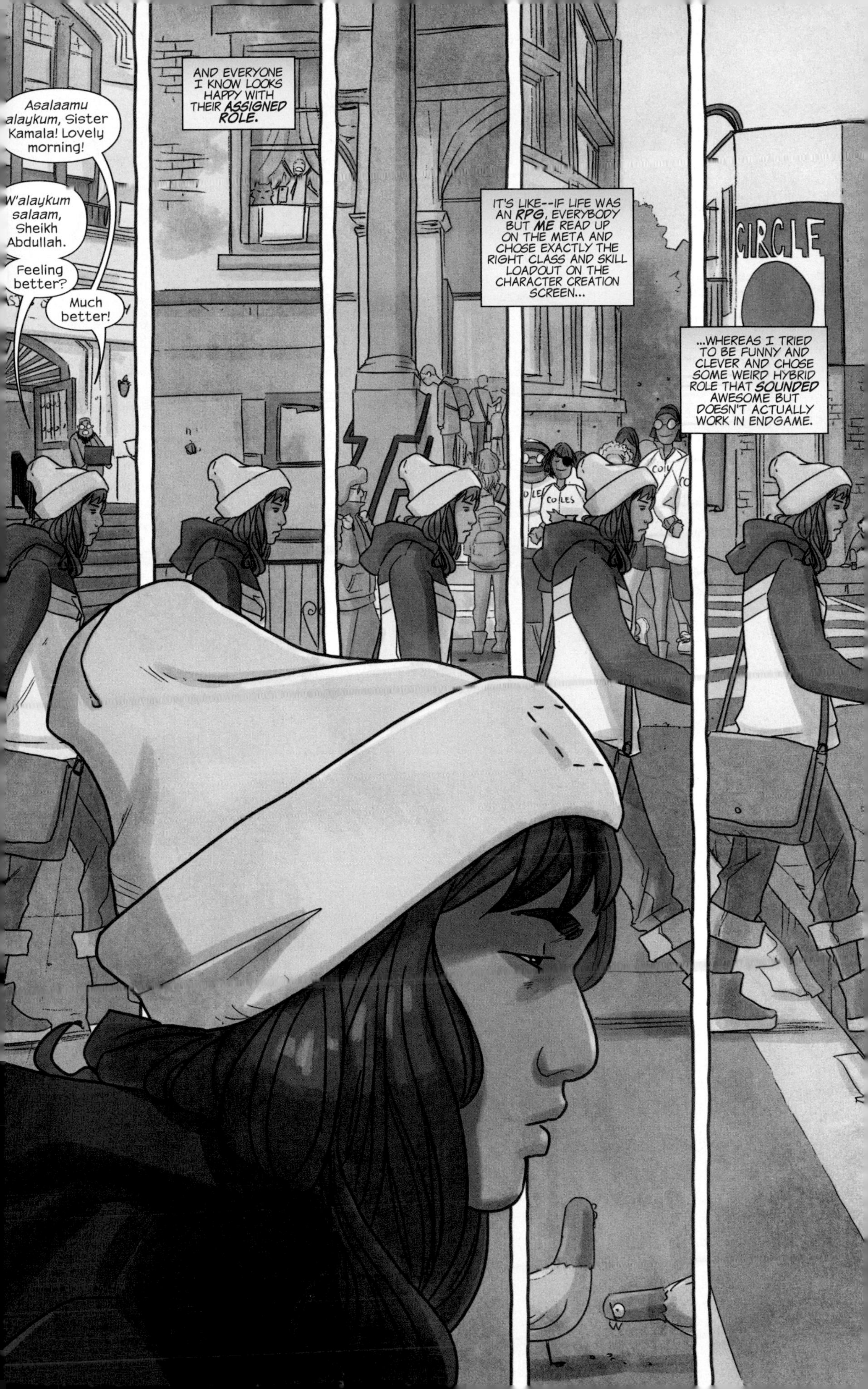
Asalaamu alaykum, Sister Kamala! Lovely morning!
W'alaykum salaam, Sheikh Abdullah.
Feeling better?
Much better!
AND EVERYONE I KNOW LOOKS HAPPY WITH THEIR ASSIGNED ROLE.
IT'S LIKE--IF LIFE WAS AN RPG, EVERYBODY BUT ME READ UP ON THE META AND CHOSE EXACTLY THE RIGHT CLASS AND SKILL LOADOUT ON THE CHARACTER CREATION SCREEN...
...WHEREAS I TRIED TO BE FUNNY AND CLEVER AND CHOSE SOME WEIRD HYBRID ROLE THAT SOUNDED AWESOME BUT DOESN'T ACTUALLY WORK IN ENDGAME.
CIRCLE

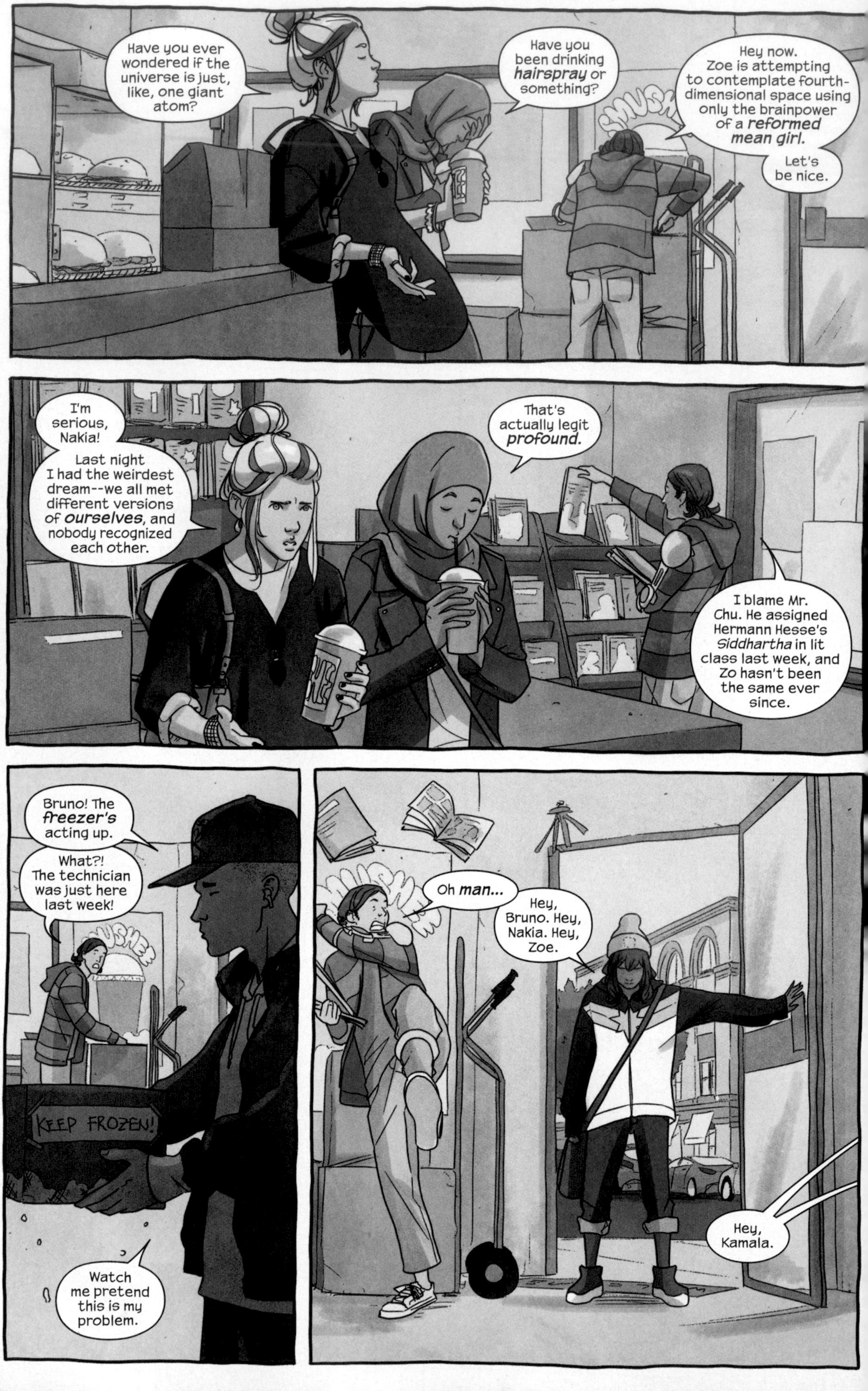
Have you ever wondered if the universe is just, like, one giant atom?
Have you been drinking hairspray or something?
Hey now. Zoe is attempting to contemplate fourth-dimensional space using only the brainpower of a reformed mean girl.
Let's be nice.
SMUSH
I'm serious, Nakia!
Last night I had the weirdest dream--we all met different versions of ourselves, and nobody recognized each other.
That's actually legit profound.
I blame Mr. Chu. He assigned Hermann Hesse's Siddhartha in lit class last week, and Zo hasn't been the same ever since.
Bruno! The freezer's acting up.
What?! The technician was just here last week!
KEEP FROZEN!
Watch me pretend this is my problem.
Oh man...
Hey, Bruno. Hey, Nakia. Hey, Zoe.
Hey, Kamala.

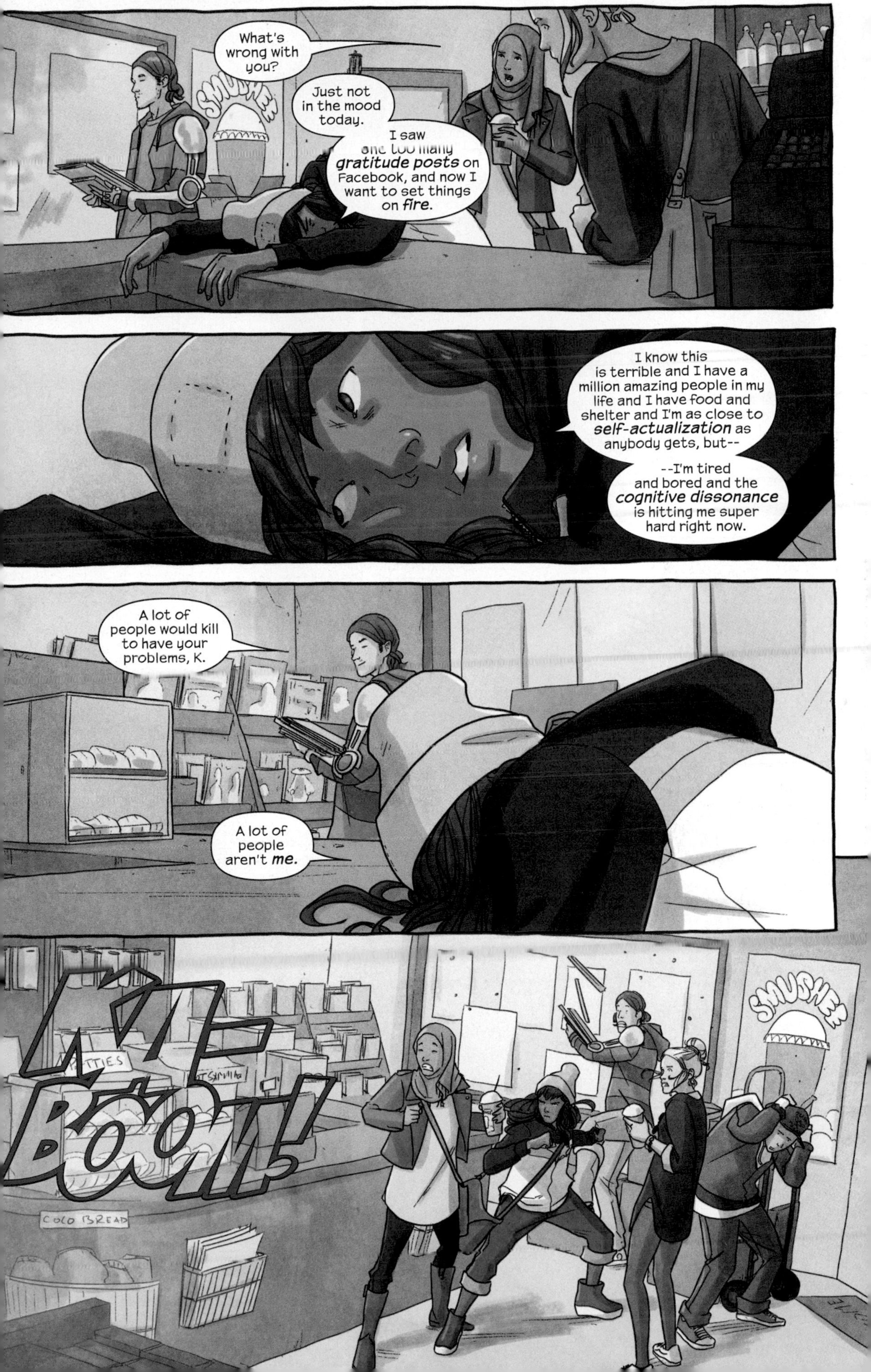
What's wrong with you?
Just not in the mood today.
SMUSHEE
I saw one too many *gratitude posts* on Facebook, and now I want to set things on *fire*.
I know this is terrible and I have a million amazing people in my life and I have food and shelter and I'm as close to *self-actualization* as anybody gets, but--
--I'm tired and bored and the *cognitive dissonance* is hitting me super hard right now.
A lot of people would kill to have your problems, K.
A lot of people aren't *me.*
KABOOM!
PATTIES
COLD BREAD
SMUSHEE

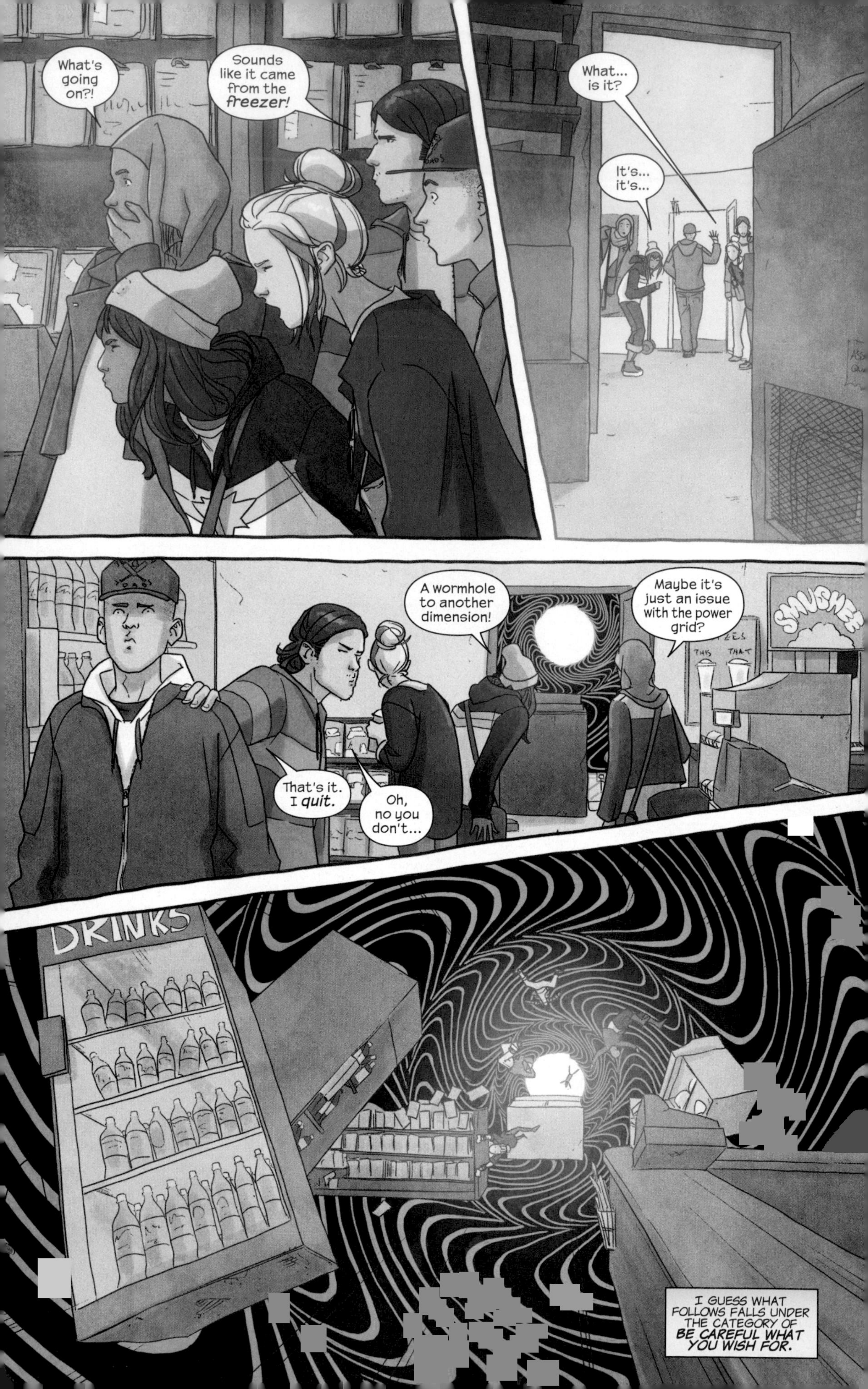
What's going on?!
Sounds like it came from the freezer!
What... is it?
It's... it's...
A wormhole to another dimension!
Maybe it's just an issue with the power grid?
SMUSHEE
That's it. I quit.
Oh, no you don't...
DRINKS
I GUESS WHAT FOLLOWS FALLS UNDER THE CATEGORY OF BE CAREFUL WHAT YOU WISH FOR.

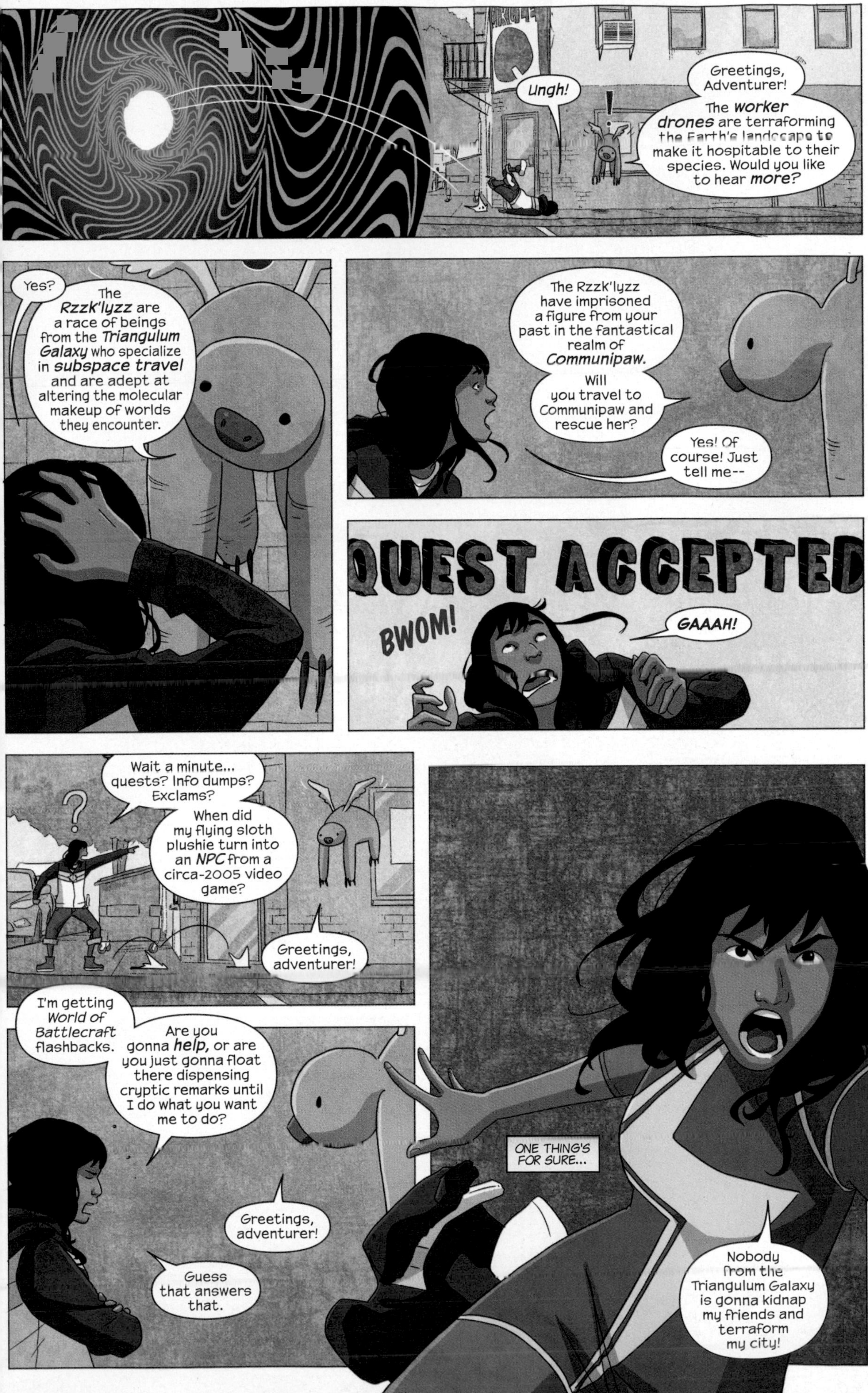
Ungh!
!
Greetings, Adventurer!
The worker drones are terraforming the Earth's landscape to make it hospitable to their species. Would you like to hear more?
Yes?
The Rzzk'lyzz are a race of beings from the Triangulum Galaxy who specialize in subspace travel and are adept at altering the molecular makeup of worlds they encounter.
The Rzzk'lyzz have imprisoned a figure from your past in the fantastical realm of Communipaw.
Will you travel to Communipaw and rescue her?
Yes! Of course! Just tell me--
QUEST ACCEPTED
BWOM!
GAAAH!
?
Wait a minute... quests? Info dumps? Exclams?
When did my flying sloth plushie turn into an NPC from a circa-2005 video game?
Greetings, adventurer!
I'm getting World of Battlecraft flashbacks.
Are you gonna help, or are you just gonna float there dispensing cryptic remarks until I do what you want me to do?
Greetings, adventurer!
Guess that answers that.
ONE THING'S FOR SURE...
Nobody from the Triangulum Galaxy is gonna kidnap my friends and terraform my city!

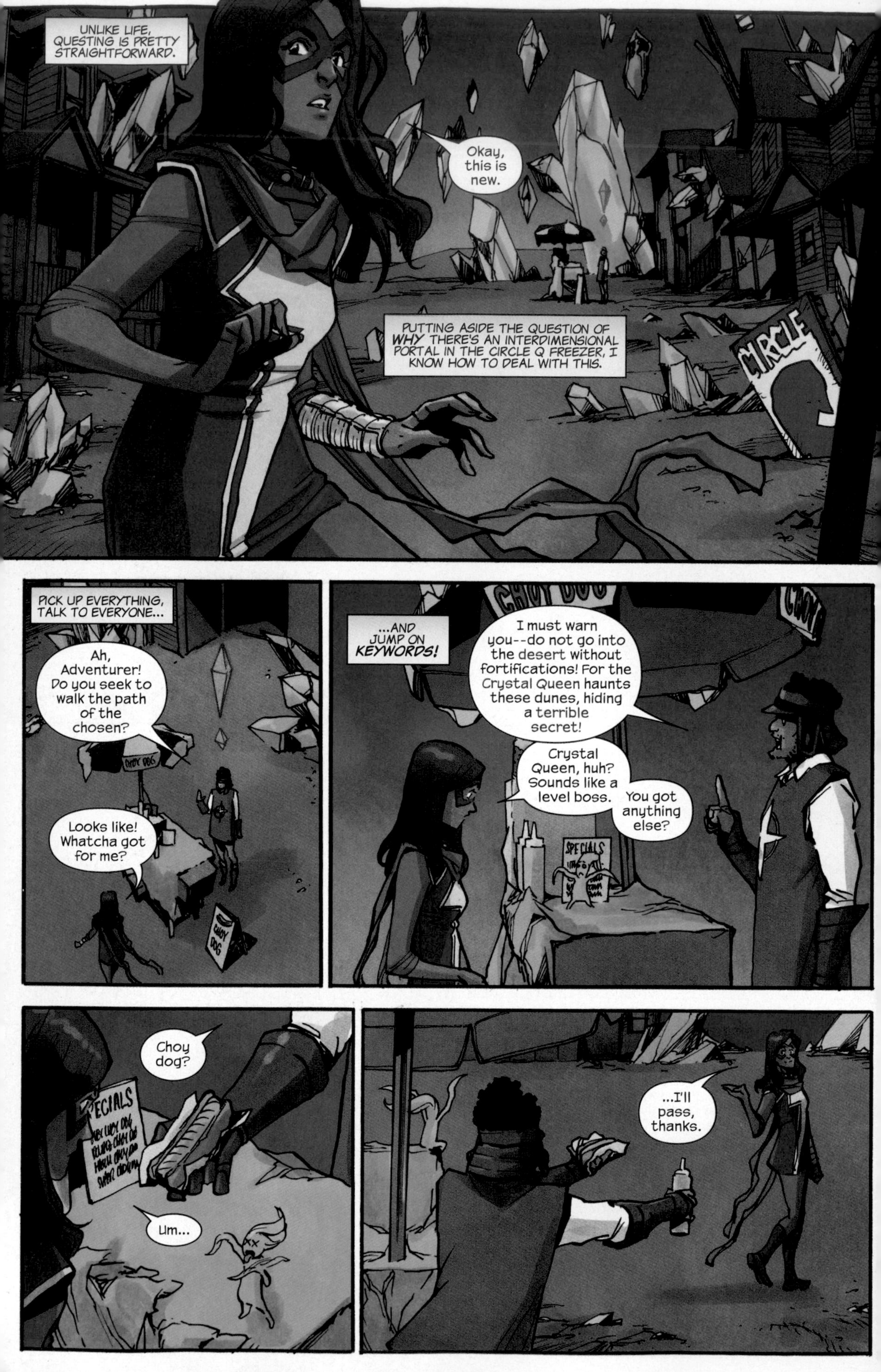
UNLIKE LIFE, QUESTING IS PRETTY STRAIGHTFORWARD.
Okay, this is new.
PUTTING ASIDE THE QUESTION OF *WHY* THERE'S AN INTERDIMENSIONAL PORTAL IN THE CIRCLE Q FREEZER, I KNOW HOW TO DEAL WITH THIS.
CIRCLE Q
PICK UP EVERYTHING, TALK TO EVERYONE...
Ah, Adventurer! Do you seek to walk the path of the chosen?
Looks like! Whatcha got for me?
CHOY DOG
...AND JUMP ON ***KEYWORDS!***
I must warn you--do not go into the desert without fortifications! For the Crystal Queen haunts these dunes, hiding a terrible secret!
Crystal Queen, huh? Sounds like a level boss.
You got anything else?
SPECIALS
Choy dog?
Um...
...I'll pass, thanks.

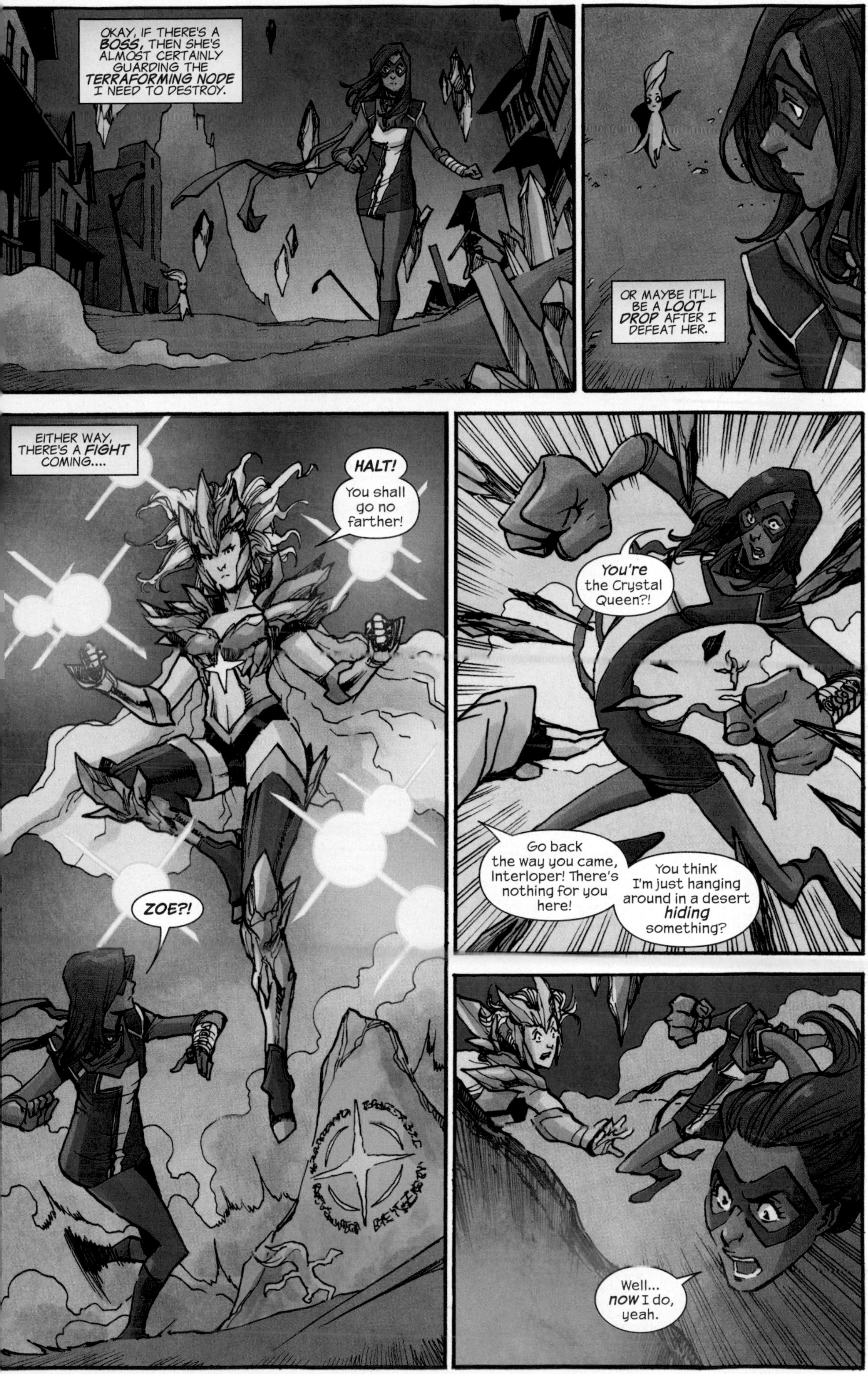
OKAY, IF THERE'S A BOSS, THEN SHE'S ALMOST CERTAINLY GUARDING THE TERRAFORMING NODE I NEED TO DESTROY.
OR MAYBE IT'LL BE A LOOT DROP AFTER I DEFEAT HER.
EITHER WAY, THERE'S A FIGHT COMING....
HALT! You shall go no farther!
ZOE?!
You're the Crystal Queen?!
Go back the way you came, Interloper! There's nothing for you here!
You think I'm just hanging around in a desert hiding something?
Well... now I do, yeah.

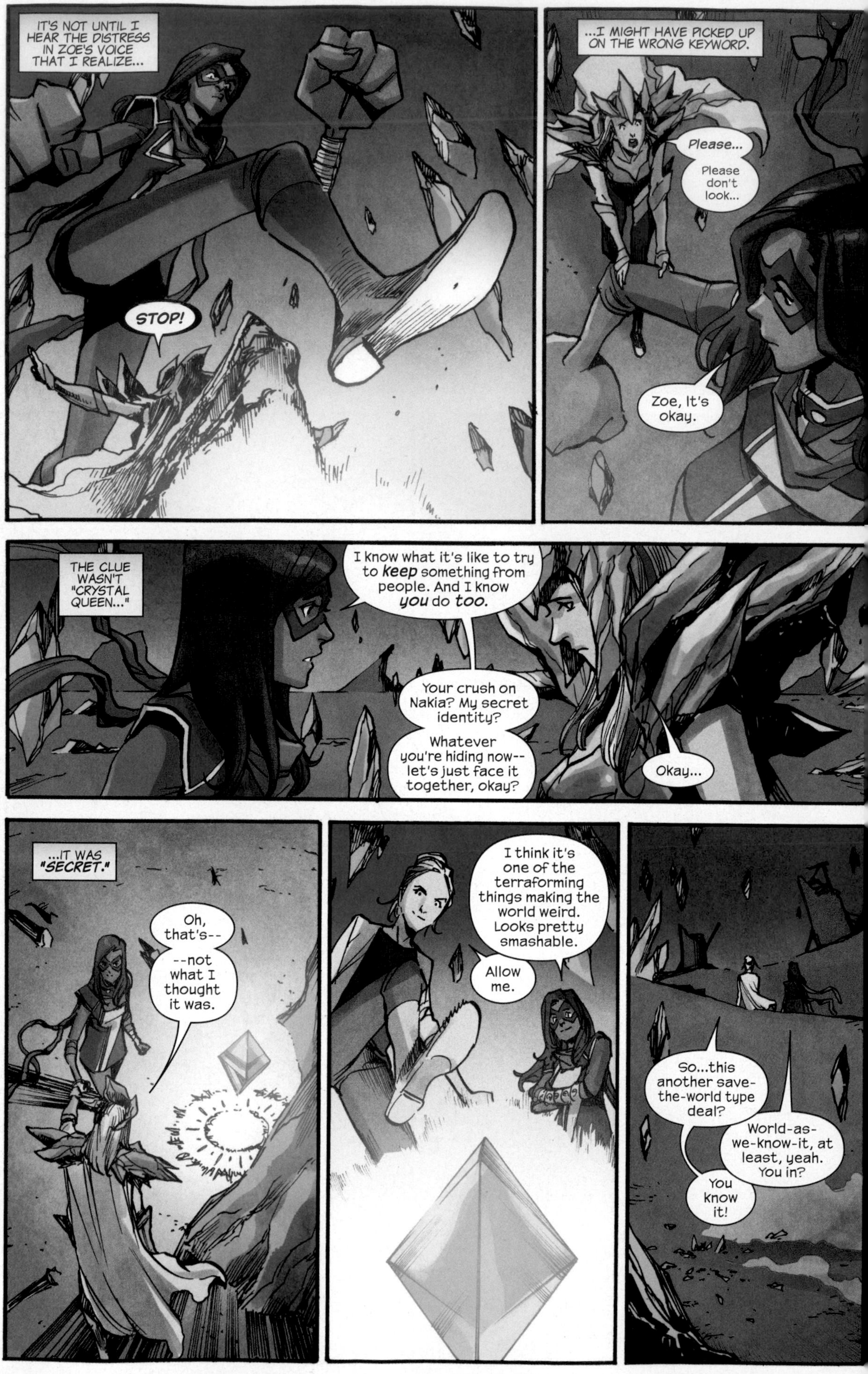
IT'S NOT UNTIL I HEAR THE DISTRESS IN ZOE'S VOICE THAT I REALIZE...
STOP!
...I MIGHT HAVE PICKED UP ON THE WRONG KEYWORD.
Please...
Please don't look...
Zoe, It's okay.
THE CLUE WASN'T "CRYSTAL QUEEN..."
I know what it's like to try to keep something from people. And I know you do too.
Your crush on Nakia? My secret identity?
Whatever you're hiding now-- let's just face it together, okay?
Okay...
...IT WAS "SECRET."
Oh, that's--
--not what I thought it was.
I think it's one of the terraforming things making the world weird. Looks pretty smashable.
Allow me.
So...this another save-the-world type deal?
World-as-we-know-it, at least, yeah. You in?
You know it!

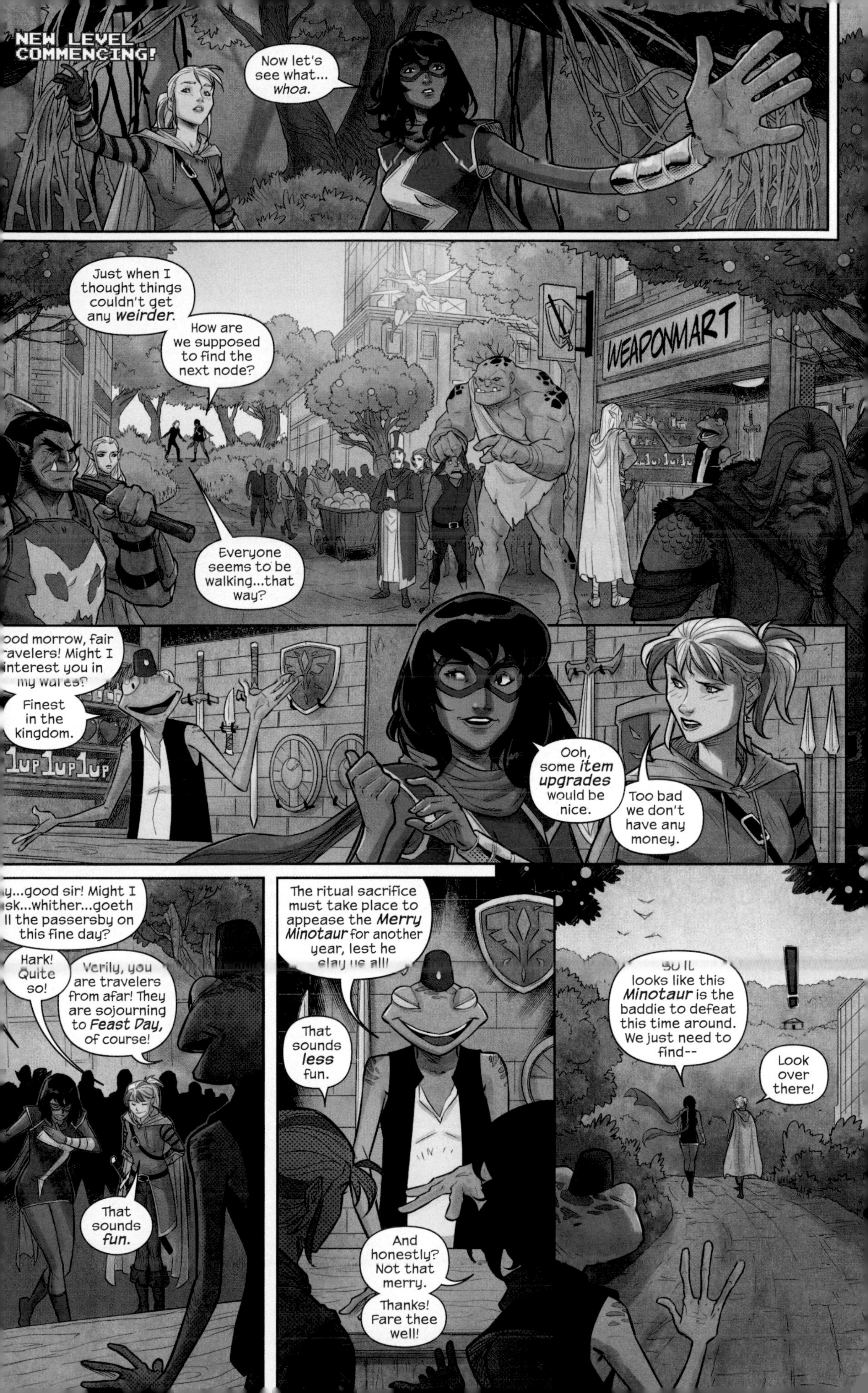
NEW LEVEL COMMENCING!
Now let's see what... *whoa.*
Just when I thought things couldn't get any **weirder**.
How are we supposed to find the next node?
Everyone seems to be walking...that way?
WEAPONMART
ood morrow, fair ravelers! Might I interest you in my wares?
Finest in the kingdom.
1UP 1UP 1UP
Ooh, some **item upgrades** would be nice.
Too bad we don't have any money.
y...good sir! Might I sk...whither...goeth ll the passersby on this fine day?
Hark! Quite so!
Verily, you are travelers from afar! They are sojourning to *Feast Day,* of course!
That sounds *fun.*
The ritual sacrifice must take place to appease the *Merry Minotaur* for another year, lest he slay us all!
That sounds *less* fun.
And honestly? Not that merry.
Thanks! Fare thee well!
So it looks like this *Minotaur* is the baddie to defeat this time around. We just need to find--
Look over there!

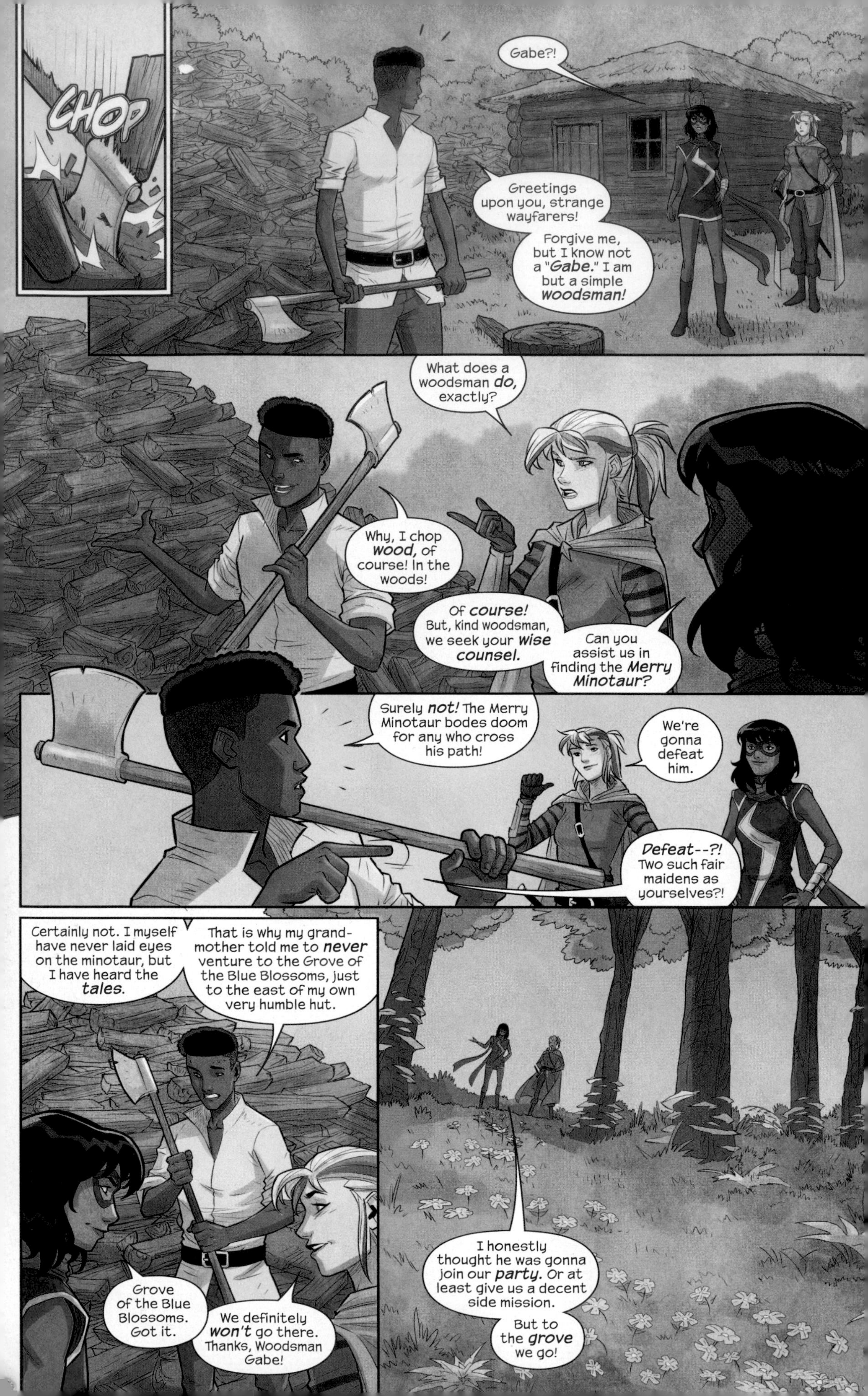
CHOP
Gabe?!
Greetings upon you, strange wayfarers!
Forgive me, but I know not a "Gabe." I am but a simple woodsman!
What does a woodsman do, exactly?
Why, I chop wood, of course! In the woods!
Of course! But, kind woodsman, we seek your wise counsel.
Can you assist us in finding the Merry Minotaur?
Surely not! The Merry Minotaur bodes doom for any who cross his path!
We're gonna defeat him.
Defeat--?! Two such fair maidens as yourselves?!
Certainly not. I myself have never laid eyes on the minotaur, but I have heard the tales.
That is why my grand-mother told me to never venture to the Grove of the Blue Blossoms, just to the east of my own very humble hut.
Grove of the Blue Blossoms. Got it.
We definitely won't go there. Thanks, Woodsman Gabe!
I honestly thought he was gonna join our party. Or at least give us a decent side mission.
But to the grove we go!

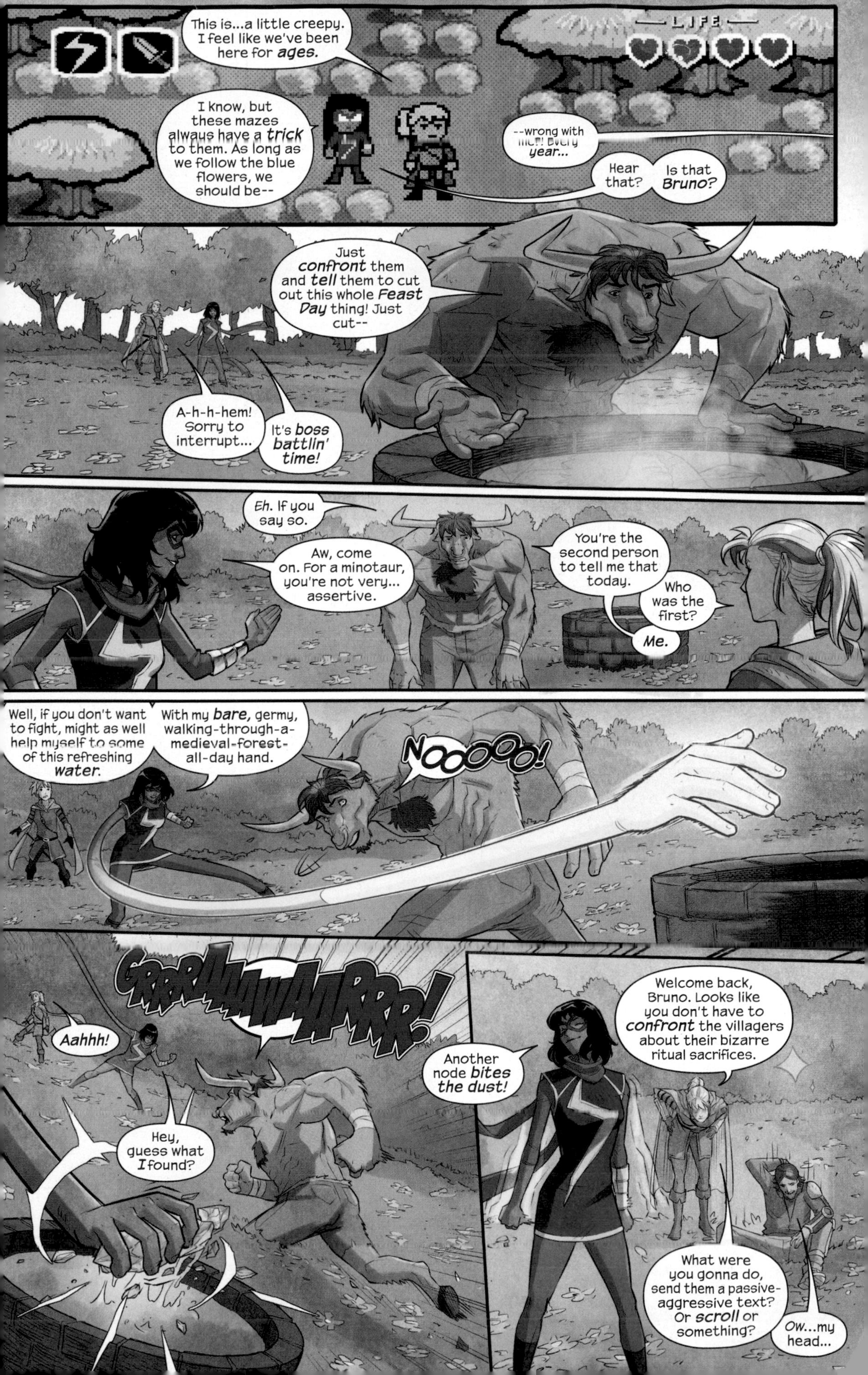

LIFE
This is...a little creepy. I feel like we've been here for *ages.*
I know, but these mazes always have a *trick* to them. As long as we follow the blue flowers, we should be--
--wrong with
year...
Hear that?
Is that *Bruno?*
Just *confront* them and *tell* them to cut out this whole *Feast Day* thing! Just cut--
A-h-h-hem! Sorry to interrupt...
It's *boss battlin' time!*
Eh. If you say so.
Aw, come on. For a minotaur, you're not very... assertive.
You're the second person to tell me that today.
Who was the first?
Me.
Well, if you don't want to fight, might as well help myself to some of this refreshing *water.*
With my *bare,* germy, walking-through-a-medieval-forest-all-day hand.
NOOOOOO!
GRRRAAAAWAARRRR!
Aahhh!
Hey, guess what *I* found?
Another node *bites the dust!*
Welcome back, Bruno. Looks like you don't have to *confront* the villagers about their bizarre ritual sacrifices.
What were you gonna do, send them a passive-aggressive text? Or *scroll* or something?
Ow...my head...

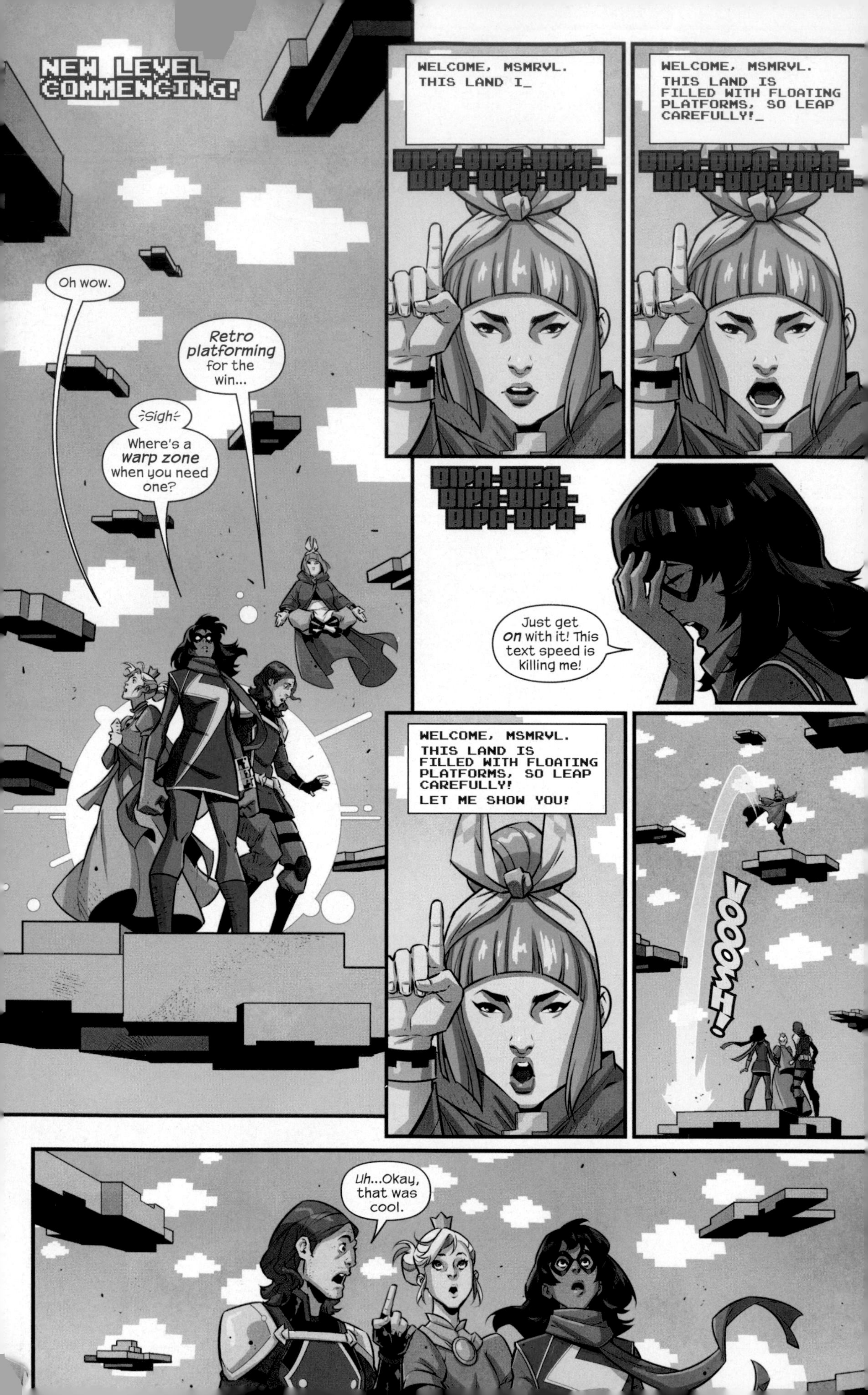

NEW LEVEL COMMENCING!
Oh wow.
Retro platforming for the win...
Sigh
Where's a warp zone when you need one?
WELCOME, MSMRVL. THIS LAND I_
BIPA-BIPA-BIPA-BIPA-BIPA-BIPA-
WELCOME, MSMRVL. THIS LAND IS FILLED WITH FLOATING PLATFORMS, SO LEAP CAREFULLY!_
BIPA-BIPA-BIPA-BIPA-BIPA-BIPA-
BIPA-BIPA-BIPA-BIPA-BIPA-BIPA-
Just get on with it! This text speed is killing me!
WELCOME, MSMRVL. THIS LAND IS FILLED WITH FLOATING PLATFORMS, SO LEAP CAREFULLY! LET ME SHOW YOU!
VOOOOSH!
Uh...Okay, that was cool.

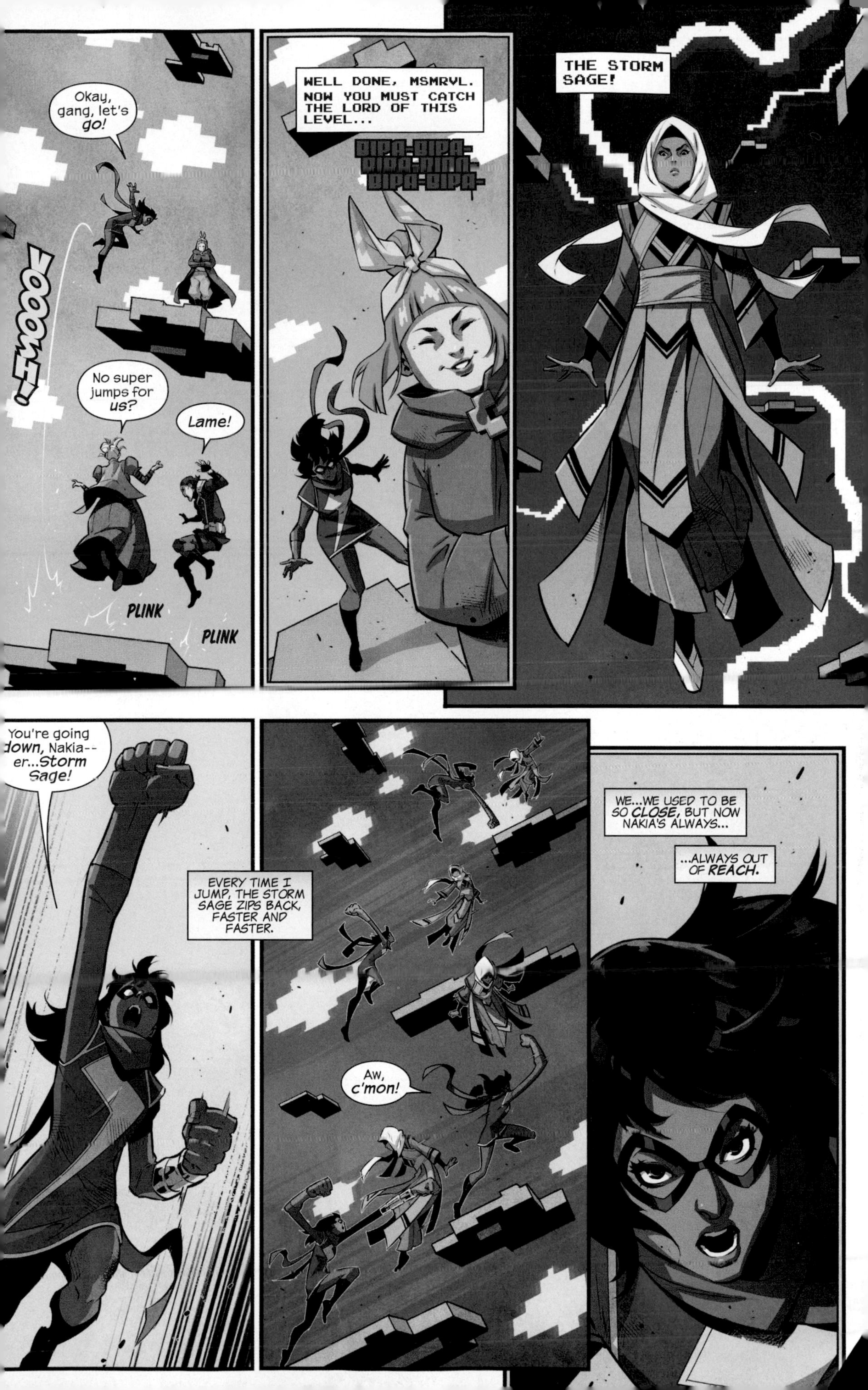
Okay, gang, let's go!
SHOOOOM
No super jumps for us?
Lame!
PLINK
PLINK
WELL DONE, MSMRVL. NOW YOU MUST CATCH THE LORD OF THIS LEVEL...
BIPA-BIPA-BIPA-NINN-BIPA-BIPA-
THE STORM SAGE!
You're going down, Nakia-- er...Storm Sage!
EVERY TIME I JUMP, THE STORM SAGE ZIPS BACK, FASTER AND FASTER.
Aw, c'mon!
WE...WE USED TO BE SO CLOSE, BUT NOW NAKIA'S ALWAYS...
...ALWAYS OUT OF REACH.

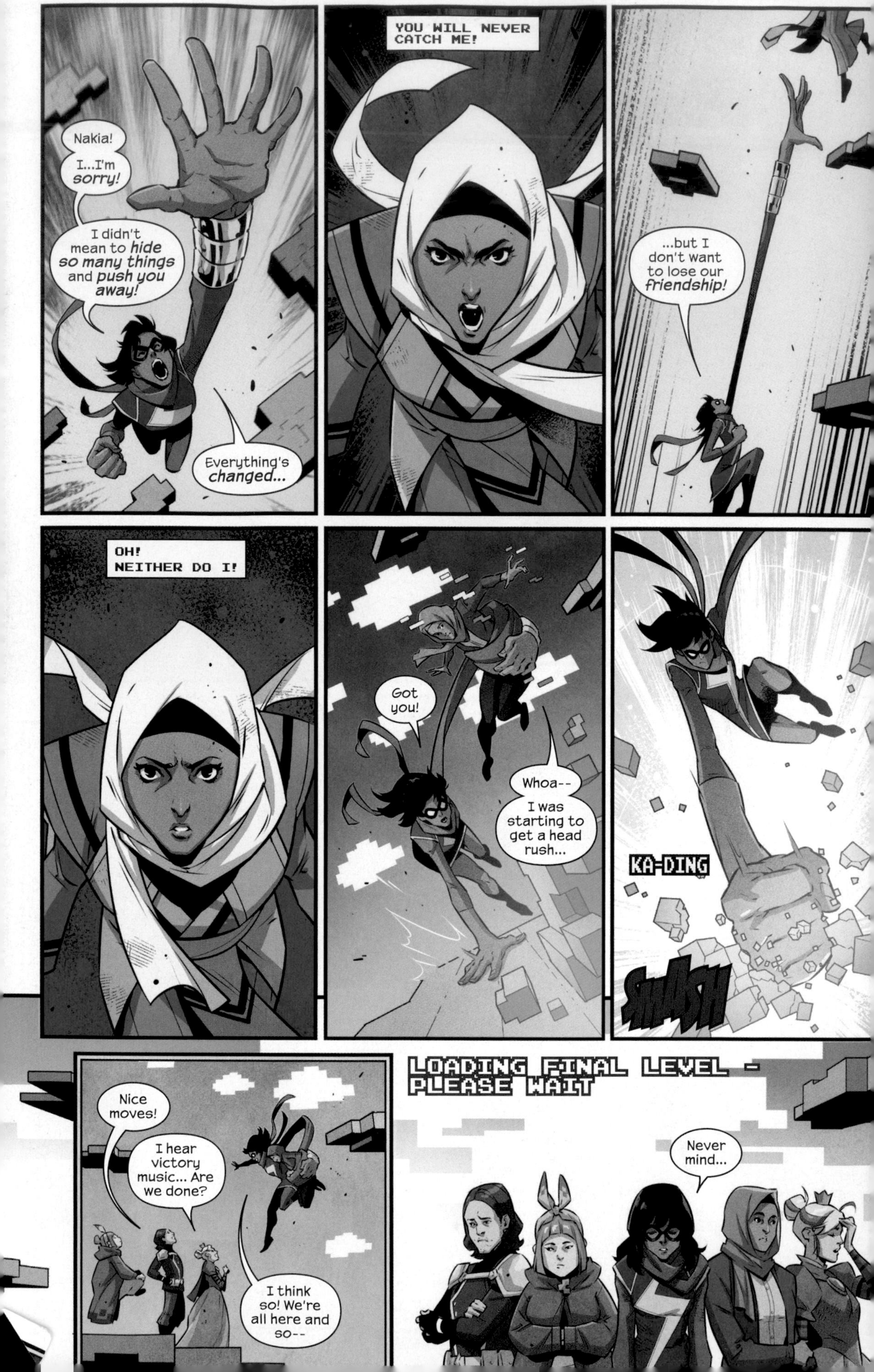

Nakia!
I...I'm sorry!
I didn't mean to hide so many things and push you away!
Everything's changed...
YOU WILL NEVER CATCH ME!
...but I don't want to lose our friendship!
OH! NEITHER DO I!
Got you!
Whoa-- I was starting to get a head rush...
KA-DING
SMASH
Nice moves!
I hear victory music... Are we done?
I think so! We're all here and so--
LOADING FINAL LEVEL - PLEASE WAIT
Never mind...

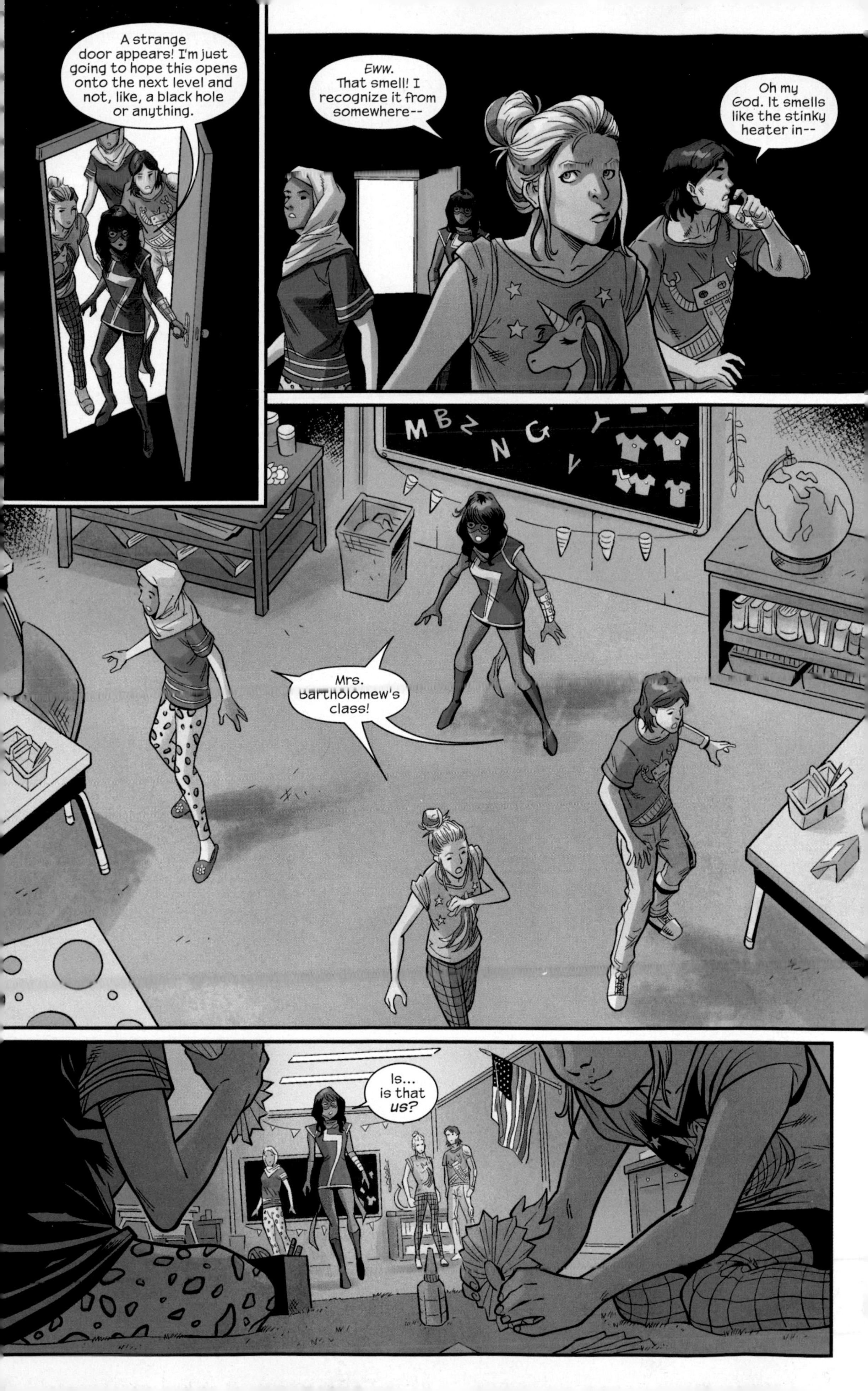
A strange door appears! I'm just going to hope this opens onto the next level and not, like, a black hole or anything.
Eww. That smell! I recognize it from somewhere--
Oh my God. It smells like the stinky heater in--
MB N G Y
Mrs. Bartholomew's class!
Is... is that us?

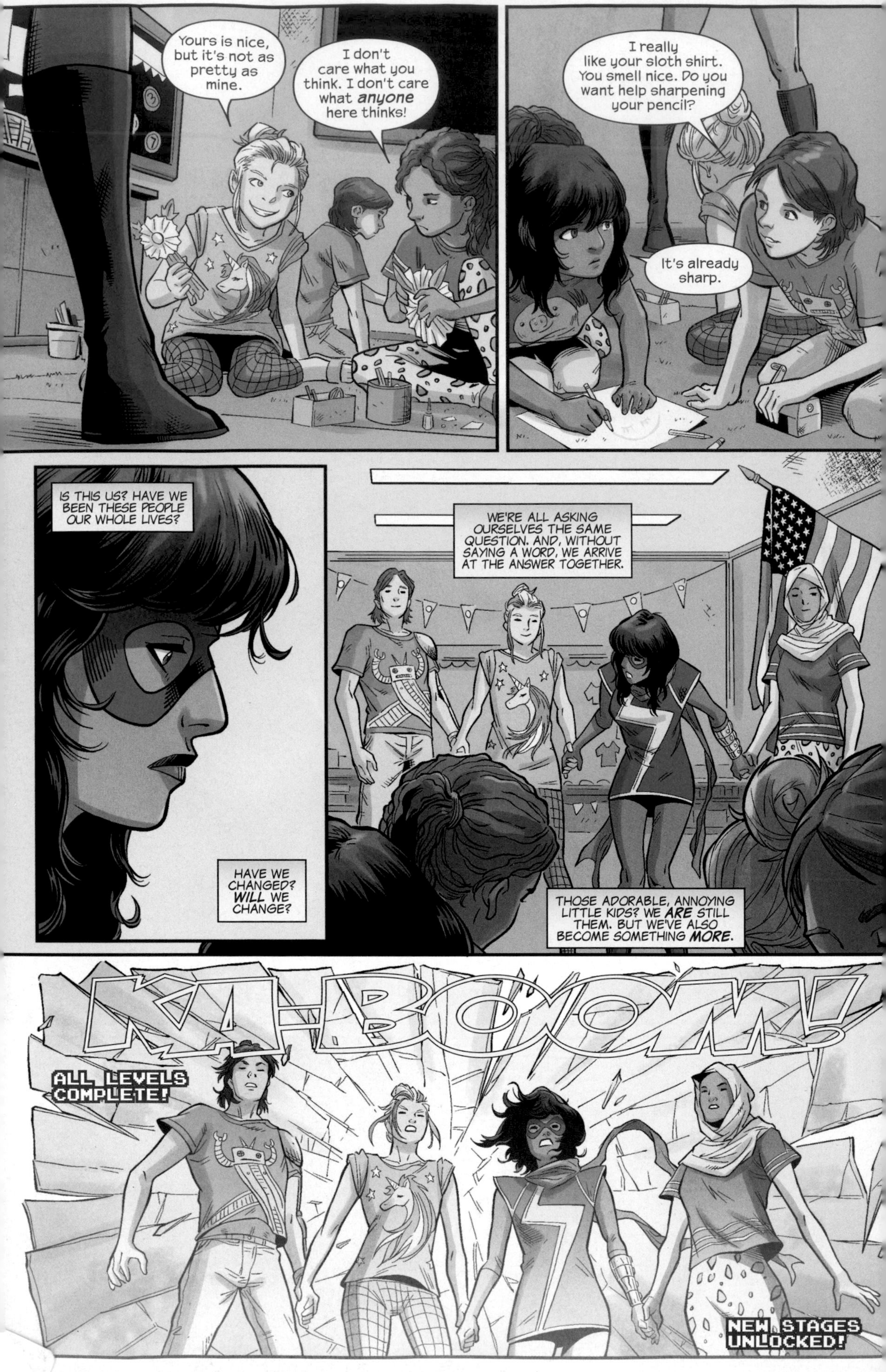
Yours is nice, but it's not as pretty as mine.
I don't care what you think. I don't care what *anyone* here thinks!
I really like your sloth shirt. You smell nice. Do you want help sharpening your pencil?
It's already sharp.
IS THIS US? HAVE WE BEEN THESE PEOPLE OUR WHOLE LIVES?
HAVE WE CHANGED? *WILL* WE CHANGE?
WE'RE ALL ASKING OURSELVES THE SAME QUESTION. AND, WITHOUT SAYING A WORD, WE ARRIVE AT THE ANSWER TOGETHER.
THOSE ADORABLE, ANNOYING LITTLE KIDS? WE *ARE* STILL THEM. BUT WE'VE ALSO BECOME SOMETHING *MORE*.
KA-BOOM!
ALL LEVELS COMPLETE!
NEW STAGES UNLOCKED!

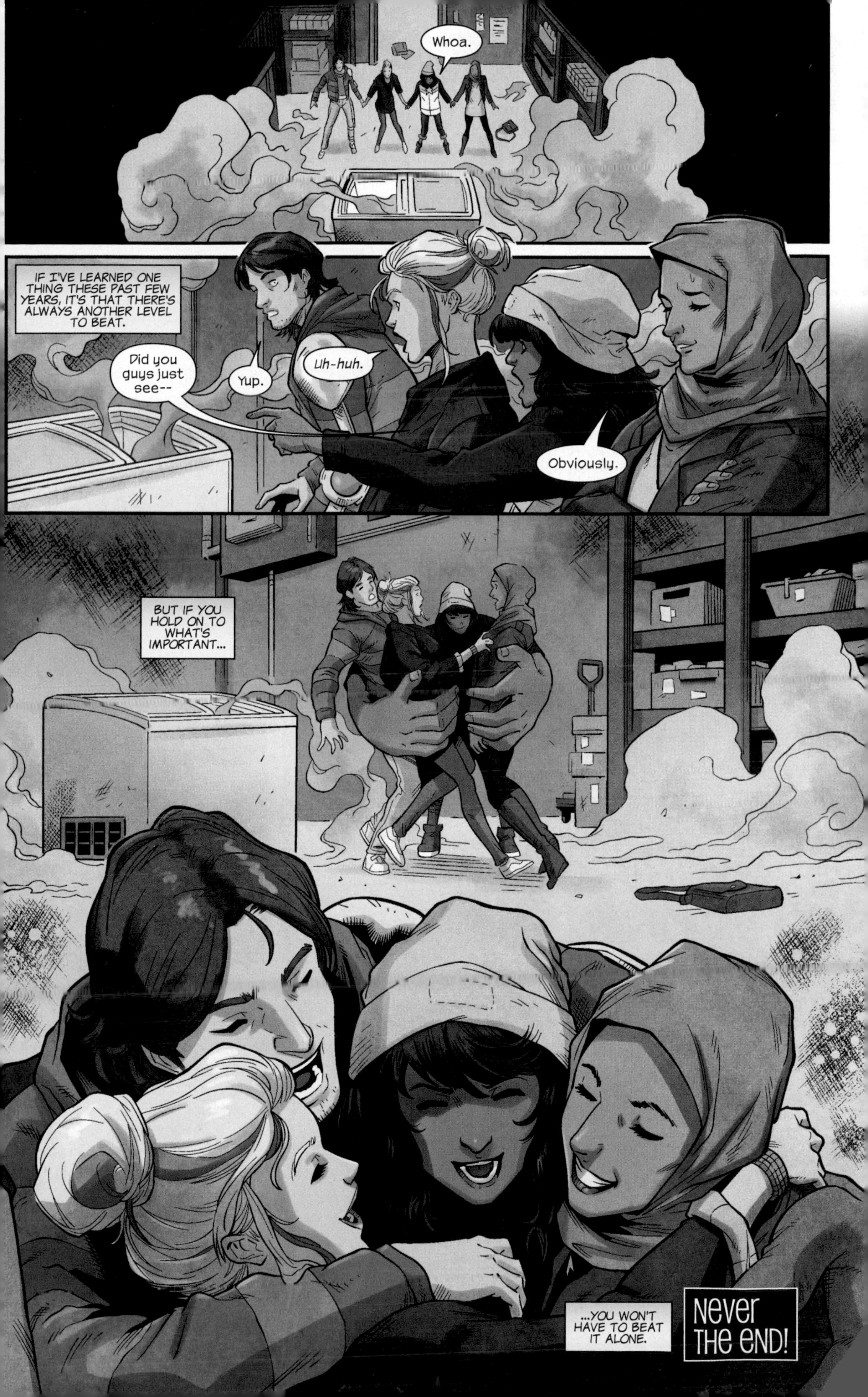
Whoa.
IF I'VE LEARNED ONE THING THESE PAST FEW YEARS, IT'S THAT THERE'S ALWAYS ANOTHER LEVEL TO BEAT.
Did you guys just see--
Yup.
Uh-huh.
Obviously.
BUT IF YOU HOLD ON TO WHAT'S IMPORTANT...
...YOU WON'T HAVE TO BEAT IT ALONE.
Never THE END!

PETE'S PRICEY PETROL

BZZZTT--

TAP
    TAP
TAP
    TAP

HEY, WHAT ARE YOU UP TO?

DRINK! SMUSHE ON EDGE OF TOWN.

"ALL THE WAY OUT THERE?"

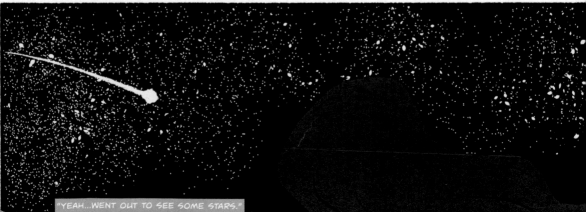

"YEAH...WENT OUT TO SEE SOME STARS."

Being part of the genesis of Kamala Khan has been one of the greatest honors of my life. From my puzzlement during that first telephone conversation with Sana in 2012 — I was pregnant, frazzled from a long book tour and in disbelief (You want to launch a new character? In this market?) — to my stunned amazement when the first issue went into its seventh printing, to my glee when Sana handed the first trade paperback to the president of the United States, this journey has been pure joy.

Sana and I initially had very modest expectations for this book. Our goal was to get to ten issues. It was going to be a fun side project — a young adult Muslim super hero! At Marvel! — that would have the lifespan of fun side projects. I budgeted a year for it. But by the time the first trade paperback hit the *New York Times* Graphic Books Best Sellers list, I realized Kamala was quickly becoming the center of my life.

And that is in no small part thanks to you, the readers. Your enthusiasm has propelled this character to greater and greater heights. Never in my life did I imagine I would walk into my local drugstore and see something I created staring back at me from T-shirts and action figures. Yet it's the experiences I've had meeting readers that have changed me on an elemental level. At signings, at conventions, at classroom visits, we've laughed and cried together. I've met your kids, seen pictures of your dogs, held your hands while you talked about your most difficult experiences. Kamala is not just what you read on the page or watch on TV — she is this community. And she has made all of us better human beings.

In February, I will have written 60 issues of this book — five years of Kamala's story. She is now something much bigger than the miniseries Sana and I planned years ago. She will, in all likelihood, outlive us all. I couldn't be happier about it — and by that same token, it means that my part in Kamala's adventures must eventually come to an end. Great super heroes stay fresh and relevant because they are the work of many storytellers, all of whom bring their unique perspectives and experiences to the character. Earlier this year, I began to have the persistent feeling that I was in danger of repeating myself every time I sat down to write a new script. It was a sign: time to start planning my exit.

I was delighted when Saladin said yes to taking over writing duties on MS. MARVEL. His plans for Kamala are incredibly exciting, and it's been a lot of fun getting an inside look at where the series is heading under his direction. I was blown away by his work on BLACK BOLT, which gave me the same sense of endless possibility that reading *Sandman* gave me as a teenager. You're in for a treat.

I will miss working with the phenomenal roster of artists that has made this series one of the best-looking books on the shelf year after year — Adrian Alphona, whose genius character and environmental designs gave this series its distinct look; Jamie McKelvie, whose design sense is already legendary, for the costume that so quickly became iconic; Takeshi Miyazawa, whose kinetic, gleeful style was impossible not to love; and Nico Leon, who is basically my blood brother at this point and for whom no action sequence is too weird. The amazing Ian Herring, who has colored EVERY SINGLE ISSUE of this book for five straight years and whose flawless palette gives the book stylistic continuity no matter who is drawing it. And Joe Caramagna, letterer extraordinaire, who has spent half a decade putting up with my last-minute edits when he really shouldn't have had to. (I love you, Joe. I'm sorry, Joe.)

I may be stepping down as the writer of MS. MARVEL, but I will be a fan for life.

G. Willow Wilson

⚡⚡⚡⚡⚡⚡

I remember telling our publisher, Dan Buckley, that I would stop editing MS. MARVEL when I was dead. I think I had an expectation to edit this book even if I was fired, assuming I could negotiate it in my severance. Ah, Sana, you were so…dramatic.

I am hoping my flair for drama is somewhat understandable, though. As you fans of MS. MARVEL know, this book is different. It was truly a labor of love, not just for Willow and me, but for everyone who has come across this comic in some capacity. Whether you were a creator behind the page, or a fan in front of it, Kamala has found a way into all of our hearts. This special anniversary issue is a testament to that fact as voices across the Marvel Universe come together in that shared love. Now, as Kamala embarks on her next chapter with the magnificent team of Saladin Ahmed and Minkyu Jung, she's set to become a big part of our Marvel legacy.

Over the last five years, there have been many think pieces on who Ms. Marvel is and what she means. Is she a political statement? Is she destroying the comics industry? Is she fighting Islamophobia? It is incredible to me that a super hero has cultivated this much dialogue and even contention. She is in academic syllabi, documentaries and fan films. Everyone has an opinion on who Kamala is to him or her. And that's amazing. That is what we want. We want you to feel something about her. We want you to get to know her. Even if you don't necessarily like her. Because at least you now know there can be heroes like this. Not just in the funny books, but also out there in the world.

Speaking of real-life heroes, I want to share my love and gratefulness to the entire creative team. To Willow, whose collaboration and genius on this will be one of my most treasured experiences. To Adrian Alphona who built Kamala's wonderland with charming personality and heart. Takeshi Miyazawa and Nico Leon who continued to expand Kamala's world with a sense of love and personality. Ian Herring who literally lit up her pages in a symphony of colors. Jamie McKelvie who gave us the visual direction of the hero Kamala would become. Joe Caramagna for the thoughtful attention to crafting the words around her. To Devin Lewis, Charles Beacham and Mark Basso, my personal "Brunos," I couldn't have done these books without you. And last, but definitely not least, my dear friend and former boss Stephen Wacker, whose curiosity and creative guidance made the sheer possibility of Kamala a reality.

So, as I pass off the editorial baton to the very talented Alanna Smith, I'd like to make sure that we continue to uphold the spirit of Ms. Marvel. That disruption of the norms, that seeking of the unknown, that reminder that we are far more connected than we realize. You have our word Kamala will always be out there, fighting the good fight — taking down the bad guys and helping those who need it. She just hopes that you will be too.

Remember: good is a thing you do, not a thing you are.

Embiggen!

Sana Amanat

MS. MARVEL #31 VARIANT
BY STEPHANIE HANS

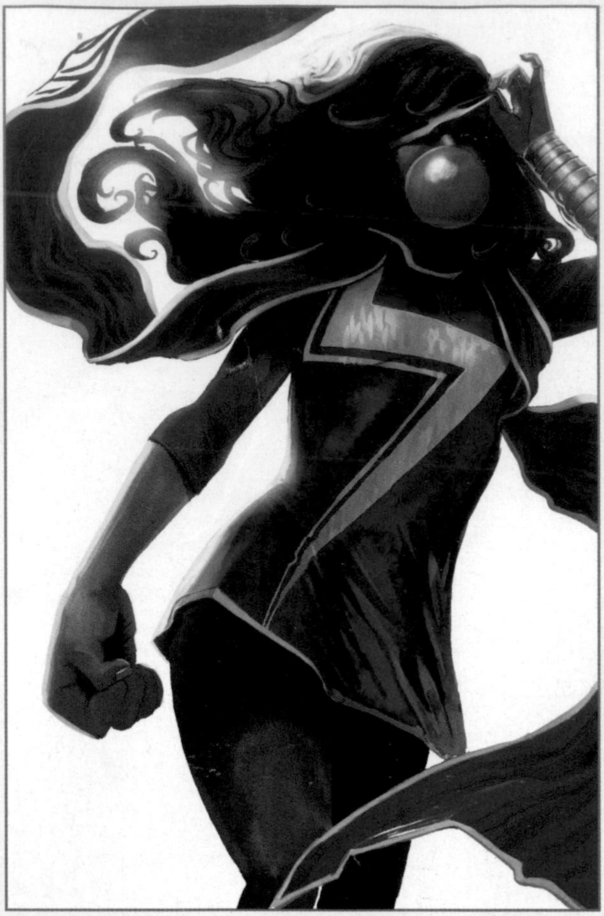

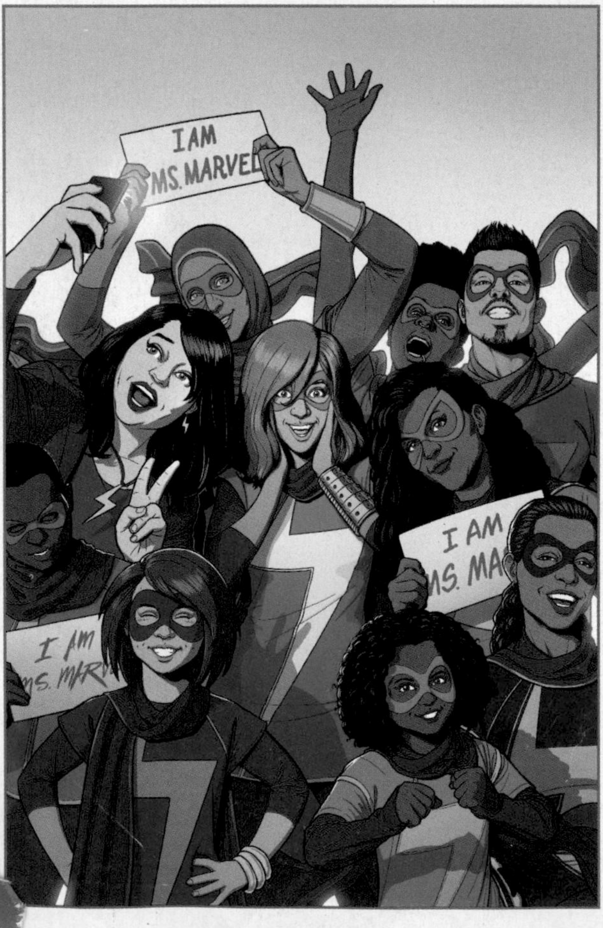
I AM MS. MARVEL
I AM MS. MA
I AM MS. MAR

MS. MARVEL #37 VARIANT
BY JAMIE McKELVIE